You hold in your hands a comic that has been repro-
duced as faithfully as possible to the original Japanese
work. None of the images have been rearranged or
altered. This work truly represents the vision of the
original author.

Confused?

Simply read the work from right to left. Start with
what you'd traditionally consider the "last page" and
continue through the book from right to left, page by
page. Within each page, start with the rightmost top
panel, and continue right to left, top to bottom. We
hope that you enjoy this work in its original format.

Directions:

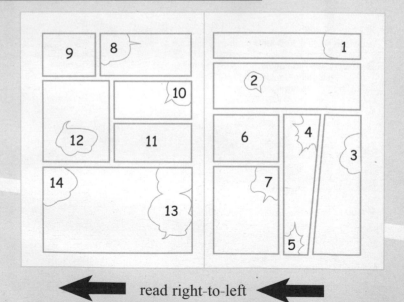

read right-to-left

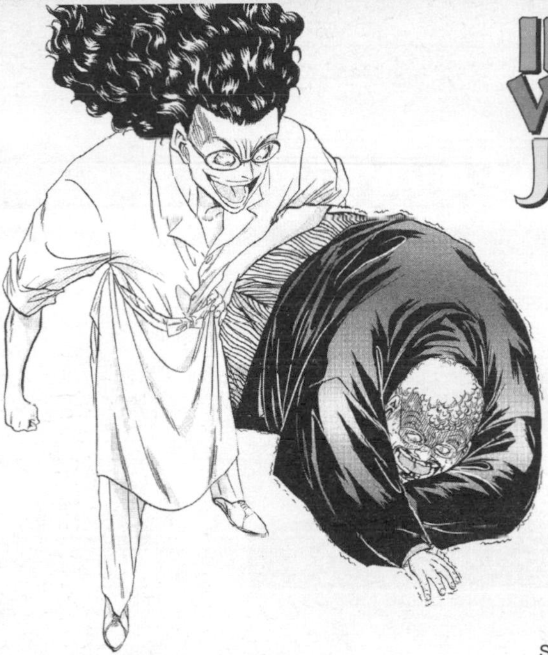

ISBN4-253-05205-3
Iron Wok Jan! 10

Publisher
ComicsOne Corporation
48531 Warm Springs Blvd., Suite 408
Fremont, CA 94539
www.ComicsOne.com

First Edition: October 2004
ISBN 1-58899-000-1

Translator
Sahe Kawahara

Editors
Shawn Sanders
Kevin P. Croall

Production Artist
Mei Chun Cheng

US Cover Design
Mei Chun Cheng

Production Manager
Janice Chang

Art Director
Yuki Chung

Marketing
Nicole Curry

President
Robin Kuo

IRON WOK JAN!

10

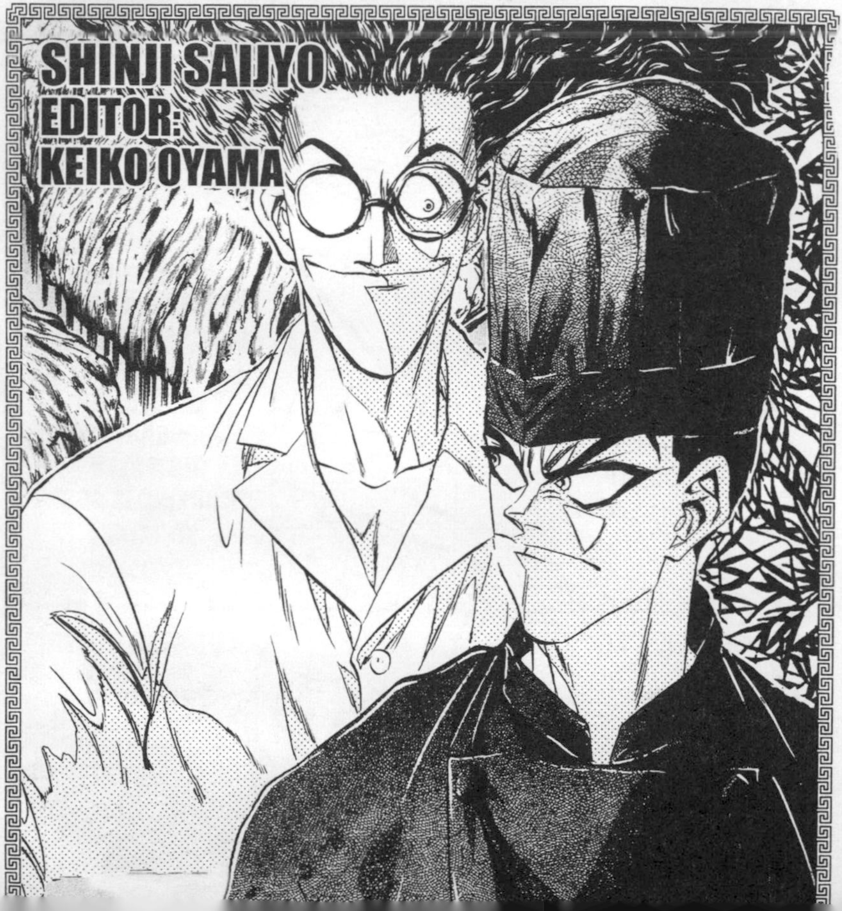
SHINJI SAIJYO
EDITOR:
KEIKO OYAMA

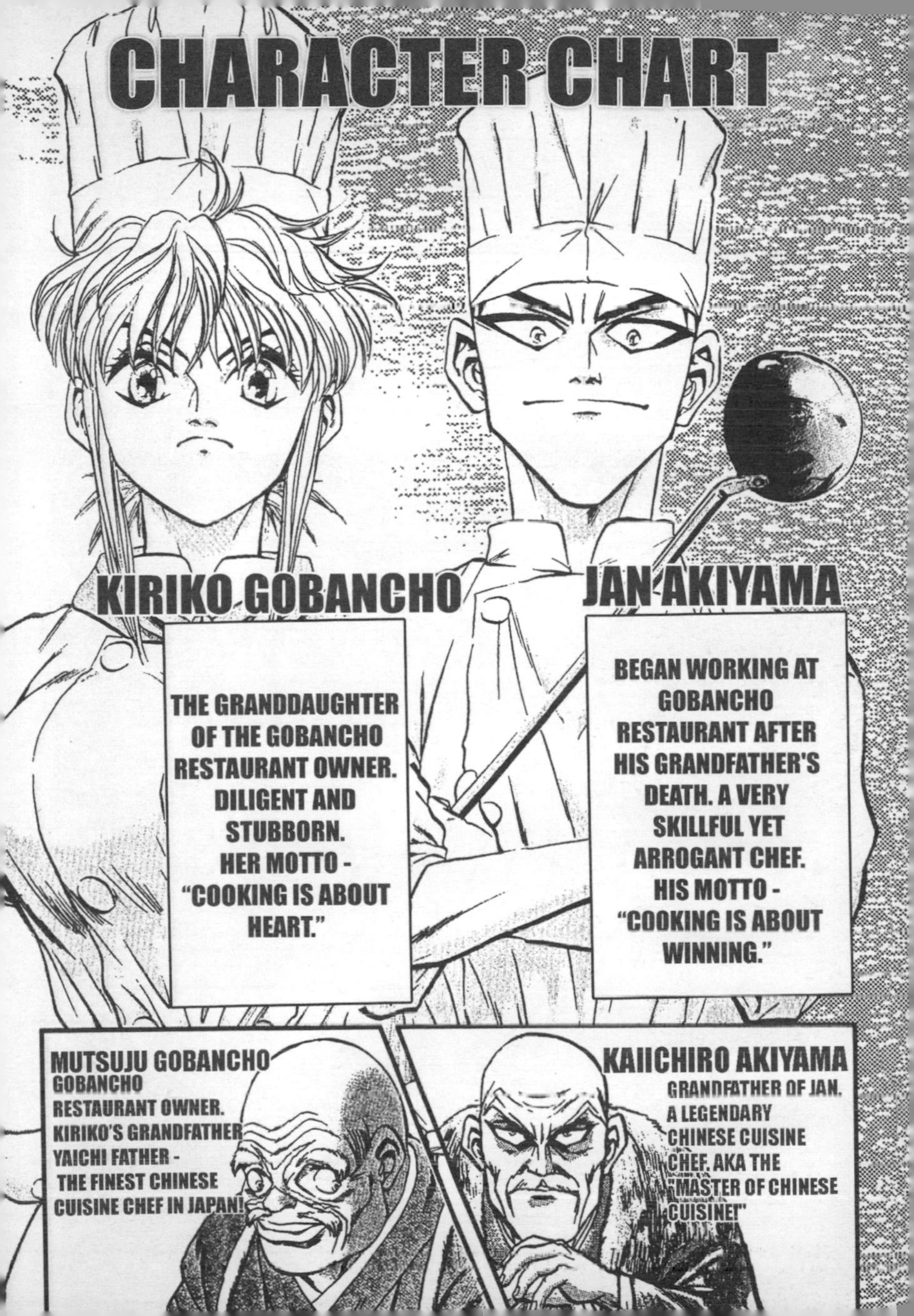
CHARACTER CHART
JAN AKIYAMA
BEGAN WORKING AT GOBANCHO RESTAURANT AFTER HIS GRANDFATHER'S DEATH. A VERY SKILLFUL YET ARROGANT CHEF. HIS MOTTO - "COOKING IS ABOUT WINNING."
KIRIKO GOBANCHO
THE GRANDDAUGHTER OF THE GOBANCHO RESTAURANT OWNER. DILIGENT AND STUBBORN. HER MOTTO - "COOKING IS ABOUT HEART."
KAIICHIRO AKIYAMA
GRANDFATHER OF JAN. A LEGENDARY CHINESE CUISINE CHEF. AKA THE "MASTER OF CHINESE CUISINE!"
MUTSUJU GOBANCHO
GOBANCHO RESTAURANT OWNER. KIRIKO'S GRANDFATHER YAICHI FATHER - THE FINEST CHINESE CUISINE CHEF IN JAPAN!

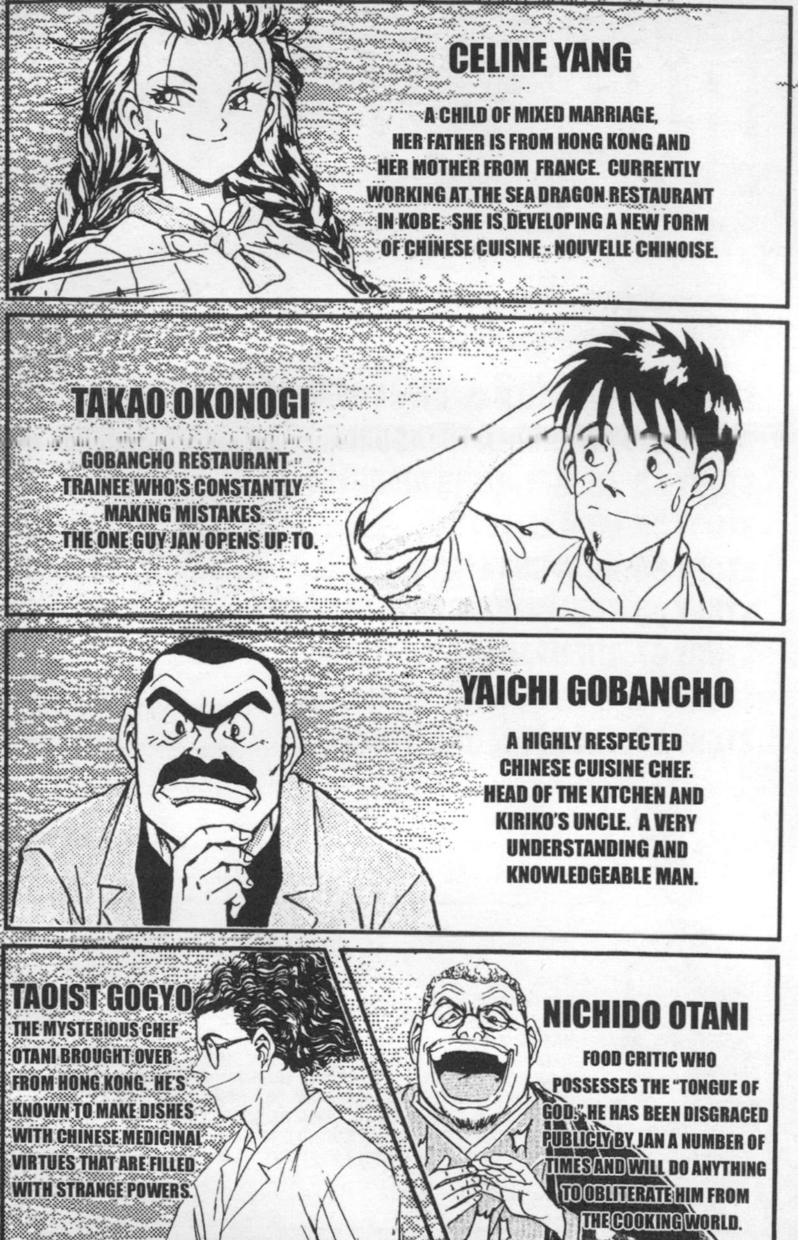
CELINE YANG
A CHILD OF MIXED MARRIAGE, HER FATHER IS FROM HONG KONG AND HER MOTHER FROM FRANCE. CURRENTLY WORKING AT THE SEA DRAGON RESTAURANT IN KOBE. SHE IS DEVELOPING A NEW FORM OF CHINESE CUISINE - NOUVELLE CHINOISE.
TAKAO OKONOGI
GOBANCHO RESTAURANT TRAINEE WHO'S CONSTANTLY MAKING MISTAKES. THE ONE GUY JAN OPENS UP TO.
YAICHI GOBANCHO
A HIGHLY RESPECTED CHINESE CUISINE CHEF. HEAD OF THE KITCHEN AND KIRIKO'S UNCLE. A VERY UNDERSTANDING AND KNOWLEDGEABLE MAN.
NICHIDO OTANI
FOOD CRITIC WHO POSSESSES THE "TONGUE OF GOD." HE HAS BEEN DISGRACED PUBLICLY BY JAN A NUMBER OF TIMES AND WILL DO ANYTHING TO OBLITERATE HIM FROM THE COOKING WORLD.
TAOIST GOGYO
THE MYSTERIOUS CHEF OTANI BROUGHT OVER FROM HONG KONG. HE'S KNOWN TO MAKE DISHES WITH CHINESE MEDICINAL VIRTUES THAT ARE FILLED WITH STRANGE POWERS.

IRON WOK JAN!

VOL. 10 TABLE OF CONTENTS

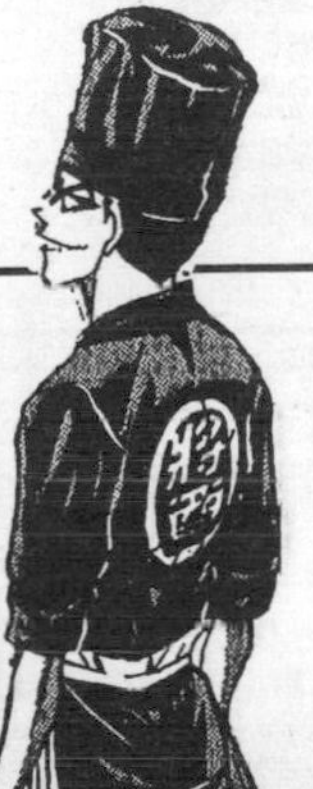

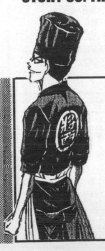

SYNOPSIS

OTANI, THE COOKING ADVISOR OF THE CHINESE RESTAURANT THE MIRAGE INSIDE A NEW GRAND HOTEL, IS TAKING ADVANTAGE OF JAN TO RAISE THE POPULARITY OF THE MIRAGE. OTANI HAS BROUGHT A CHEF FROM HONG KONG, TAOIST GOGYO AND ARRANGED A COOKING BATTLE THAT'LL CRUSH JAN TO DEFEAT. A 5-ROUND COOKING BATTLE BETWEEN JAN AND GOGYO IS BROADCASTED LIVE FROM ODAIBA SEA PARK. JAN WHO WAS CREAMED DURING THE FIRST TWO ROUNDS CAME BACK AND WIPED GOGYO OUT IN THE ROUND 3 "STAMINA DISH" BATTLE. JAN'S 1 FOR 2 AND ROUND 4 IS ABOUT TO BEGIN! THE TOPIC IS...!?

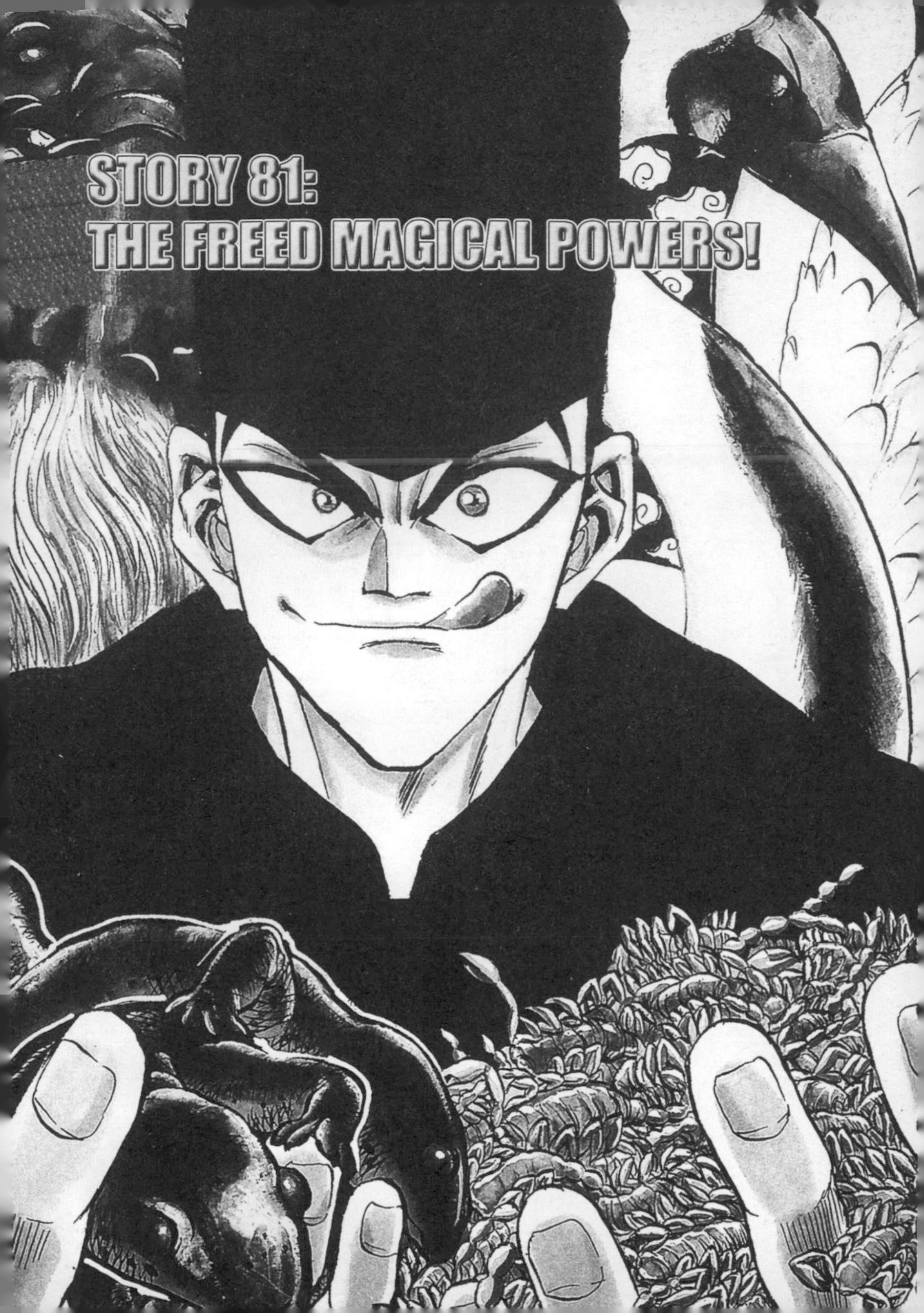
STORY 81:
THE FREED MAGICAL POWERS!

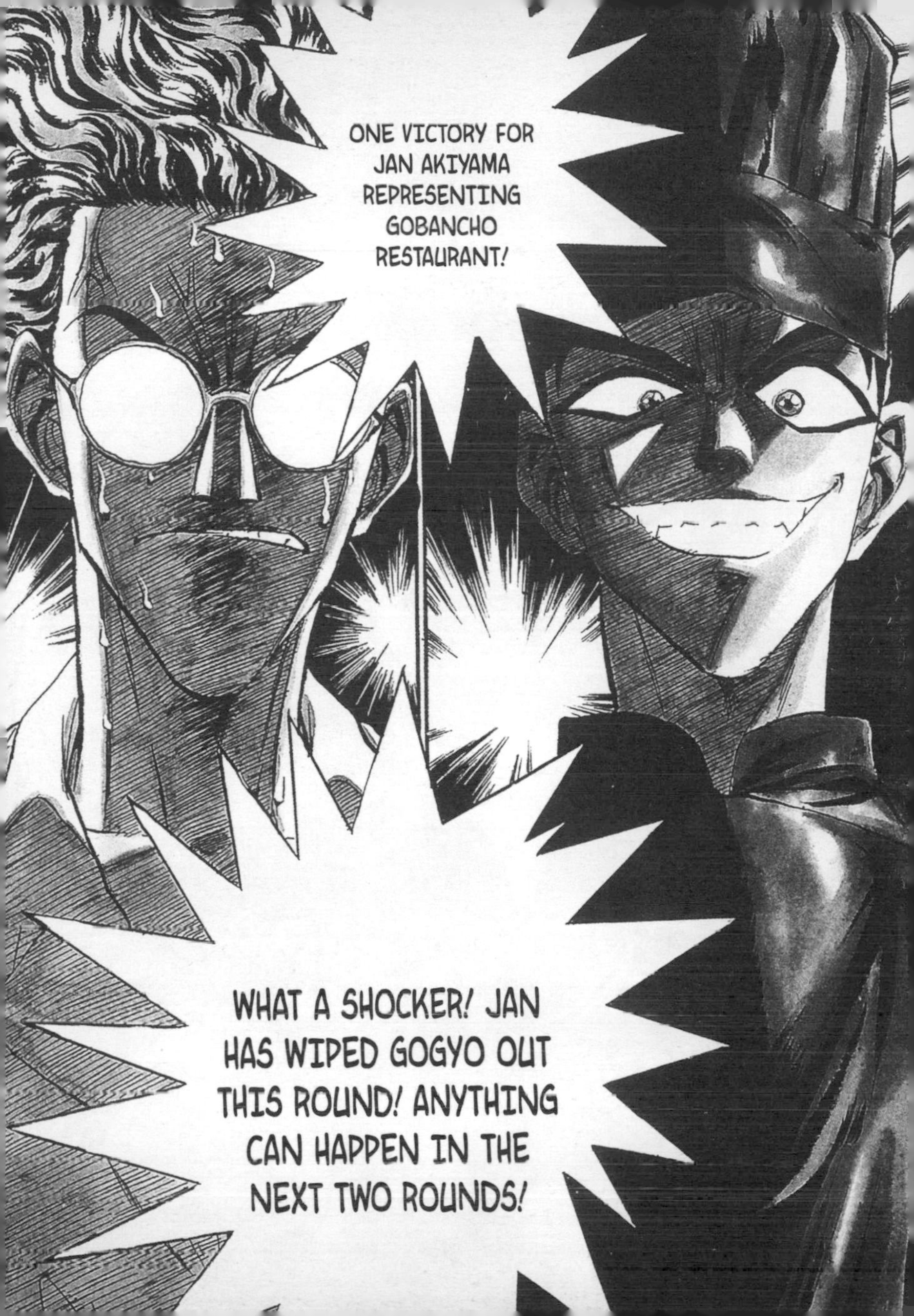
ONE VICTORY FOR JAN AKIYAMA REPRESENTING GOBANCHO RESTAURANT!
WHAT A SHOCKER! JAN HAS WIPED GOGYO OUT THIS ROUND! ANYTHING CAN HAPPEN IN THE NEXT TWO ROUNDS!

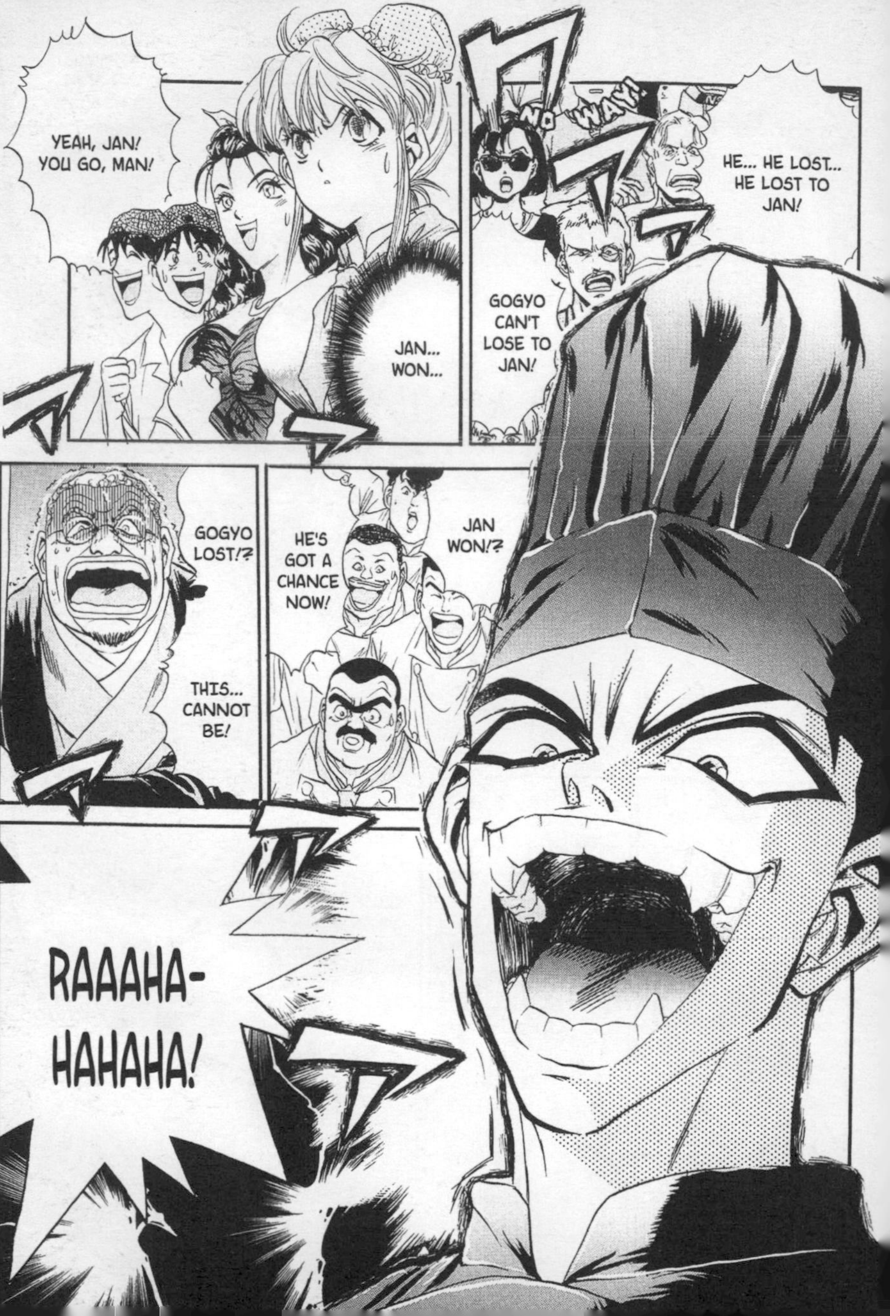
NO WAY!
HE... HE LOST... HE LOST TO JAN!
GOGYO CAN'T LOSE TO JAN!
YEAH, JAN! YOU GO, MAN!
JAN... WON...
JAN WON!?
HE'S GOT A CHANCE NOW!
GOGYO LOST!?
THIS... CANNOT BE!
RAAAHA-HAHAHA!

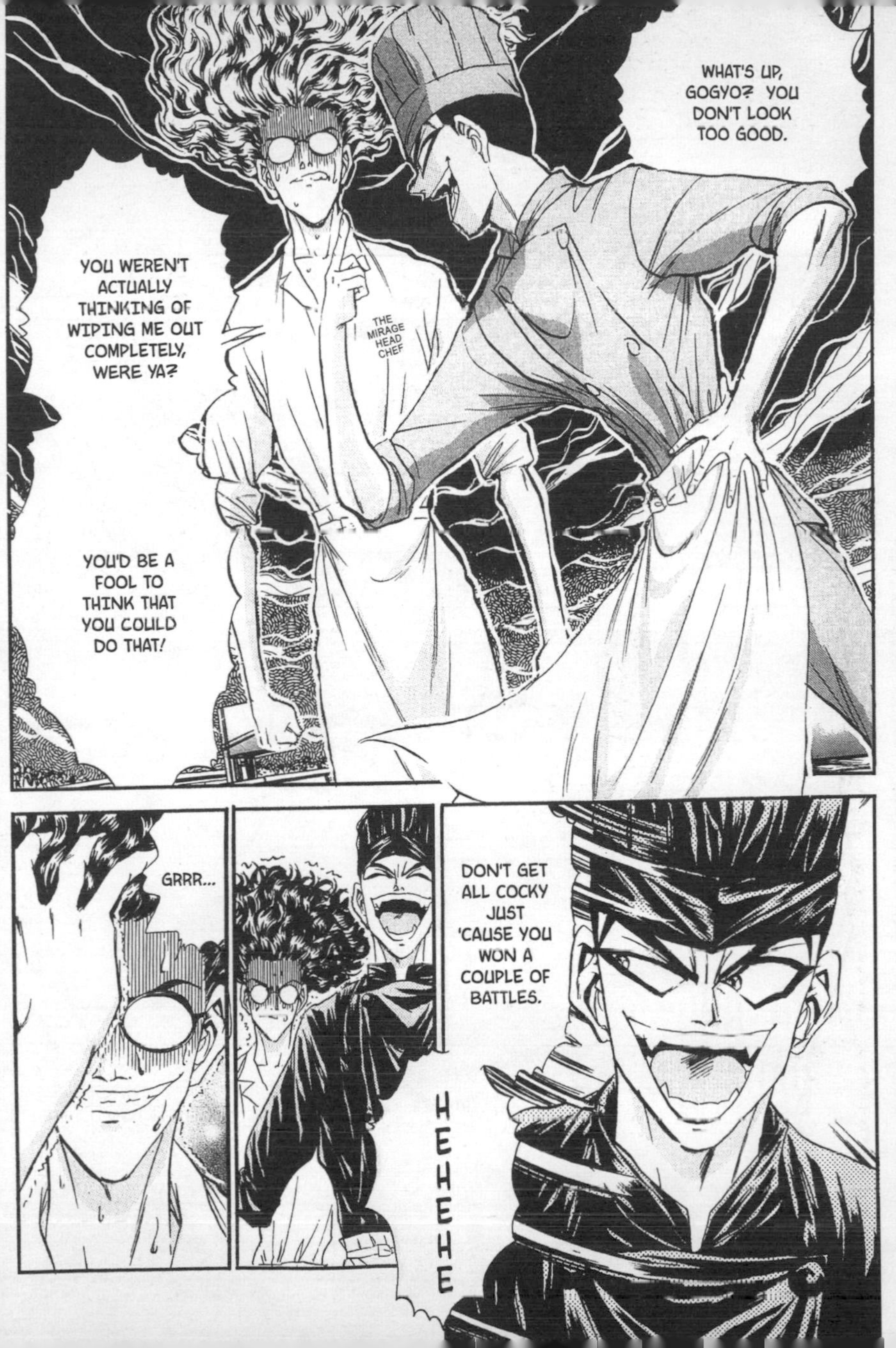
WHAT'S UP, GOGYO? YOU DON'T LOOK TOO GOOD.
THE MIRAGE HEAD CHEF
YOU WEREN'T ACTUALLY THINKING OF WIPING ME OUT COMPLETELY, WERE YA?
YOU'D BE A FOOL TO THINK THAT YOU COULD DO THAT!
DON'T GET ALL COCKY JUST 'CAUSE YOU WON A COUPLE OF BATTLES.
HEHEHE
GRRR...

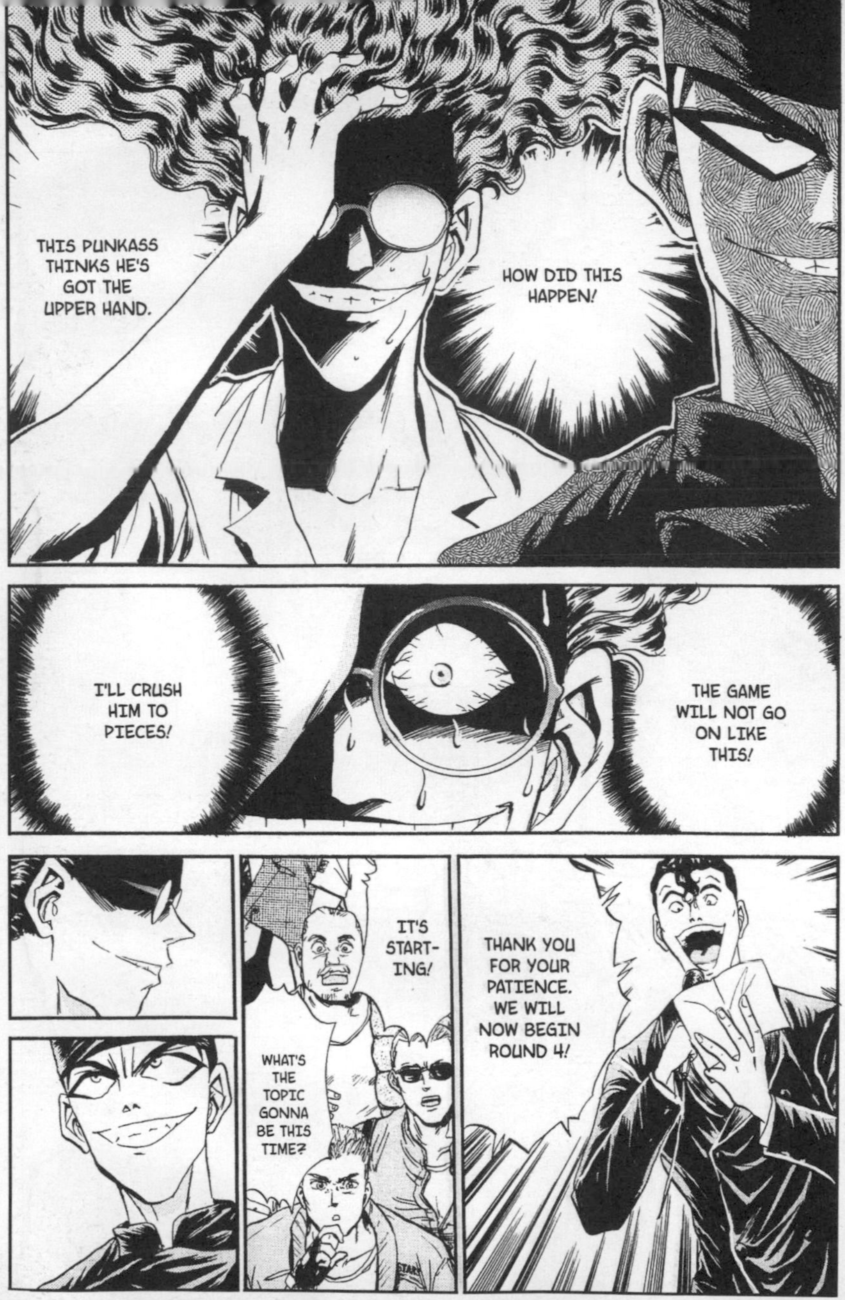
HOW DID THIS HAPPEN!
THIS PUNKASS THINKS HE'S GOT THE UPPER HAND.
THE GAME WILL NOT GO ON LIKE THIS!
I'LL CRUSH HIM TO PIECES!
THANK YOU FOR YOUR PATIENCE. WE WILL NOW BEGIN ROUND 4!
IT'S START-ING!
WHAT'S THE TOPIC GONNA BE THIS TIME?

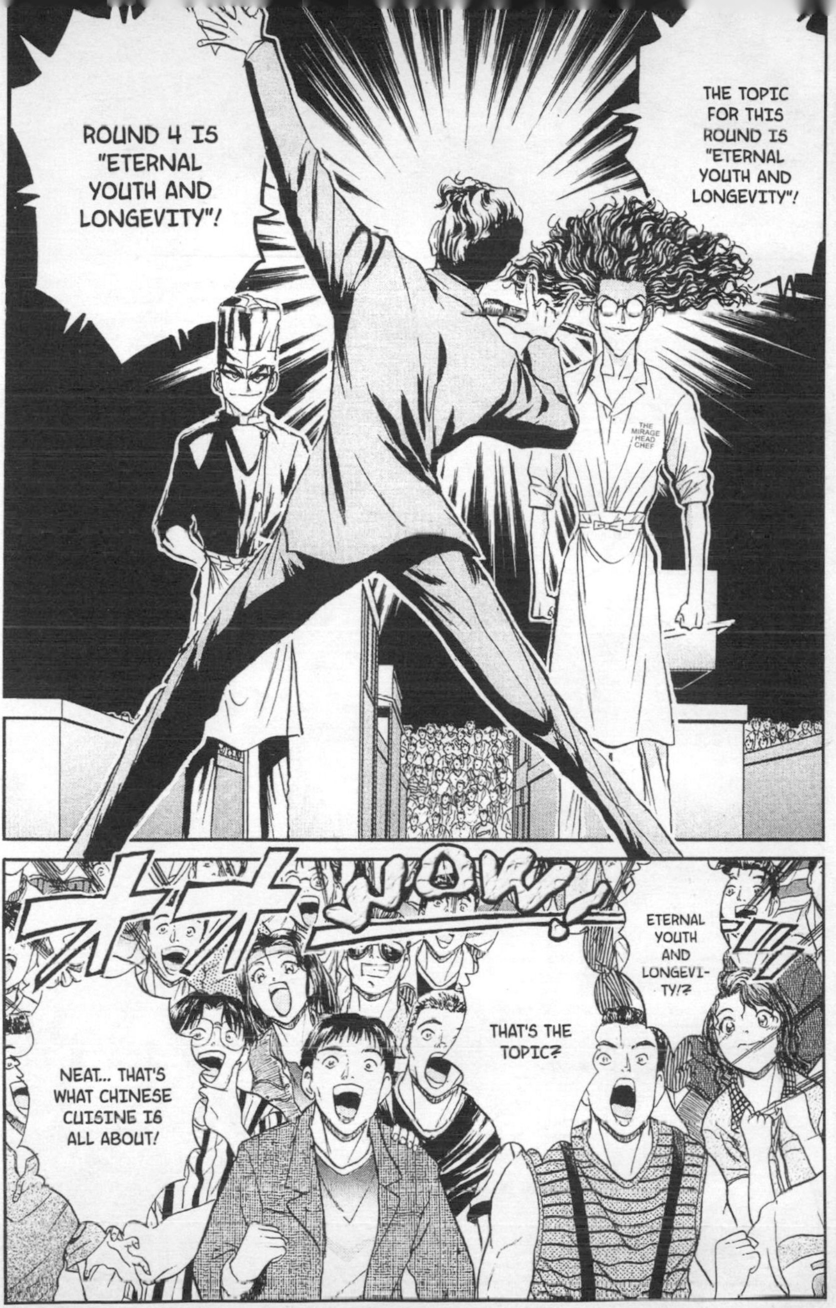
THE TOPIC FOR THIS ROUND IS "ETERNAL YOUTH AND LONGEVITY"!
ROUND 4 IS "ETERNAL YOUTH AND LONGEVITY"!
THE MIRAGE HEAD CHEF
オオ
WOW!
ETERNAL YOUTH AND LONGEVI-TY!?
THAT'S THE TOPIC?
NEAT... THAT'S WHAT CHINESE CUISINE IS ALL ABOUT!

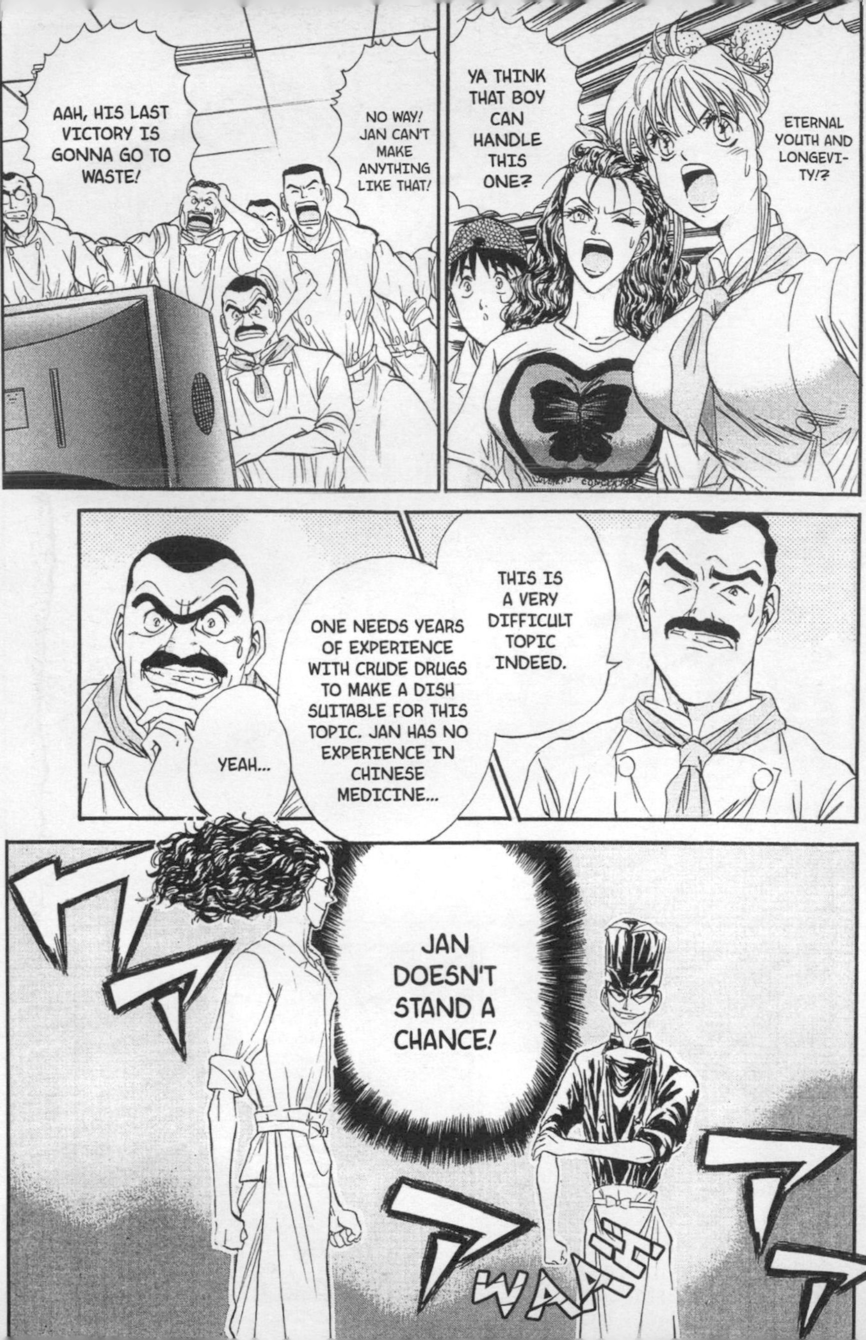
ETERNAL YOUTH AND LONGEVITY!?
YA THINK THAT BOY CAN HANDLE THIS ONE?
NO WAY! JAN CAN'T MAKE ANYTHING LIKE THAT!
AAH, HIS LAST VICTORY IS GONNA GO TO WASTE!
THIS IS A VERY DIFFICULT TOPIC INDEED.
ONE NEEDS YEARS OF EXPERIENCE WITH CRUDE DRUGS TO MAKE A DISH SUITABLE FOR THIS TOPIC. JAN HAS NO EXPERIENCE IN CHINESE MEDICINE...
YEAH...
JAN DOESN'T STAND A CHANCE!
WAAI

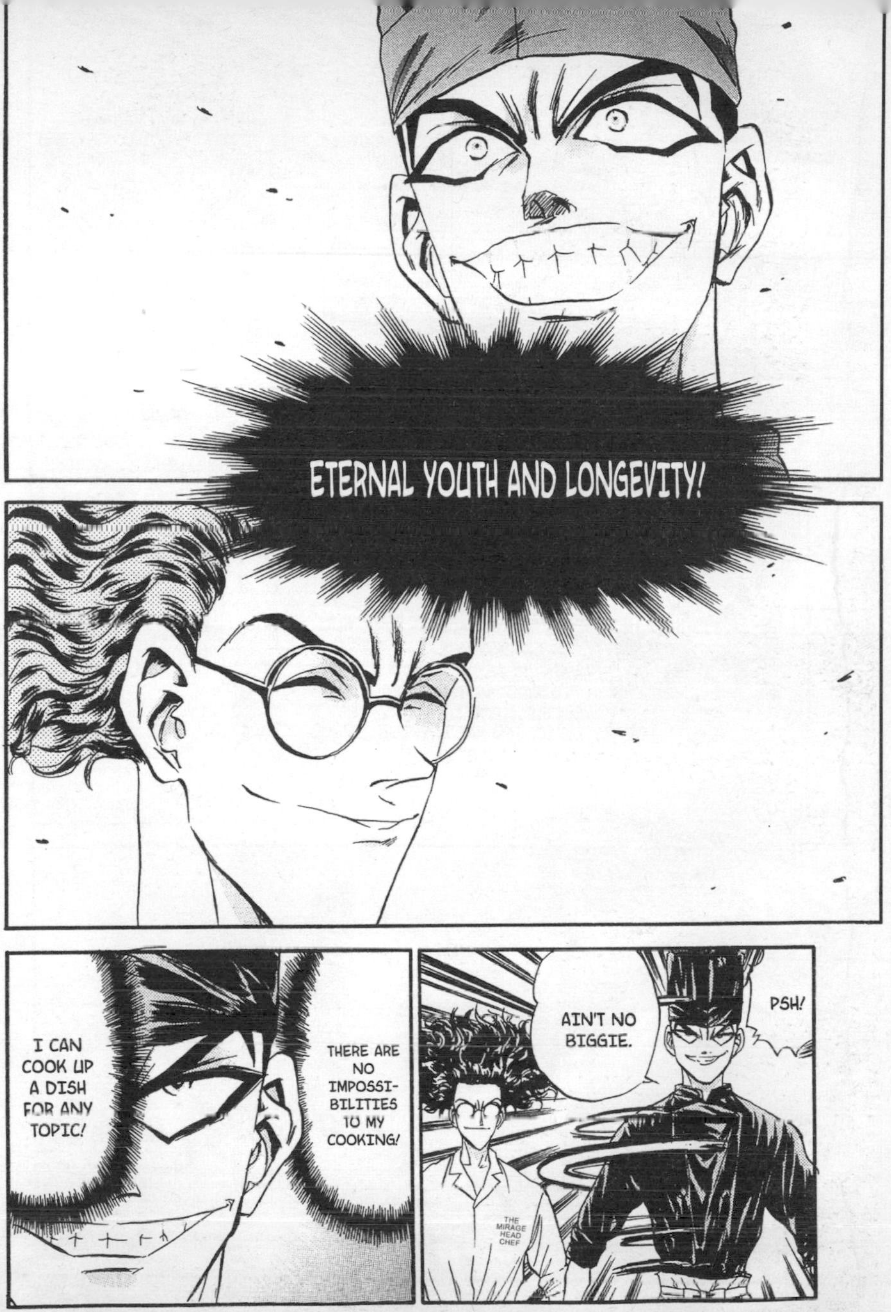
ETERNAL YOUTH AND LONGEVITY!
PSH!
AIN'T NO BIGGIE.
THE MIRAGE HEAD CHEF
THERE ARE NO IMPOSSIBILITIES TO MY COOKING!
I CAN COOK UP A DISH FOR ANY TOPIC!

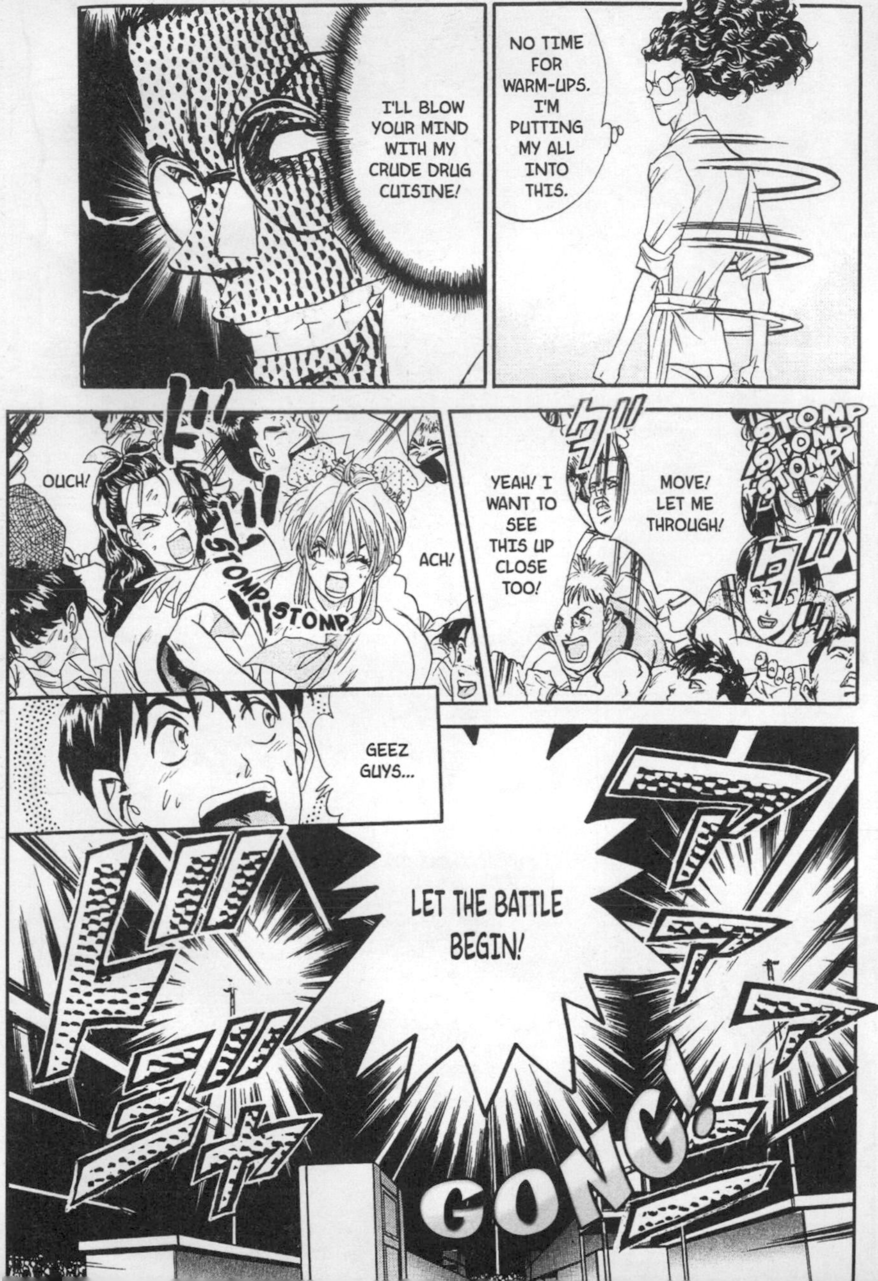
NO TIME FOR WARM-UPS. I'M PUTTING MY ALL INTO THIS.
I'LL BLOW YOUR MIND WITH MY CRUDE DRUG CUISINE!
STOMP STOMP STOMP
MOVE! LET ME THROUGH!
YEAH! I WANT TO SEE THIS UP CLOSE TOO!
ACH!
STOMP STOMP
OUCH!
GEEZ GUYS...
LET THE BATTLE BEGIN!
GONG!

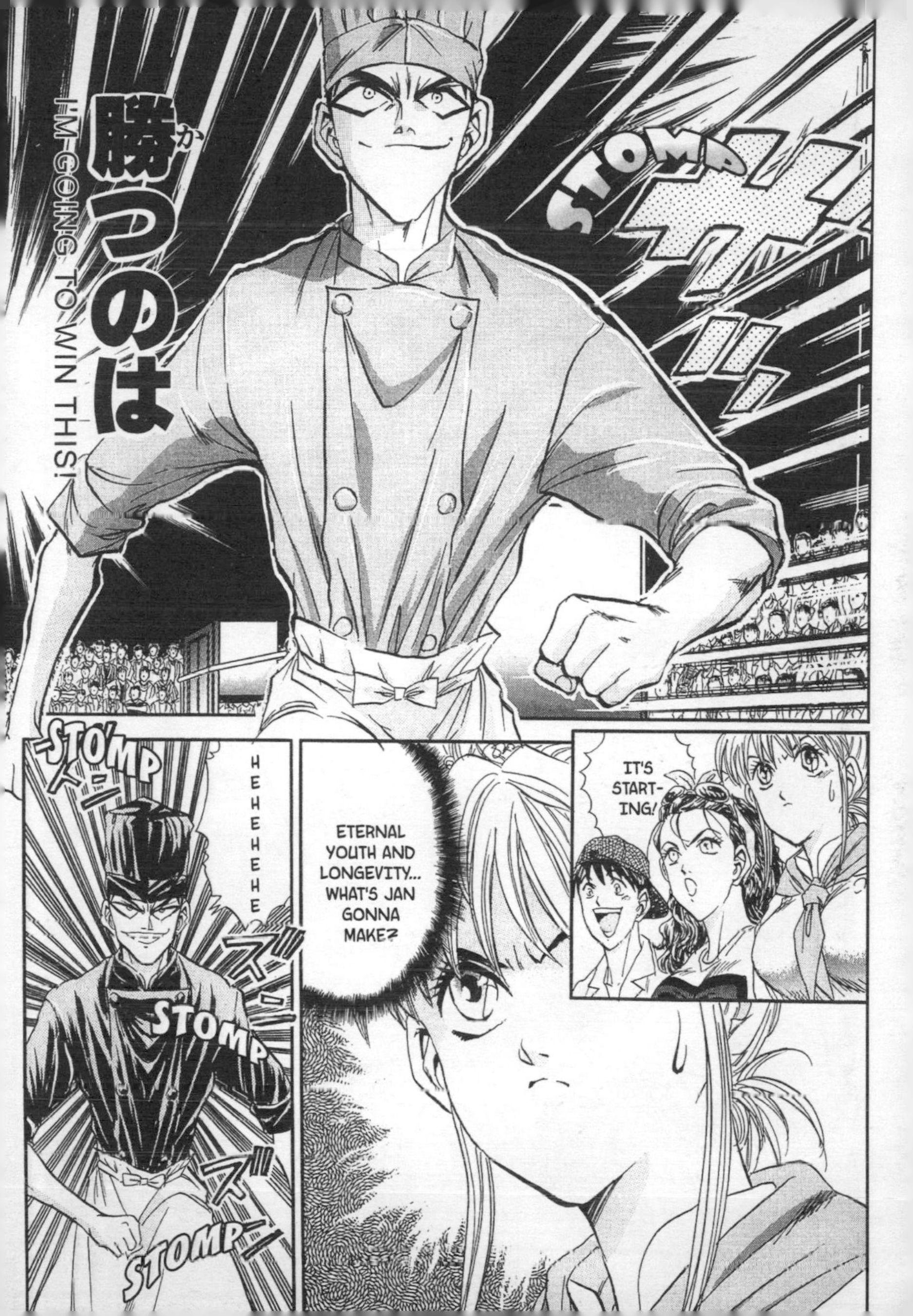

勝つのは
I'M GOING TO WIN THIS!
STOMP
IT'S START-ING!
ETERNAL YOUTH AND LONGEVITY... WHAT'S JAN GONNA MAKE?
STOMP
HEHEHEHEHEHE
STOMP
STOMP

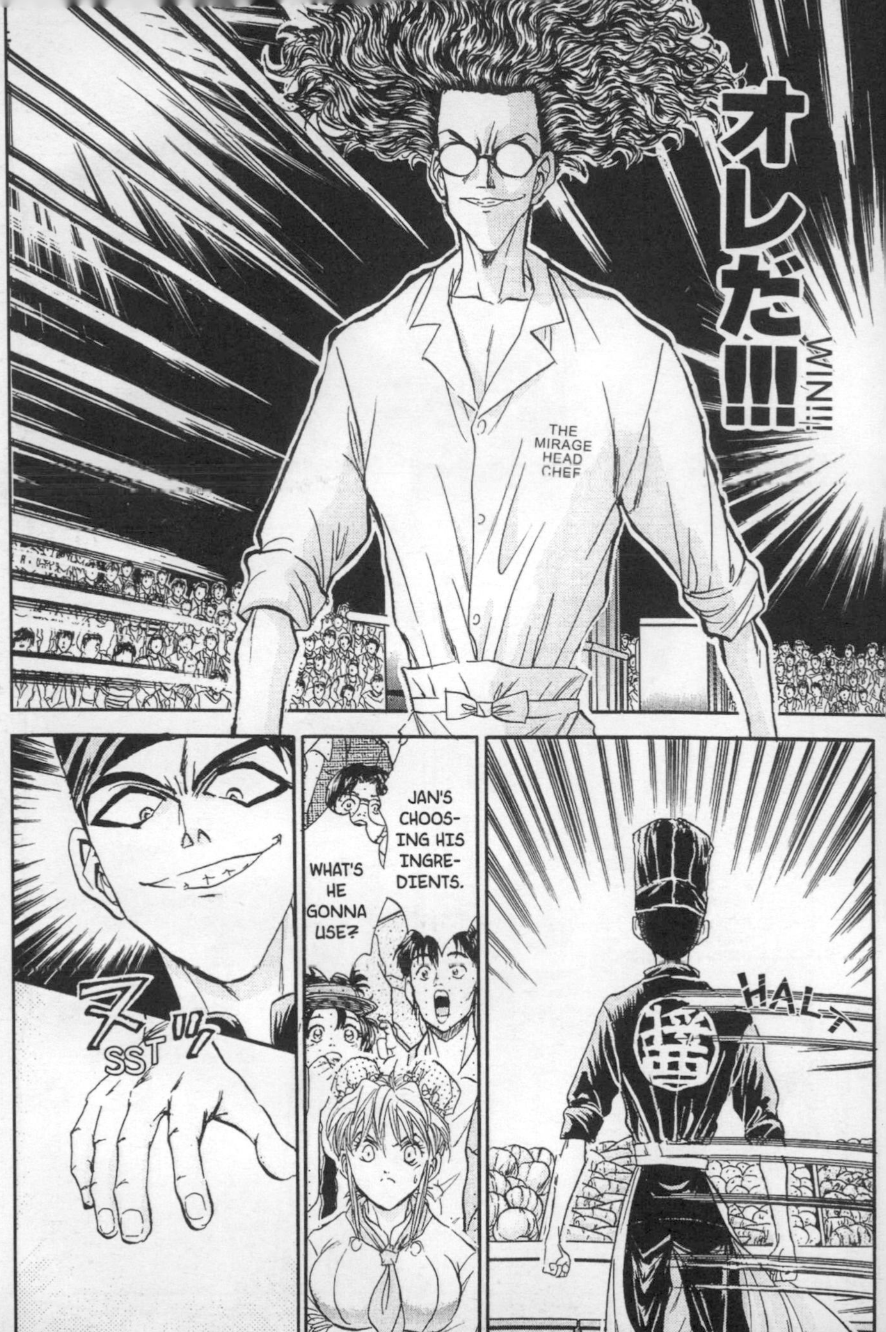
オレだ!!!
WIN!!!
THE MIRAGE HEAD CHEF
HALT
JAN'S CHOOSING HIS INGREDIENTS.
WHAT'S HE GONNA USE?
スッ
SST

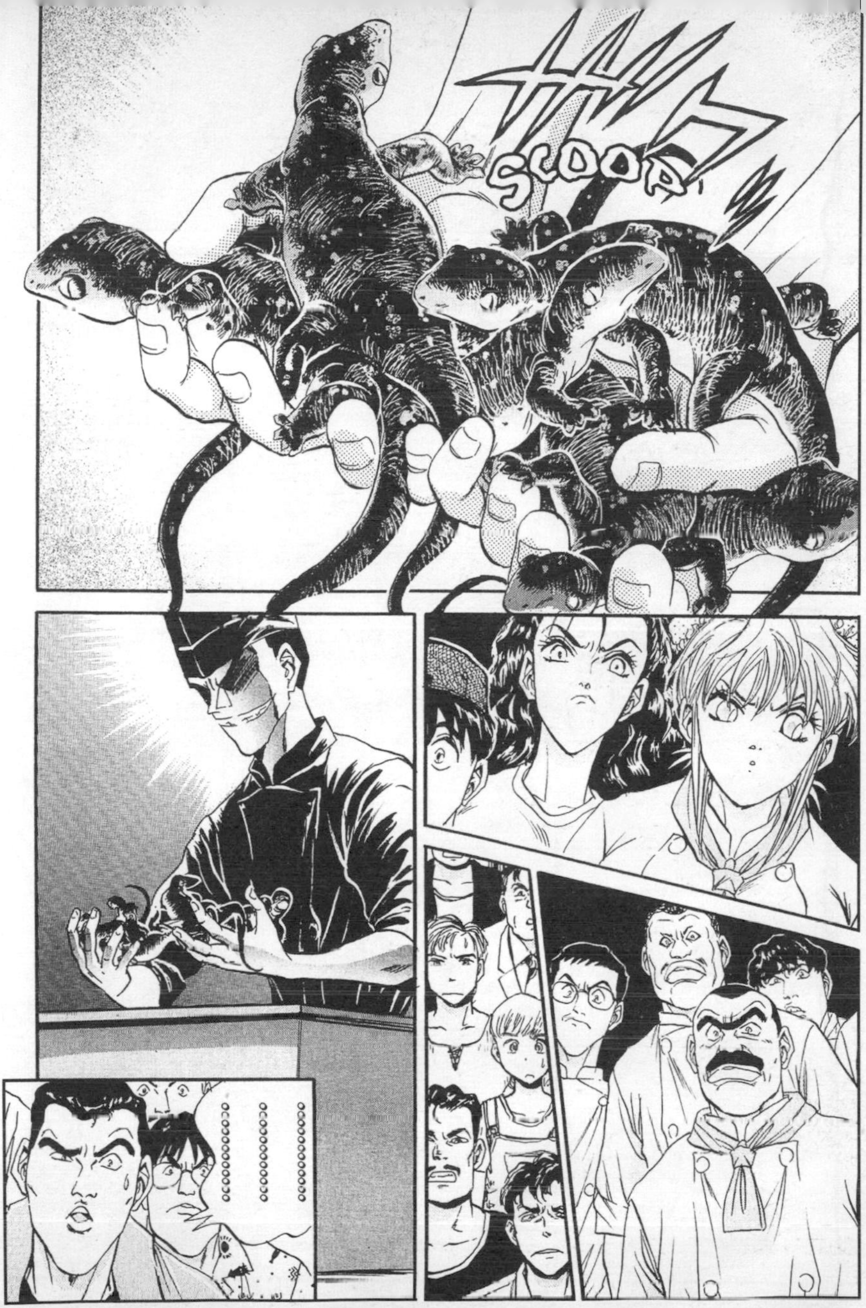
SLOOP!

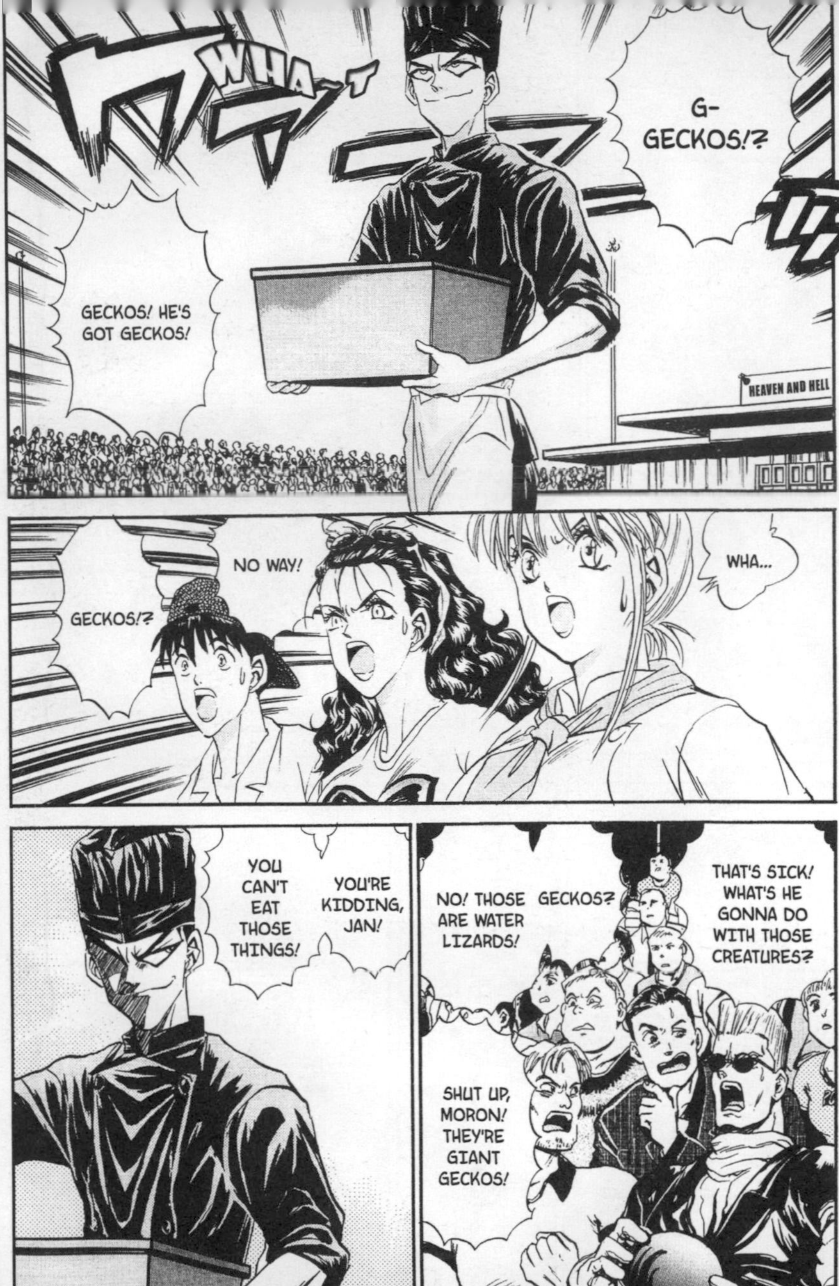
G-
GECKOS!?
WHA-T
GECKOS! HE'S GOT GECKOS!
HEAVEN AND HELL
WHA...
NO WAY!
GECKOS!?
THAT'S SICK! WHAT'S HE GONNA DO WITH THOSE CREATURES?
GECKOS?
NO! THOSE ARE WATER LIZARDS!
SHUT UP, MORON! THEY'RE GIANT GECKOS!
YOU'RE KIDDING, JAN!
YOU CAN'T EAT THOSE THINGS!

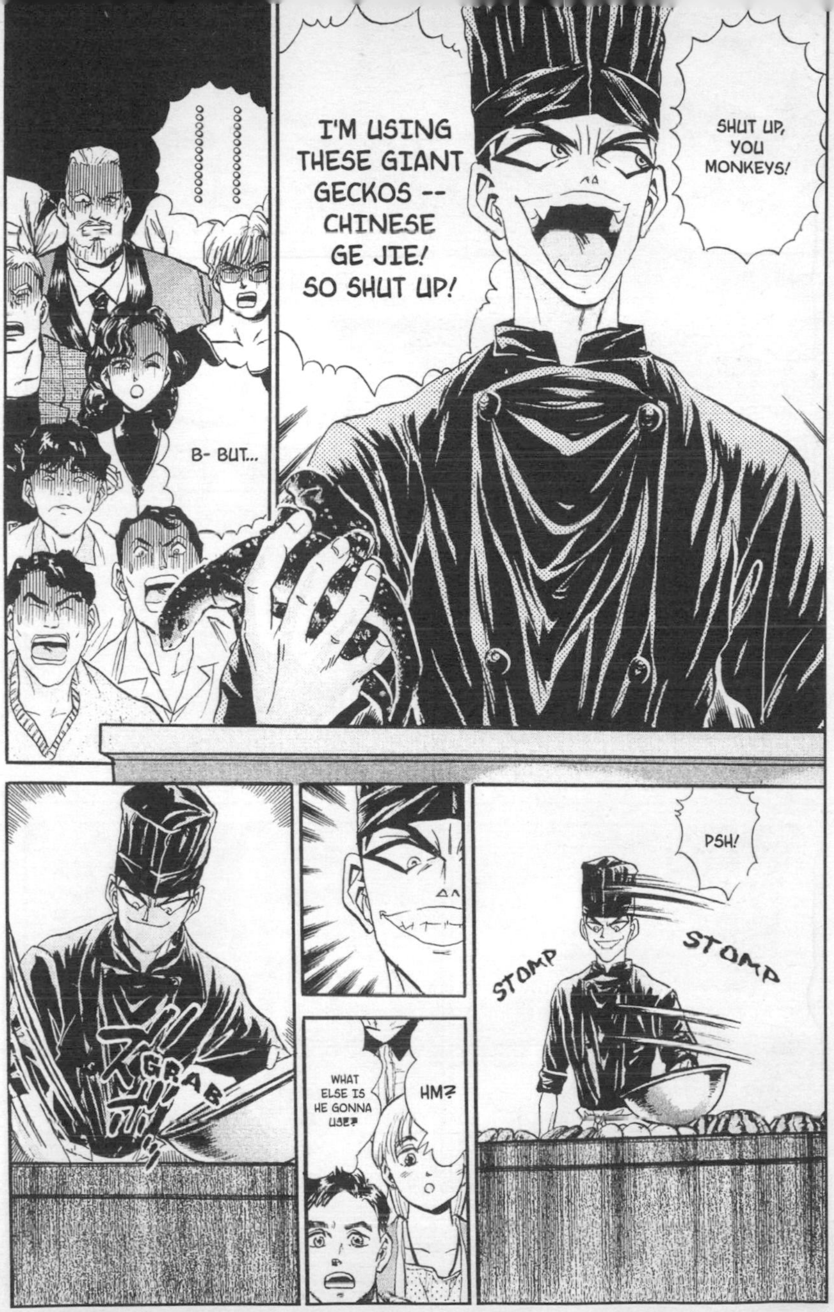
SHUT UP, YOU MONKEYS!
I'M USING THESE GIANT GECKOS -- CHINESE GE JIE! SO SHUT UP!
B- BUT...
PSH!
STOMP
STOMP
HM?
WHAT ELSE IS HE GONNA USE?
GRAB

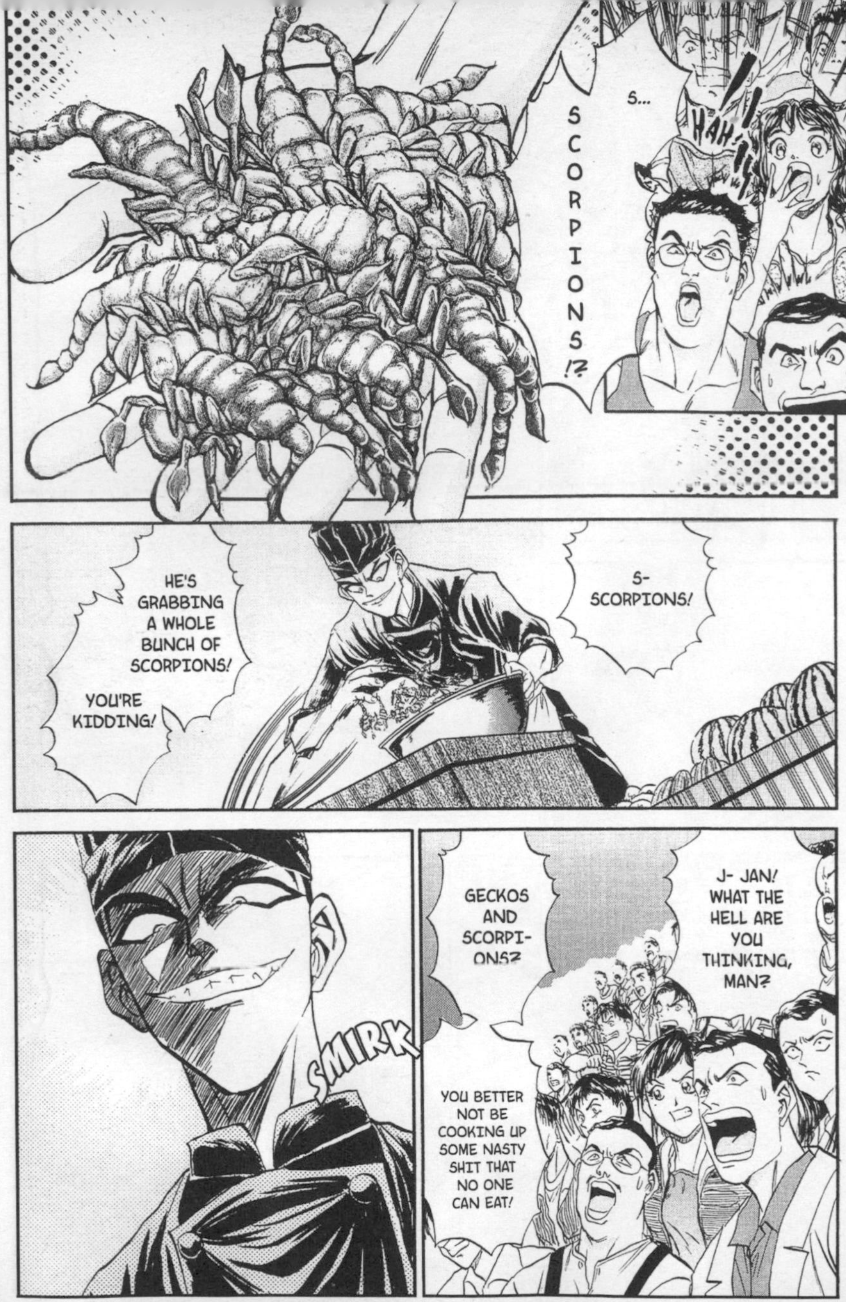
HAH!!
S...
SCORPIONS!?
S- SCORPIONS!
HE'S GRABBING A WHOLE BUNCH OF SCORPIONS!
YOU'RE KIDDING!
J- JAN! WHAT THE HELL ARE YOU THINKING, MAN?
GECKOS AND SCORPI-ONS?
YOU BETTER NOT BE COOKING UP SOME NASTY SHIT THAT NO ONE CAN EAT!
SMIRK

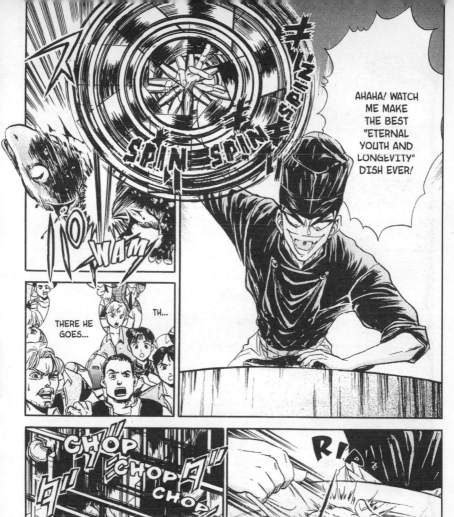

AHAHA! WATCH ME MAKE THE BEST "ETERNAL YOUTH AND LONGEVITY" DISH EVER!

SPIN SPIN SPIN

WAM

TH...

THERE HE GOES...

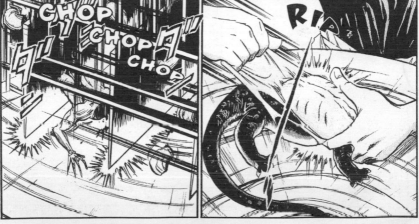

CHOP CHOP CHOP

RIP

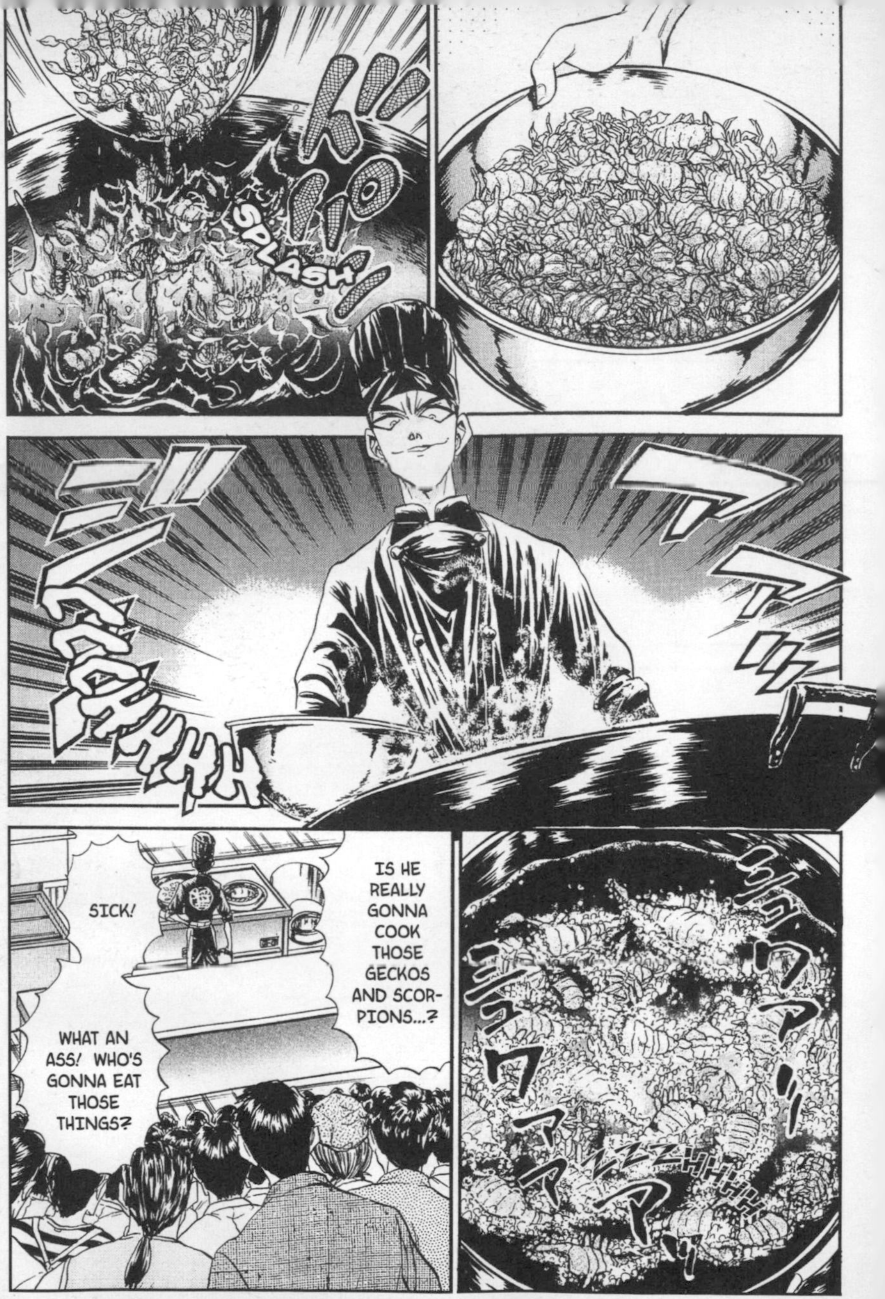
SPLASH
CHHHHHH
ZZZZHHHHH
IS HE REALLY GONNA COOK THOSE GECKOS AND SCORPIONS...?
SICK!
WHAT AN ASS! WHO'S GONNA EAT THOSE THINGS?

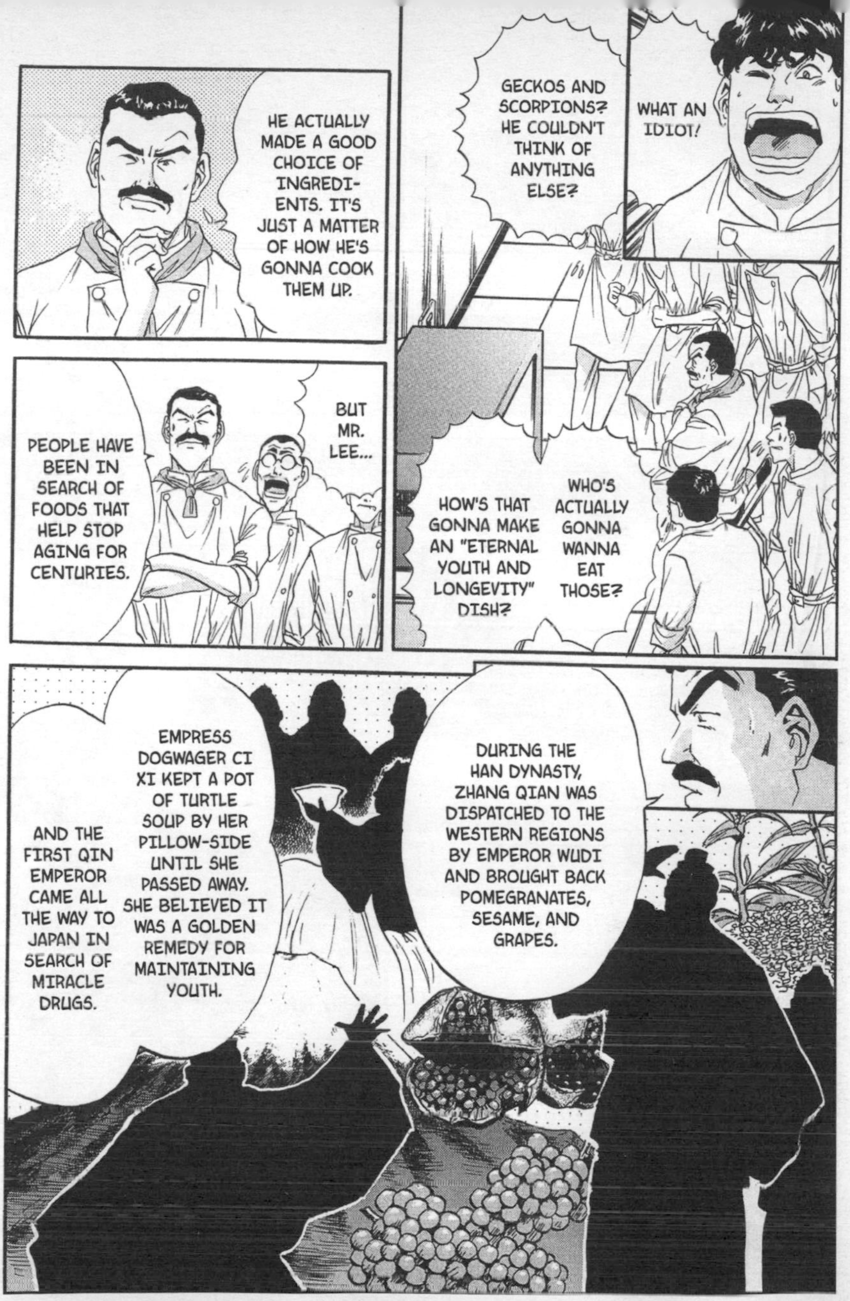
WHAT AN IDIOT!
GECKOS AND SCORPIONS? HE COULDN'T THINK OF ANYTHING ELSE?
WHO'S ACTUALLY GONNA WANNA EAT THOSE?
HOW'S THAT GONNA MAKE AN "ETERNAL YOUTH AND LONGEVITY" DISH?
HE ACTUALLY MADE A GOOD CHOICE OF INGREDI- ENTS. IT'S JUST A MATTER OF HOW HE'S GONNA COOK THEM UP.
BUT MR. LEE...
PEOPLE HAVE BEEN IN SEARCH OF FOODS THAT HELP STOP AGING FOR CENTURIES.
DURING THE HAN DYNASTY, ZHANG QIAN WAS DISPATCHED TO THE WESTERN REGIONS BY EMPEROR WUDI AND BROUGHT BACK POMEGRANATES, SESAME, AND GRAPES.
EMPRESS DOGWAGER CI XI KEPT A POT OF TURTLE SOUP BY HER PILLOW-SIDE UNTIL SHE PASSED AWAY. SHE BELIEVED IT WAS A GOLDEN REMEDY FOR MAINTAINING YOUTH.
AND THE FIRST QIN EMPEROR CAME ALL THE WAY TO JAPAN IN SEARCH OF MIRACLE DRUGS.

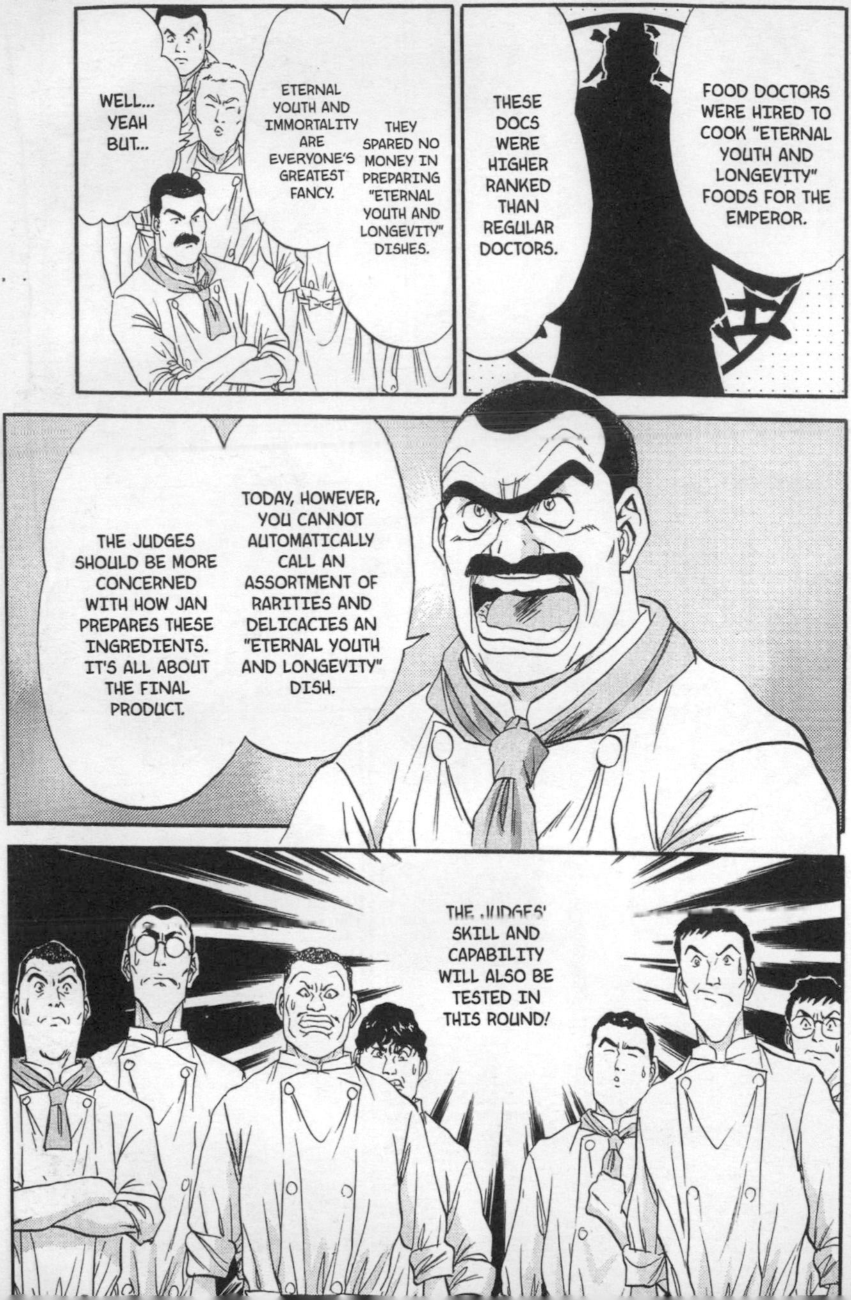

FOOD DOCTORS WERE HIRED TO COOK "ETERNAL YOUTH AND LONGEVITY" FOODS FOR THE EMPEROR.
THESE DOCS WERE HIGHER RANKED THAN REGULAR DOCTORS.
ETERNAL YOUTH AND IMMORTALITY ARE EVERYONE'S GREATEST FANCY.
THEY SPARED NO MONEY IN PREPARING "ETERNAL YOUTH AND LONGEVITY" DISHES.
WELL... YEAH BUT...
TODAY, HOWEVER, YOU CANNOT AUTOMATICALLY CALL AN ASSORTMENT OF RARITIES AND DELICACIES AN "ETERNAL YOUTH AND LONGEVITY" DISH.
THE JUDGES SHOULD BE MORE CONCERNED WITH HOW JAN PREPARES THESE INGREDIENTS. IT'S ALL ABOUT THE FINAL PRODUCT.
THE JUDGES' SKILL AND CAPABILITY WILL ALSO BE TESTED IN THIS ROUND!

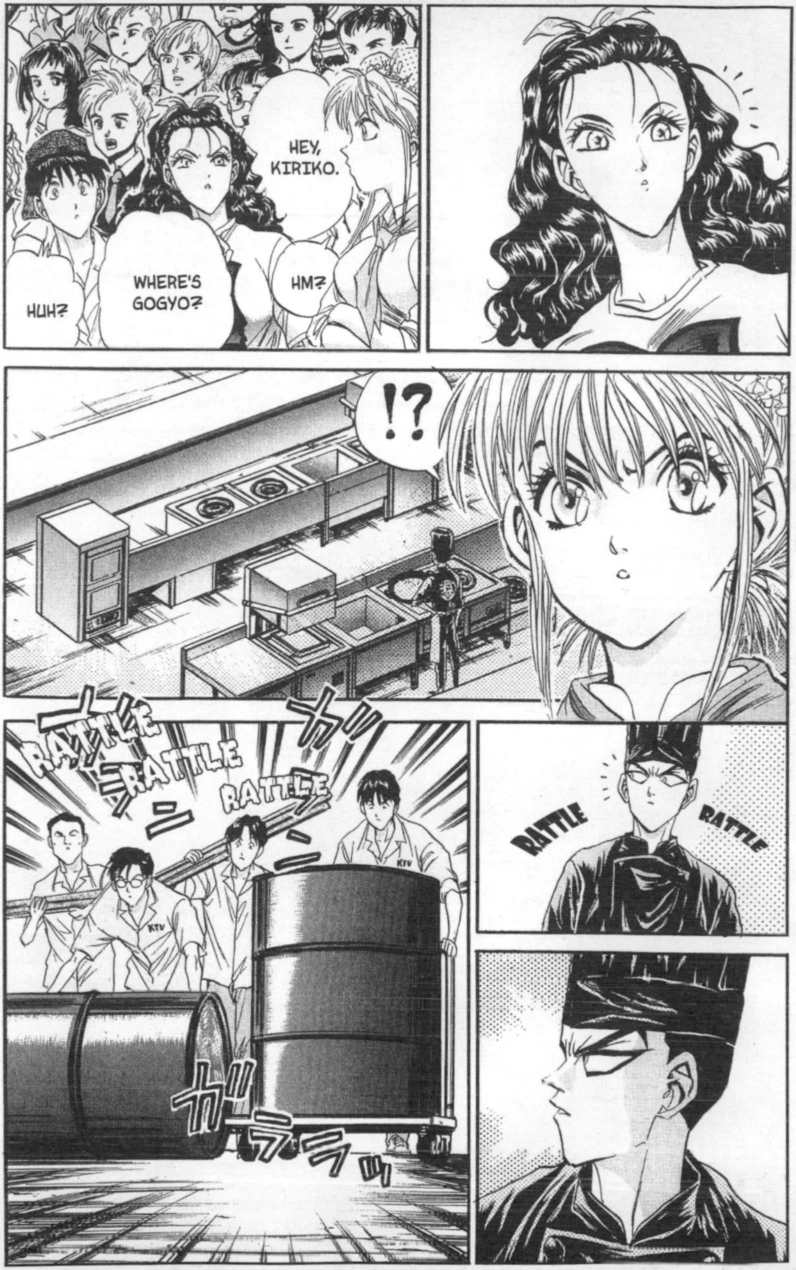
HEY, KIRIKO.
HM?
WHERE'S GOGYO?
HUH?
!?
RATTLE RATTLE
RATTLE RATTLE RATTLE

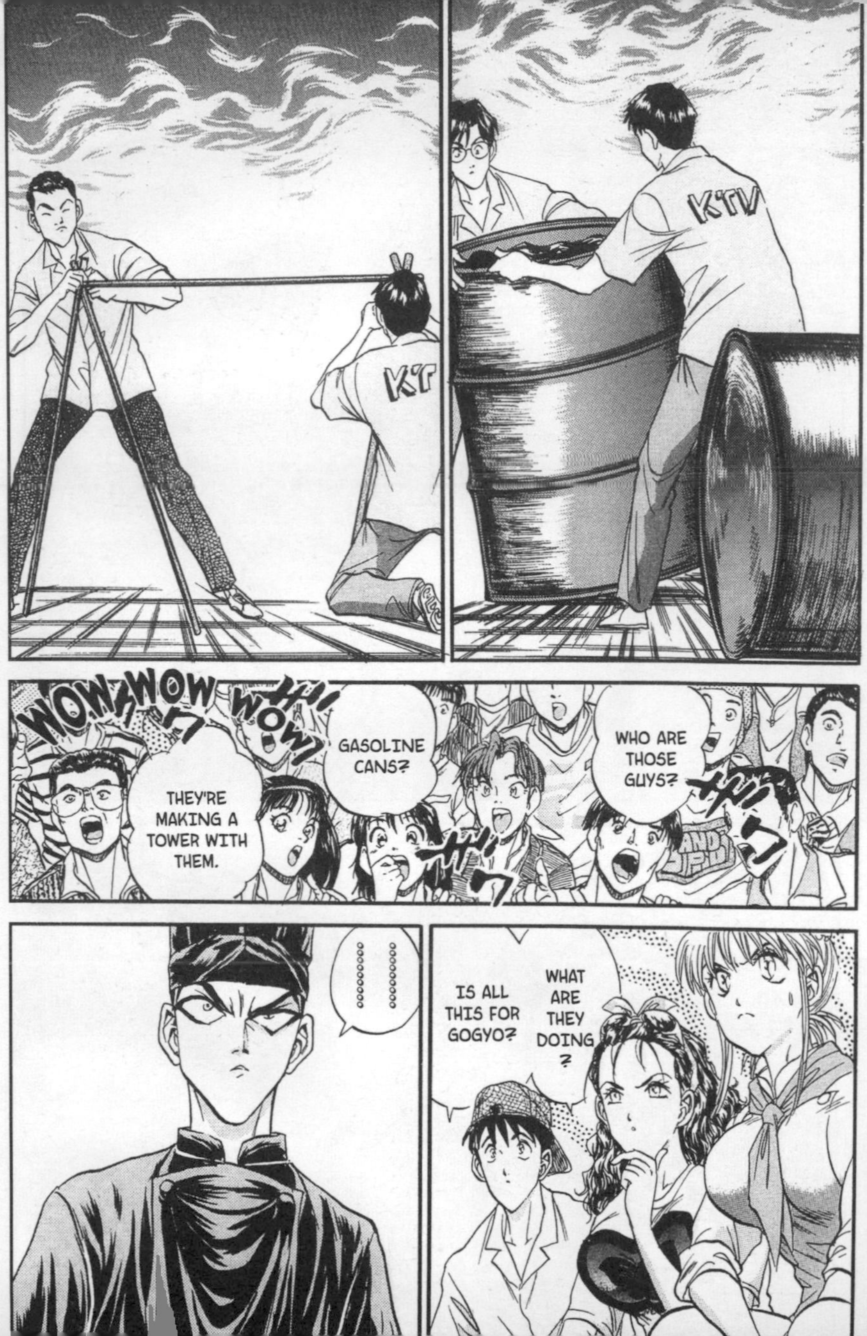
K'TV
WHO ARE THOSE GUYS?
GASOLINE CANS?
THEY'RE MAKING A TOWER WITH THEM.
WOW WOW WOW WOW!
WHAT ARE THEY DOING?
IS ALL THIS FOR GOGYO?
....

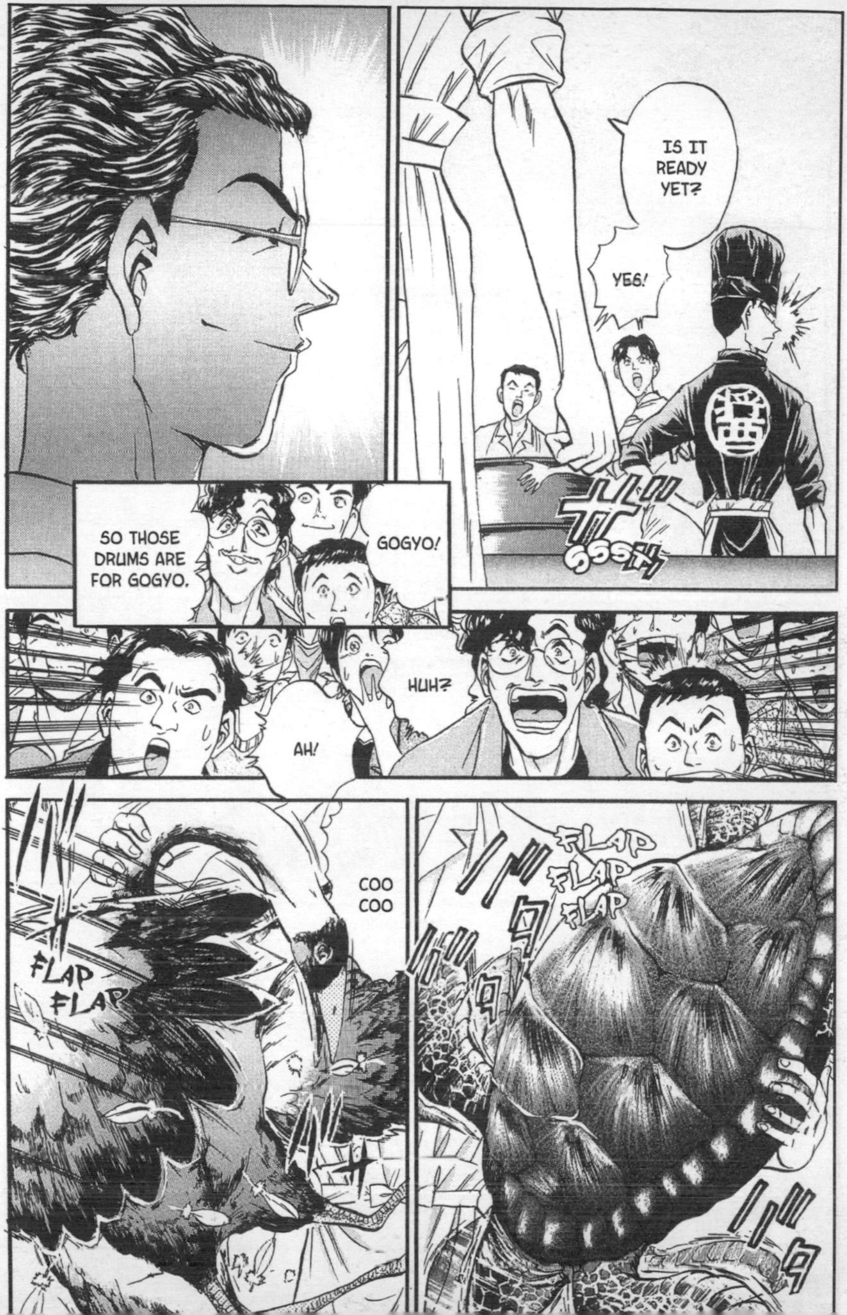
IS IT READY YET?
YES!
GOSSH
GOGYO!
SO THOSE DRUMS ARE FOR GOGYO.
HUH?
AH!
FLAP
FLAP
FLAP
COO COO
FLAP FLAP

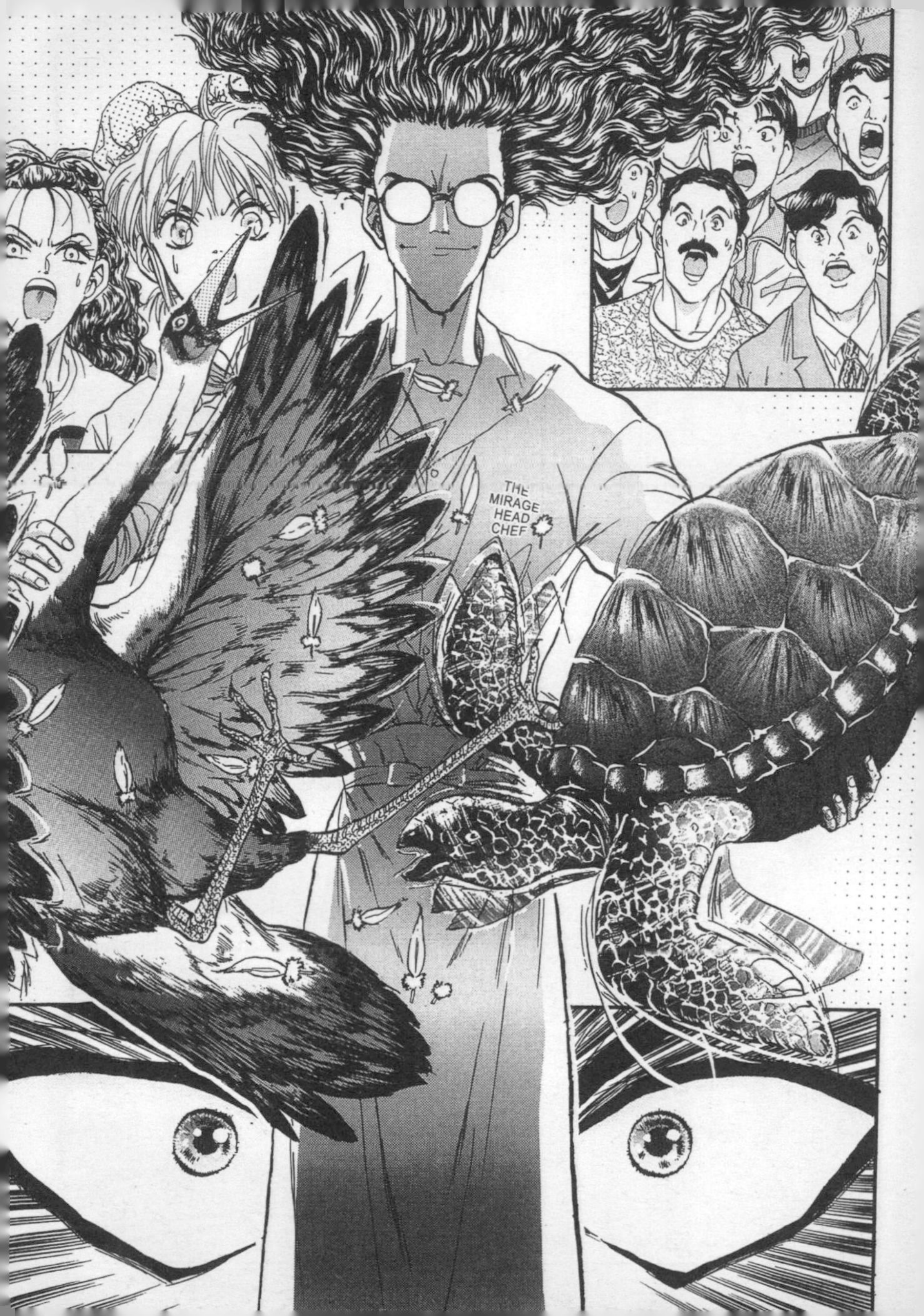
THE MIRAGE HEAD CHEF

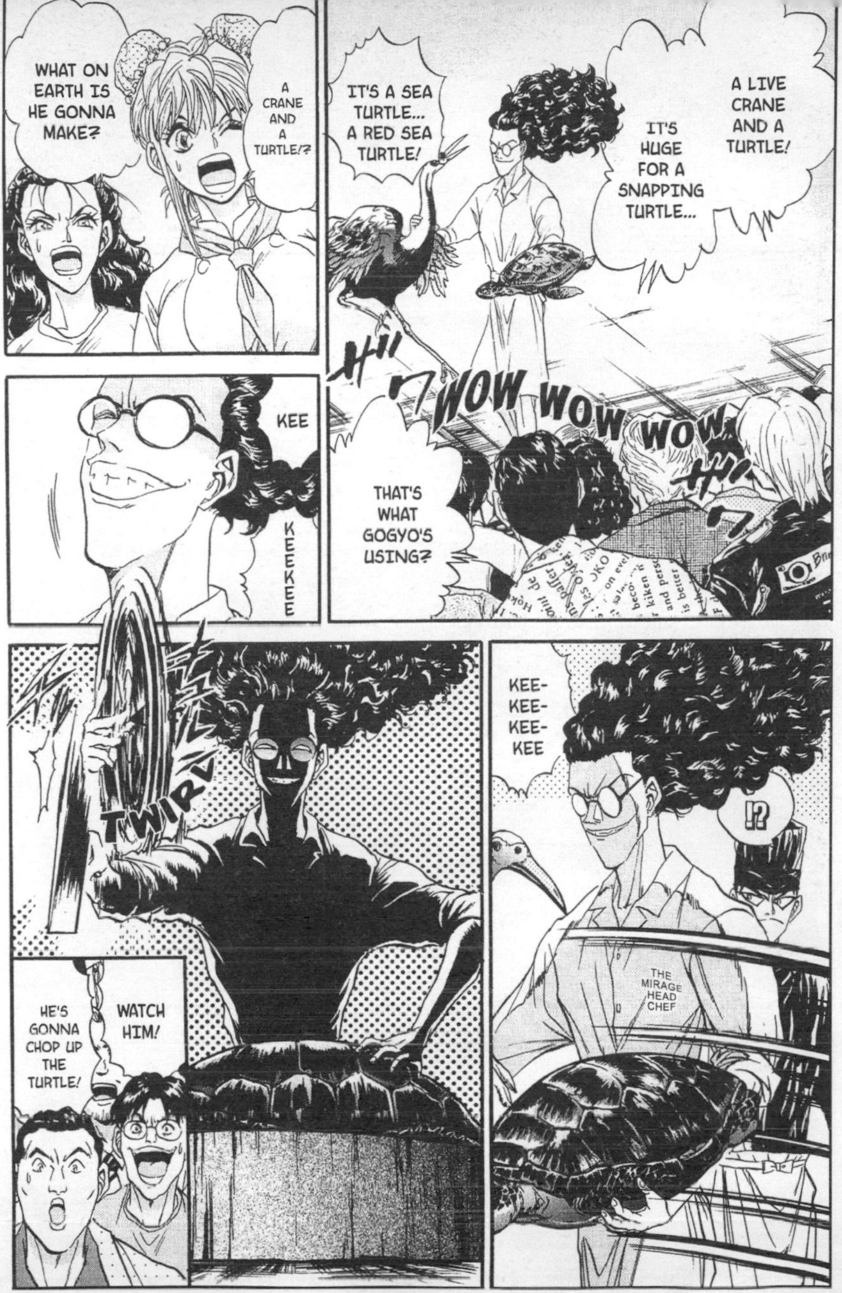
A LIVE CRANE AND A TURTLE!
IT'S HUGE FOR A SNAPPING TURTLE...
IT'S A SEA TURTLE... A RED SEA TURTLE!
A CRANE AND A TURTLE!?
WHAT ON EARTH IS HE GONNA MAKE?
ザワ
WOW WOW WOW
ザワ
THAT'S WHAT GOGYO'S USING?
KEE
KEEKEE
KEE-KEE-KEE-KEE
!?
THE MIRAGE HEAD CHEF
TWIRL
WATCH HIM!
HE'S GONNA CHOP UP THE TURTLE!

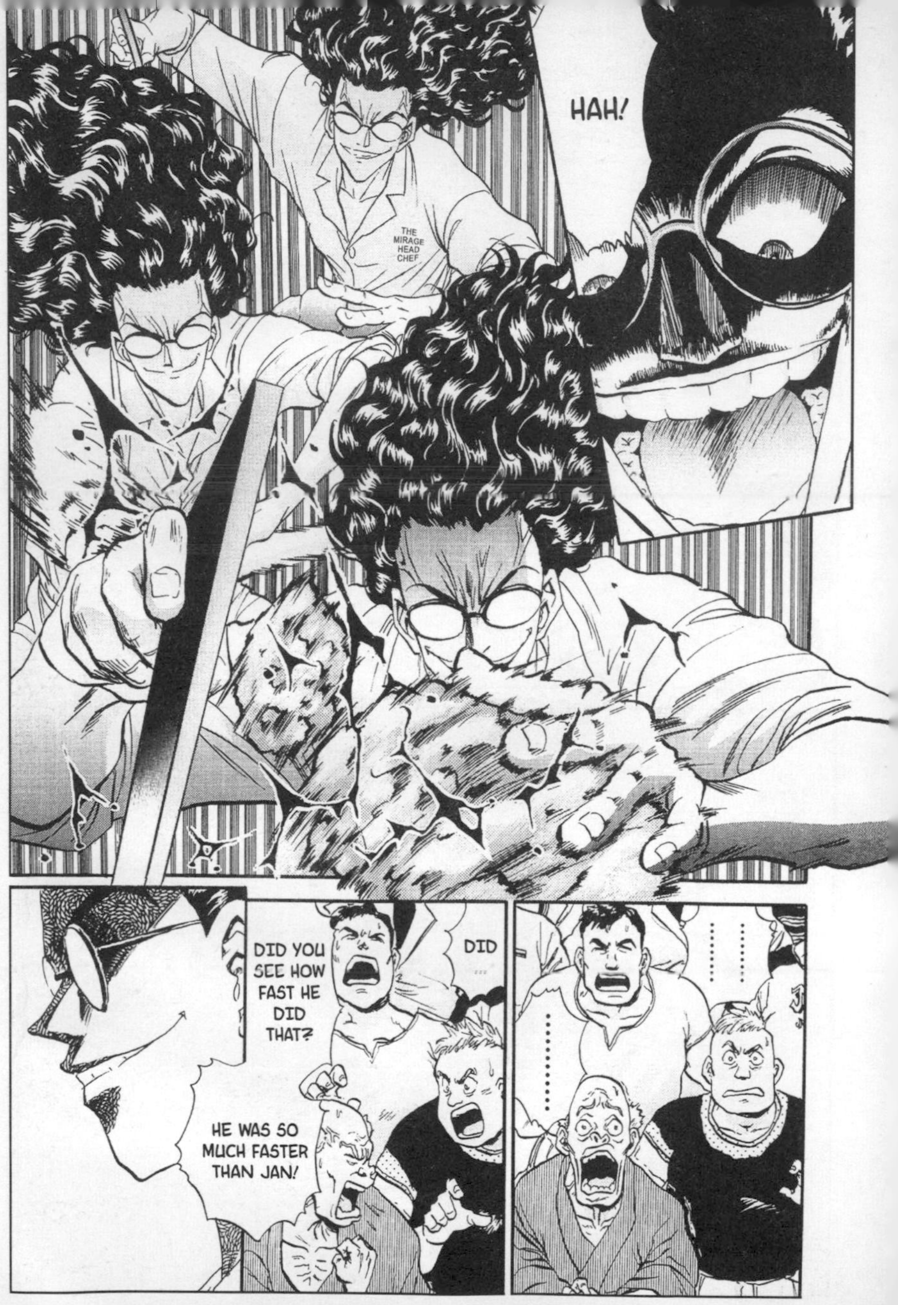
HAH!
THE MIRAGE HEAD CHEF
......
......
DID ...
DID YOU SEE HOW FAST HE DID THAT?
HE WAS SO MUCH FASTER THAN JAN!

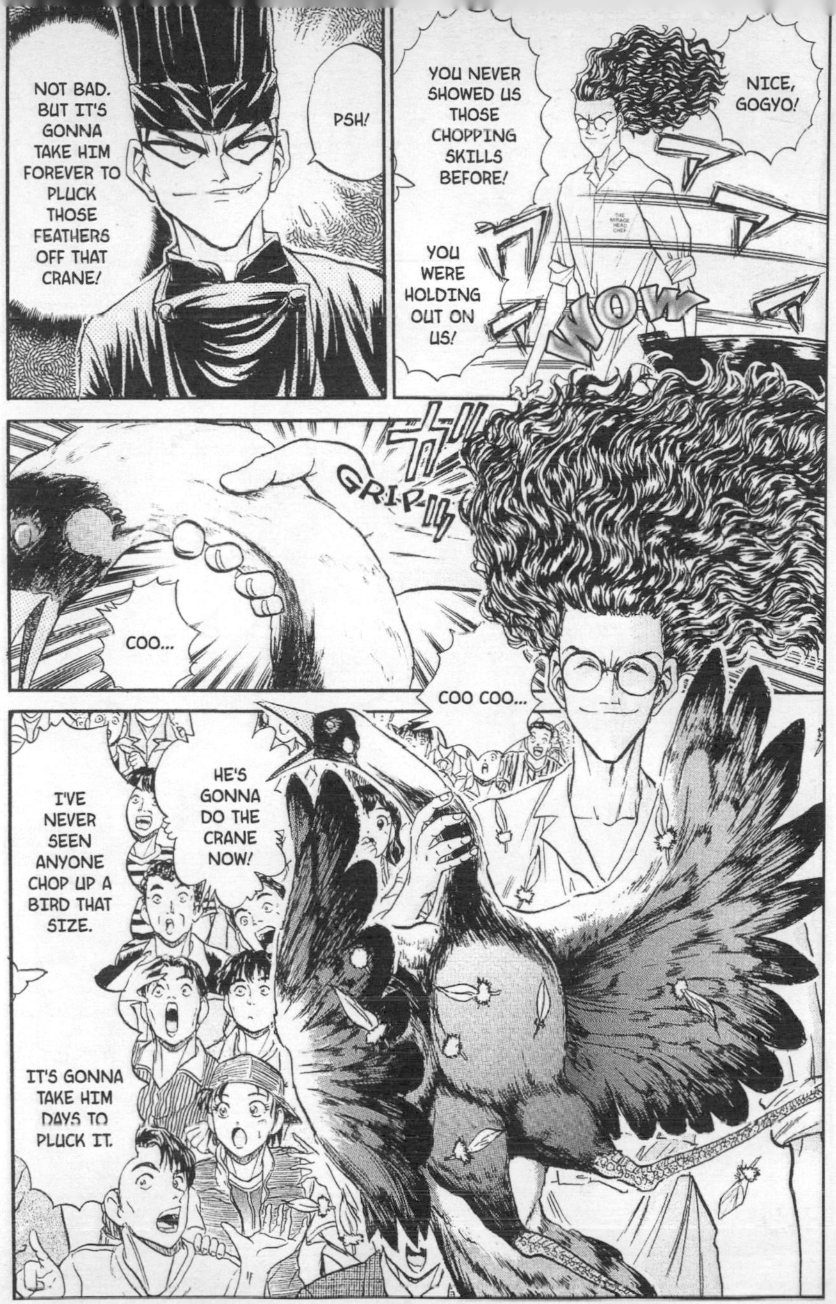
NICE, GOGYO!
YOU NEVER SHOWED US THOSE CHOPPING SKILLS BEFORE!
THE MIRAGE HEAD CHEF
YOU WERE HOLDING OUT ON US!
WOW
PSH!
NOT BAD. BUT IT'S GONNA TAKE HIM FOREVER TO PLUCK THOSE FEATHERS OFF THAT CRANE!
GRI-P-D
COO...
COO COO...
HE'S GONNA DO THE CRANE NOW!
I'VE NEVER SEEN ANYONE CHOP UP A BIRD THAT SIZE.
IT'S GONNA TAKE HIM DAYS TO PLUCK IT.

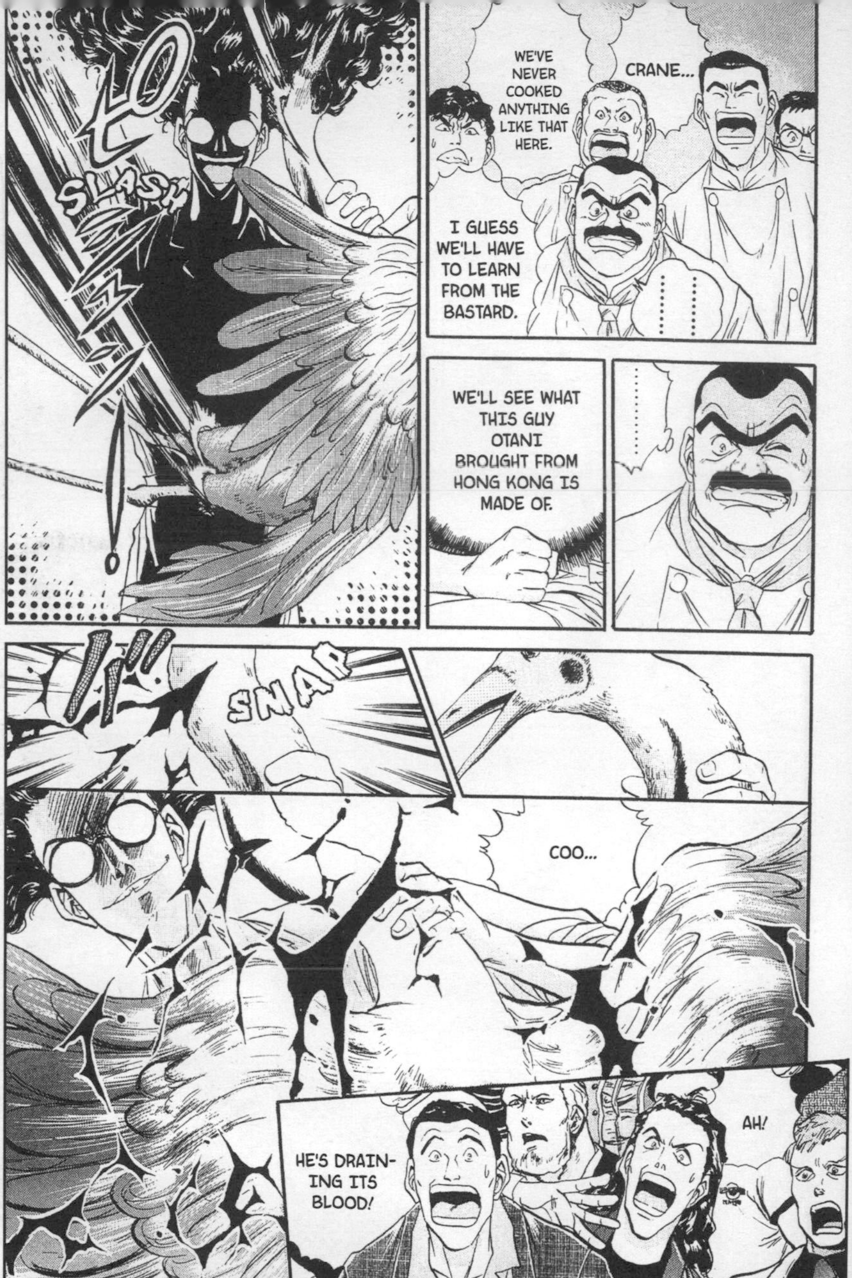
CRANE...
WE'VE NEVER COOKED ANYTHING LIKE THAT HERE.
I GUESS WE'LL HAVE TO LEARN FROM THE BASTARD.
WE'LL SEE WHAT THIS GUY OTANI BROUGHT FROM HONG KONG IS MADE OF.
SLASH
SNAP
COO...
AH!
HE'S DRAIN-ING ITS BLOOD!

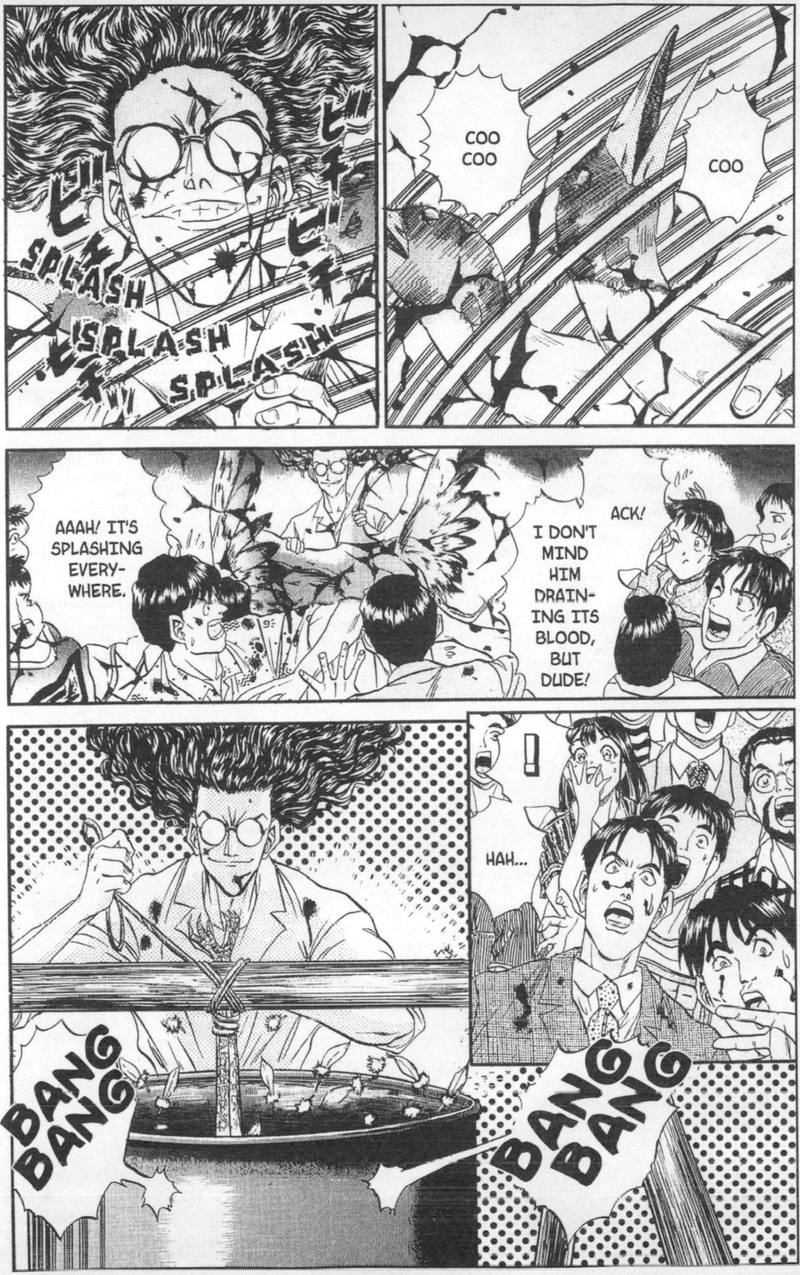
COO
COO
COO
SPLASH
SPLASH
SPLASH
ACK!
I DON'T MIND HIM DRAIN-ING ITS BLOOD, BUT DUDE!
AAAH! IT'S SPLASHING EVERY-WHERE.
!
HAH...
BANG BANG
BANG BANG

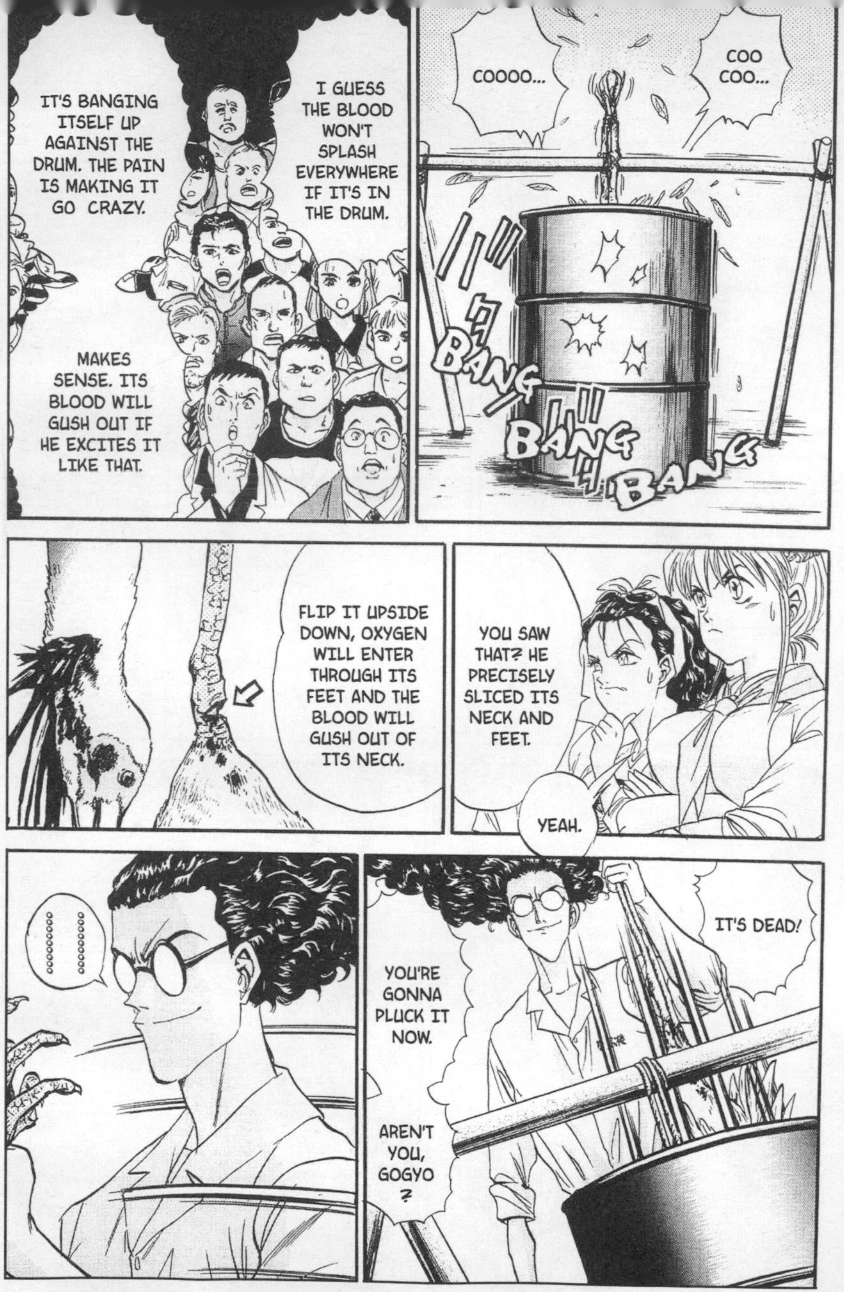
COO COO...
COOOO...
BANG
BANG
BANG
I GUESS THE BLOOD WON'T SPLASH EVERYWHERE IF IT'S IN THE DRUM.
IT'S BANGING ITSELF UP AGAINST THE DRUM. THE PAIN IS MAKING IT GO CRAZY.
MAKES SENSE. ITS BLOOD WILL GUSH OUT IF HE EXCITES IT LIKE THAT.
YOU SAW THAT? HE PRECISELY SLICED ITS NECK AND FEET.
YEAH.
FLIP IT UPSIDE DOWN, OXYGEN WILL ENTER THROUGH ITS FEET AND THE BLOOD WILL GUSH OUT OF ITS NECK.
IT'S DEAD!
YOU'RE GONNA PLUCK IT NOW.
AREN'T YOU, GOGYO?

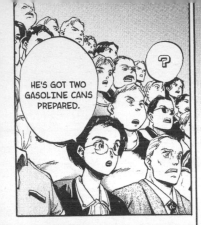

STOMP
?
HE'S GOT TWO GASOLINE CANS PREPARED.
??
WHAT'S THE OTHER DRUM FOR?
DIP
THE MIRAGE HEAD CHEF
HUH!? HE'S DIPPING THE CRANE INTO THE OTHER CAN.
SHOULD-N'T HE BE PLUCKING THE BIRD INSTEAD?
WHAT KIND OF SECRET POTION DOES HE HAVE IN THERE?
GRIN

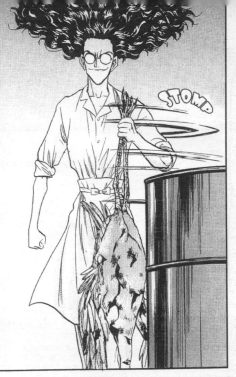

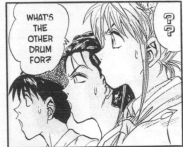

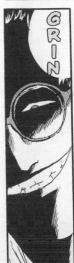

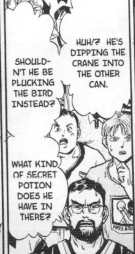

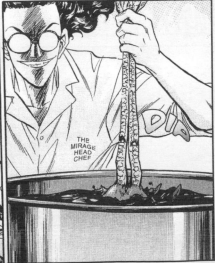

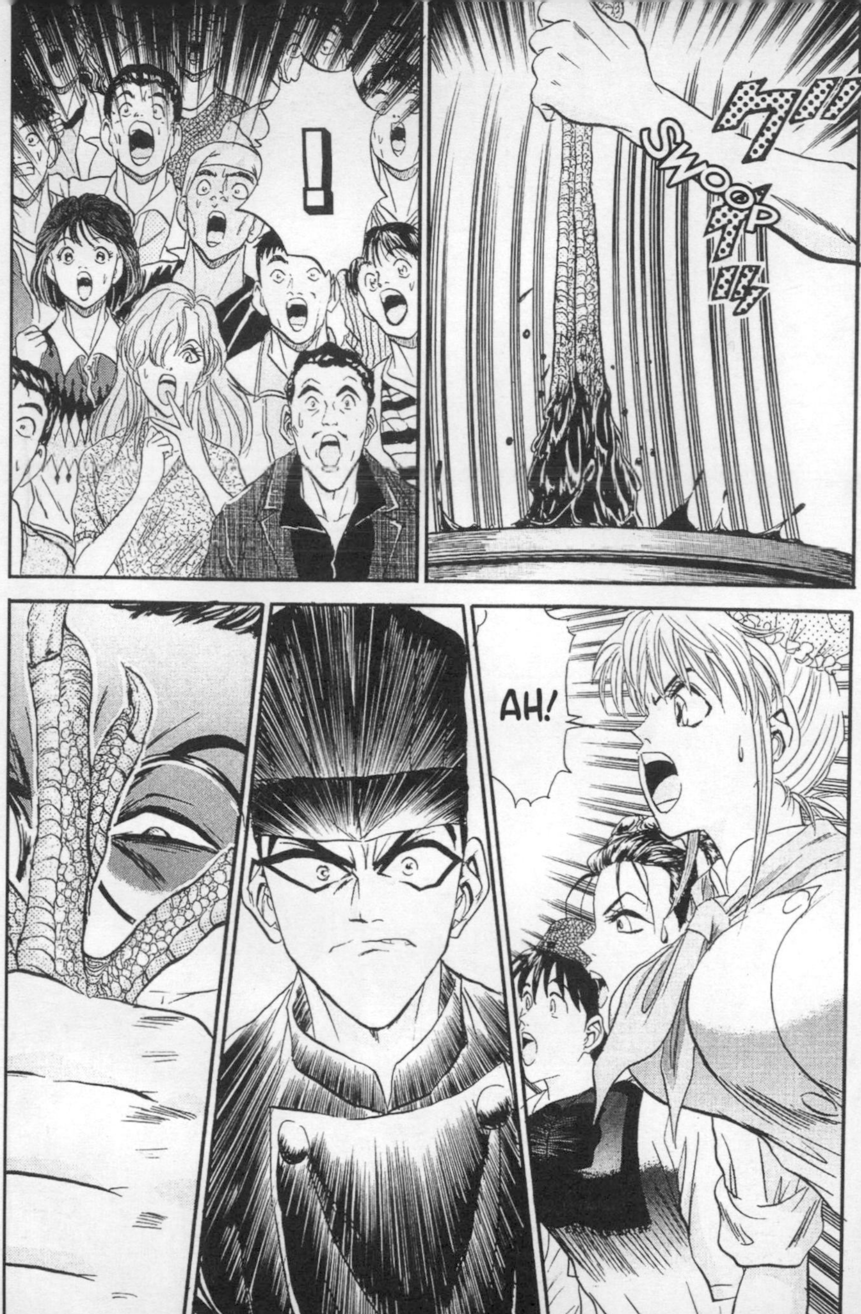
SWOOP
!
AH!

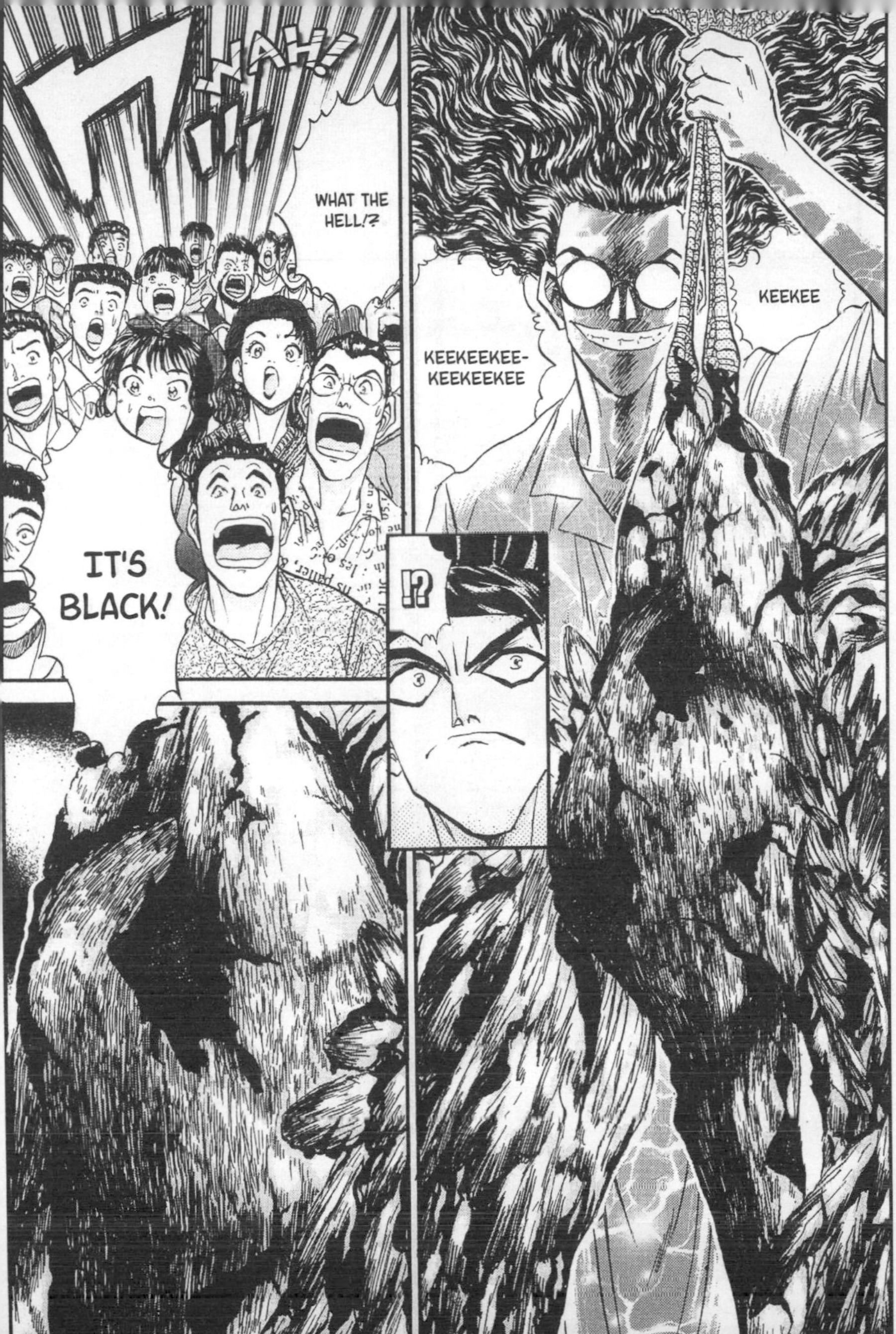
KEEKEE
KEEKEEKEE-KEEKEEKEE
YAH!
WHAT THE HELL!?
IT'S BLACK!
!?

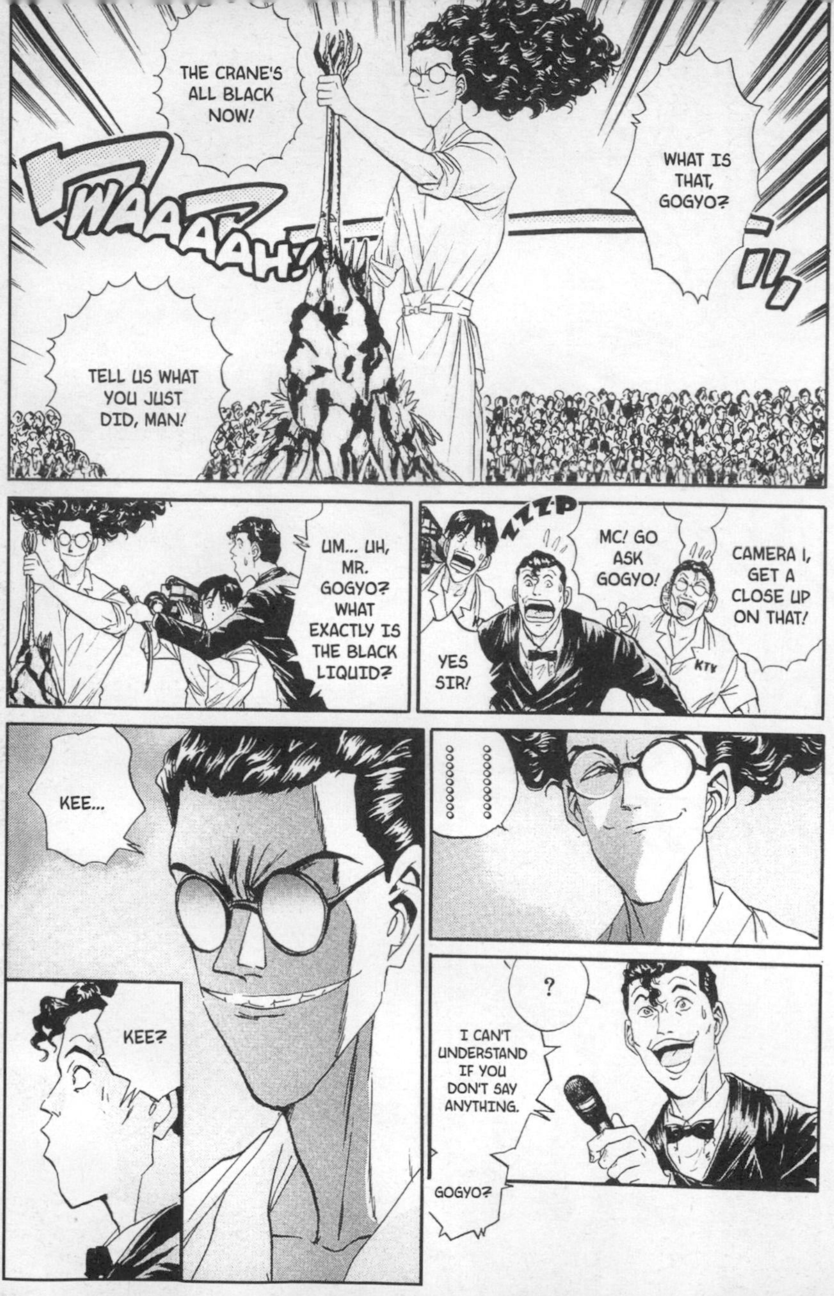

WHAT IS THAT, GOGYO?
THE CRANE'S ALL BLACK NOW!
WAAAAAH!
TELL US WHAT YOU JUST DID, MAN!
CAMERA 1, GET A CLOSE UP ON THAT!
MC! GO ASK GOGYO!
ZZZ·P
YES SIR!
UM... UH, MR. GOGYO? WHAT EXACTLY IS THE BLACK LIQUID?
....
?
I CAN'T UNDERSTAND IF YOU DON'T SAY ANYTHING.
GOGYO?
KEE...
KEE?

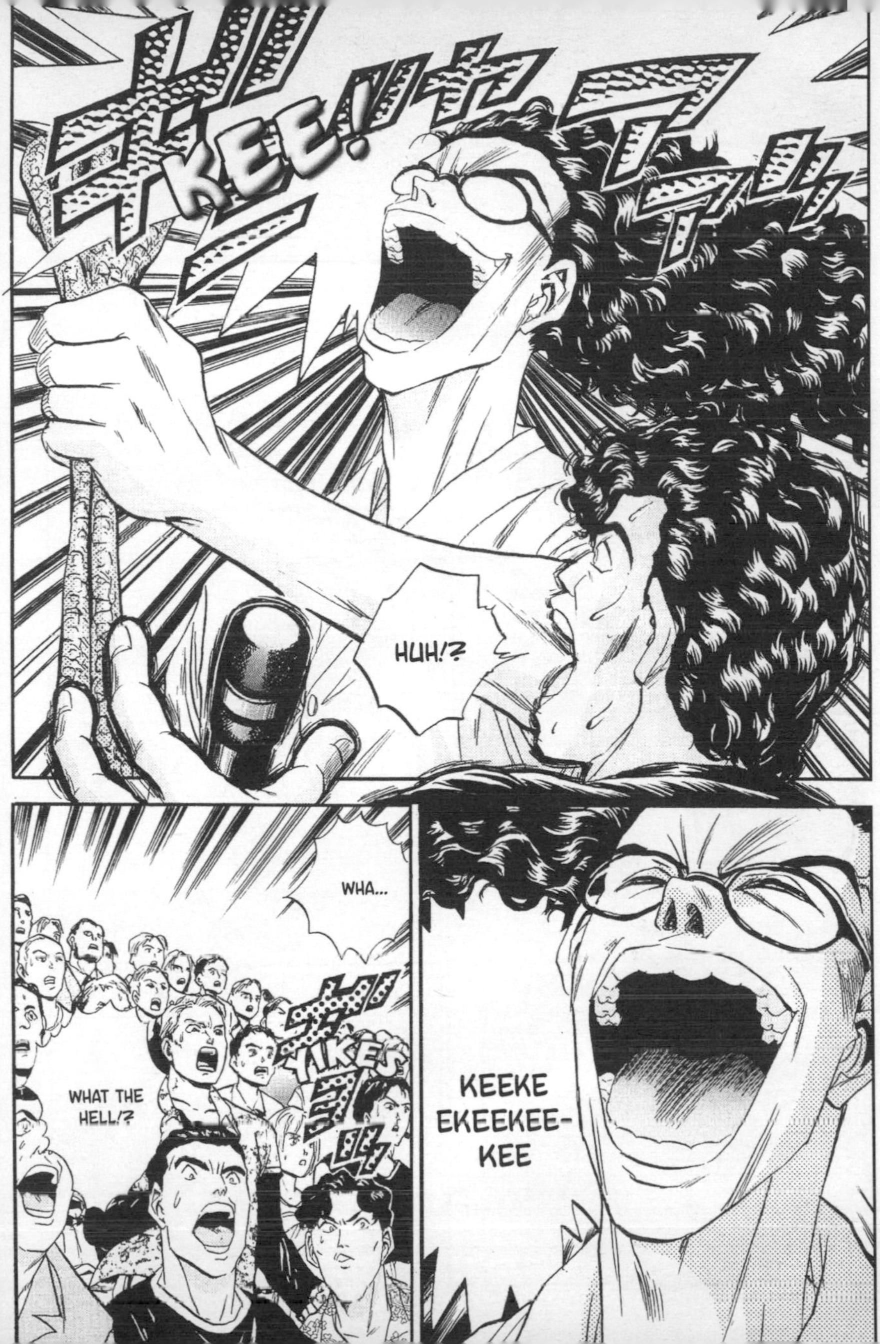
KEE!!
HUH!?
KEEKE EKEEKEE-KEE
WHA...
YIKES
WHAT THE HELL!?

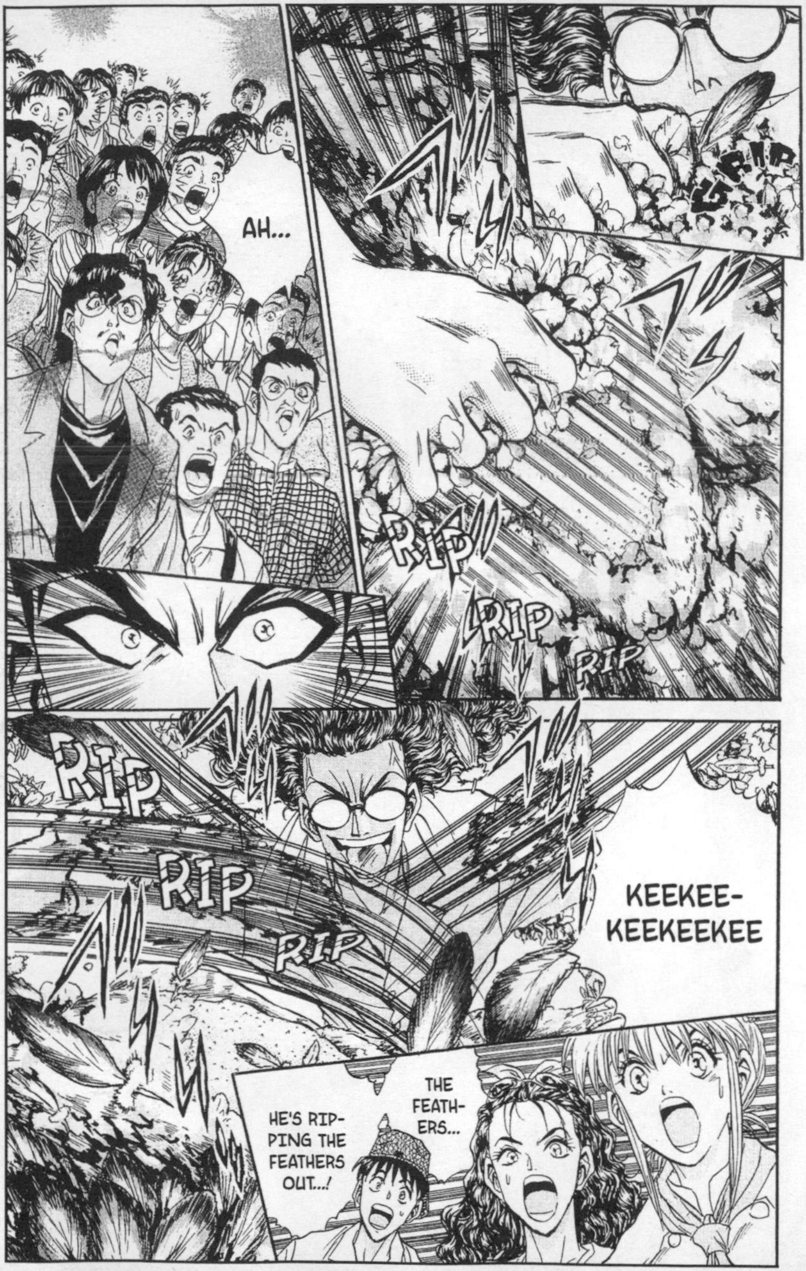
RIP
RIP
RIP
RIP
AH...
KEEKEE-
KEEKEEKEE
RIP
RIP
RIP
THE FEATH-ERS...
HE'S RIP-PING THE FEATHERS OUT...!

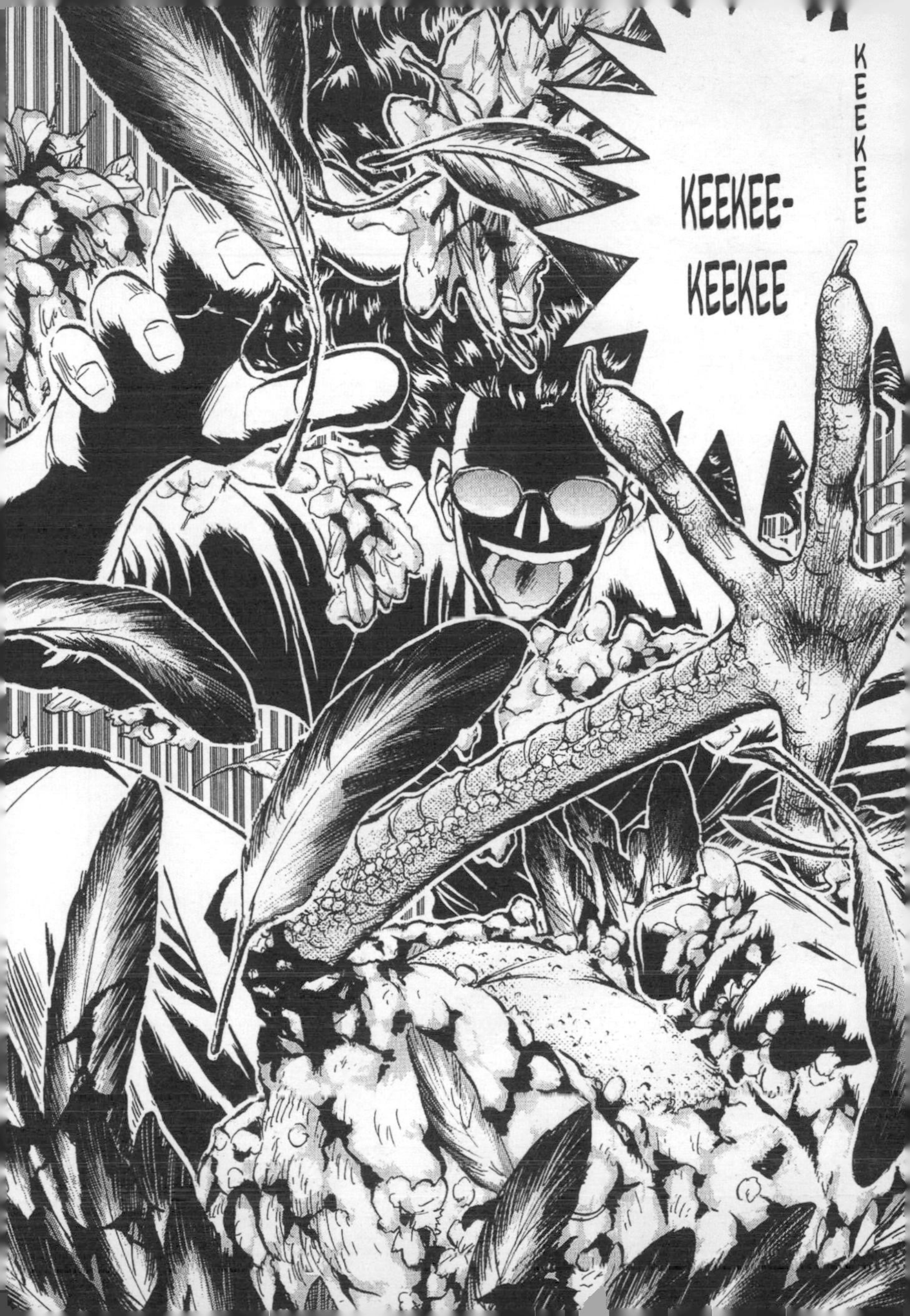
KEEKEE
KEEKEE-
KEEKEE

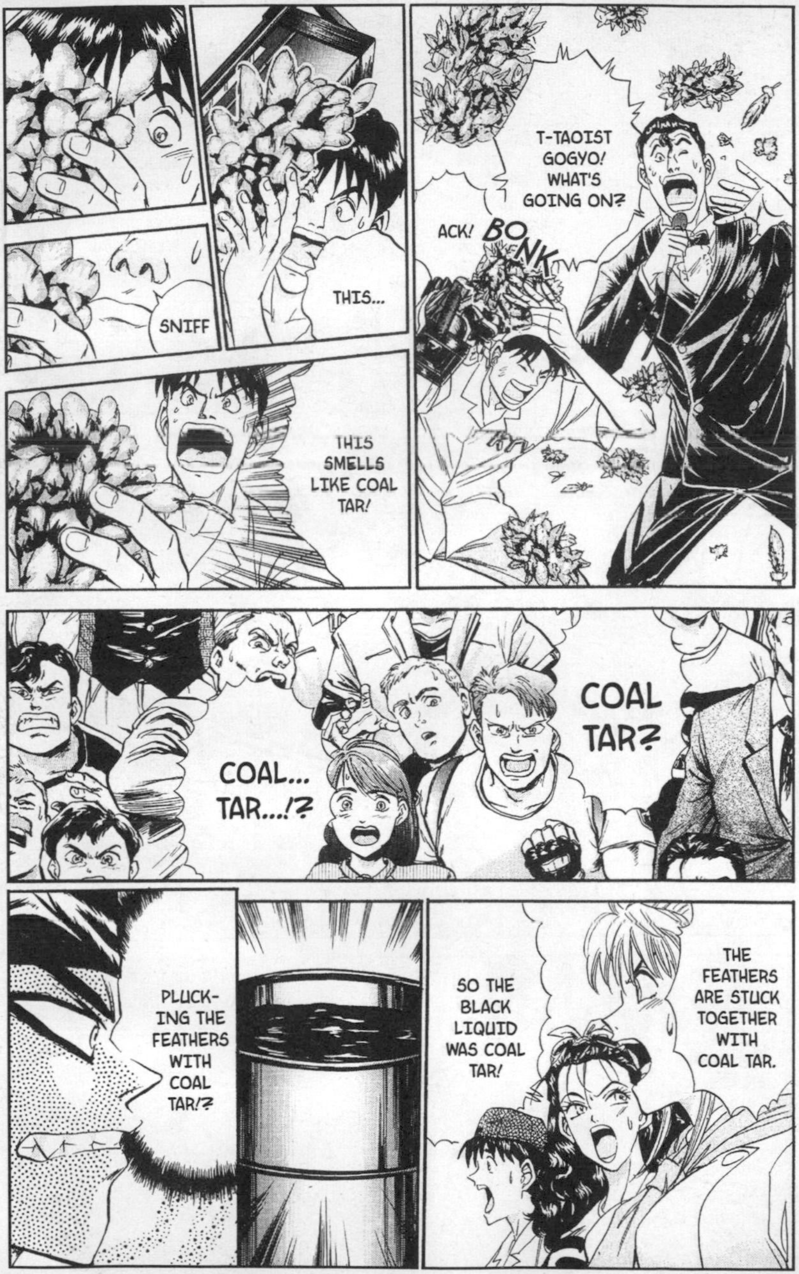
T-TAOIST GOGYO! WHAT'S GOING ON?
ACK!
BONK
THIS...
SNIFF
THIS SMELLS LIKE COAL TAR!
COAL TAR?
COAL... TAR...!?
THE FEATHERS ARE STUCK TOGETHER WITH COAL TAR.
SO THE BLACK LIQUID WAS COAL TAR!
PLUCKING THE FEATHERS WITH COAL TAR!?

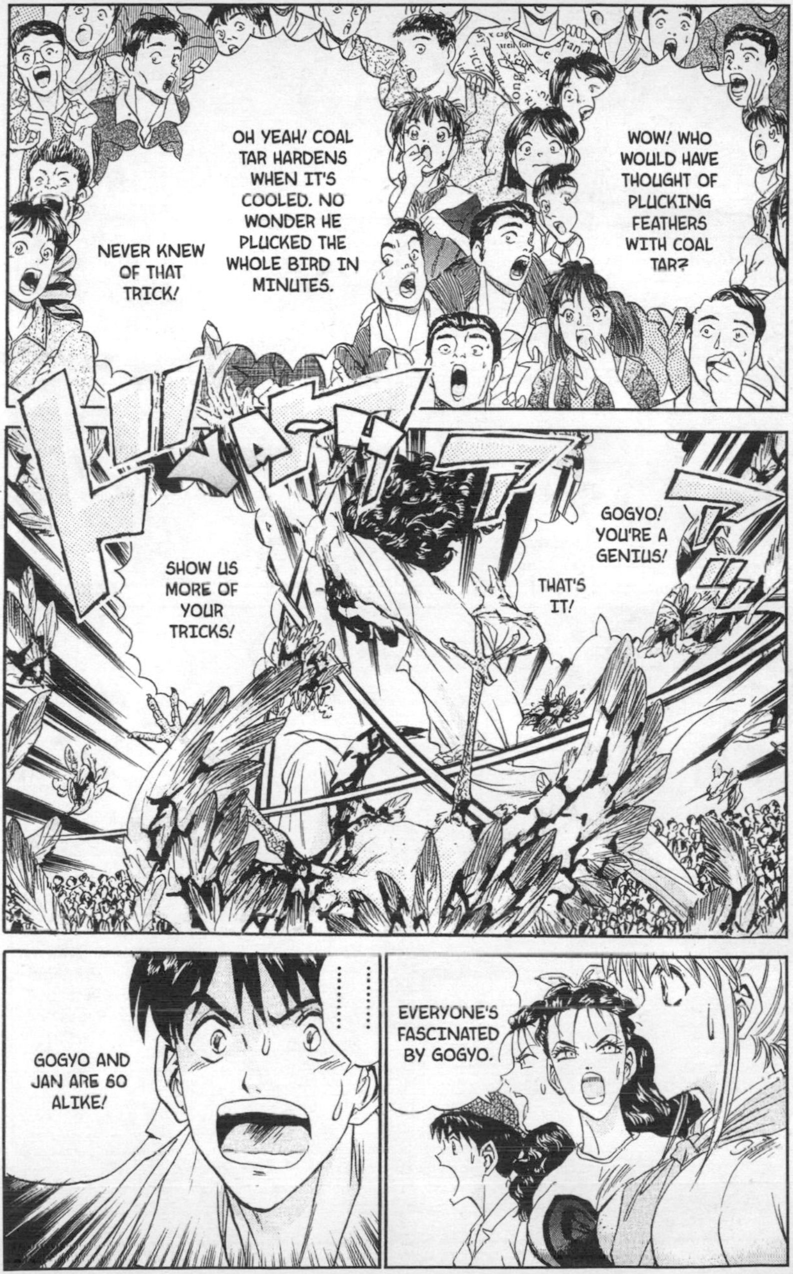
WOW! WHO WOULD HAVE THOUGHT OF PLUCKING FEATHERS WITH COAL TAR?
OH YEAH! COAL TAR HARDENS WHEN IT'S COOLED. NO WONDER HE PLUCKED THE WHOLE BIRD IN MINUTES.
NEVER KNEW OF THAT TRICK!
GOGYO! YOU'RE A GENIUS!
THAT'S IT!
SHOW US MORE OF YOUR TRICKS!
EVERYONE'S FASCINATED BY GOGYO.
......
GOGYO AND JAN ARE SO ALIKE!

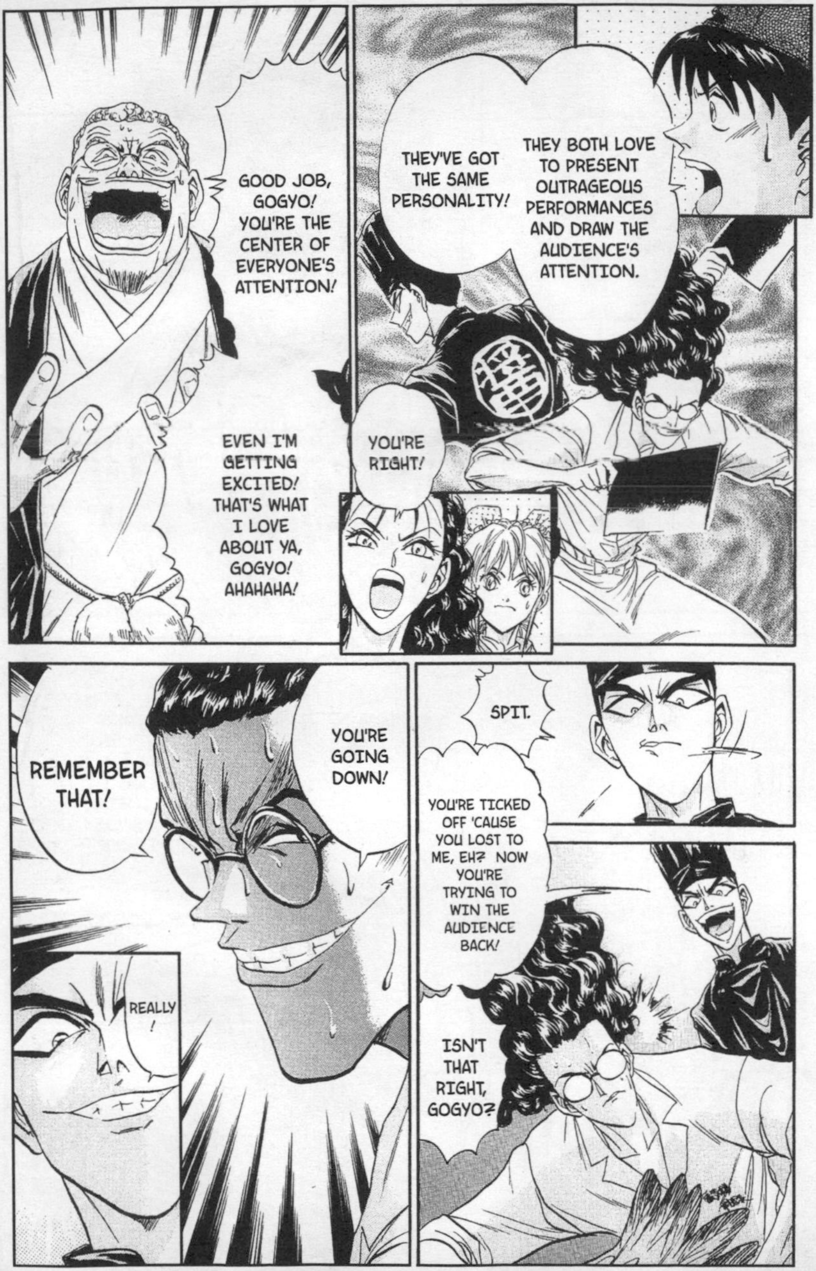

THEY BOTH LOVE TO PRESENT OUTRAGEOUS PERFORMANCES AND DRAW THE AUDIENCE'S ATTENTION.
THEY'VE GOT THE SAME PERSONALITY!
YOU'RE RIGHT!
GOOD JOB, GOGYO! YOU'RE THE CENTER OF EVERYONE'S ATTENTION!
EVEN I'M GETTING EXCITED! THAT'S WHAT I LOVE ABOUT YA, GOGYO! AHAHAHA!
SPIT.
YOU'RE TICKED OFF 'CAUSE YOU LOST TO ME, EH? NOW YOU'RE TRYING TO WIN THE AUDIENCE BACK!
ISN'T THAT RIGHT, GOGYO?
YOU'RE GOING DOWN!
REMEMBER THAT!
REALLY!

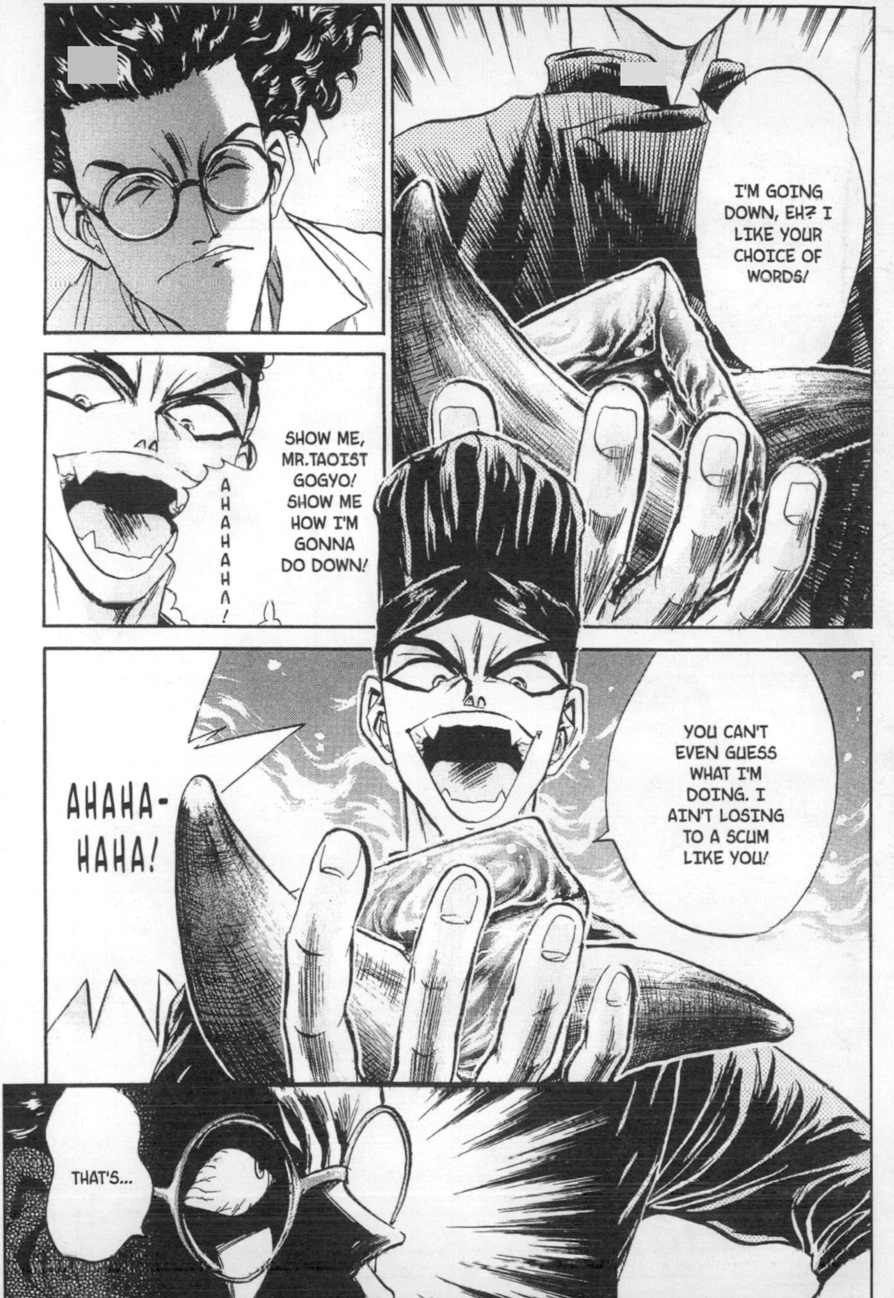
I'M GOING DOWN, EH? I LIKE YOUR CHOICE OF WORDS!
SHOW ME, MR.TAOIST GOGYO! SHOW ME HOW I'M GONNA DO DOWN!
AHAHAHAHA!
YOU CAN'T EVEN GUESS WHAT I'M DOING. I AIN'T LOSING TO A SCUM LIKE YOU!
AHAHA-HAHA!
THAT'S...

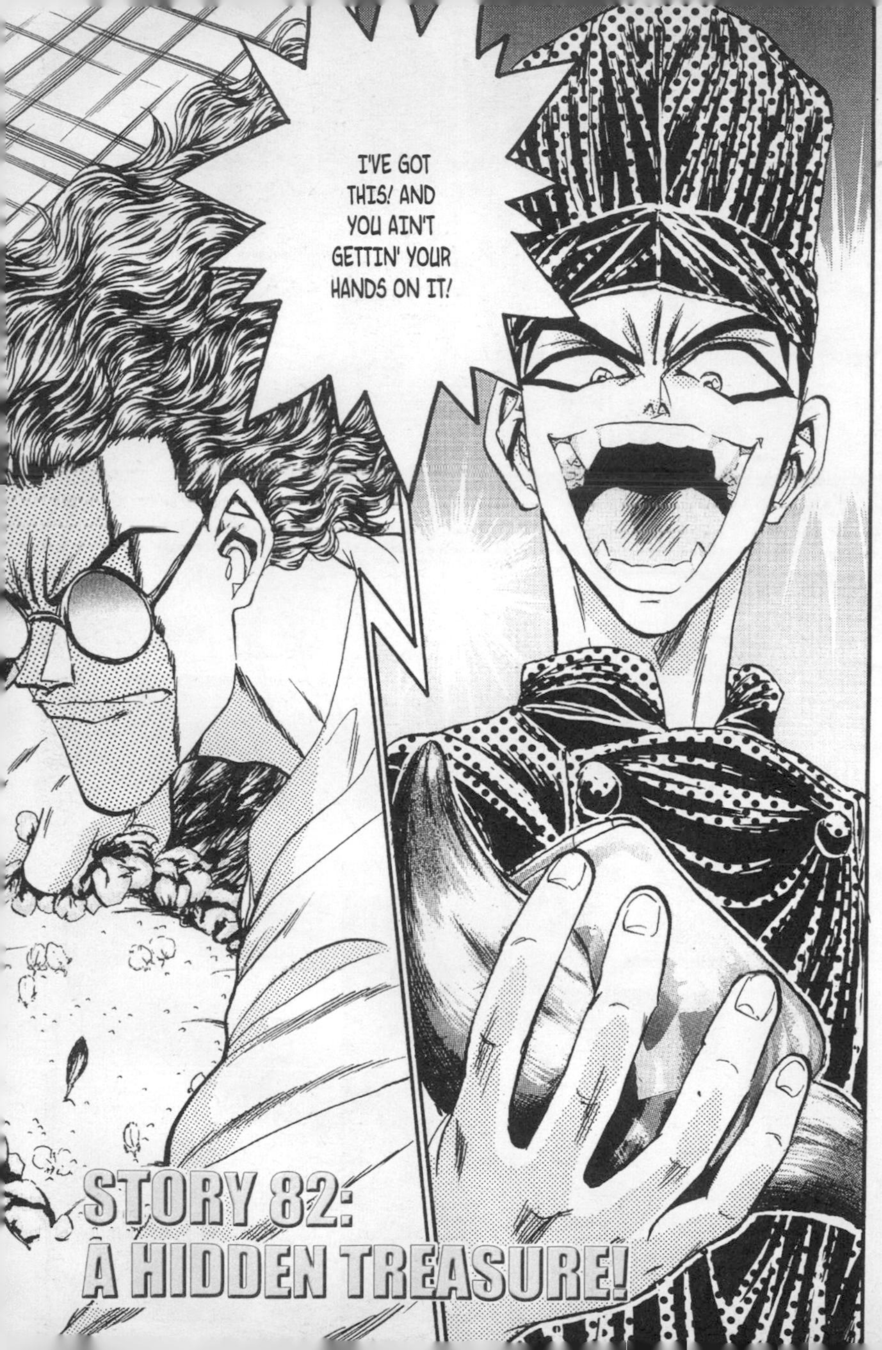
I'VE GOT THIS! AND YOU AIN'T GETTIN' YOUR HANDS ON IT!
STORY 82: A HIDDEN TREASURE!

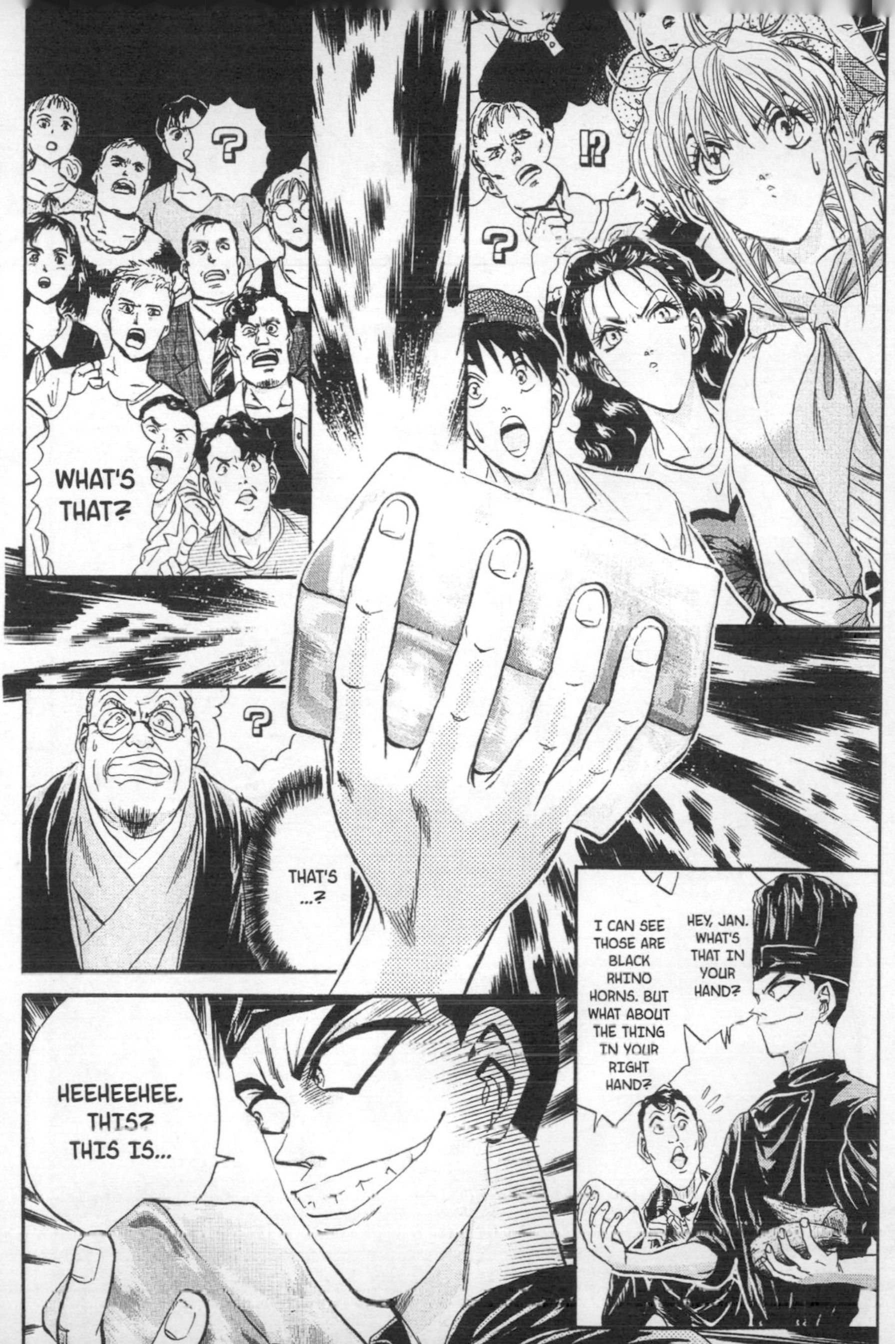
!?
?
?
WHAT'S THAT?
?
THAT'S ...?
HEY, JAN. WHAT'S THAT IN YOUR HAND?
I CAN SEE THOSE ARE BLACK RHINO HORNS. BUT WHAT ABOUT THE THING IN YOUR RIGHT HAND?
HEEHEEHEE. THIS? THIS IS...

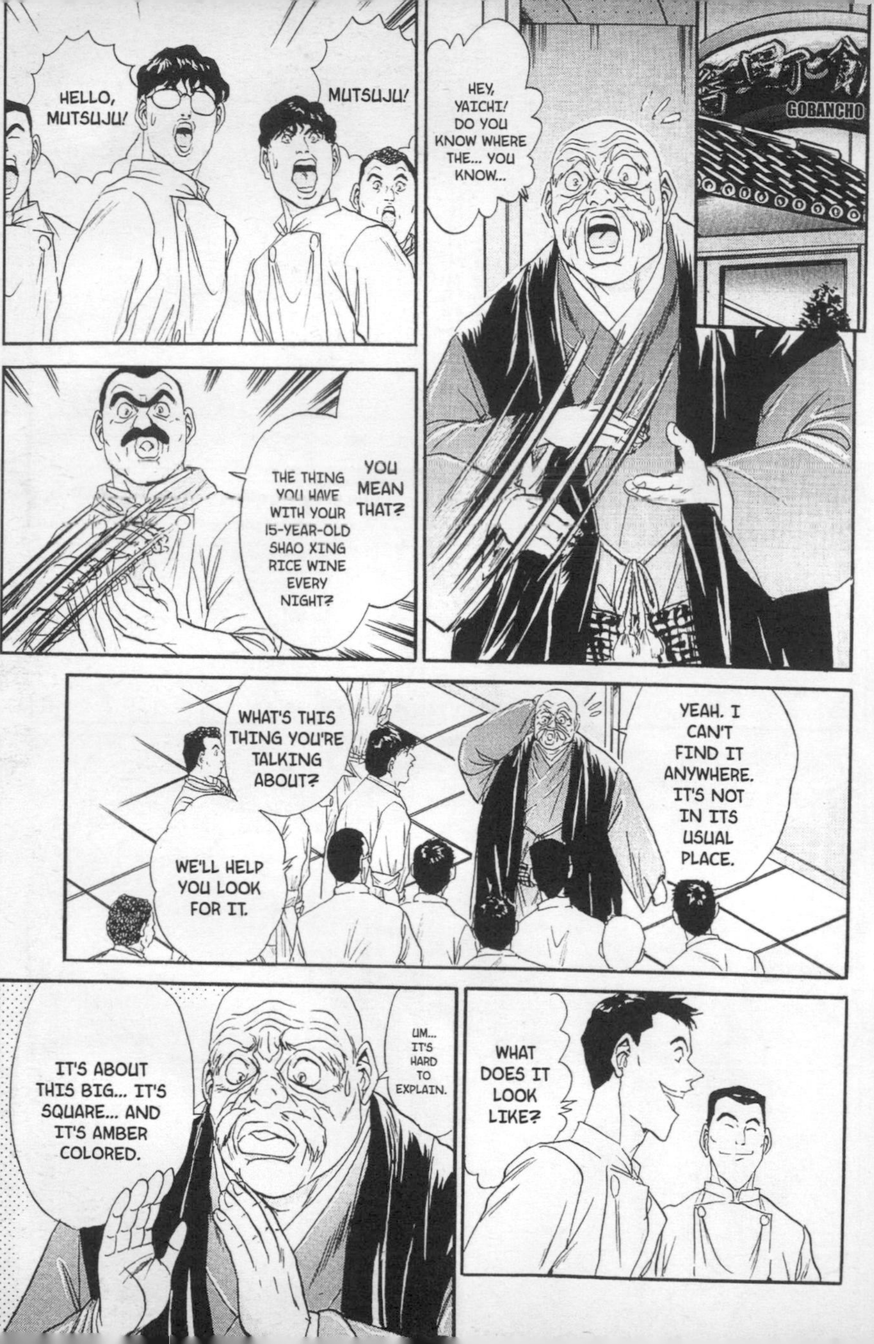
GOBANCHO
HEY, YAICHI! DO YOU KNOW WHERE THE... YOU KNOW...
MUTSUJU!
HELLO, MUTSUJU!
YOU MEAN THAT?
THE THING YOU HAVE WITH YOUR 15-YEAR-OLD SHAO XING RICE WINE EVERY NIGHT?
YEAH. I CAN'T FIND IT ANYWHERE. IT'S NOT IN ITS USUAL PLACE.
WHAT'S THIS THING YOU'RE TALKING ABOUT?
WE'LL HELP YOU LOOK FOR IT.
WHAT DOES IT LOOK LIKE?
UM... IT'S HARD TO EXPLAIN.
IT'S ABOUT THIS BIG... IT'S SQUARE... AND IT'S AMBER COLORED.

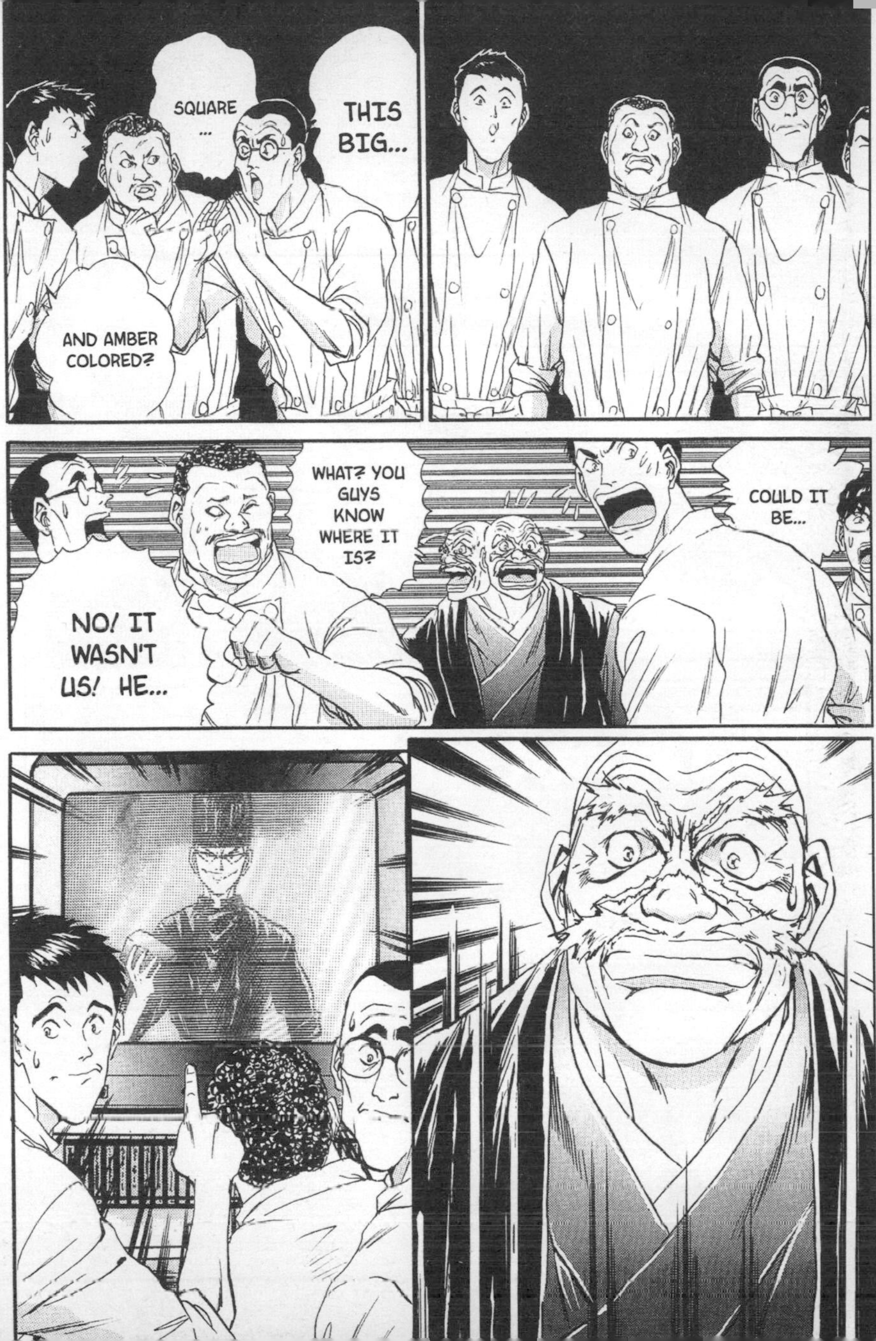
THIS BIG...
SQUARE ...
AND AMBER COLORED?
COULD IT BE...
WHAT? YOU GUYS KNOW WHERE IT IS?
NO! IT WASN'T US! HE...

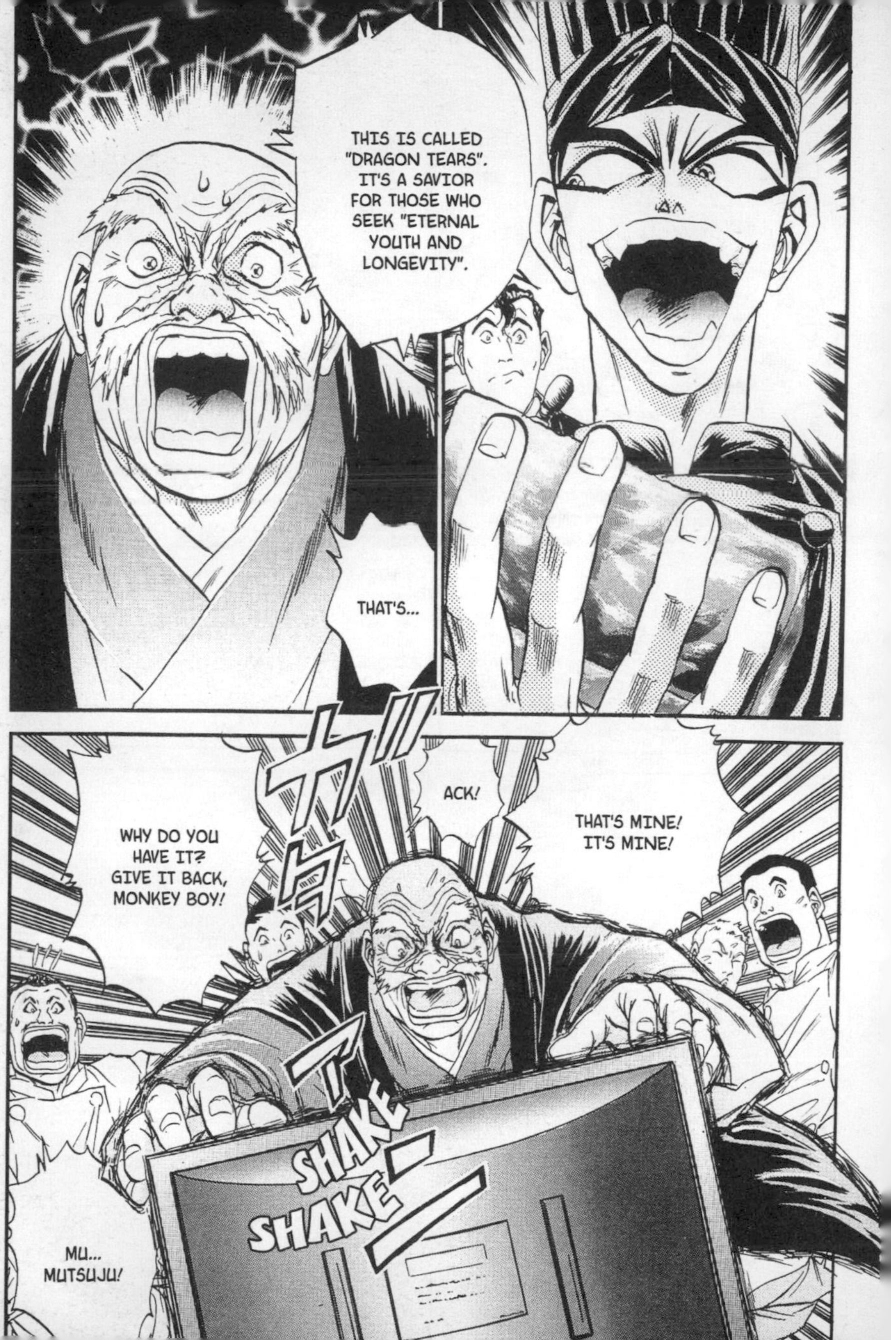
THIS IS CALLED "DRAGON TEARS". IT'S A SAVIOR FOR THOSE WHO SEEK "ETERNAL YOUTH AND LONGEVITY".
THAT'S...
THAT'S MINE! IT'S MINE!
ACK!
WHY DO YOU HAVE IT? GIVE IT BACK, MONKEY BOY!
SHAKE
SHAKE
MU... MUTSUJU!

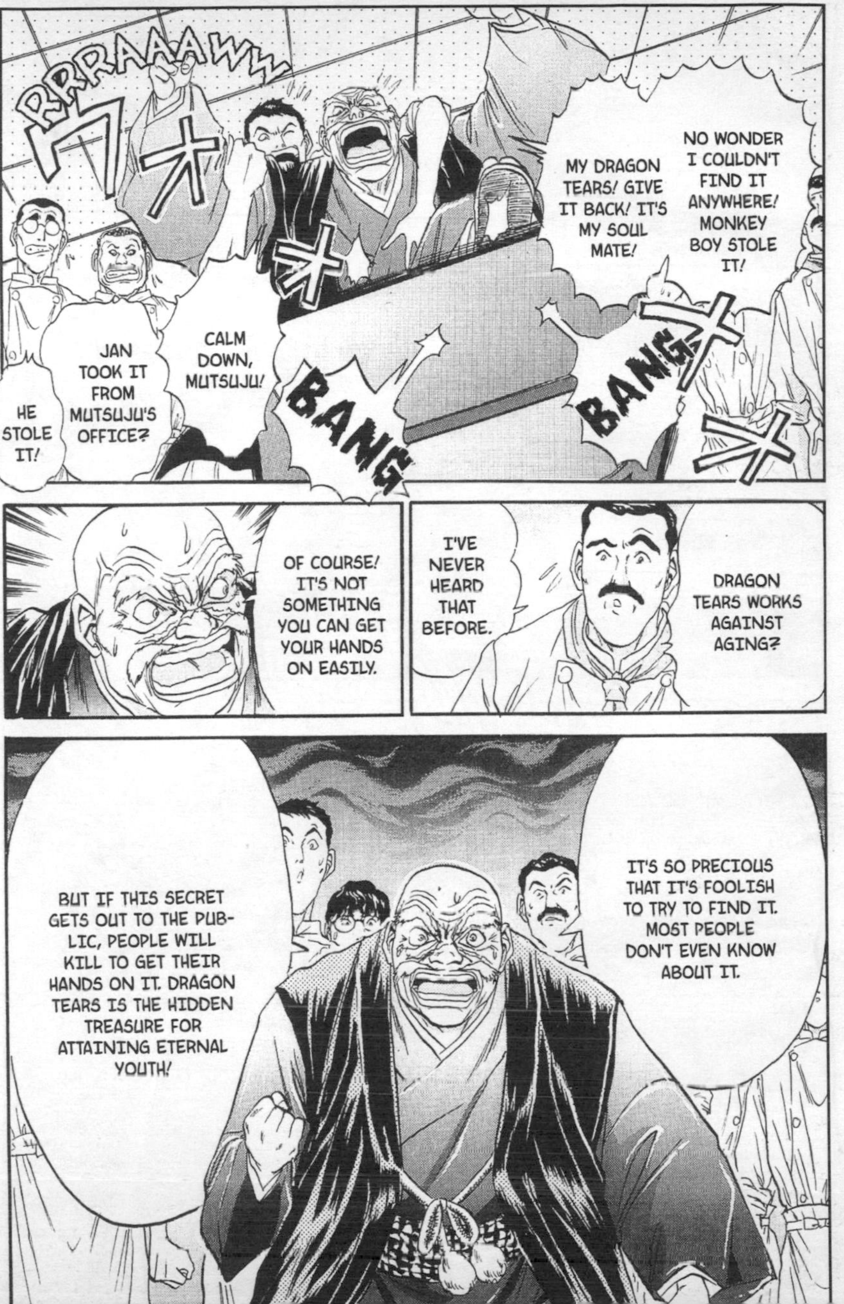
NO WONDER I COULDN'T FIND IT ANYWHERE! MONKEY BOY STOLE IT!
MY DRAGON TEARS! GIVE IT BACK! IT'S MY SOUL MATE!
BRRAAAWW
BANG
BANG
CALM DOWN, MUTSUJU!
JAN TOOK IT FROM MUTSUJU'S OFFICE?
HE STOLE IT!
DRAGON TEARS WORKS AGAINST AGING?
I'VE NEVER HEARD THAT BEFORE.
OF COURSE! IT'S NOT SOMETHING YOU CAN GET YOUR HANDS ON EASILY.
IT'S SO PRECIOUS THAT IT'S FOOLISH TO TRY TO FIND IT. MOST PEOPLE DON'T EVEN KNOW ABOUT IT.
BUT IF THIS SECRET GETS OUT TO THE PUB-LIC, PEOPLE WILL KILL TO GET THEIR HANDS ON IT. DRAGON TEARS IS THE HIDDEN TREASURE FOR ATTAINING ETERNAL YOUTH!

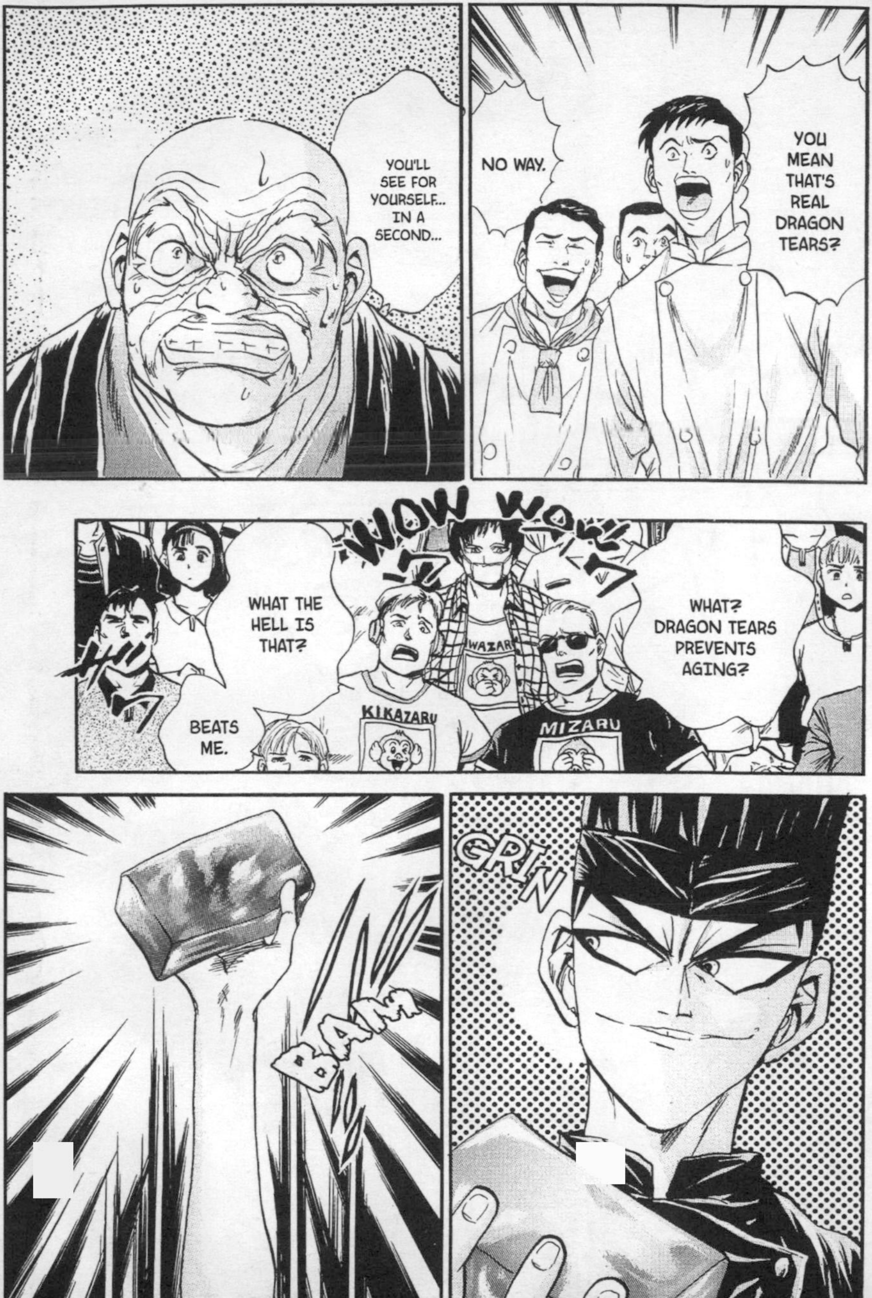
YOU MEAN THAT'S REAL DRAGON TEARS?
NO WAY.
YOU'LL SEE FOR YOURSELF... IN A SECOND...
WOW WOW
WHAT? DRAGON TEARS PREVENTS AGING?
WHAT THE HELL IS THAT?
BEATS ME.
MIZARU
KIKAZARU
GRIN
BAM

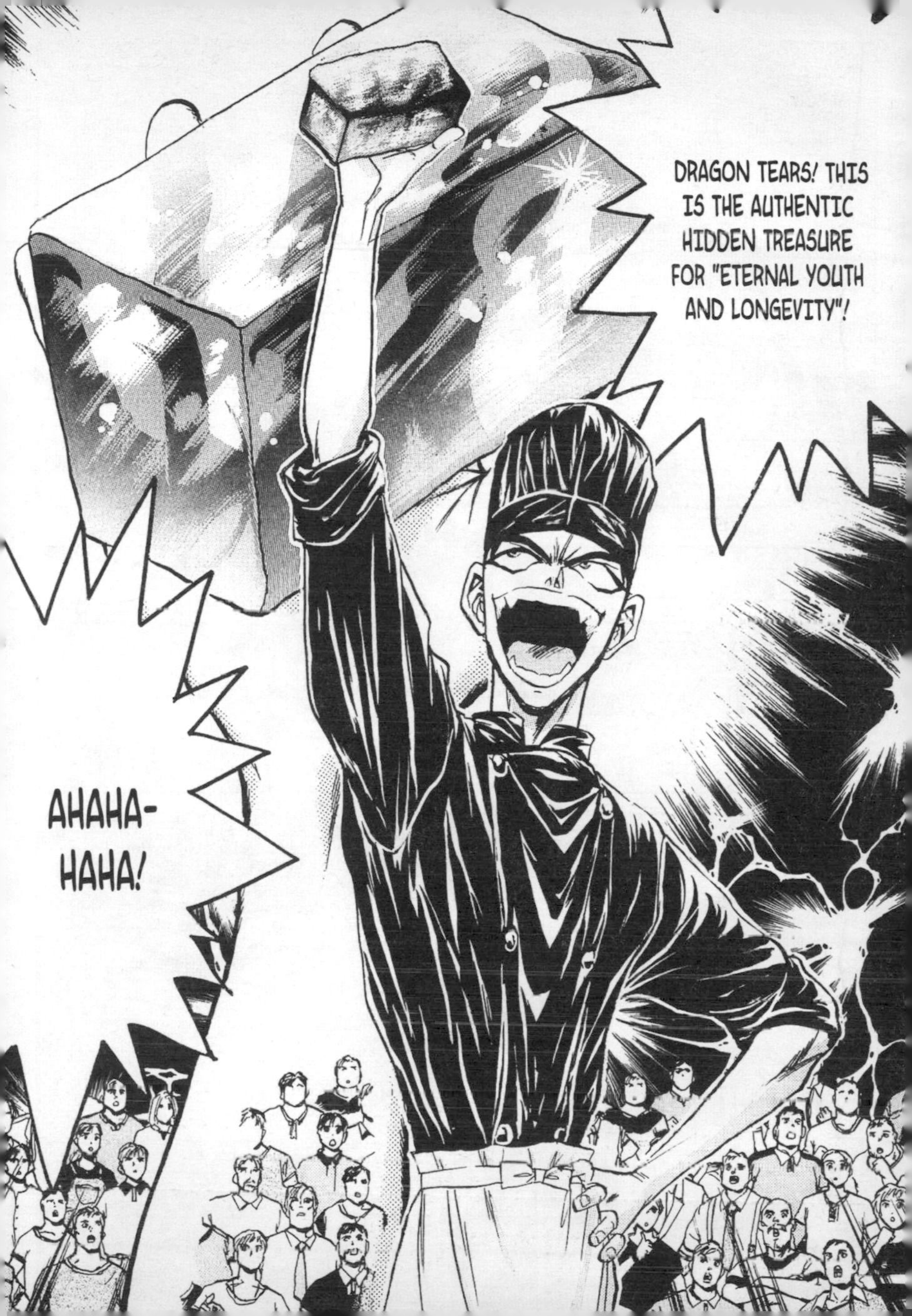
DRAGON TEARS! THIS IS THE AUTHENTIC HIDDEN TREASURE FOR "ETERNAL YOUTH AND LONGEVITY"!
AHAHA-HAHA!

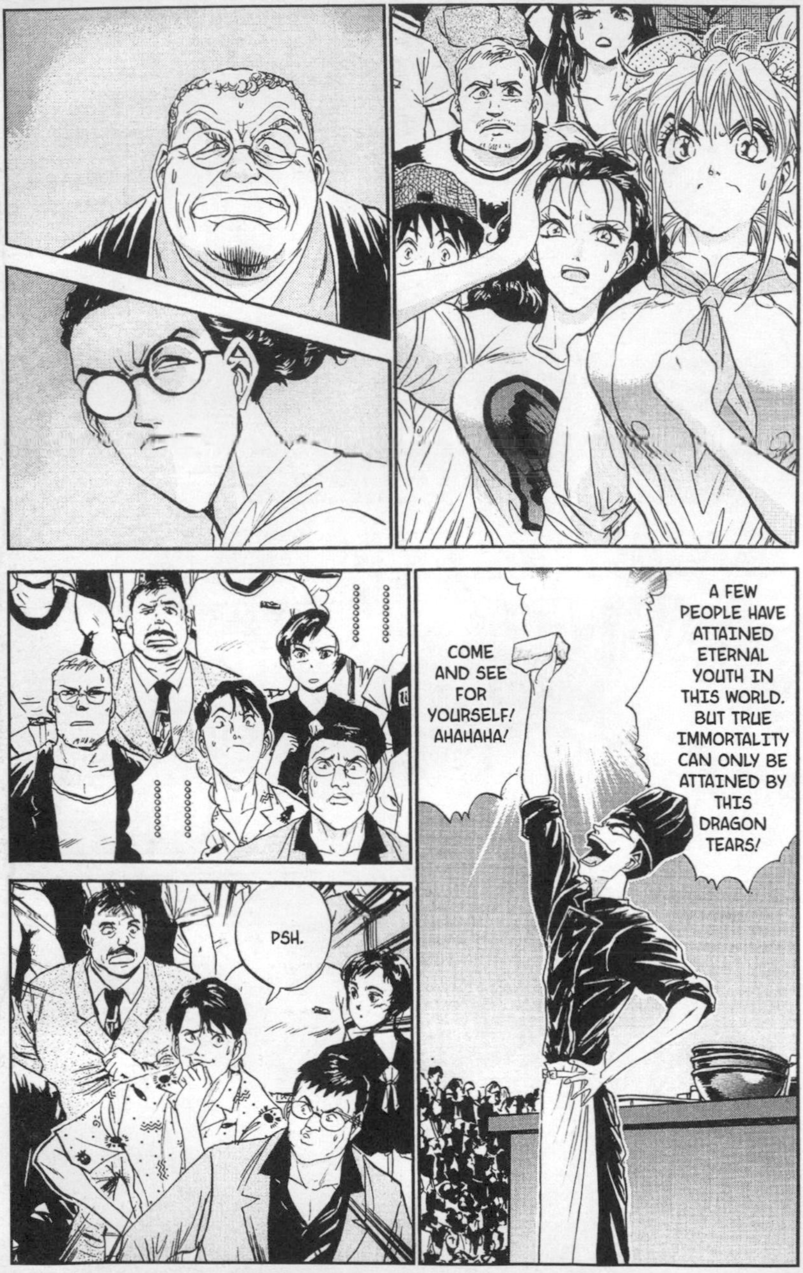
A FEW PEOPLE HAVE ATTAINED ETERNAL YOUTH IN THIS WORLD. BUT TRUE IMMORTALITY CAN ONLY BE ATTAINED BY THIS DRAGON TEARS!
COME AND SEE FOR YOURSELF! AHAHAHA!
PSH.

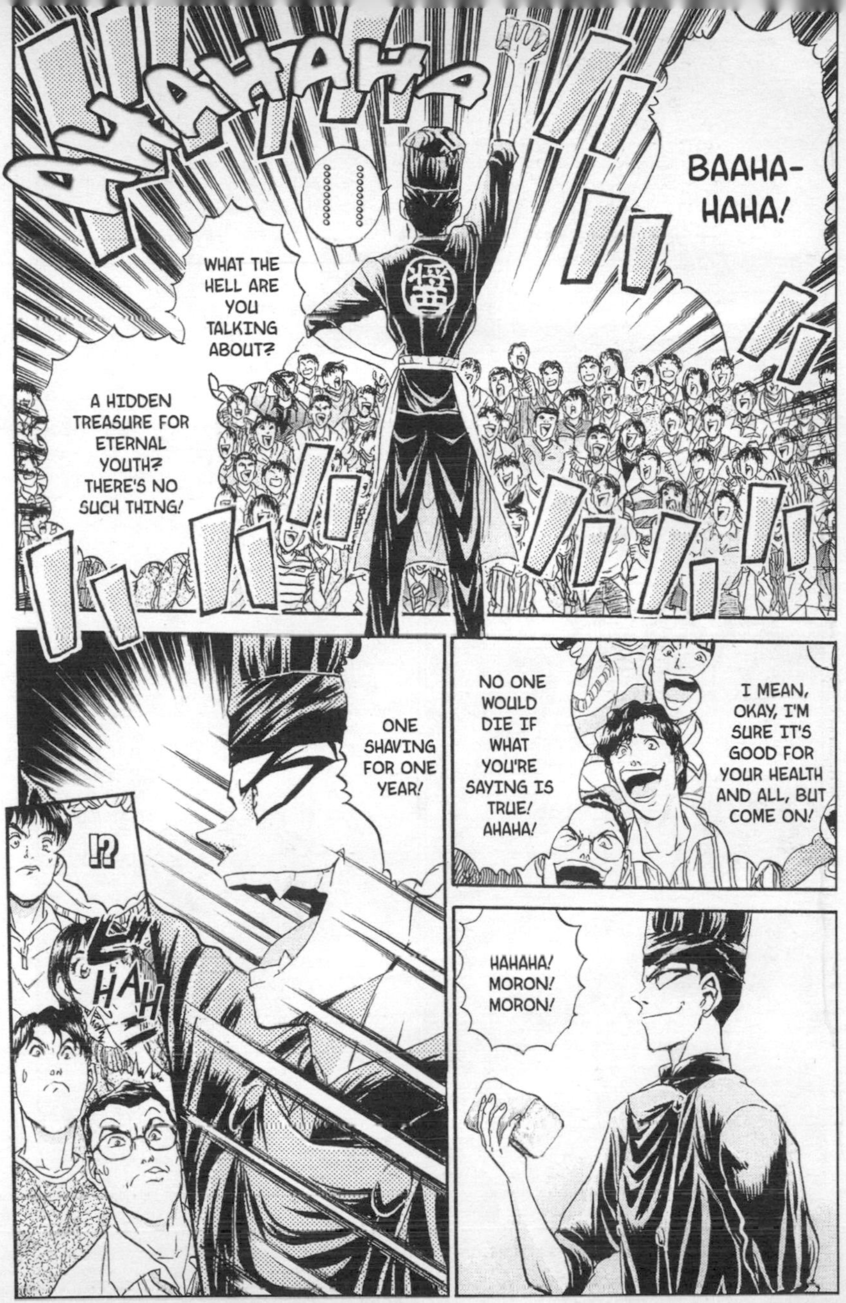
BAAHA-HAHA!
AHAHAHA
WHAT THE HELL ARE YOU TALKING ABOUT?
A HIDDEN TREASURE FOR ETERNAL YOUTH? THERE'S NO SUCH THING!
I MEAN, OKAY, I'M SURE IT'S GOOD FOR YOUR HEALTH AND ALL, BUT COME ON!
NO ONE WOULD DIE IF WHAT YOU'RE SAYING IS TRUE! AHAHA!
HAHAHA! MORON! MORON!
ONE SHAVING FOR ONE YEAR!
!?
HAH HAH

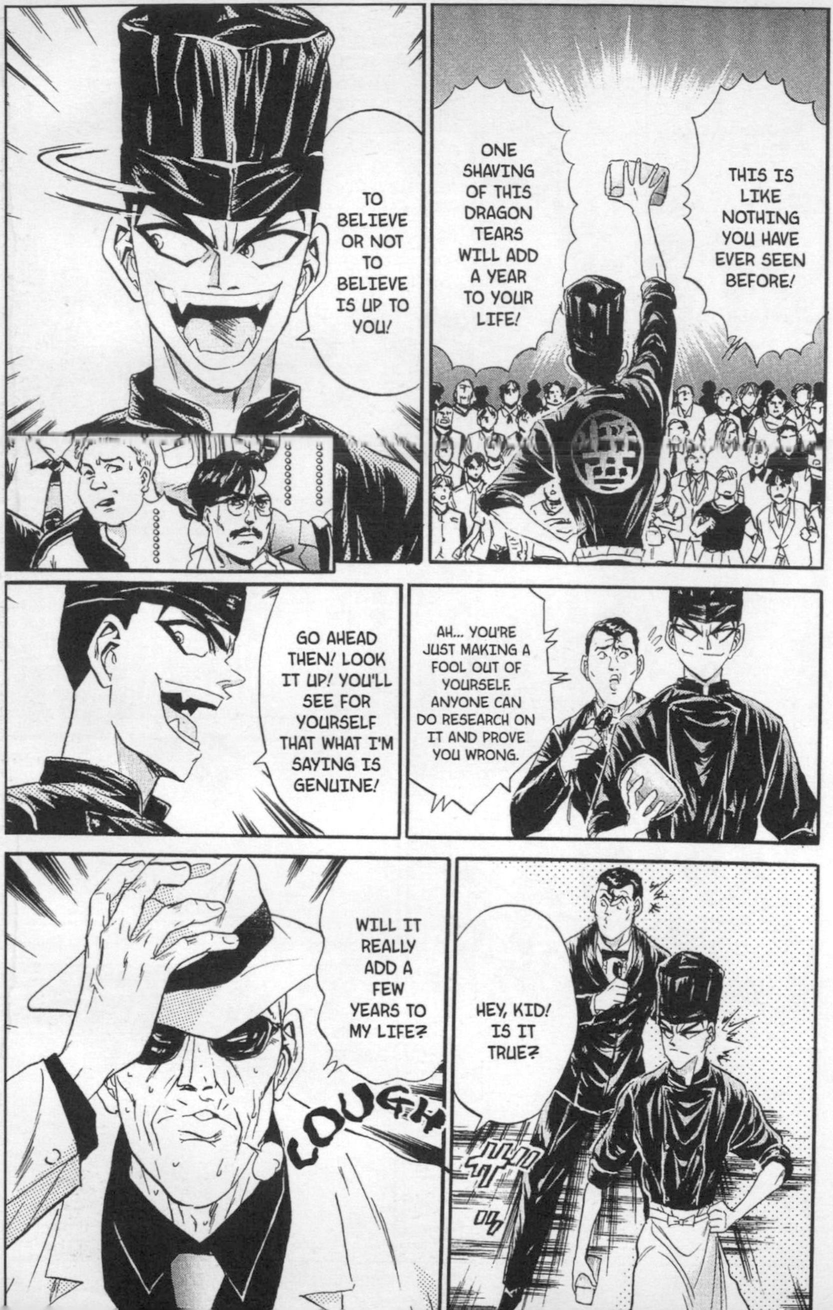
THIS IS LIKE NOTHING YOU HAVE EVER SEEN BEFORE!
ONE SHAVING OF THIS DRAGON TEARS WILL ADD A YEAR TO YOUR LIFE!
TO BELIEVE OR NOT TO BELIEVE IS UP TO YOU!
AH... YOU'RE JUST MAKING A FOOL OUT OF YOURSELF. ANYONE CAN DO RESEARCH ON IT AND PROVE YOU WRONG.
GO AHEAD THEN! LOOK IT UP! YOU'LL SEE FOR YOURSELF THAT WHAT I'M SAYING IS GENUINE!
HEY, KID! IS IT TRUE?
WILL IT REALLY ADD A FEW YEARS TO MY LIFE?
COUGH

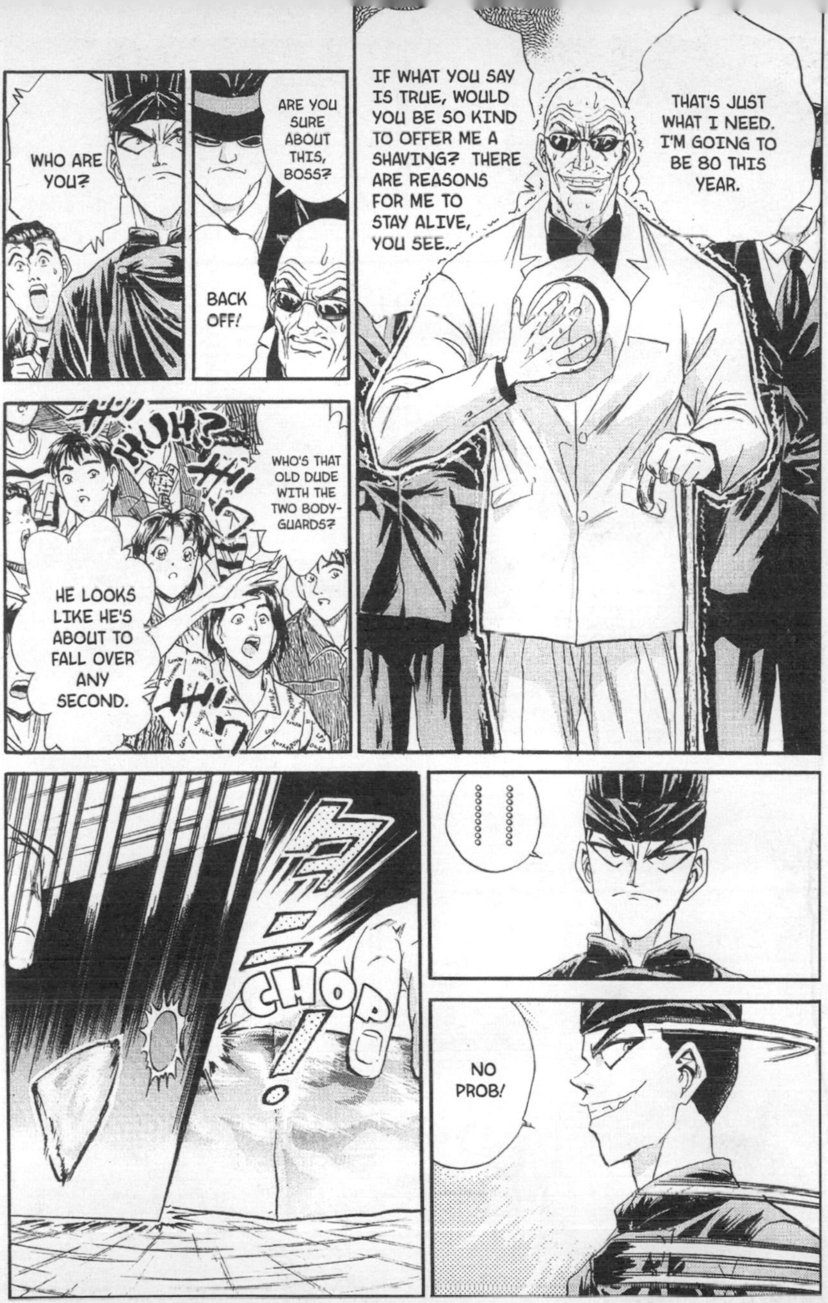
IF WHAT YOU SAY IS TRUE, WOULD YOU BE SO KIND TO OFFER ME A SHAVING? THERE ARE REASONS FOR ME TO STAY ALIVE, YOU SEE...
THAT'S JUST WHAT I NEED. I'M GOING TO BE 80 THIS YEAR.
ARE YOU SURE ABOUT THIS, BOSS?
BACK OFF!
WHO ARE YOU?
HUH?
WHO'S THAT OLD DUDE WITH THE TWO BODY-GUARDS?
HE LOOKS LIKE HE'S ABOUT TO FALL OVER ANY SECOND.
......
NO PROB!
CHOP!

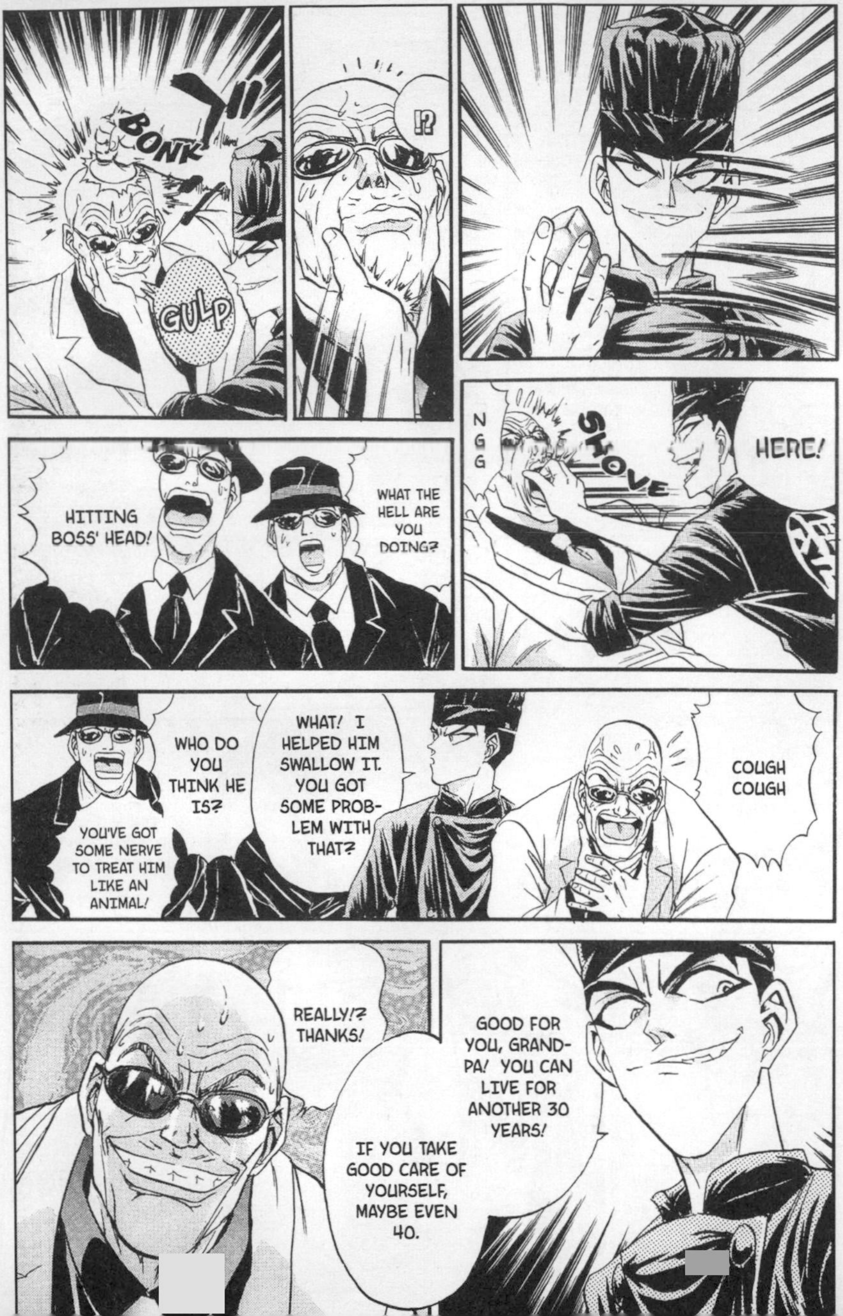
!?
BONK
GULP
HERE!
SHOVE
NGG
WHAT THE HELL ARE YOU DOING?
HITTING BOSS' HEAD!
COUGH COUGH
WHAT! I HELPED HIM SWALLOW IT. YOU GOT SOME PROBLEM WITH THAT?
WHO DO YOU THINK HE IS?
YOU'VE GOT SOME NERVE TO TREAT HIM LIKE AN ANIMAL!
GOOD FOR YOU, GRANDPA! YOU CAN LIVE FOR ANOTHER 30 YEARS!
IF YOU TAKE GOOD CARE OF YOURSELF, MAYBE EVEN 40.
REALLY!? THANKS!

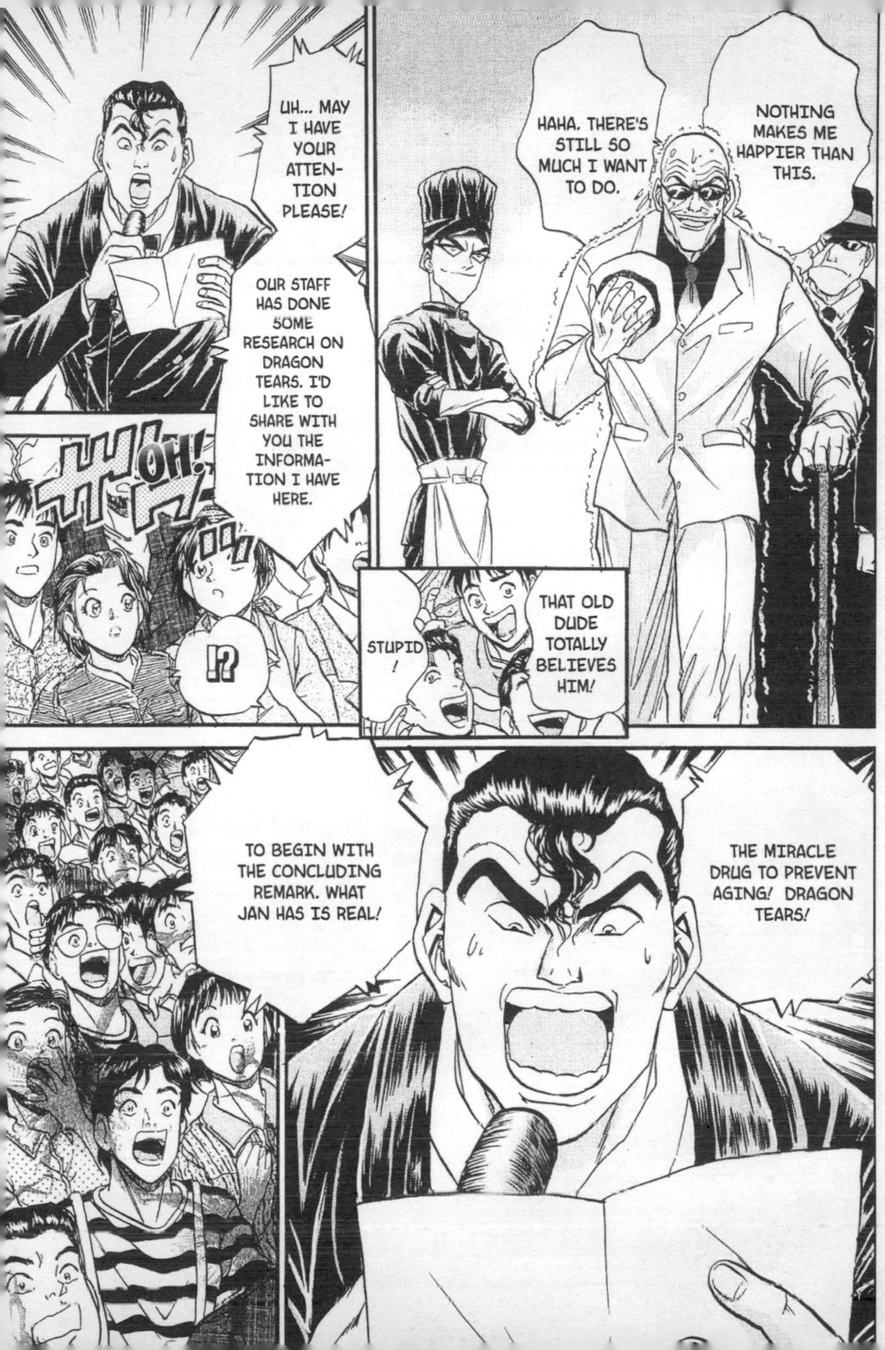
NOTHING MAKES ME HAPPIER THAN THIS.
HAHA. THERE'S STILL SO MUCH I WANT TO DO.
THAT OLD DUDE TOTALLY BELIEVES HIM!
STUPID!
UH... MAY I HAVE YOUR ATTENTION PLEASE!
OUR STAFF HAS DONE SOME RESEARCH ON DRAGON TEARS. I'D LIKE TO SHARE WITH YOU THE INFORMATION I HAVE HERE.
OH!
!?
TO BEGIN WITH THE CONCLUDING REMARK. WHAT JAN HAS IS REAL!
THE MIRACLE DRUG TO PREVENT AGING! DRAGON TEARS!

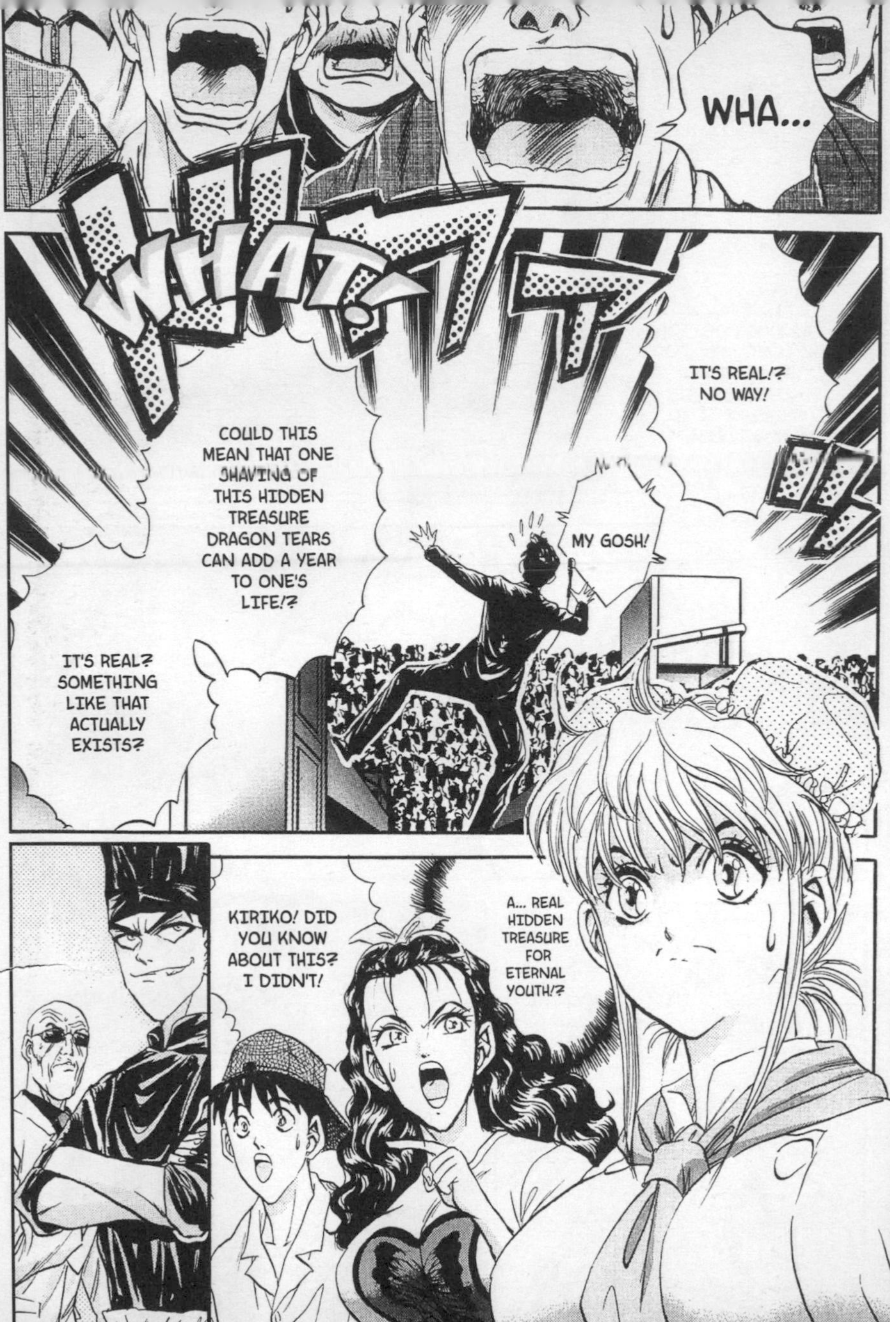
WHA...
WHAT!?
IT'S REAL!? NO WAY!
MY GOSH!
COULD THIS MEAN THAT ONE SHAVING OF THIS HIDDEN TREASURE DRAGON TEARS CAN ADD A YEAR TO ONE'S LIFE!?
IT'S REAL? SOMETHING LIKE THAT ACTUALLY EXISTS?
A... REAL HIDDEN TREASURE FOR ETERNAL YOUTH!?
KIRIKO! DID YOU KNOW ABOUT THIS? I DIDN'T!

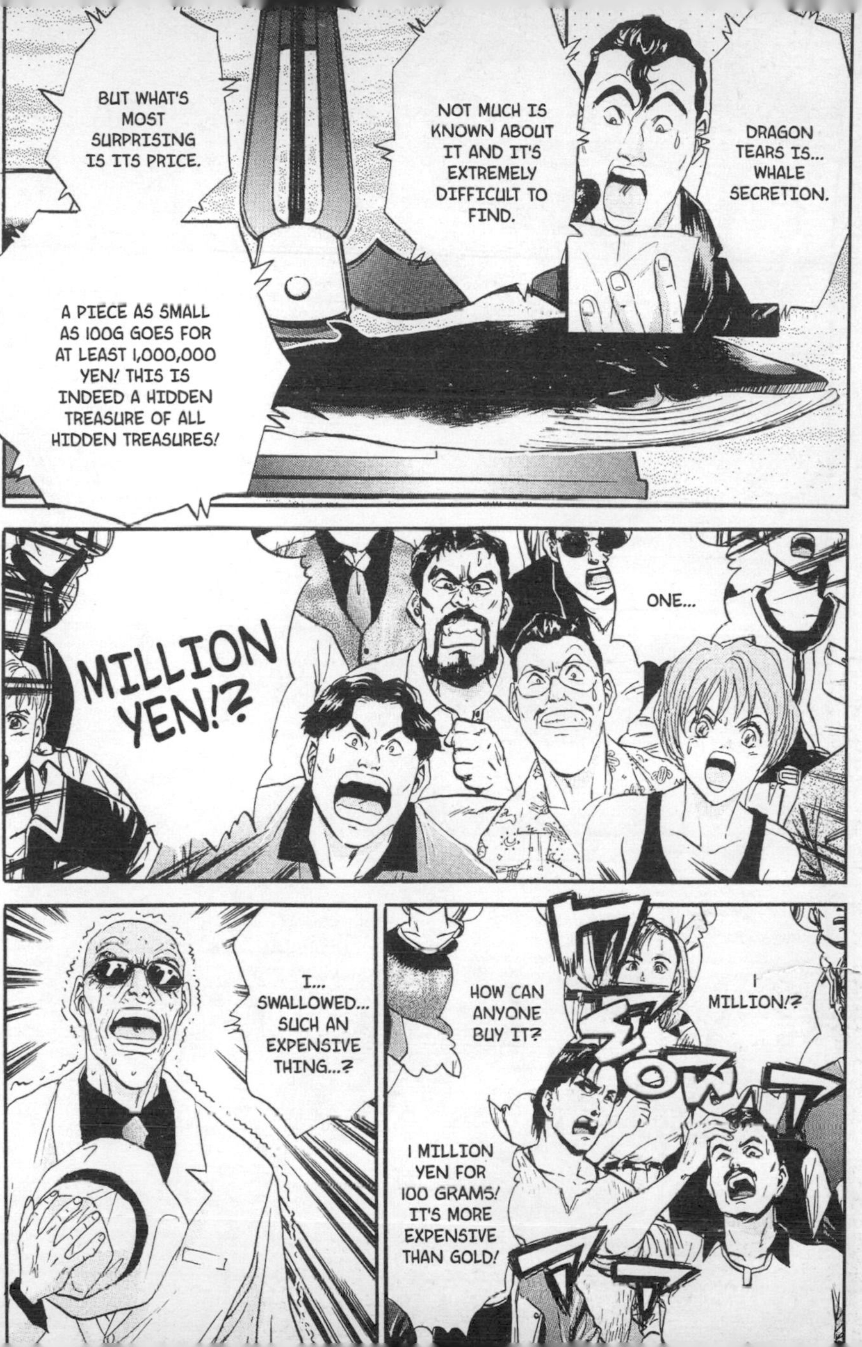
DRAGON TEARS IS... WHALE SECRETION.
NOT MUCH IS KNOWN ABOUT IT AND IT'S EXTREMELY DIFFICULT TO FIND.
BUT WHAT'S MOST SURPRISING IS ITS PRICE.
A PIECE AS SMALL AS 100G GOES FOR AT LEAST 1,000,000 YEN! THIS IS INDEED A HIDDEN TREASURE OF ALL HIDDEN TREASURES!
ONE...
MILLION YEN!?
1 MILLION!?
HOW CAN ANYONE BUY IT?
WOW
1 MILLION YEN FOR 100 GRAMS! IT'S MORE EXPENSIVE THAN GOLD!
I... SWALLOWED... SUCH AN EXPENSIVE THING...?

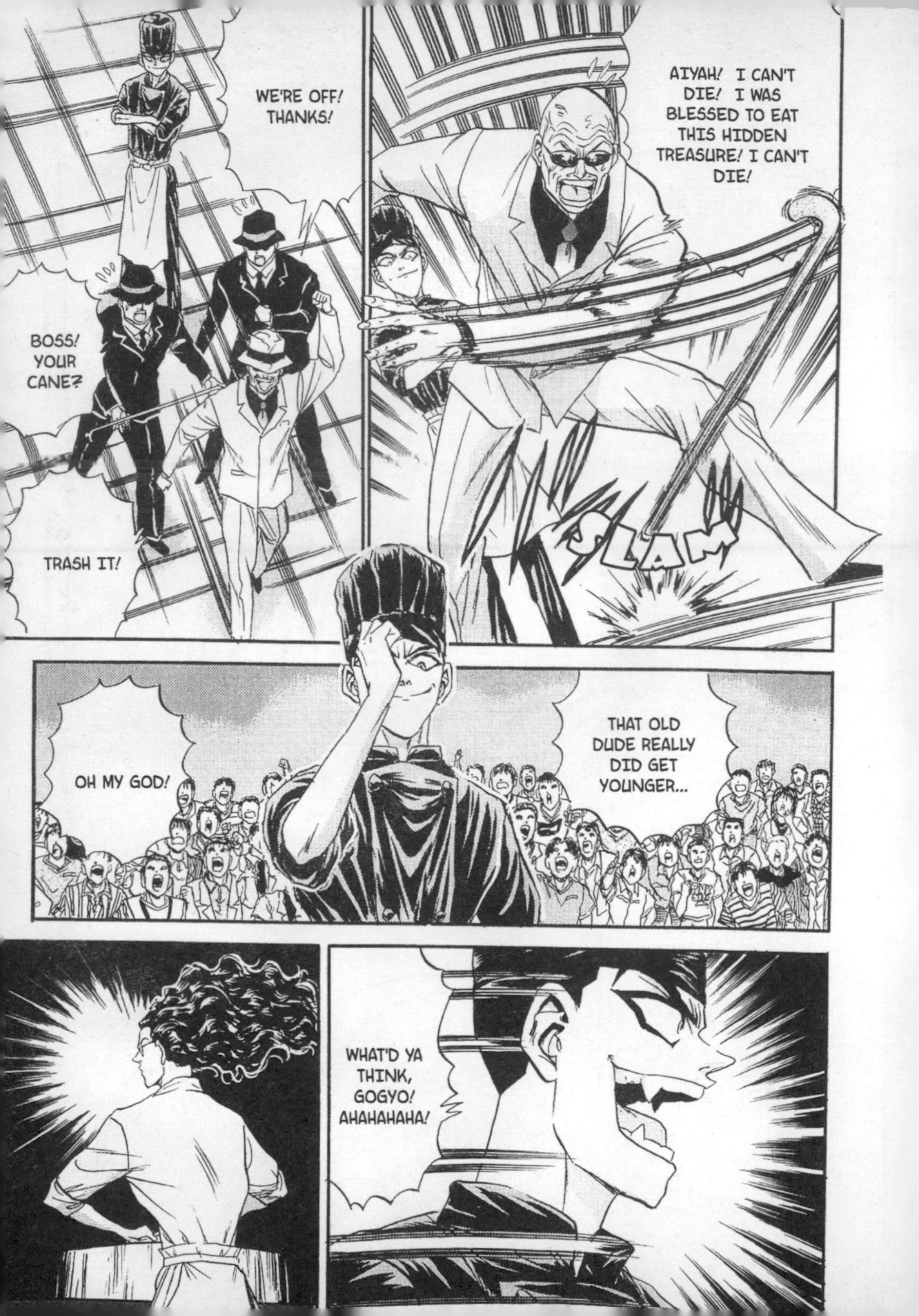
AIYAH! I CAN'T DIE! I WAS BLESSED TO EAT THIS HIDDEN TREASURE! I CAN'T DIE!
SLAM
WE'RE OFF! THANKS!
BOSS! YOUR CANE?
TRASH IT!
THAT OLD DUDE REALLY DID GET YOUNGER...
OH MY GOD!
WHAT'D YA THINK, GOGYO! AHAHAHAHA!

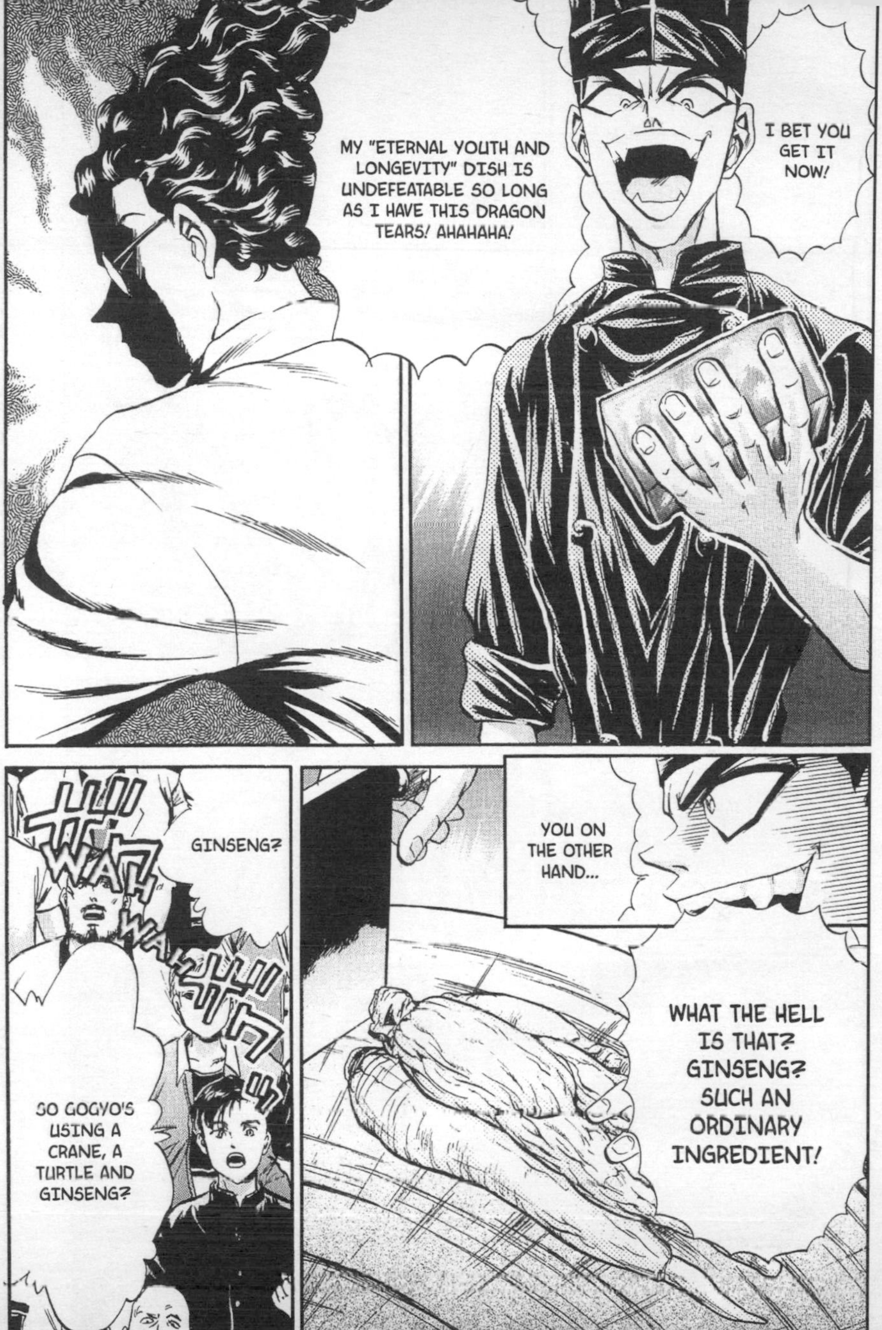
I BET YOU GET IT NOW!
MY "ETERNAL YOUTH AND LONGEVITY" DISH IS UNDEFEATABLE SO LONG AS I HAVE THIS DRAGON TEARS! AHAHAHA!
YOU ON THE OTHER HAND...
WHAT THE HELL IS THAT? GINSENG? SUCH AN ORDINARY INGREDIENT!
WAH
WAH
GINSENG?
SO GOGYO'S USING A CRANE, A TURTLE AND GINSENG?

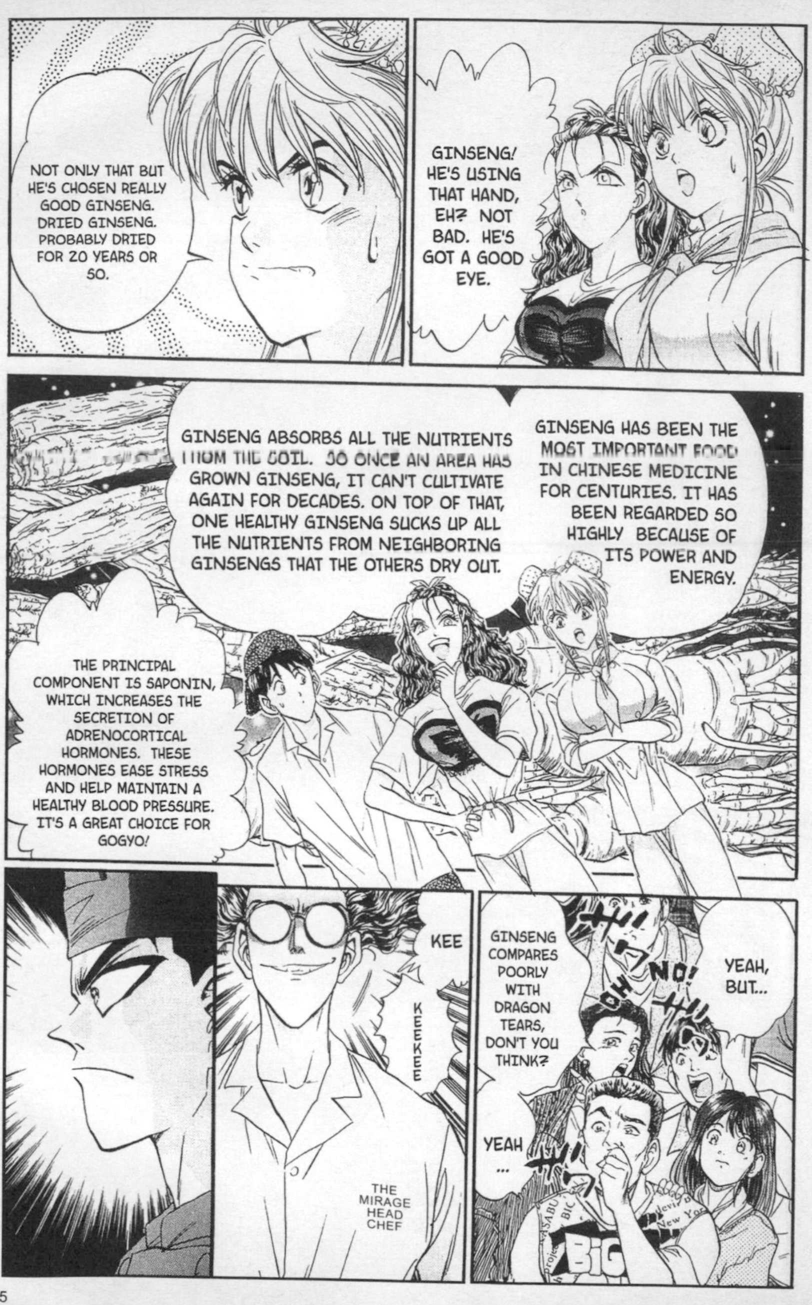
GINSENG! HE'S USING THAT HAND, EH? NOT BAD. HE'S GOT A GOOD EYE.
NOT ONLY THAT BUT HE'S CHOSEN REALLY GOOD GINSENG. DRIED GINSENG. PROBABLY DRIED FOR 20 YEARS OR SO.
GINSENG HAS BEEN THE MOST IMPORTANT FOOD IN CHINESE MEDICINE FOR CENTURIES. IT HAS BEEN REGARDED SO HIGHLY BECAUSE OF ITS POWER AND ENERGY.
GINSENG ABSORBS ALL THE NUTRIENTS FROM THE SOIL. SO ONCE AN AREA HAS GROWN GINSENG, IT CAN'T CULTIVATE AGAIN FOR DECADES. ON TOP OF THAT, ONE HEALTHY GINSENG SUCKS UP ALL THE NUTRIENTS FROM NEIGHBORING GINSENGS THAT THE OTHERS DRY OUT.
THE PRINCIPAL COMPONENT IS SAPONIN, WHICH INCREASES THE SECRETION OF ADRENOCORTICAL HORMONES. THESE HORMONES EASE STRESS AND HELP MAINTAIN A HEALTHY BLOOD PRESSURE. IT'S A GREAT CHOICE FOR GOGYO!
YEAH, BUT...
NO!
OH
GINSENG COMPARES POORLY WITH DRAGON TEARS, DON'T YOU THINK?
YEAH ...
KEE
KEEKEE
THE MIRAGE HEAD CHEF

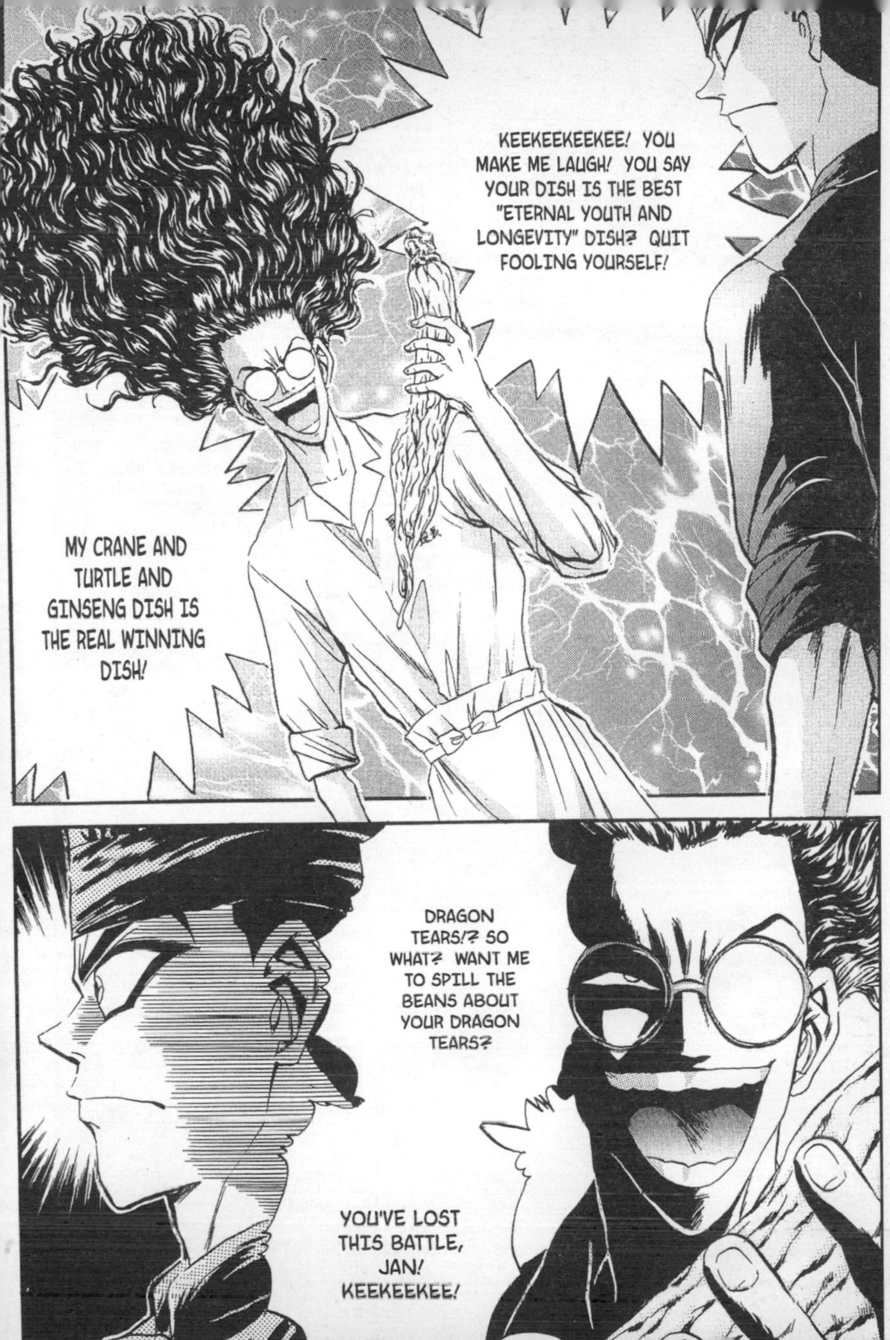
KEEKEEKEEKEE! YOU MAKE ME LAUGH! YOU SAY YOUR DISH IS THE BEST "ETERNAL YOUTH AND LONGEVITY" DISH? QUIT FOOLING YOURSELF!
MY CRANE AND TURTLE AND GINSENG DISH IS THE REAL WINNING DISH!
DRAGON TEARS!? SO WHAT? WANT ME TO SPILL THE BEANS ABOUT YOUR DRAGON TEARS?
YOU'VE LOST THIS BATTLE, JAN! KEEKEEKEE!

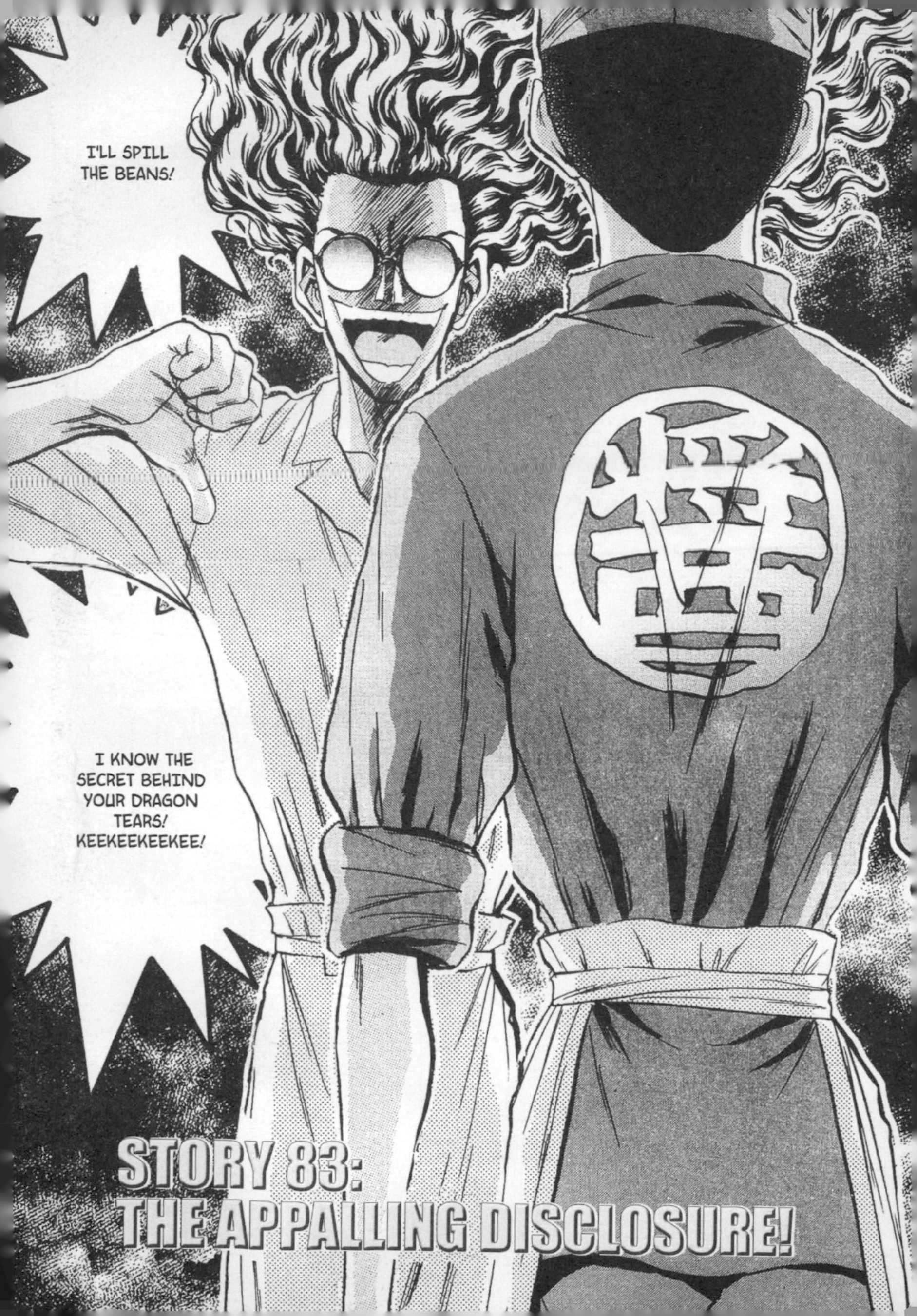
I'LL SPILL THE BEANS!
I KNOW THE SECRET BEHIND YOUR DRAGON TEARS! KEEKEEKEEKEE!
STORY 83: THE APPALLING DISCLOSURE!

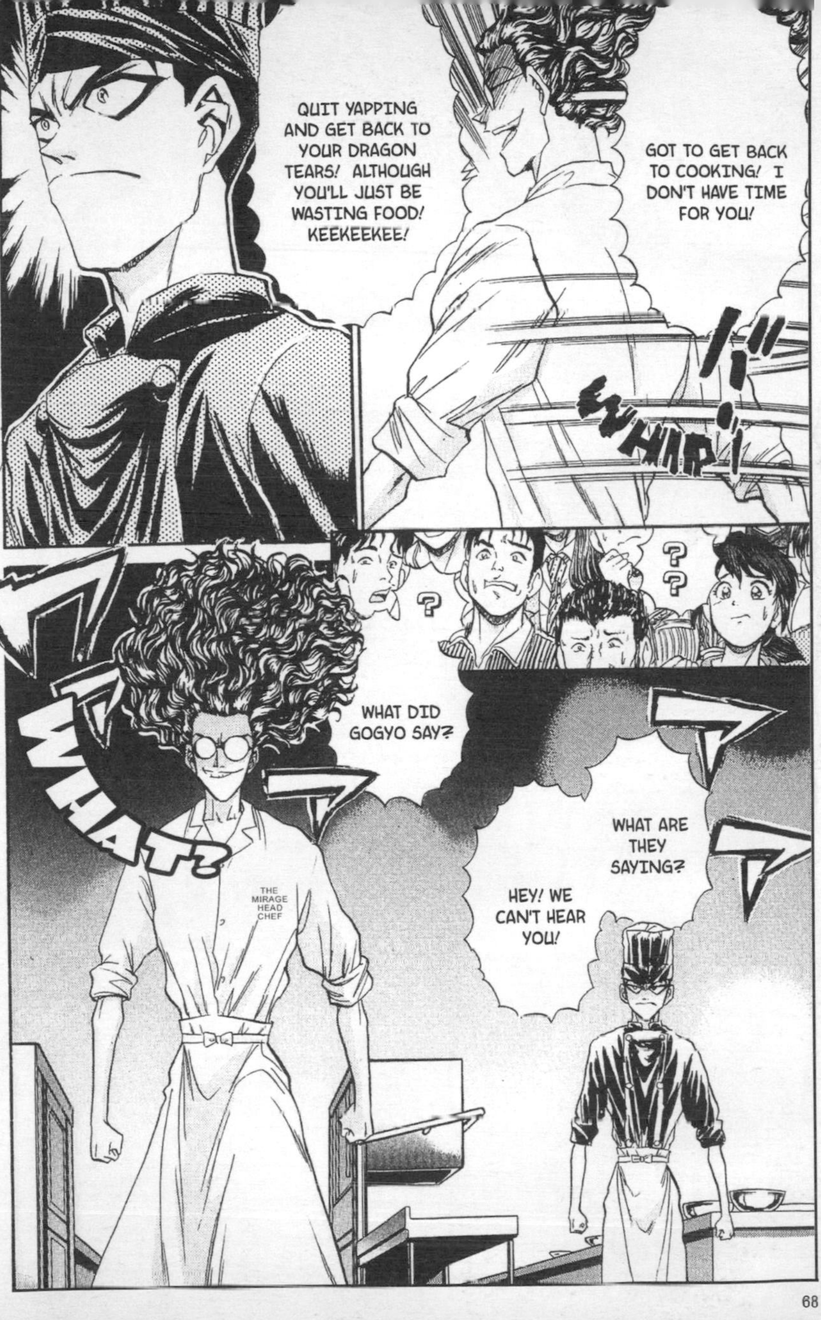
GOT TO GET BACK TO COOKING! I DON'T HAVE TIME FOR YOU!
WHIP!
QUIT YAPPING AND GET BACK TO YOUR DRAGON TEARS! ALTHOUGH YOU'LL JUST BE WASTING FOOD! KEEKEEKEE!
? ?
?
WHAT ARE THEY SAYING?
WHAT DID GOGYO SAY?
HEY! WE CAN'T HEAR YOU!
WHAT?
THE MIRAGE HEAD CHEF

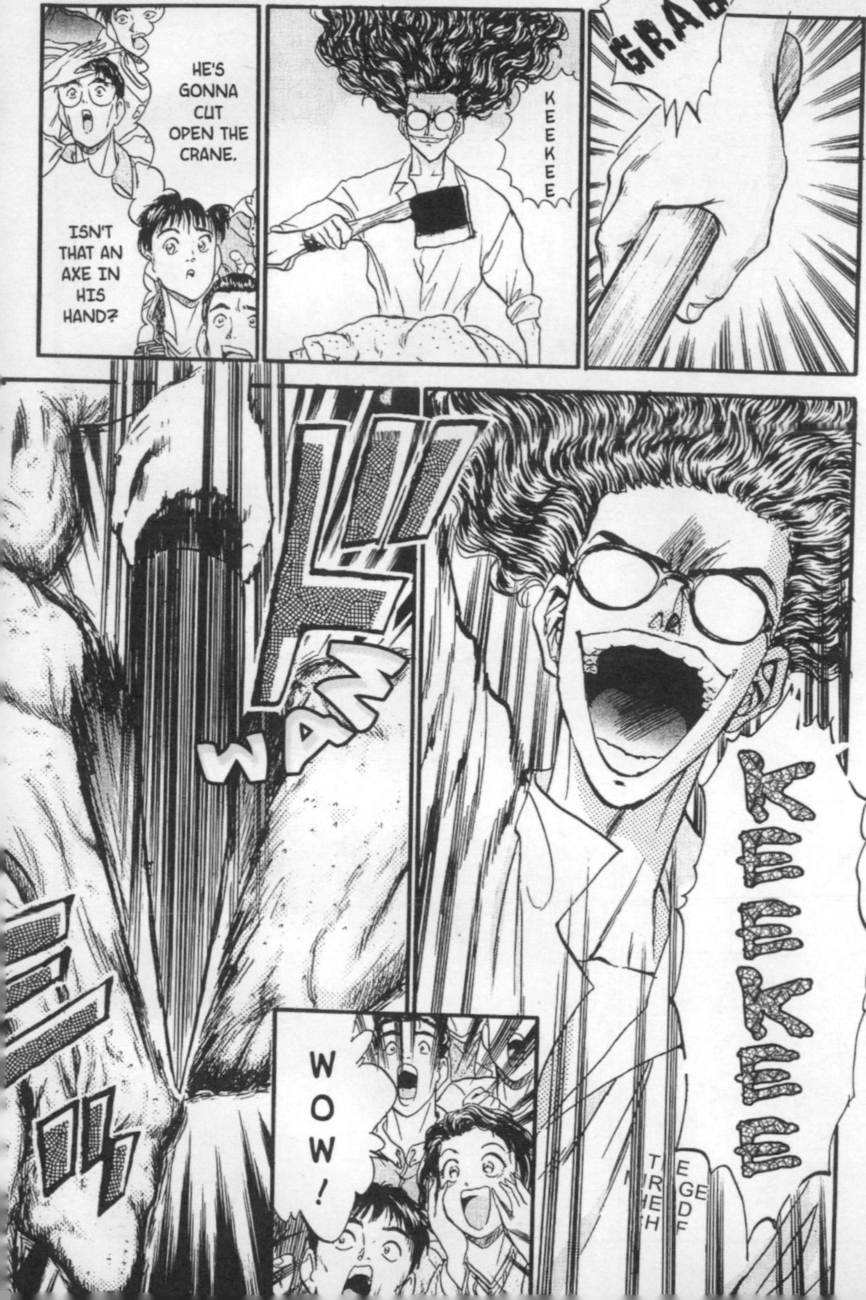
GRAB
KEEKEE
HE'S GONNA CUT OPEN THE CRANE.
ISN'T THAT AN AXE IN HIS HAND?
KEEKEE
WAM
WOW WOW!

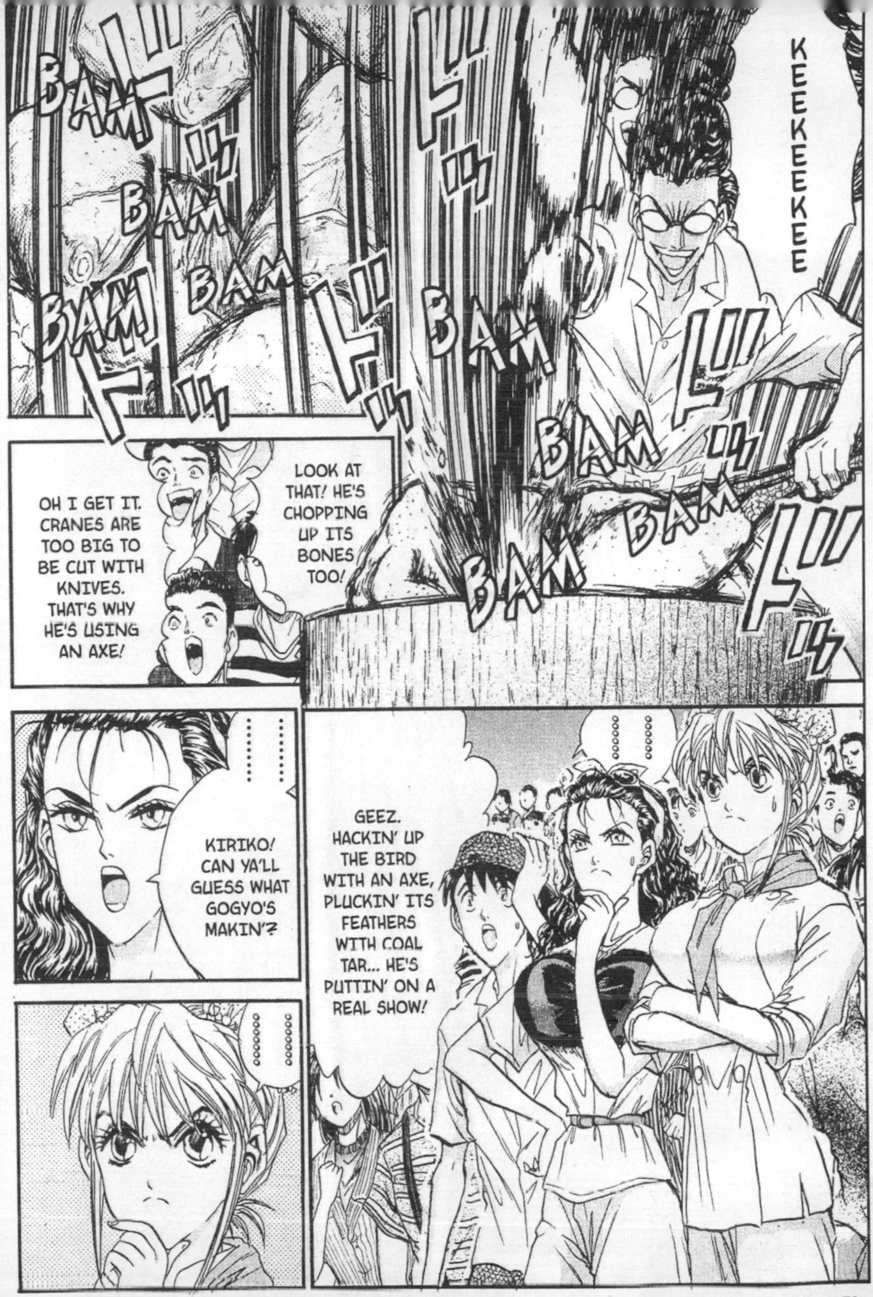
KEEKEEKEEKEE
BAM BAM BAM BAM BAM BAM BAM BAM
LOOK AT THAT! HE'S CHOPPING UP ITS BONES TOO!
OH I GET IT. CRANES ARE TOO BIG TO BE CUT WITH KNIVES. THAT'S WHY HE'S USING AN AXE!
GEEZ. HACKIN' UP THE BIRD WITH AN AXE, PLUCKIN' ITS FEATHERS WITH COAL TAR... HE'S PUTTIN' ON A REAL SHOW!
KIRIKO! CAN YA'LL GUESS WHAT GOGYO'S MAKIN'?

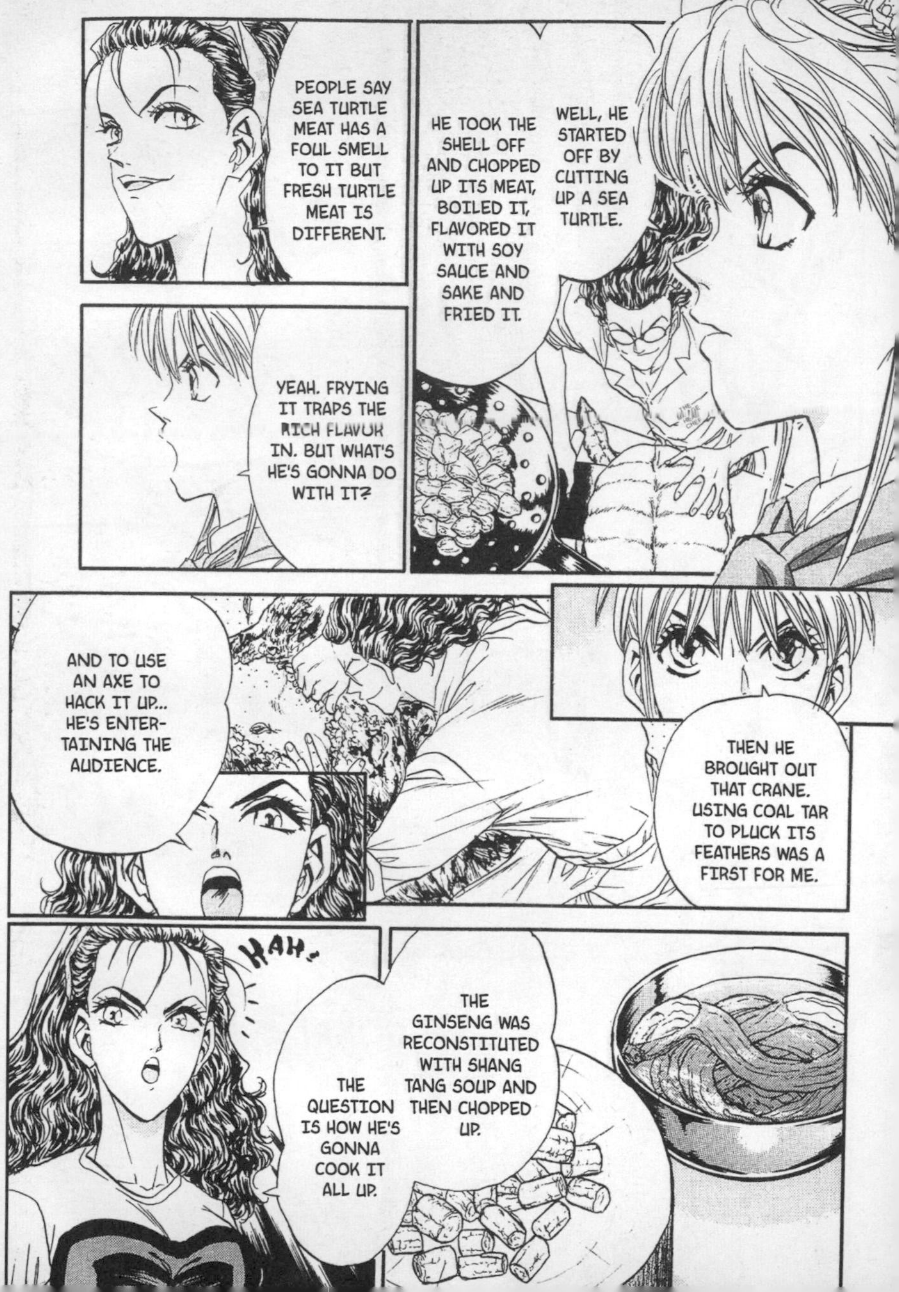
WELL, HE STARTED OFF BY CUTTING UP A SEA TURTLE.
HE TOOK THE SHELL OFF AND CHOPPED UP ITS MEAT, BOILED IT, FLAVORED IT WITH SOY SAUCE AND SAKE AND FRIED IT.
PEOPLE SAY SEA TURTLE MEAT HAS A FOUL SMELL TO IT BUT FRESH TURTLE MEAT IS DIFFERENT.
YEAH. FRYING IT TRAPS THE RICH FLAVOR IN. BUT WHAT'S HE'S GONNA DO WITH IT?
THEN HE BROUGHT OUT THAT CRANE. USING COAL TAR TO PLUCK ITS FEATHERS WAS A FIRST FOR ME.
AND TO USE AN AXE TO HACK IT UP... HE'S ENTERTAINING THE AUDIENCE.
THE GINSENG WAS RECONSTITUTED WITH SHANG TANG SOUP AND THEN CHOPPED UP.
THE QUESTION IS HOW HE'S GONNA COOK IT ALL UP.
HAH!

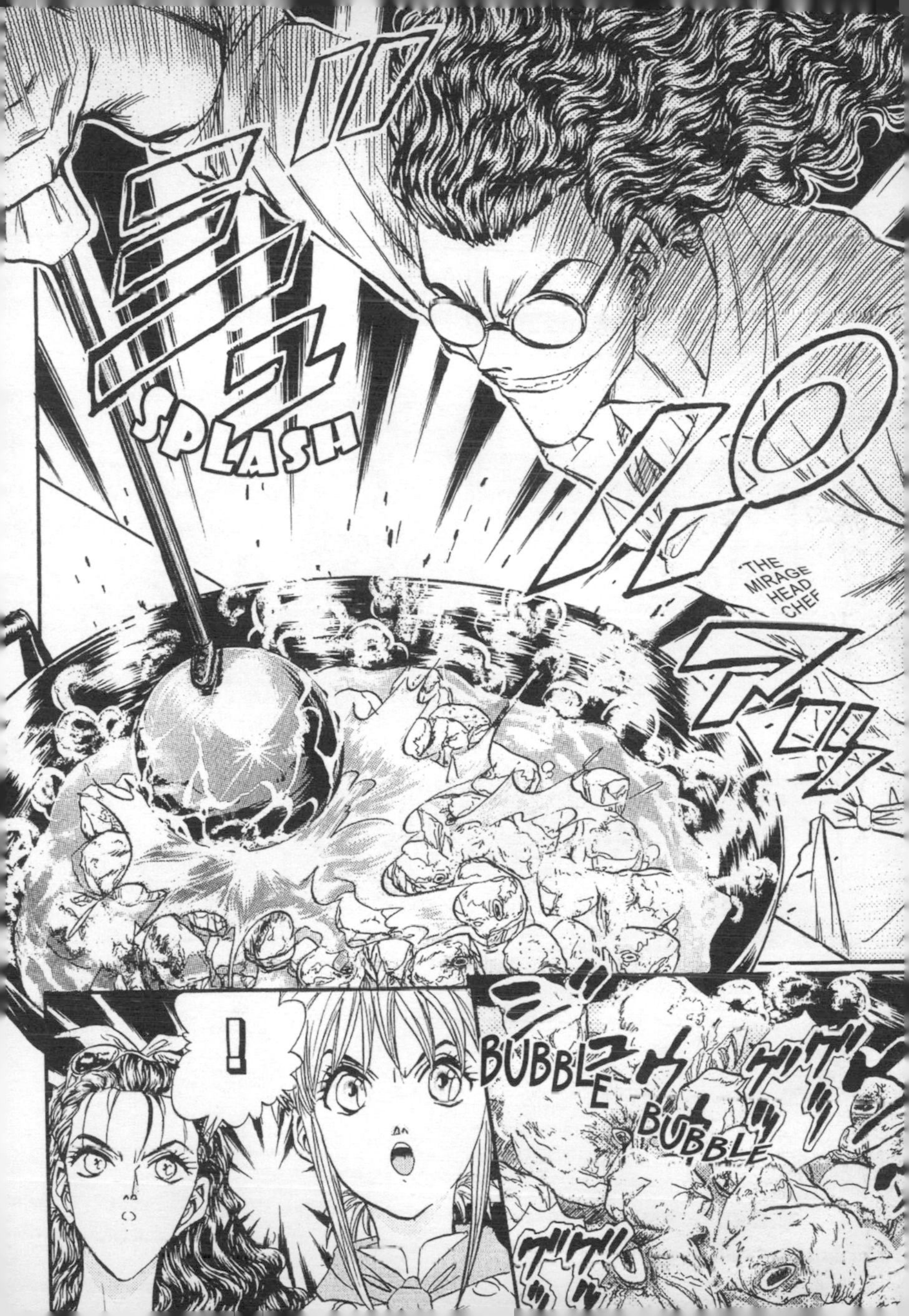
THE MIRAGE HEAD CHEF
SPLASH
!
BUBBLE
BUBBLE

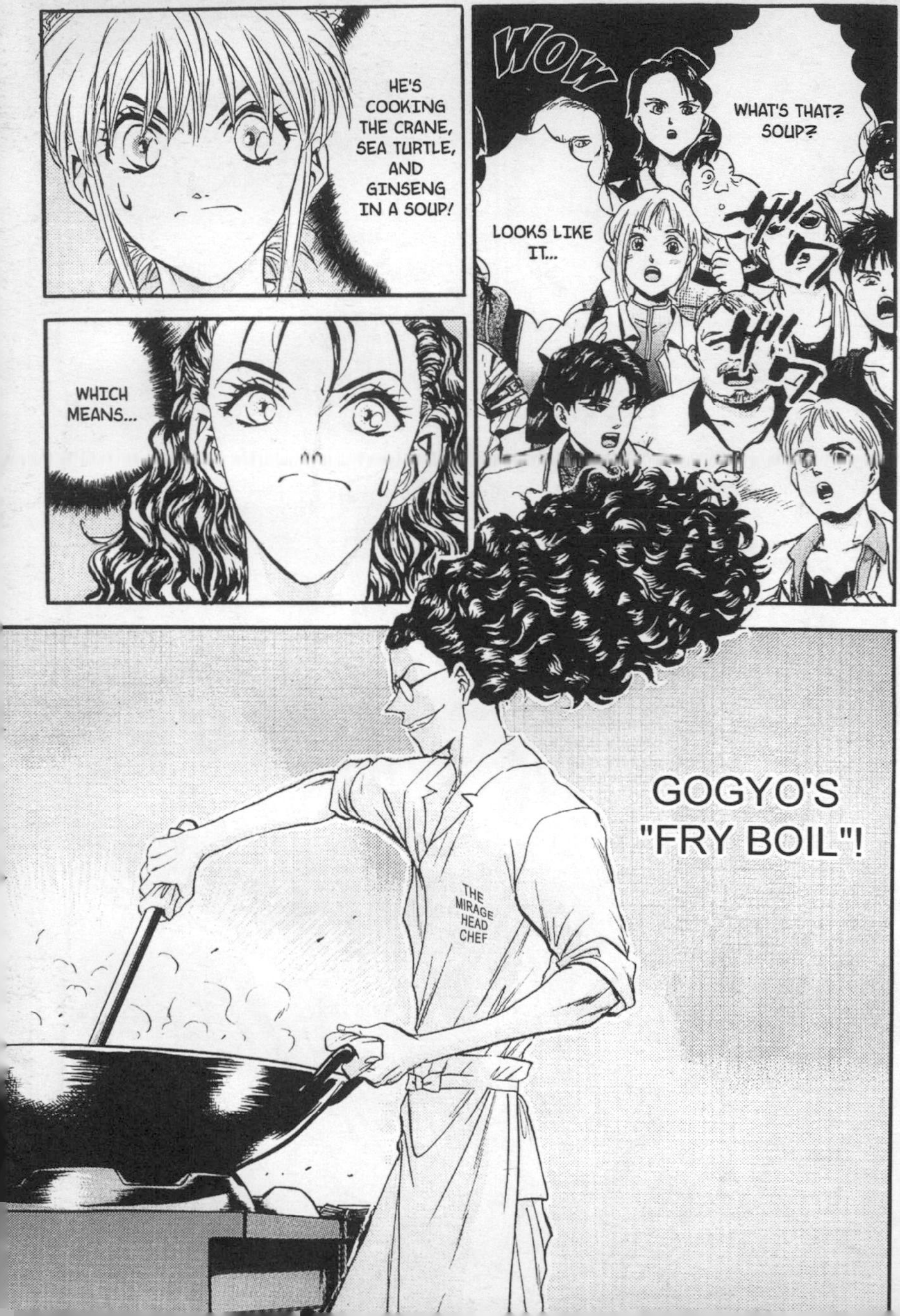
WOW
WHAT'S THAT? SOUP?
LOOKS LIKE IT...
HE'S COOKING THE CRANE, SEA TURTLE, AND GINSENG IN A SOUP!
WHICH MEANS...
THE MIRAGE HEAD CHEF
GOGYO'S "FRY BOIL"!

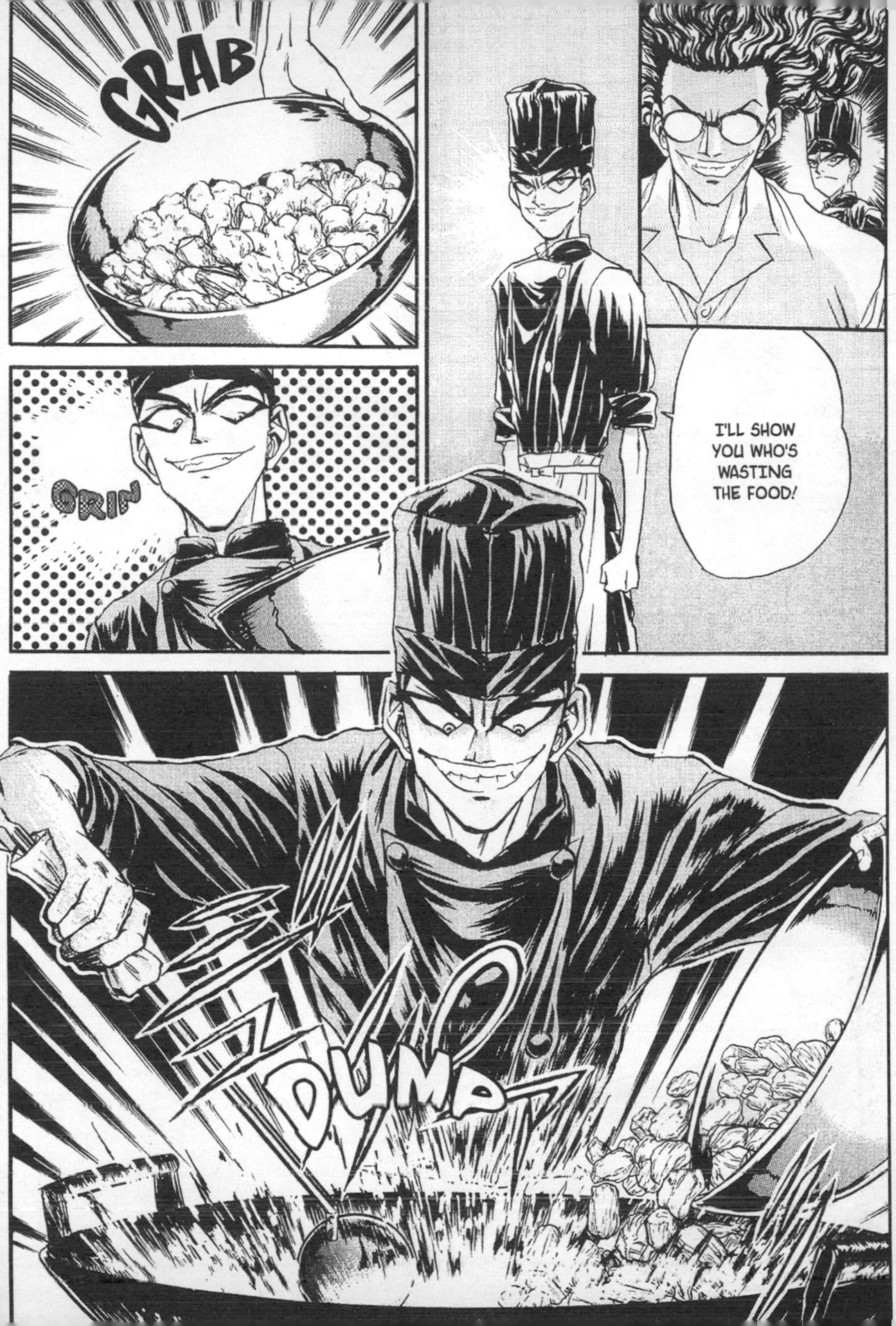
I'LL SHOW YOU WHO'S WASTING THE FOOD!
GRAB
GRIN
DUMP

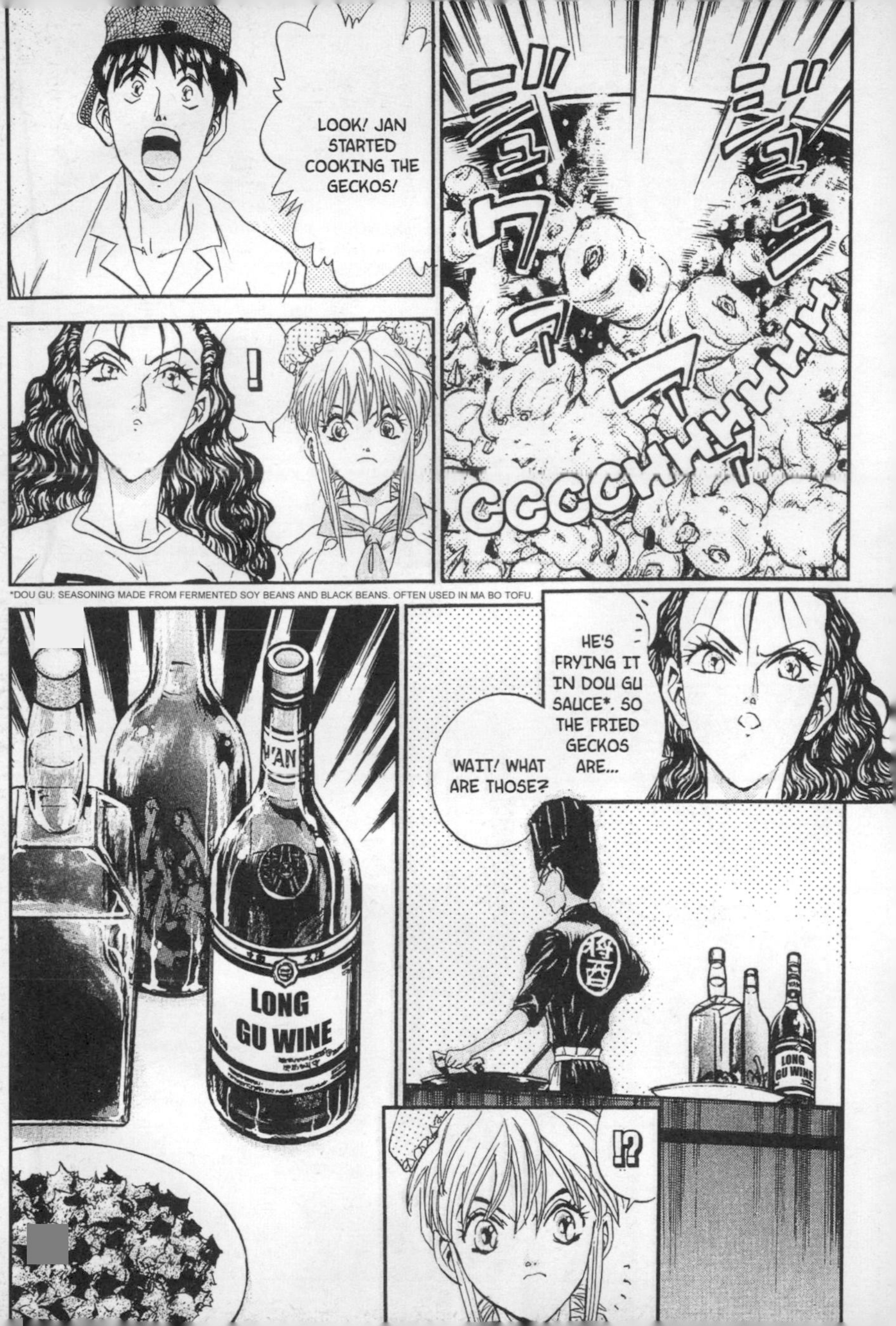
CCCCHHHHHHH
LOOK! JAN STARTED COOKING THE GECKOS!
!
HE'S FRYING IT IN DOU GU SAUCE*. SO THE FRIED GECKOS ARE...
WAIT! WHAT ARE THOSE?
LONG GU WINE
!?
LONG GU WINE

*DOU GU: SEASONING MADE FROM FERMENTED SOY BEANS AND BLACK BEANS. OFTEN USED IN MA BO TOFU.

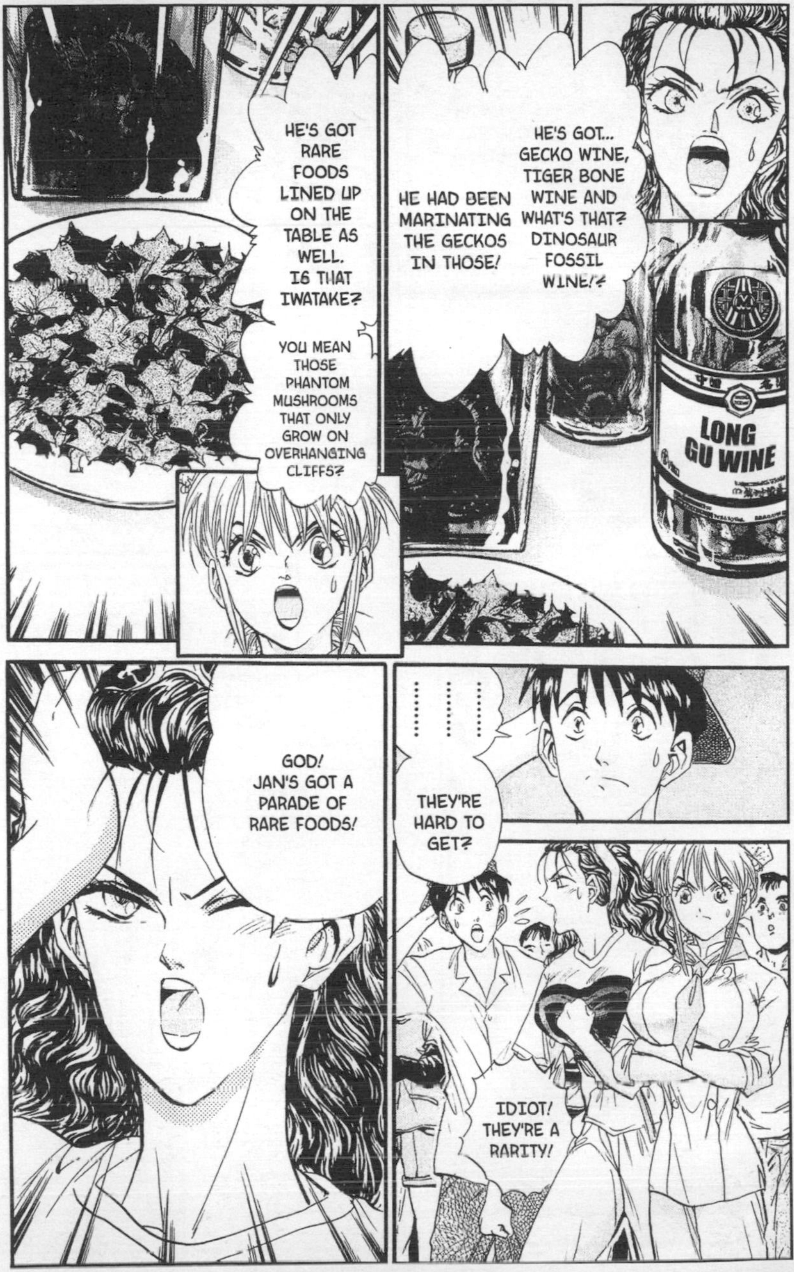
HE'S GOT... GECKO WINE, TIGER BONE WINE AND WHAT'S THAT? DINOSAUR FOSSIL WINE!?
HE HAD BEEN MARINATING THE GECKOS IN THOSE!
LONG GU WINE
HE'S GOT RARE FOODS LINED UP ON THE TABLE AS WELL. IS THAT IWATAKE?
YOU MEAN THOSE PHANTOM MUSHROOMS THAT ONLY GROW ON OVERHANGING CLIFFS?
......
THEY'RE HARD TO GET?
IDIOT! THEY'RE A RARITY!
GOD! JAN'S GOT A PARADE OF RARE FOODS!

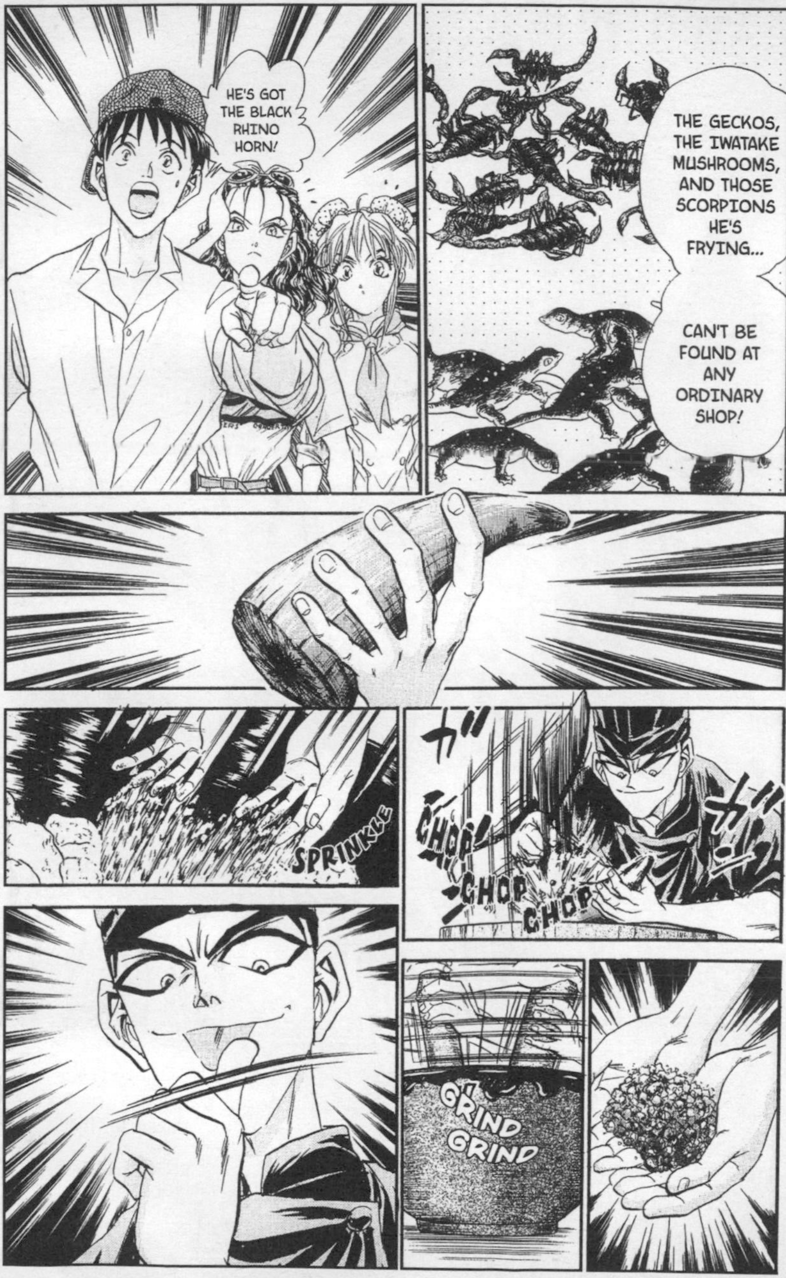
THE GECKOS, THE IWATAKE MUSHROOMS, AND THOSE SCORPIONS HE'S FRYING...
CAN'T BE FOUND AT ANY ORDINARY SHOP!
HE'S GOT THE BLACK RHINO HORN!
CHOP CHOP CHOP
SPRINKLE
GRIND GRIND

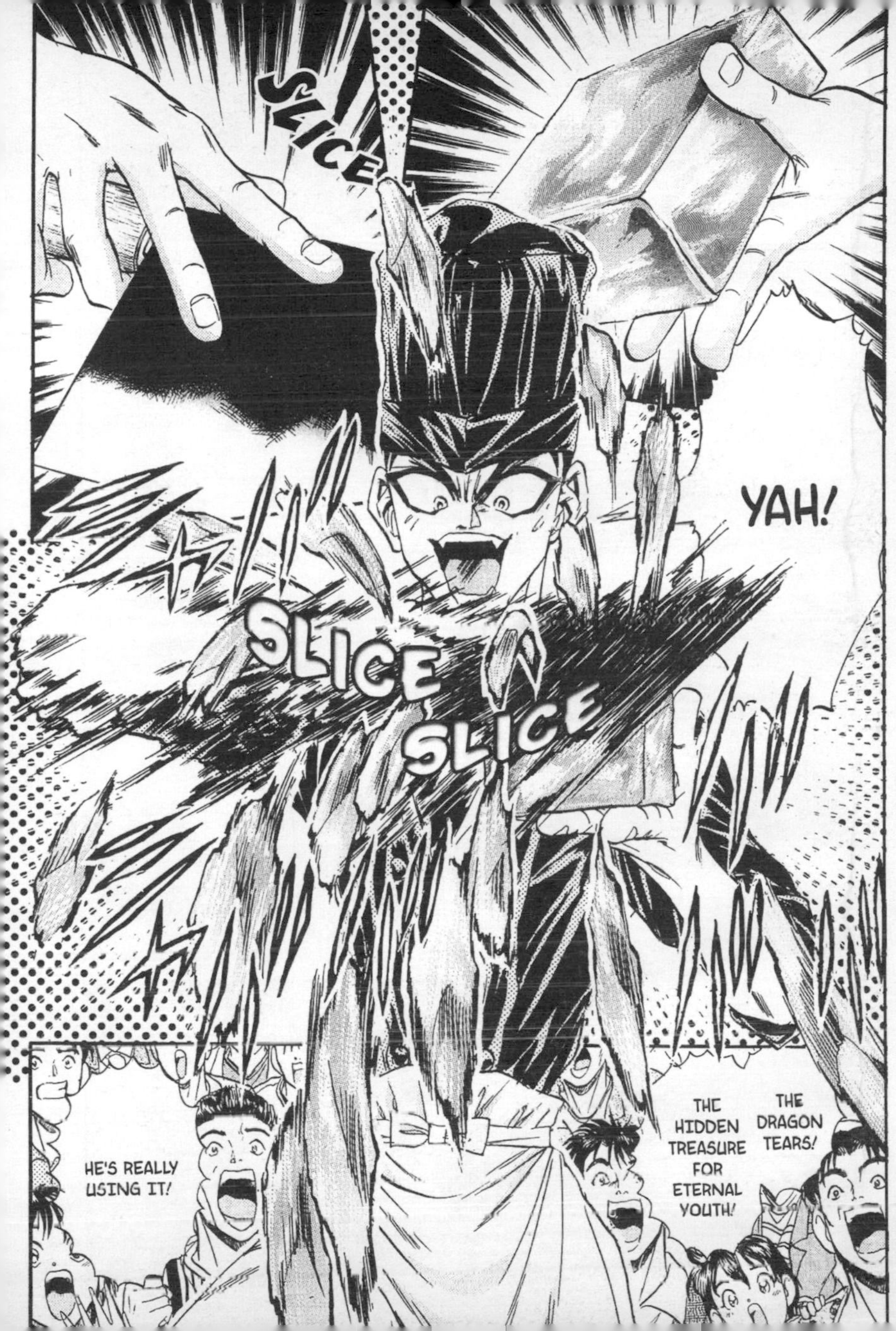
SLICE
YAH!
SLICE
SLICE
THE DRAGON TEARS!
THE HIDDEN TREASURE FOR ETERNAL YOUTH!
HE'S REALLY USING IT!

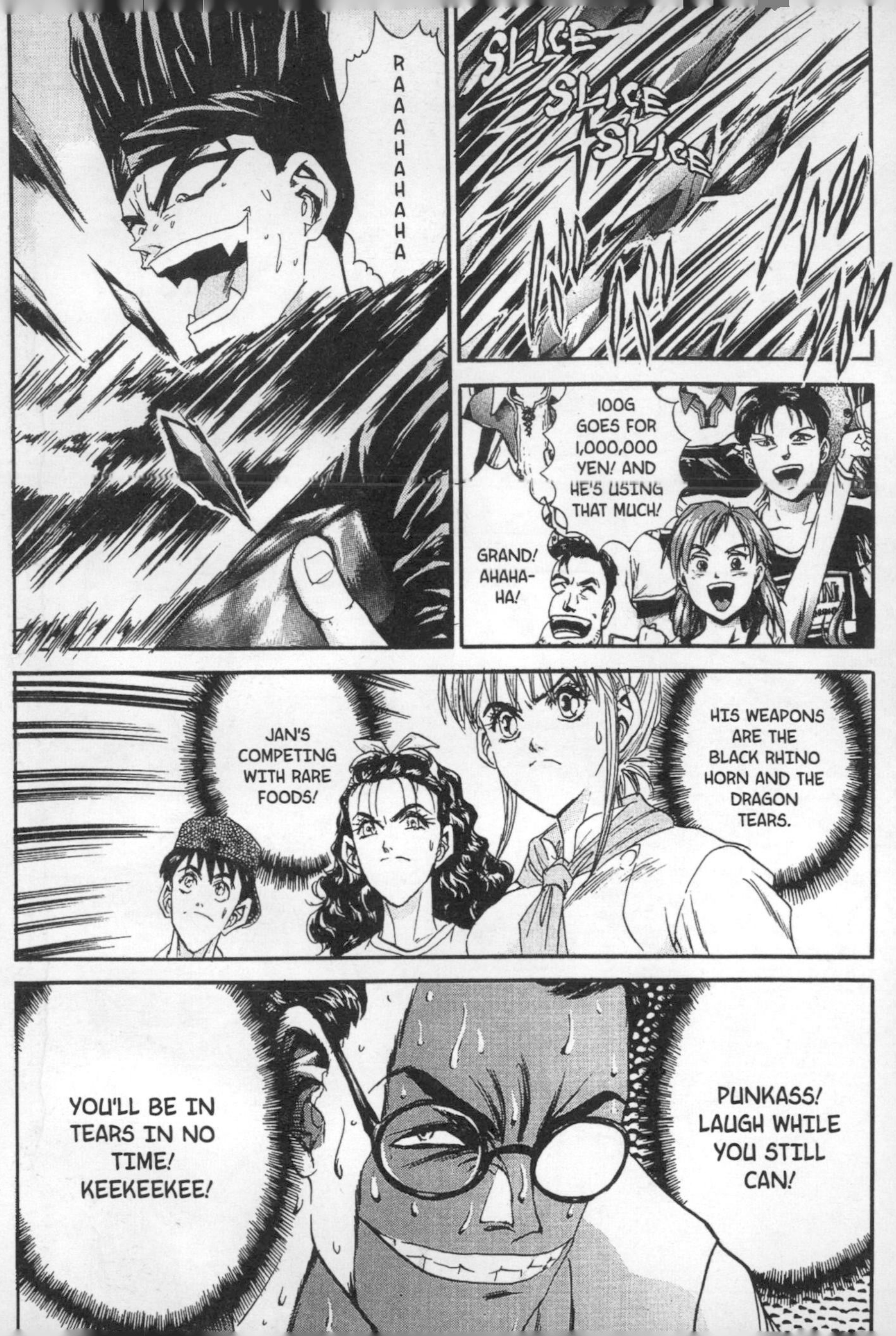
SLICE
SLICE
SLICE
100G GOES FOR 1,000,000 YEN! AND HE'S USING THAT MUCH!
GRAND! AHAHAHA!
RAAAAHAHAHAHA
HIS WEAPONS ARE THE BLACK RHINO HORN AND THE DRAGON TEARS.
JAN'S COMPETING WITH RARE FOODS!
PUNKASS! LAUGH WHILE YOU STILL CAN!
YOU'LL BE IN TEARS IN NO TIME! KEEKEEKEE!

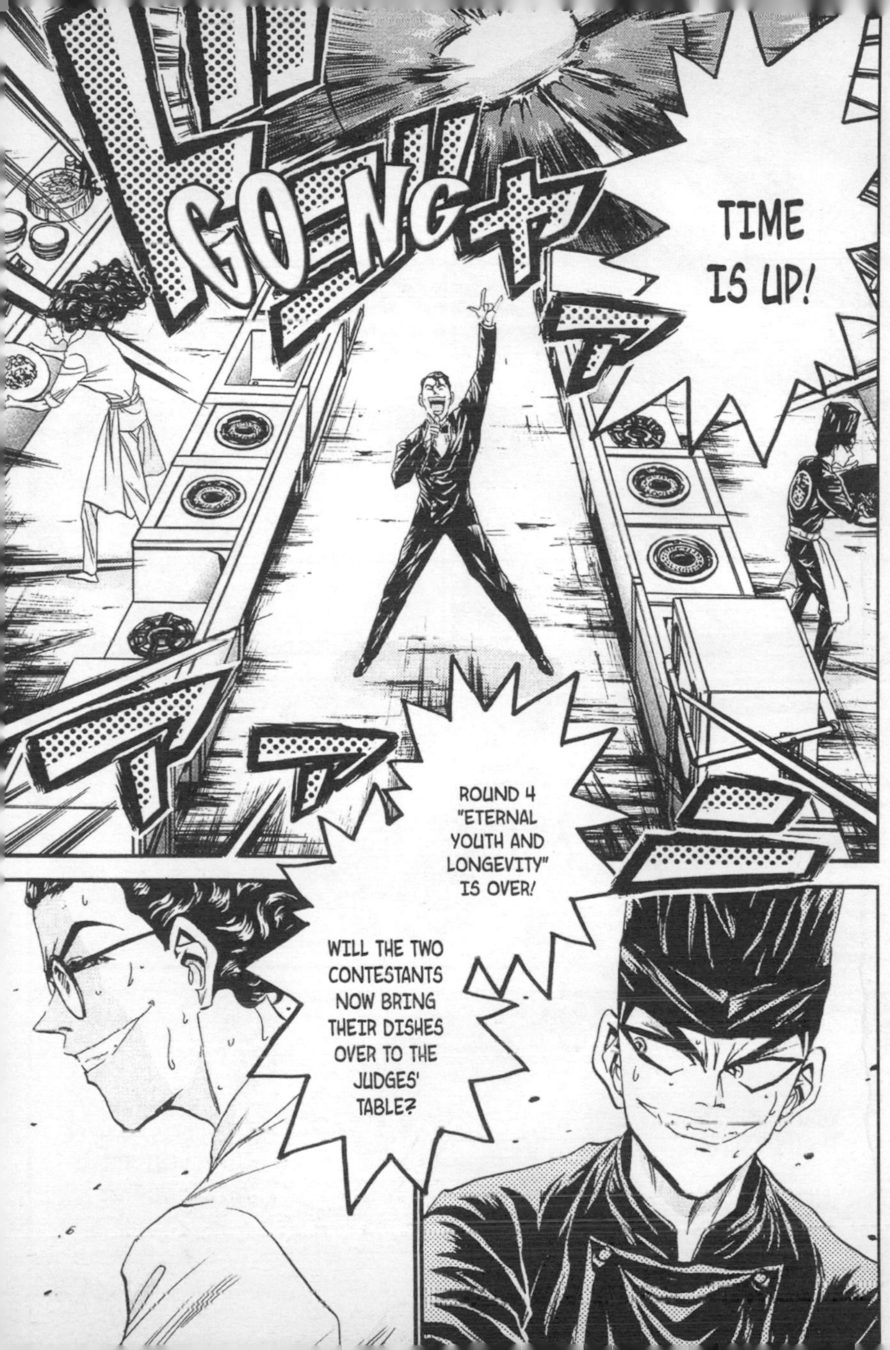
TIME IS UP!
GO-NG
ROUND 4 "ETERNAL YOUTH AND LONGEVITY" IS OVER!
WILL THE TWO CONTESTANTS NOW BRING THEIR DISHES OVER TO THE JUDGES' TABLE?

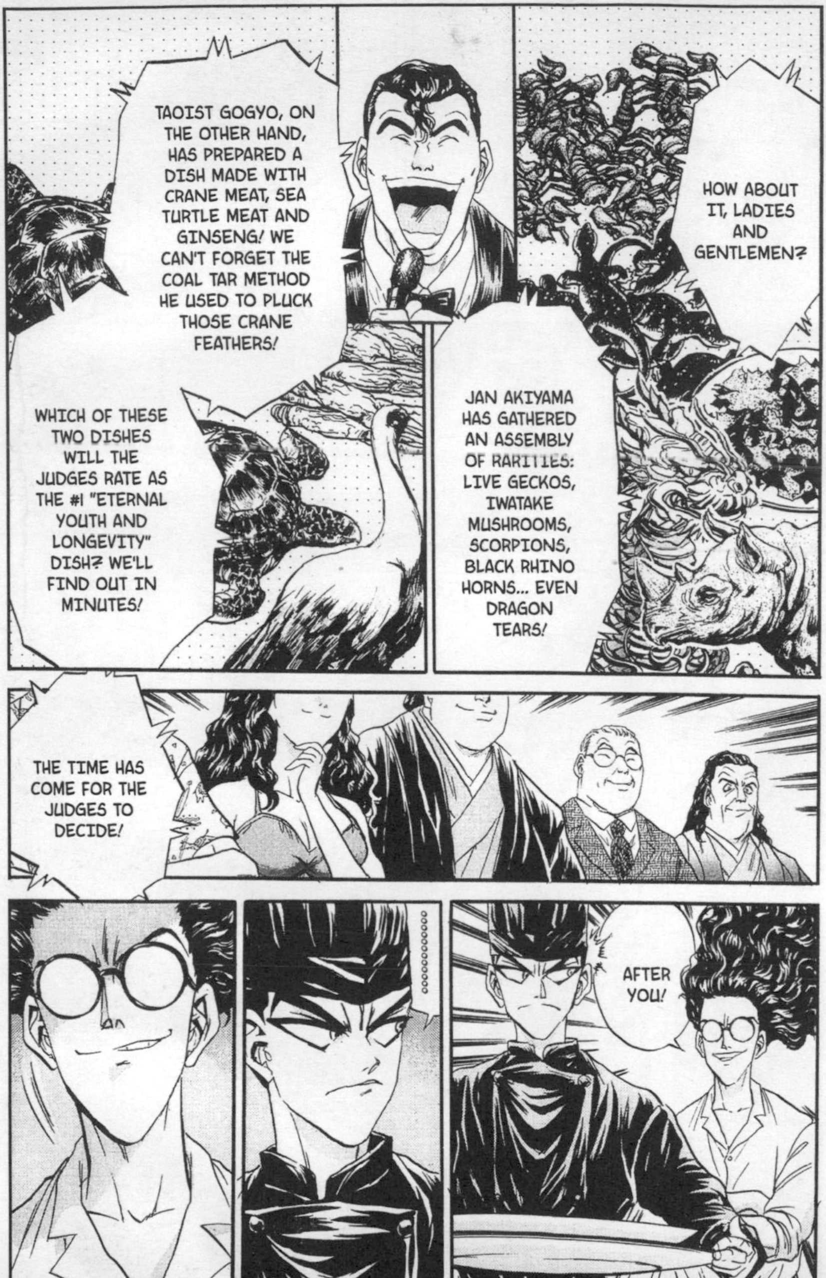

HOW ABOUT IT, LADIES AND GENTLEMEN?
JAN AKIYAMA HAS GATHERED AN ASSEMBLY OF RARITIES: LIVE GECKOS, IWATAKE MUSHROOMS, SCORPIONS, BLACK RHINO HORNS... EVEN DRAGON TEARS!
TAOIST GOGYO, ON THE OTHER HAND, HAS PREPARED A DISH MADE WITH CRANE MEAT, SEA TURTLE MEAT AND GINSENG! WE CAN'T FORGET THE COAL TAR METHOD HE USED TO PLUCK THOSE CRANE FEATHERS!
WHICH OF THESE TWO DISHES WILL THE JUDGES RATE AS THE #1 "ETERNAL YOUTH AND LONGEVITY" DISH? WE'LL FIND OUT IN MINUTES!
THE TIME HAS COME FOR THE JUDGES TO DECIDE!
AFTER YOU!

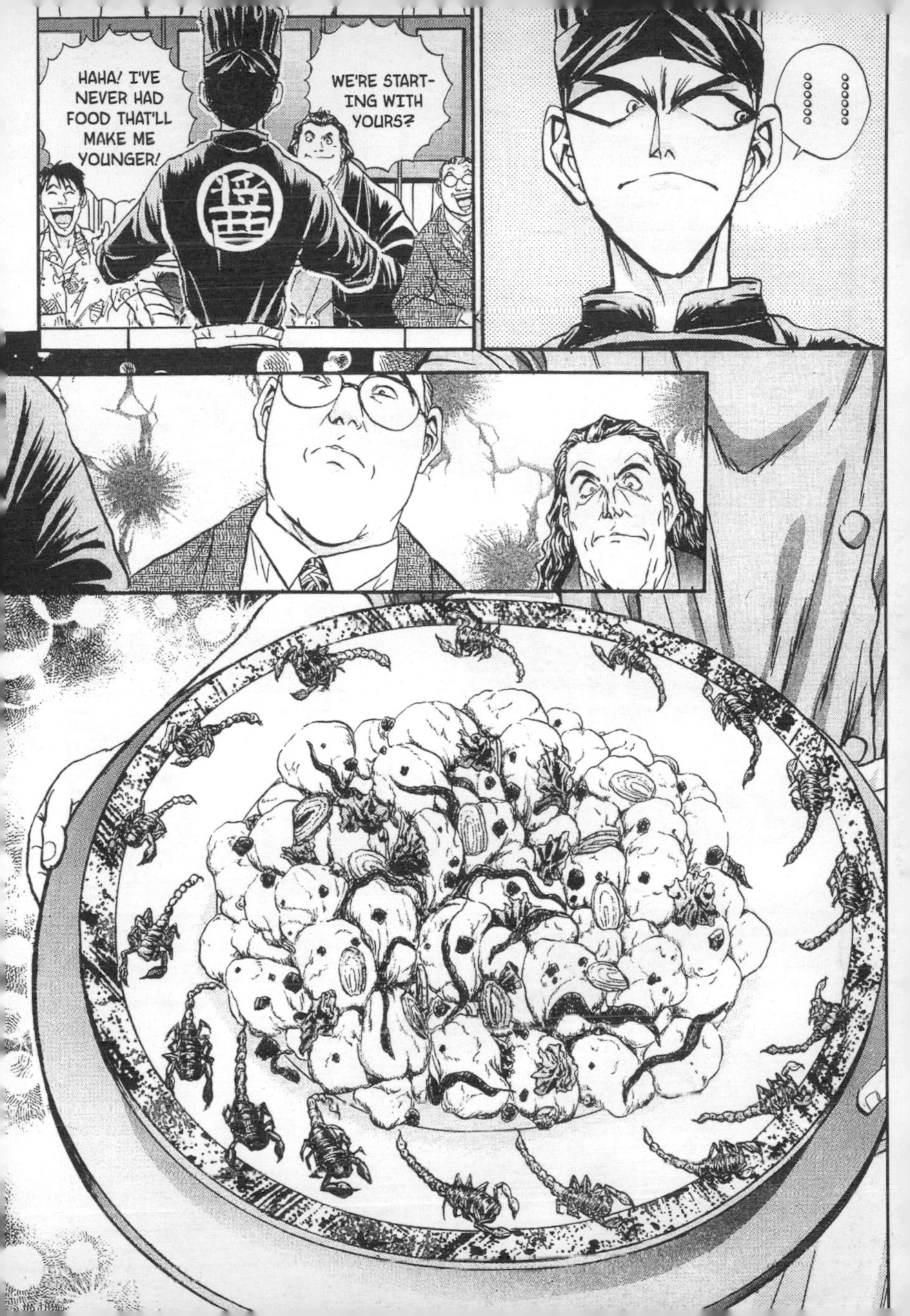
WE'RE STARTING WITH YOURS?
HAHA! I'VE NEVER HAD FOOD THAT'LL MAKE ME YOUNGER!

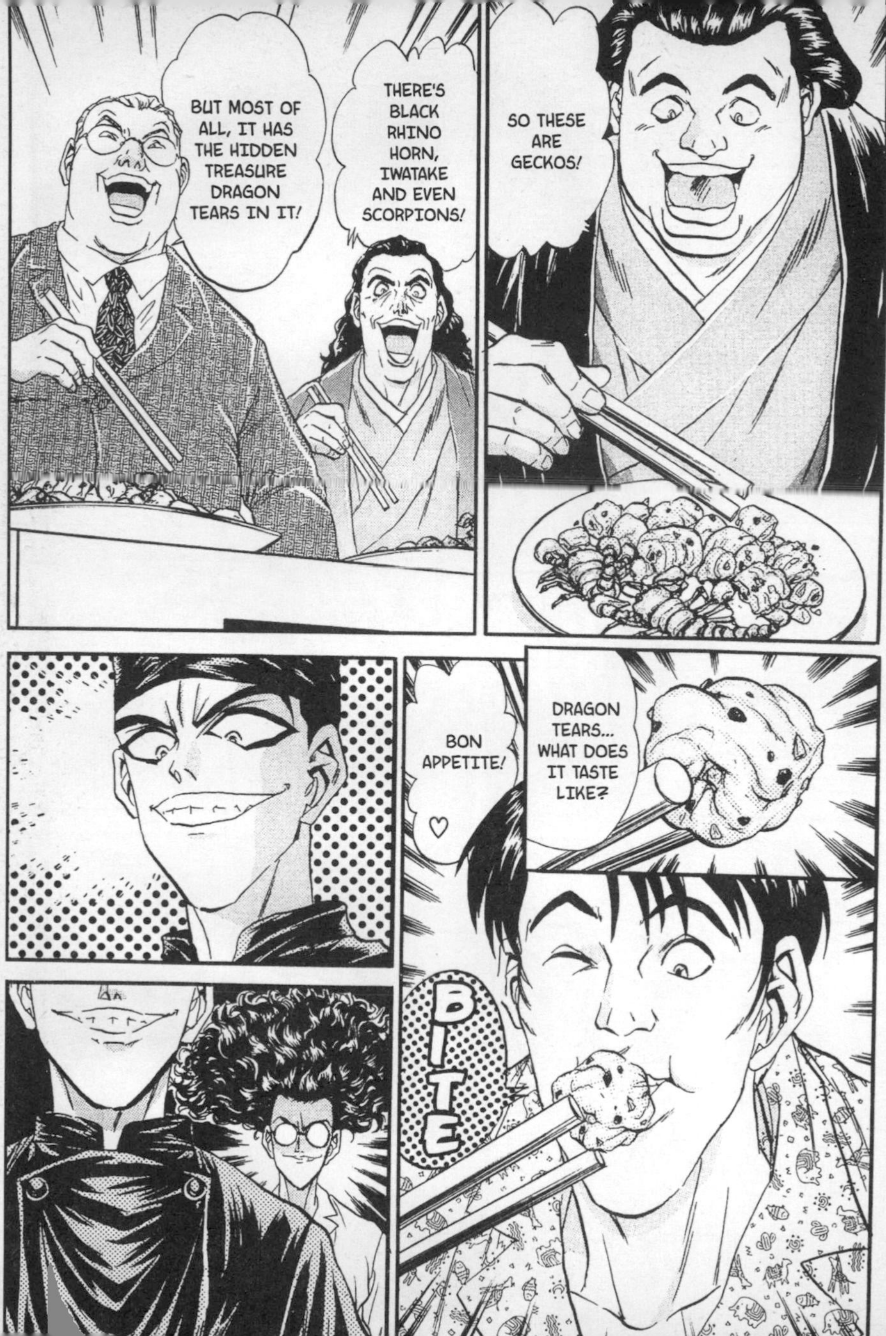
SO THESE ARE GECKOS!
THERE'S BLACK RHINO HORN, IWATAKE AND EVEN SCORPIONS!
BUT MOST OF ALL, IT HAS THE HIDDEN TREASURE DRAGON TEARS IN IT!
DRAGON TEARS... WHAT DOES IT TASTE LIKE?
BON APPETITE! ♡
BITE

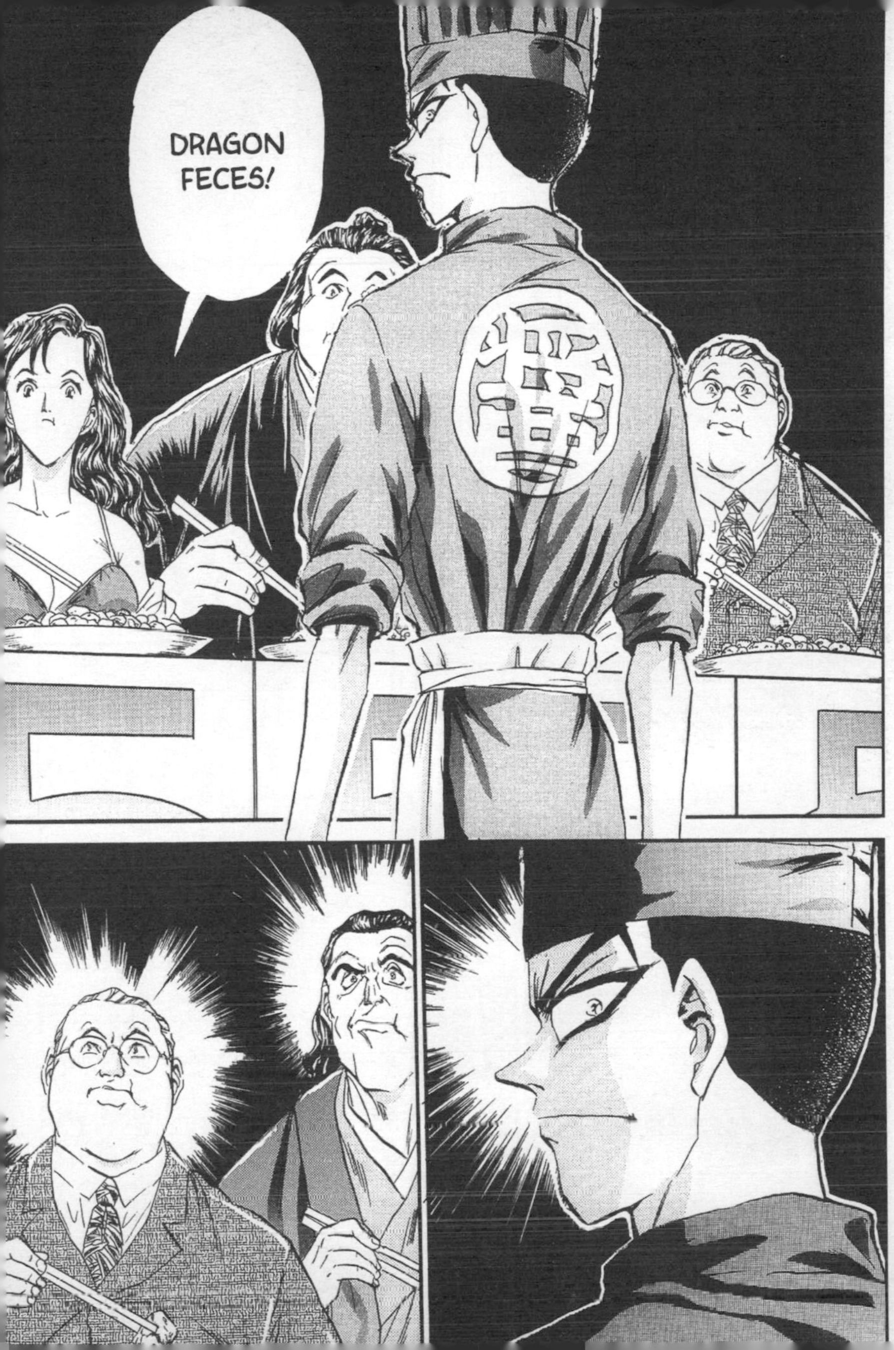
DRAGON FECES!

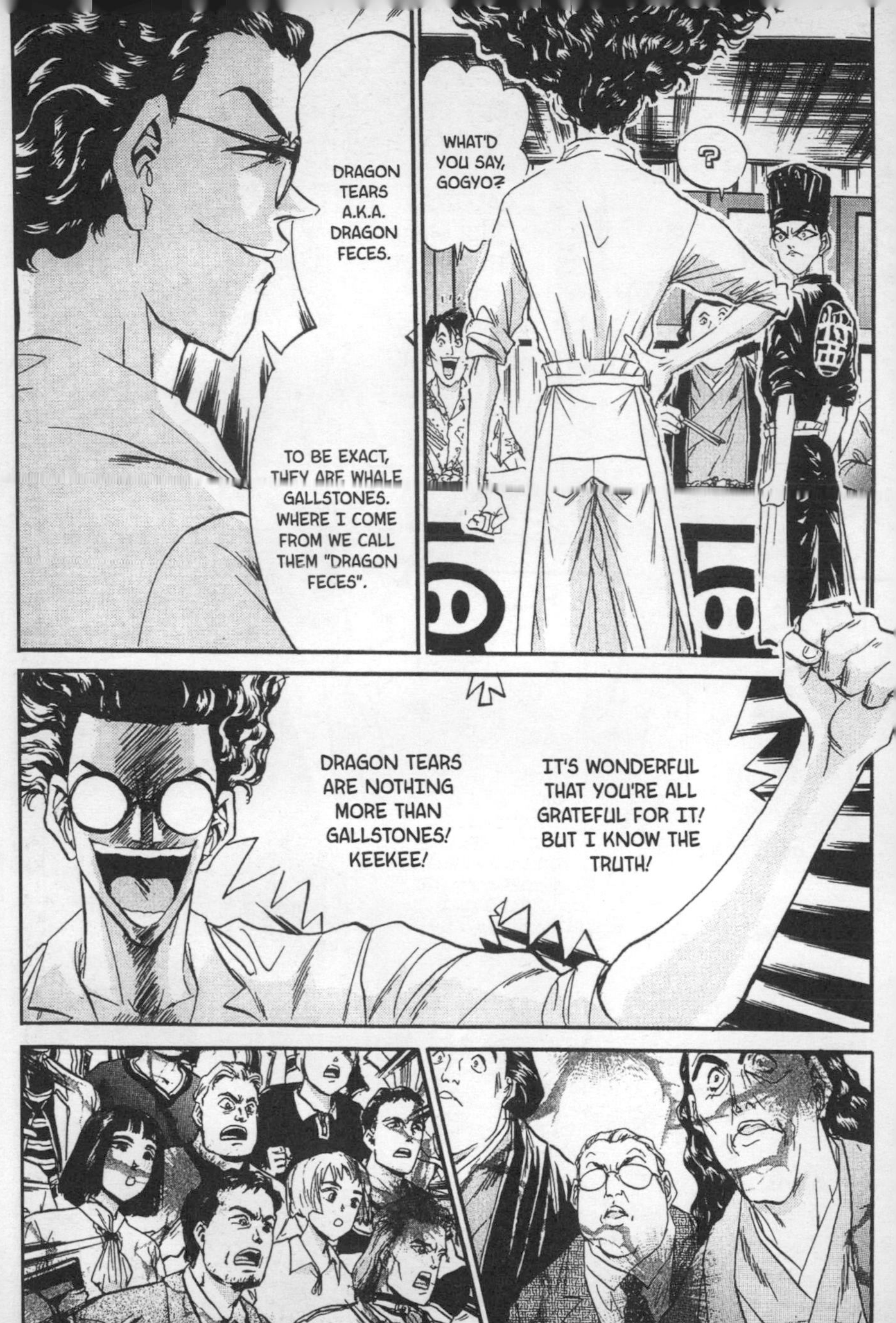
WHAT'D YOU SAY, GOGYO?
?
DRAGON TEARS A.K.A. DRAGON FECES.
TO BE EXACT, THEY ARE WHALE GALLSTONES. WHERE I COME FROM WE CALL THEM "DRAGON FECES".
IT'S WONDERFUL THAT YOU'RE ALL GRATEFUL FOR IT! BUT I KNOW THE TRUTH!
DRAGON TEARS ARE NOTHING MORE THAN GALLSTONES! KEEKEE!

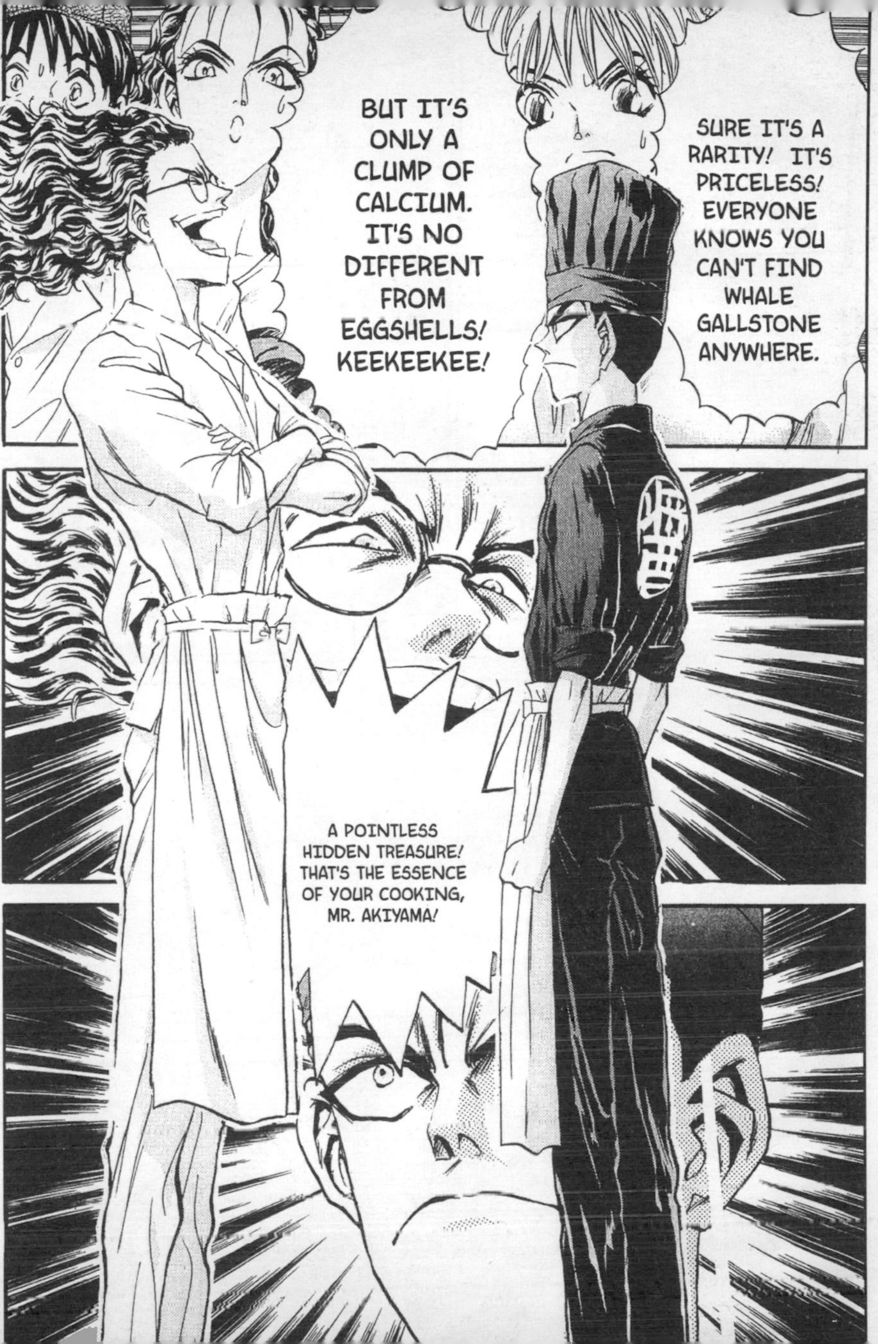
SURE IT'S A RARITY! IT'S PRICELESS! EVERYONE KNOWS YOU CAN'T FIND WHALE GALLSTONE ANYWHERE.
BUT IT'S ONLY A CLUMP OF CALCIUM. IT'S NO DIFFERENT FROM EGGSHELLS! KEEKEEKEE!
A POINTLESS HIDDEN TREASURE! THAT'S THE ESSENCE OF YOUR COOKING, MR. AKIYAMA!

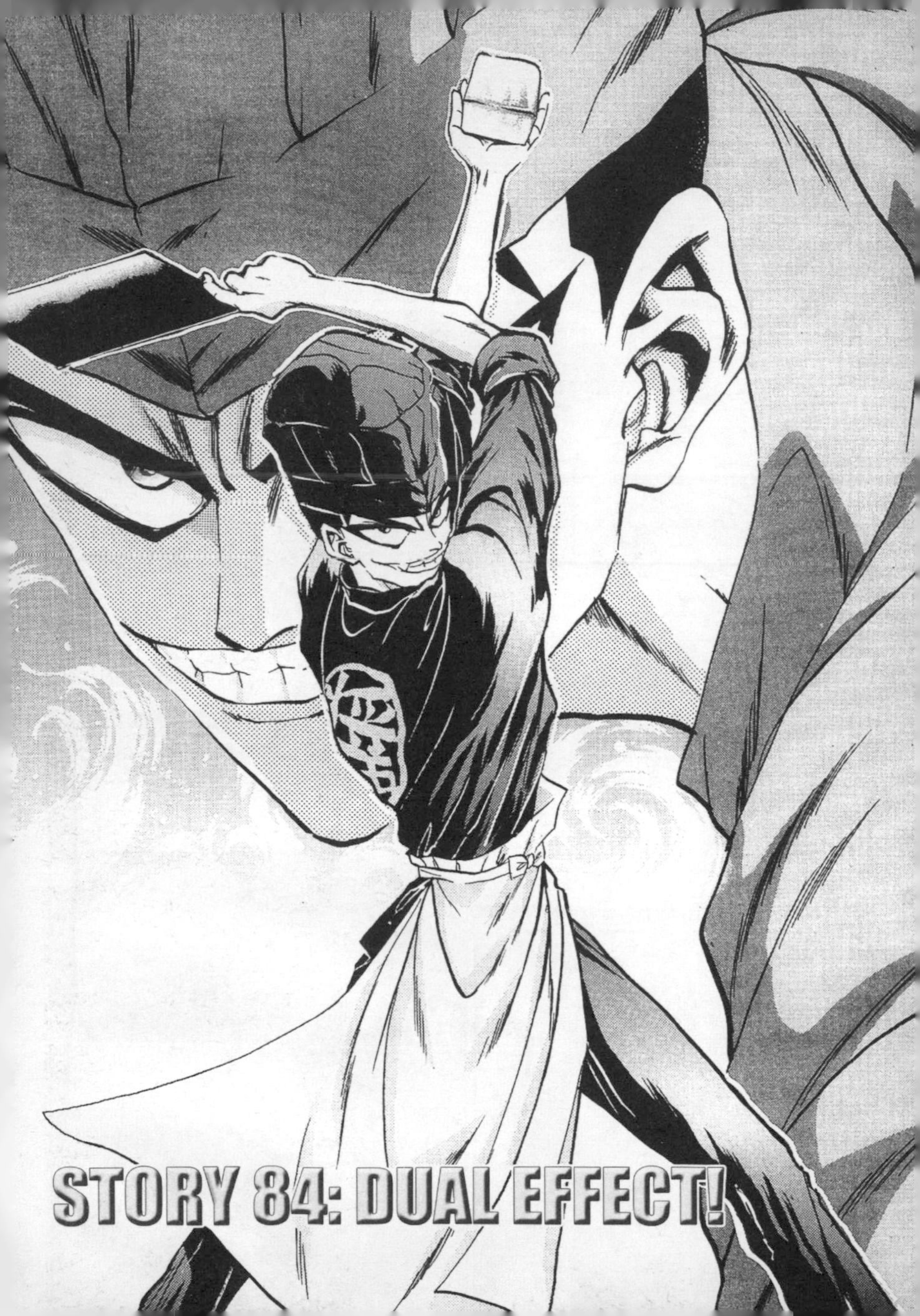
STORY 84: DUAL EFFECT!

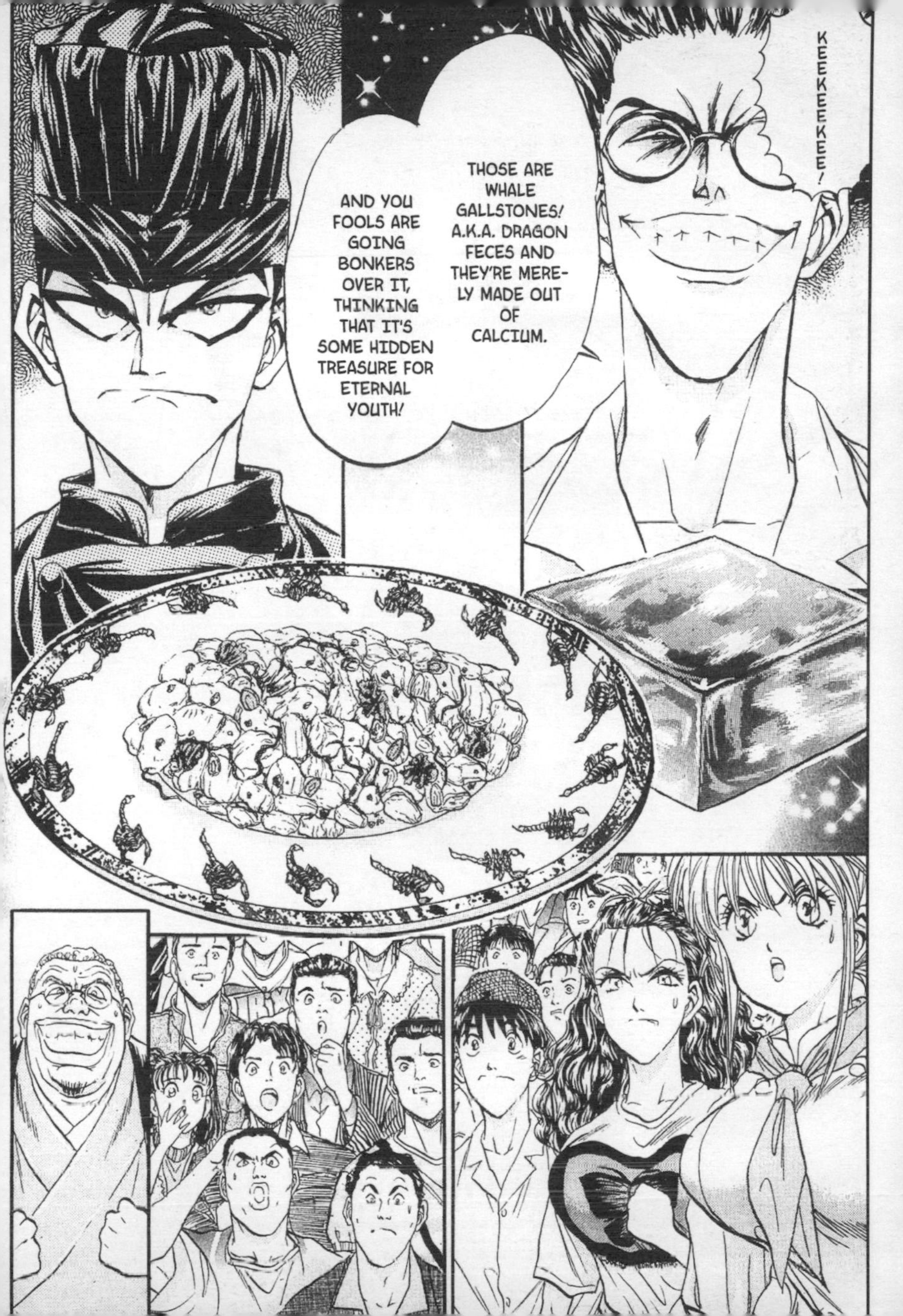
KEEKEEKEE!
THOSE ARE WHALE GALLSTONES! A.K.A. DRAGON FECES AND THEY'RE MERELY MADE OUT OF CALCIUM.
AND YOU FOOLS ARE GOING BONKERS OVER IT, THINKING THAT IT'S SOME HIDDEN TREASURE FOR ETERNAL YOUTH!

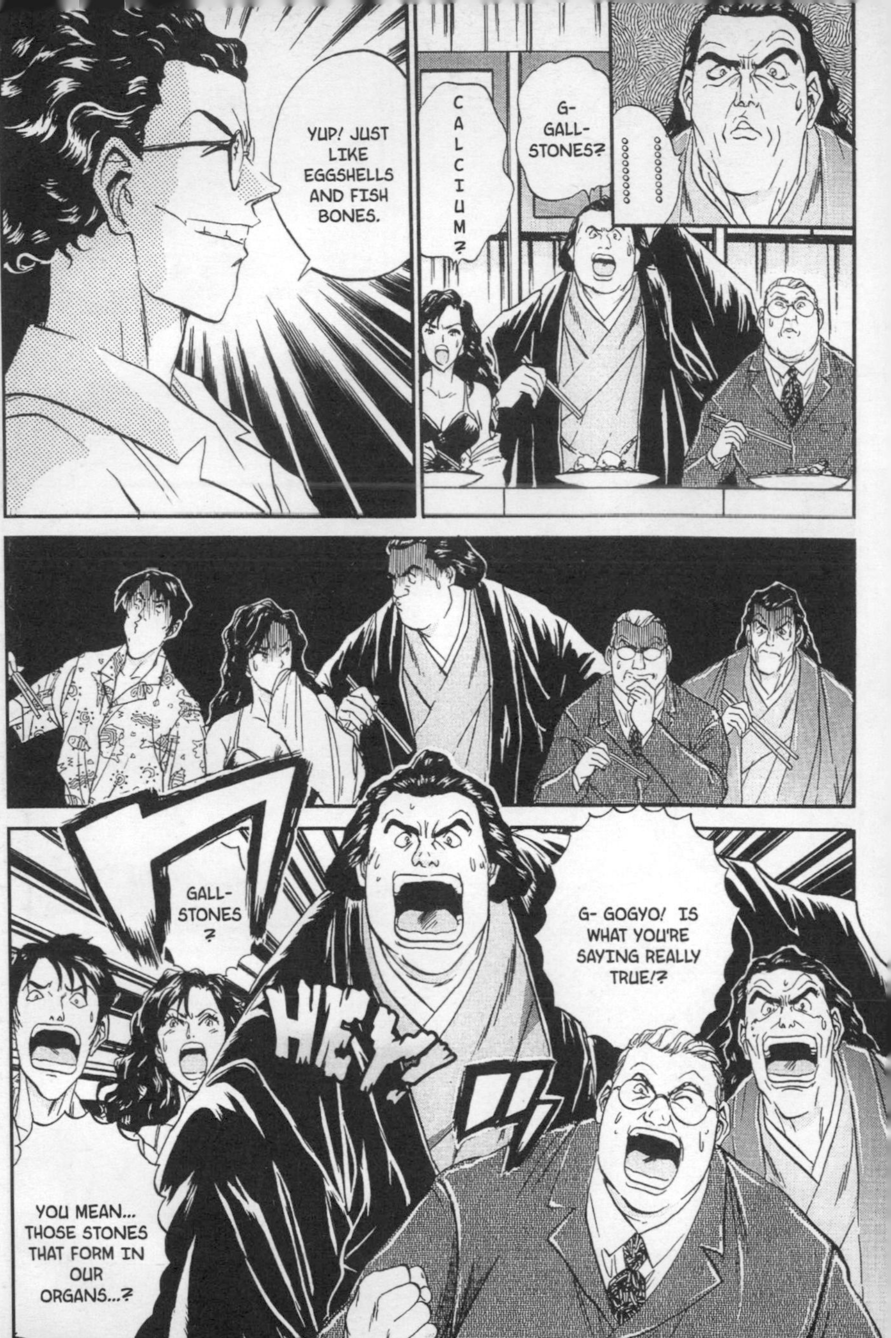

....
....
G- GALL- STONES?
CALCIUM?
YUP! JUST LIKE EGGSHELLS AND FISH BONES.
G- GOGYO! IS WHAT YOU'RE SAYING REALLY TRUE!?
HEY!!
GALL- STONES?
YOU MEAN... THOSE STONES THAT FORM IN OUR ORGANS...?

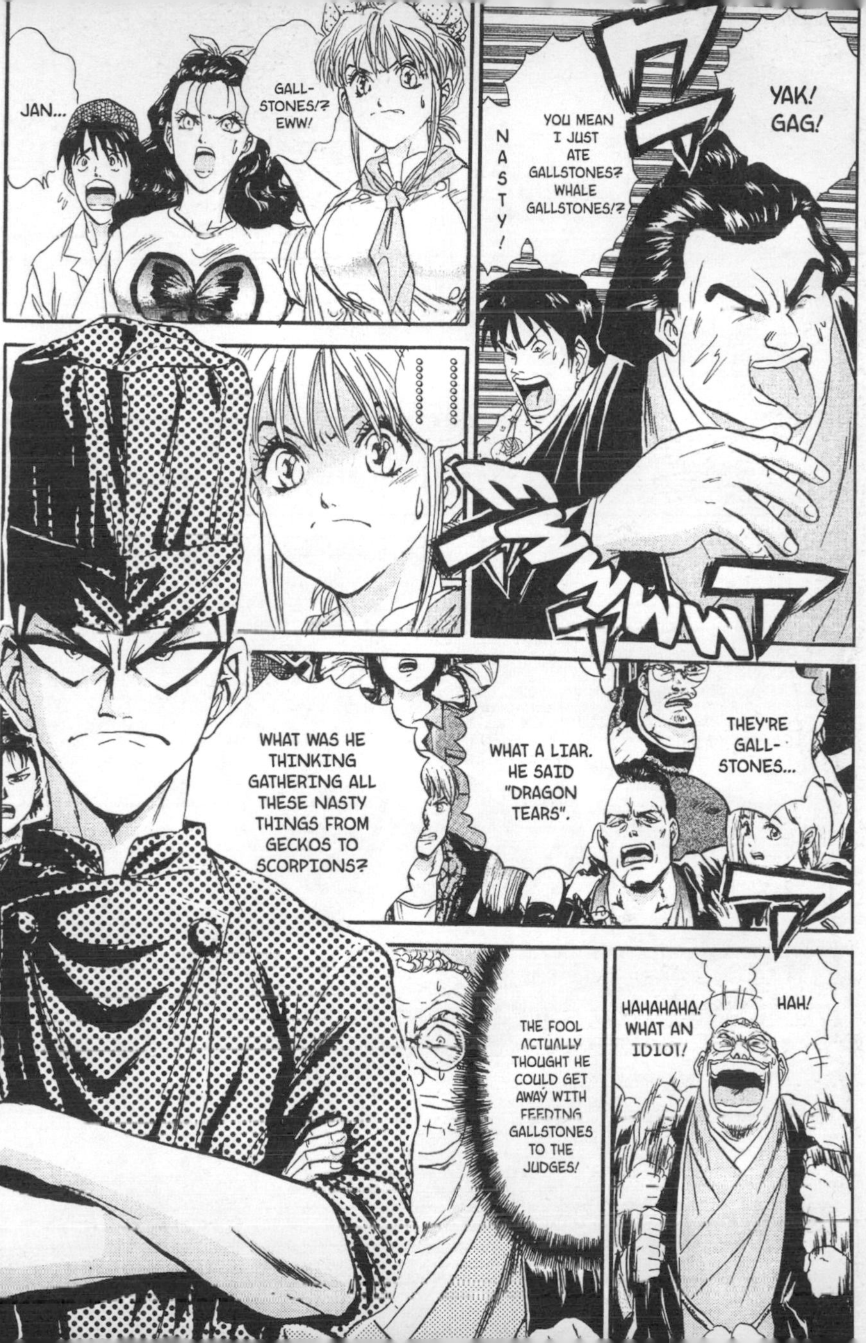
YAK! GAG!
YOU MEAN I JUST ATE GALLSTONES? WHALE GALLSTONES!?
NASTY!
GALL-STONES!? EWW!
JAN...
EWWWWW
......
THEY'RE GALL-STONES...
WHAT A LIAR. HE SAID "DRAGON TEARS".
WHAT WAS HE THINKING GATHERING ALL THESE NASTY THINGS FROM GECKOS TO SCORPIONS?
HAH!
HAHAHAHA! WHAT AN IDIOT!
THE FOOL ACTUALLY THOUGHT HE COULD GET AWAY WITH FEEDING GALLSTONES TO THE JUDGES!

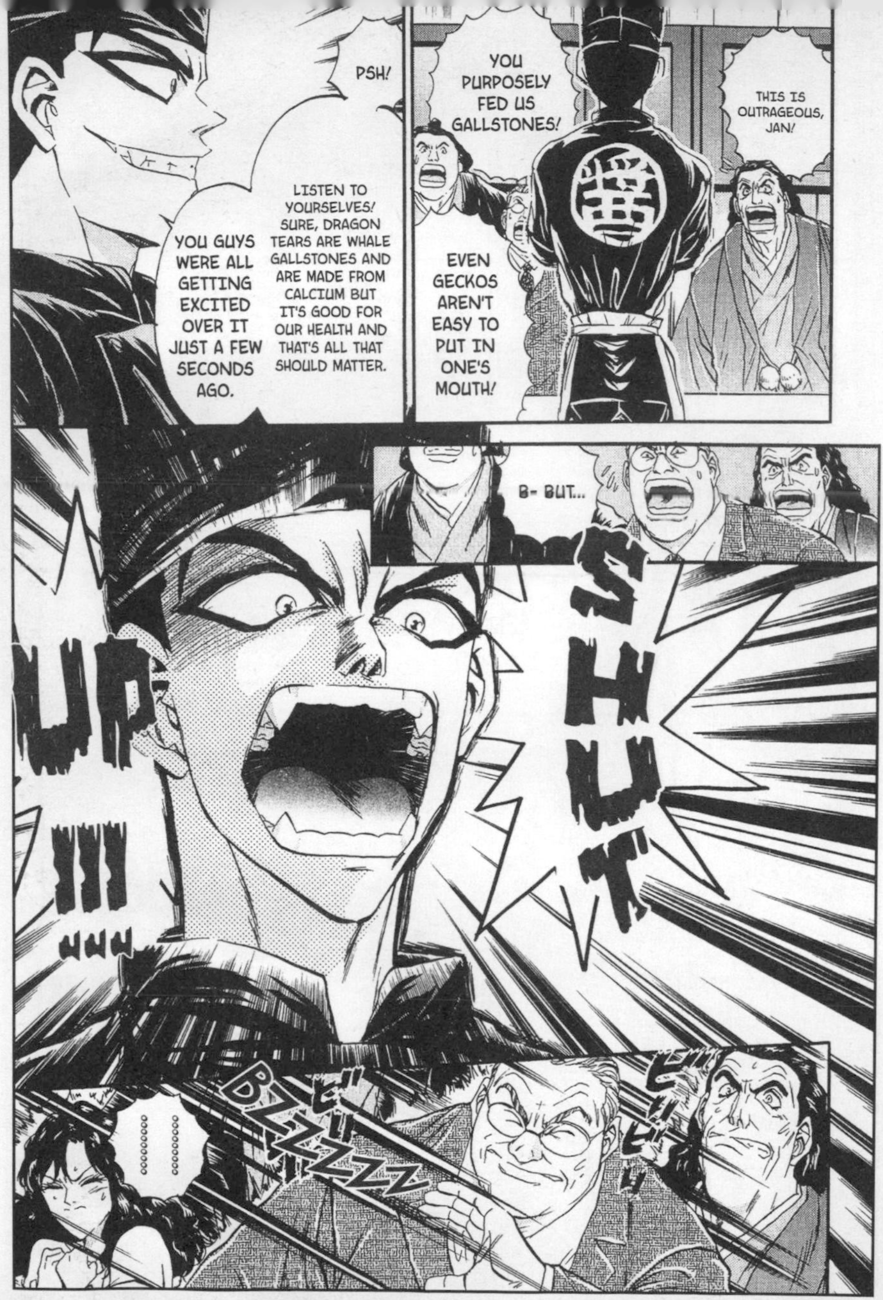
THIS IS OUTRAGEOUS, JAN!
YOU PURPOSELY FED US GALLSTONES!
EVEN GECKOS AREN'T EASY TO PUT IN ONE'S MOUTH!
PSH!
LISTEN TO YOURSELVES! SURE, DRAGON TEARS ARE WHALE GALLSTONES AND ARE MADE FROM CALCIUM BUT IT'S GOOD FOR OUR HEALTH AND THAT'S ALL THAT SHOULD MATTER.
YOU GUYS WERE ALL GETTING EXCITED OVER IT JUST A FEW SECONDS AGO.
B- BUT...
SHUT
UP!!!
BZZZZZZ

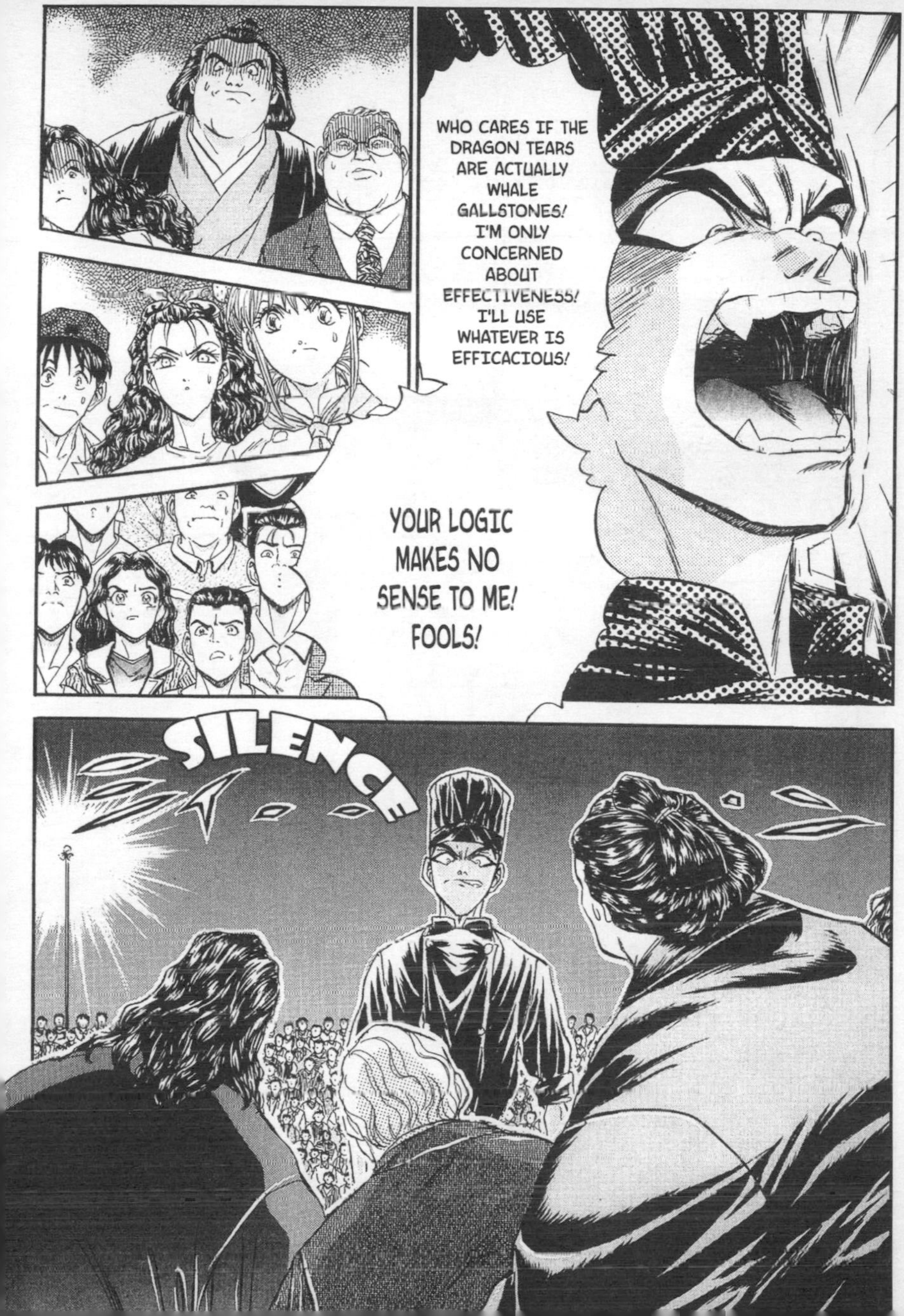
WHO CARES IF THE DRAGON TEARS ARE ACTUALLY WHALE GALLSTONES! I'M ONLY CONCERNED ABOUT EFFECTIVENESS! I'LL USE WHATEVER IS EFFICACIOUS!
YOUR LOGIC MAKES NO SENSE TO ME! FOOLS!
SILENCE

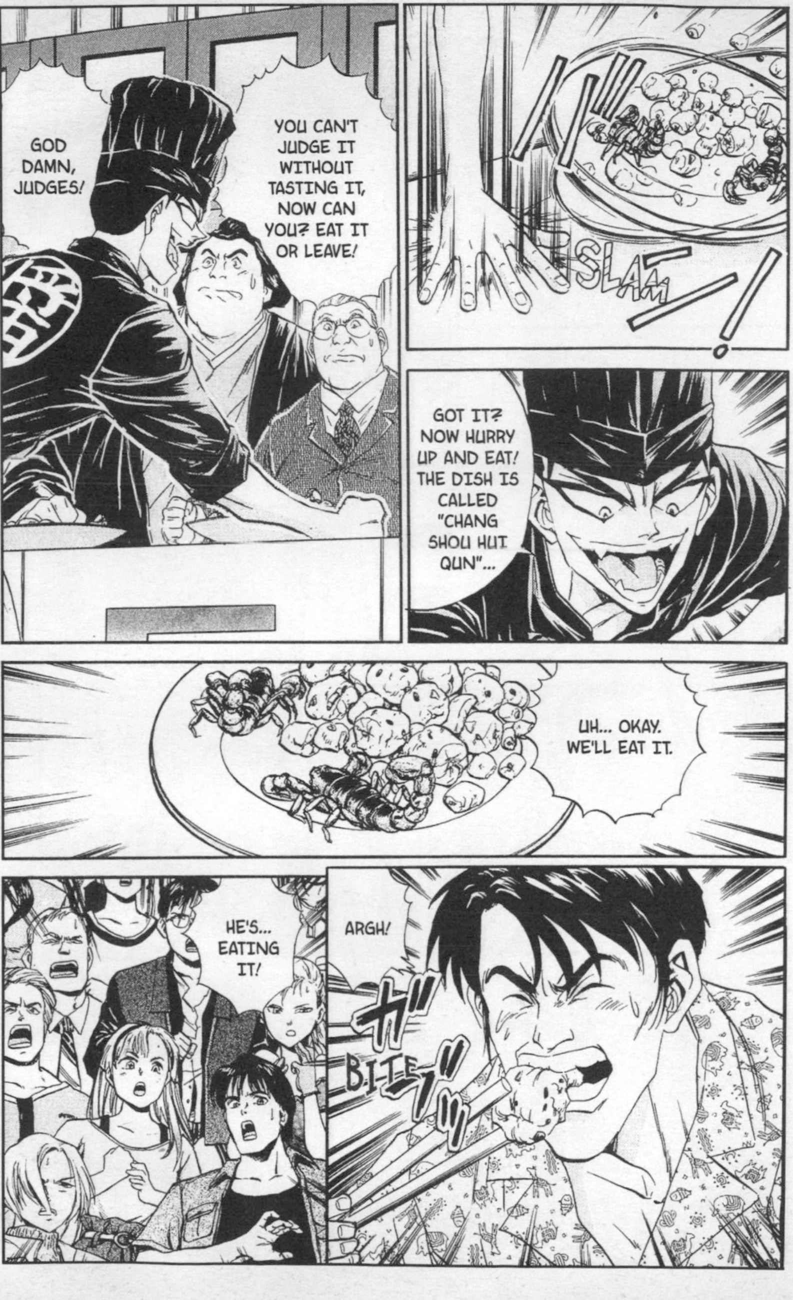
SLAM
GOT IT? NOW HURRY UP AND EAT! THE DISH IS CALLED "CHANG SHOU HUI QUN"...
YOU CAN'T JUDGE IT WITHOUT TASTING IT, NOW CAN YOU? EAT IT OR LEAVE!
GOD DAMN, JUDGES!
UH... OKAY. WE'LL EAT IT.
ARGH!
BITE
HE'S... EATING IT!

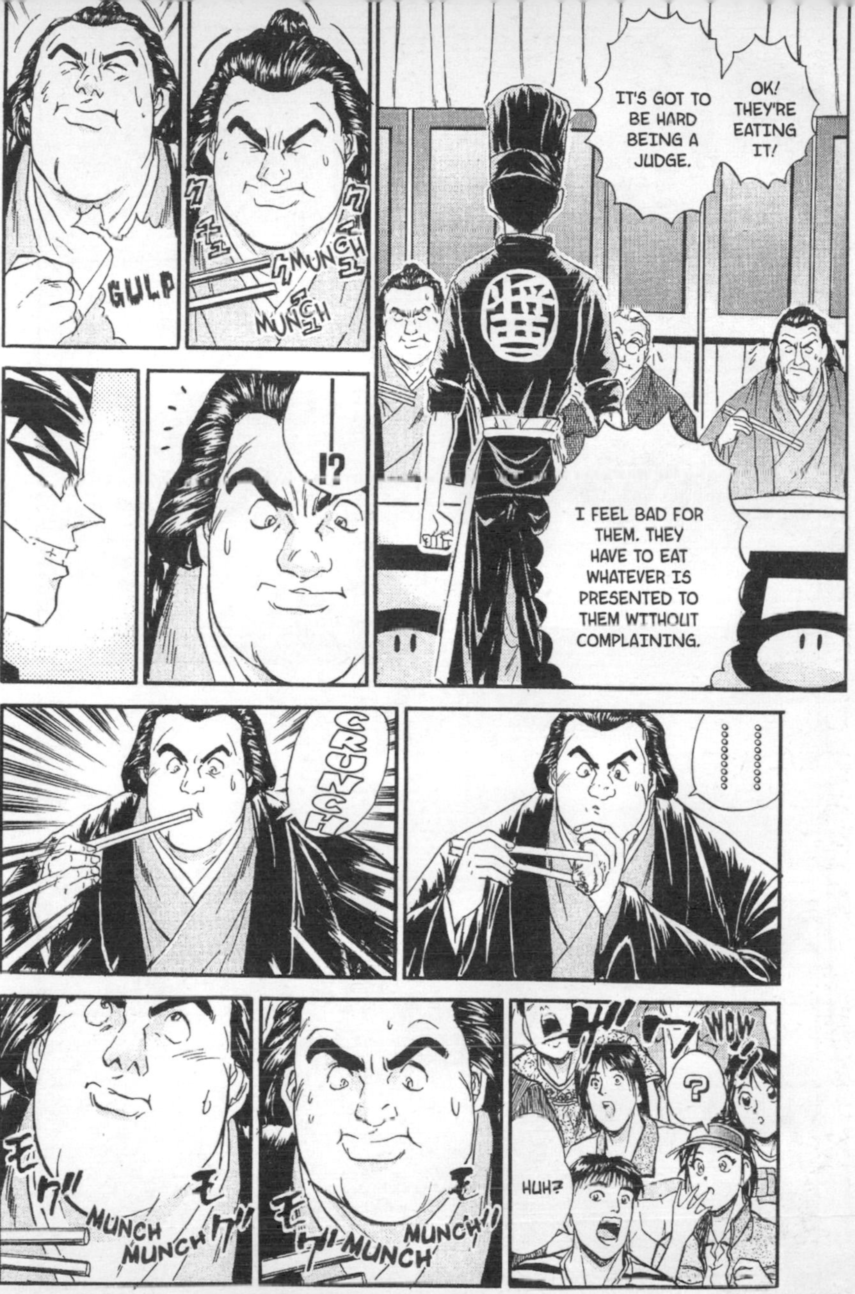
OK! THEY'RE EATING IT!
IT'S GOT TO BE HARD BEING A JUDGE.
I FEEL BAD FOR THEM. THEY HAVE TO EAT WHATEVER IS PRESENTED TO THEM WITHOUT COMPLAINING.
MUNCH MUNCH
GULP
!?
CRUNCH
WOW!!
?
HUH?
MUNCH MUNCH
MUNCH MUNCH

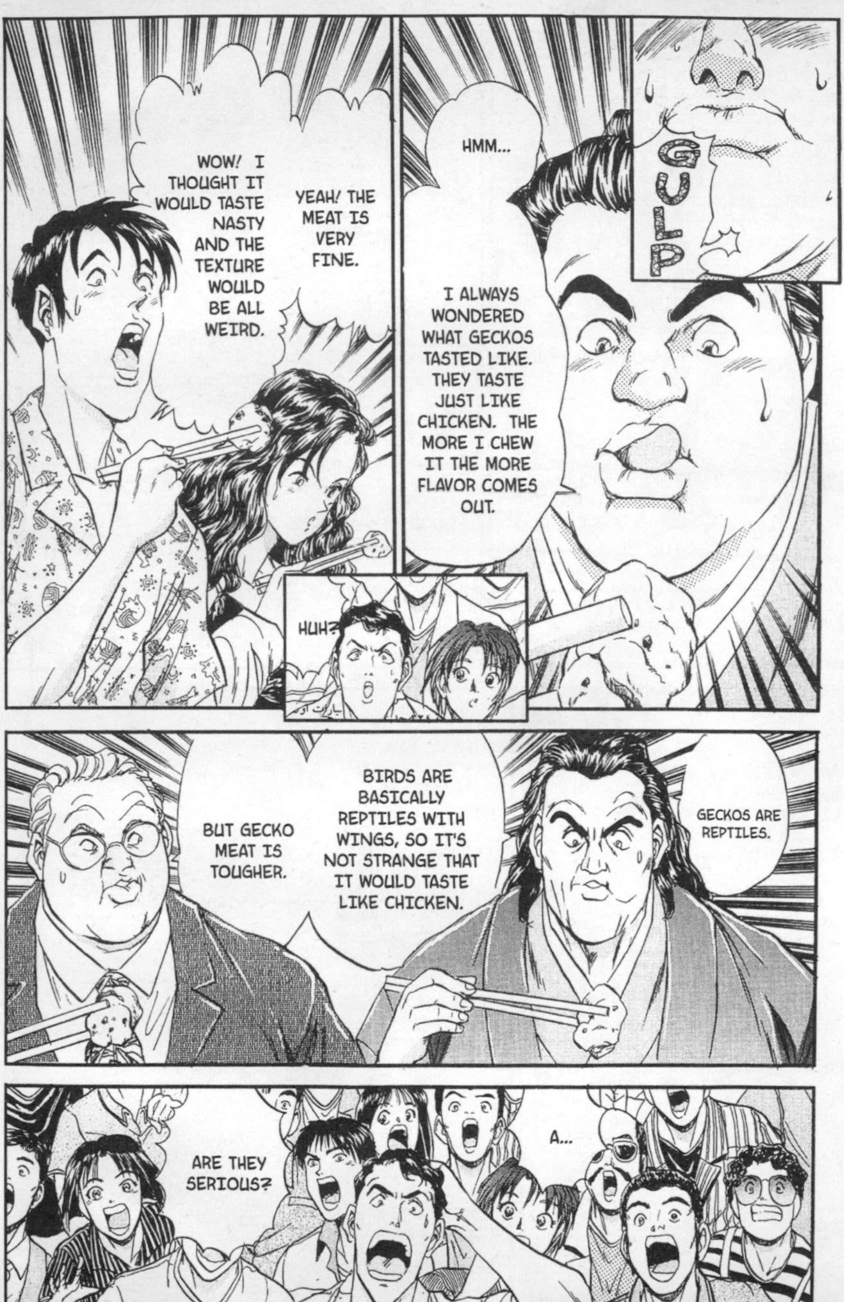
GULP
HMM...
I ALWAYS WONDERED WHAT GECKOS TASTED LIKE. THEY TASTE JUST LIKE CHICKEN. THE MORE I CHEW IT THE MORE FLAVOR COMES OUT.
WOW! I THOUGHT IT WOULD TASTE NASTY AND THE TEXTURE WOULD BE ALL WEIRD.
YEAH! THE MEAT IS VERY FINE.
HUH?
GECKOS ARE REPTILES.
BIRDS ARE BASICALLY REPTILES WITH WINGS, SO IT'S NOT STRANGE THAT IT WOULD TASTE LIKE CHICKEN.
BUT GECKO MEAT IS TOUGHER.
A...
ARE THEY SERIOUS?

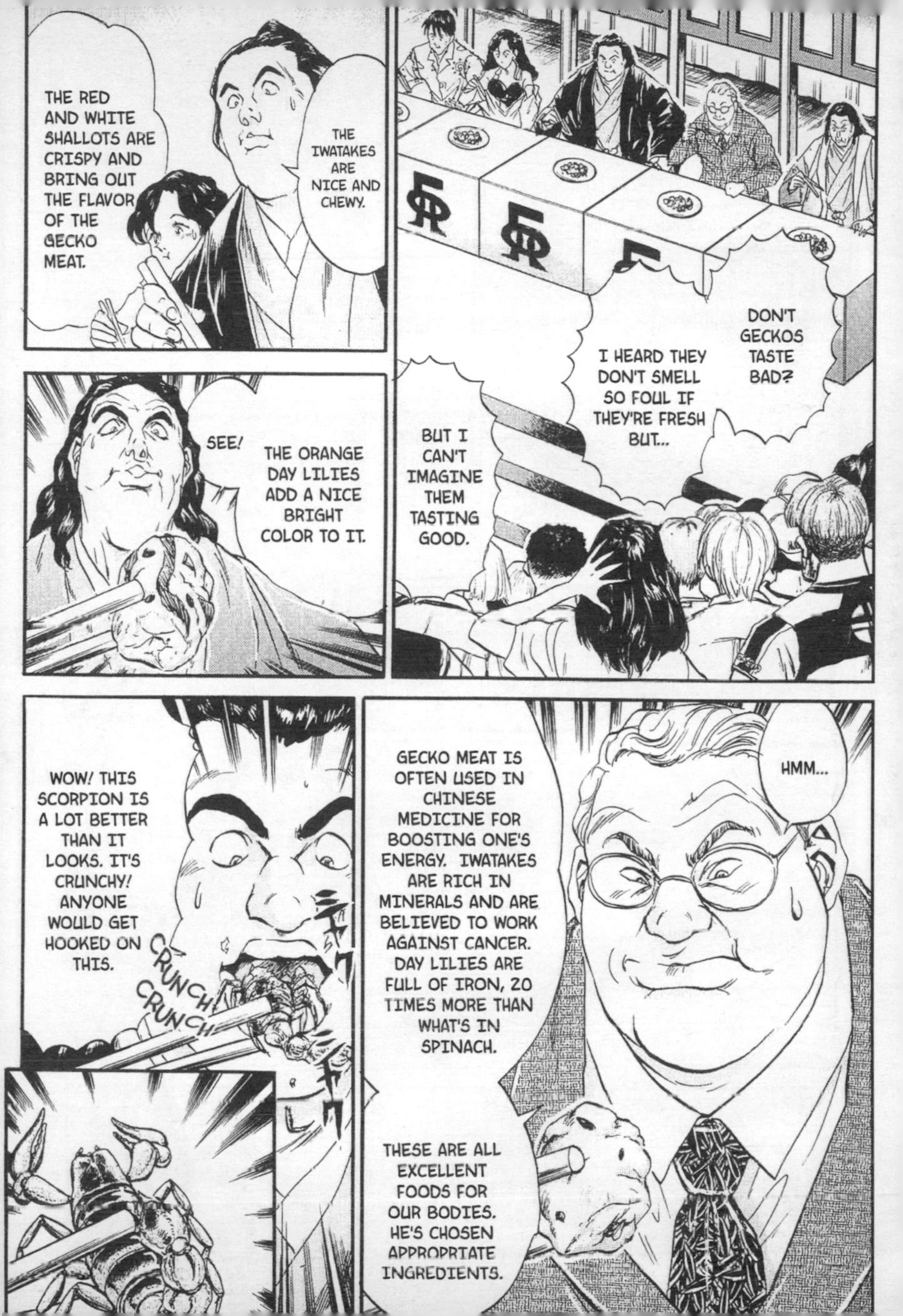
DON'T GECKOS TASTE BAD?
I HEARD THEY DON'T SMELL SO FOUL IF THEY'RE FRESH BUT...
BUT I CAN'T IMAGINE THEM TASTING GOOD.
THE IWATAKES ARE NICE AND CHEWY.
THE RED AND WHITE SHALLOTS ARE CRISPY AND BRING OUT THE FLAVOR OF THE GECKO MEAT.
THE ORANGE DAY LILIES ADD A NICE BRIGHT COLOR TO IT.
SEE!
HMM...
GECKO MEAT IS OFTEN USED IN CHINESE MEDICINE FOR BOOSTING ONE'S ENERGY. IWATAKES ARE RICH IN MINERALS AND ARE BELIEVED TO WORK AGAINST CANCER. DAY LILIES ARE FULL OF IRON, 20 TIMES MORE THAN WHAT'S IN SPINACH.
THESE ARE ALL EXCELLENT FOODS FOR OUR BODIES. HE'S CHOSEN APPROPRIATE INGREDIENTS.
WOW! THIS SCORPION IS A LOT BETTER THAN IT LOOKS. IT'S CRUNCHY! ANYONE WOULD GET HOOKED ON THIS.
CRUNCH
CRUNCH

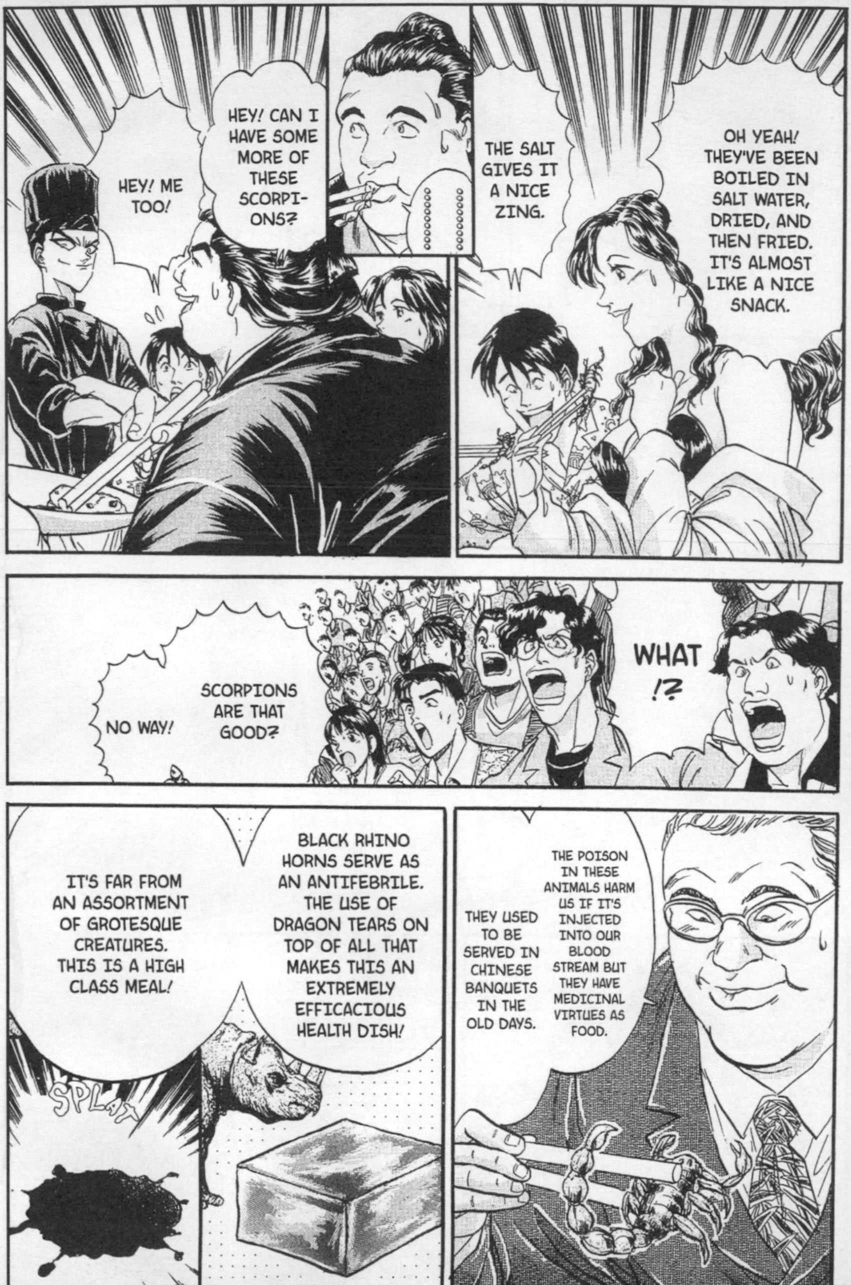
OH YEAH! THEY'VE BEEN BOILED IN SALT WATER, DRIED, AND THEN FRIED. IT'S ALMOST LIKE A NICE SNACK.
THE SALT GIVES IT A NICE ZING.
HEY! CAN I HAVE SOME MORE OF THESE SCORPI- ONS?
HEY! ME TOO!
WHAT !?
SCORPIONS ARE THAT GOOD?
NO WAY!
THE POISON IN THESE ANIMALS HARM US IF IT'S INJECTED INTO OUR BLOOD STREAM BUT THEY HAVE MEDICINAL VIRTUES AS FOOD.
THEY USED TO BE SERVED IN CHINESE BANQUETS IN THE OLD DAYS.
BLACK RHINO HORNS SERVE AS AN ANTIFEBRILE. THE USE OF DRAGON TEARS ON TOP OF ALL THAT MAKES THIS AN EXTREMELY EFFICACIOUS HEALTH DISH!
IT'S FAR FROM AN ASSORTMENT OF GROTESQUE CREATURES. THIS IS A HIGH CLASS MEAL!
SPLAT

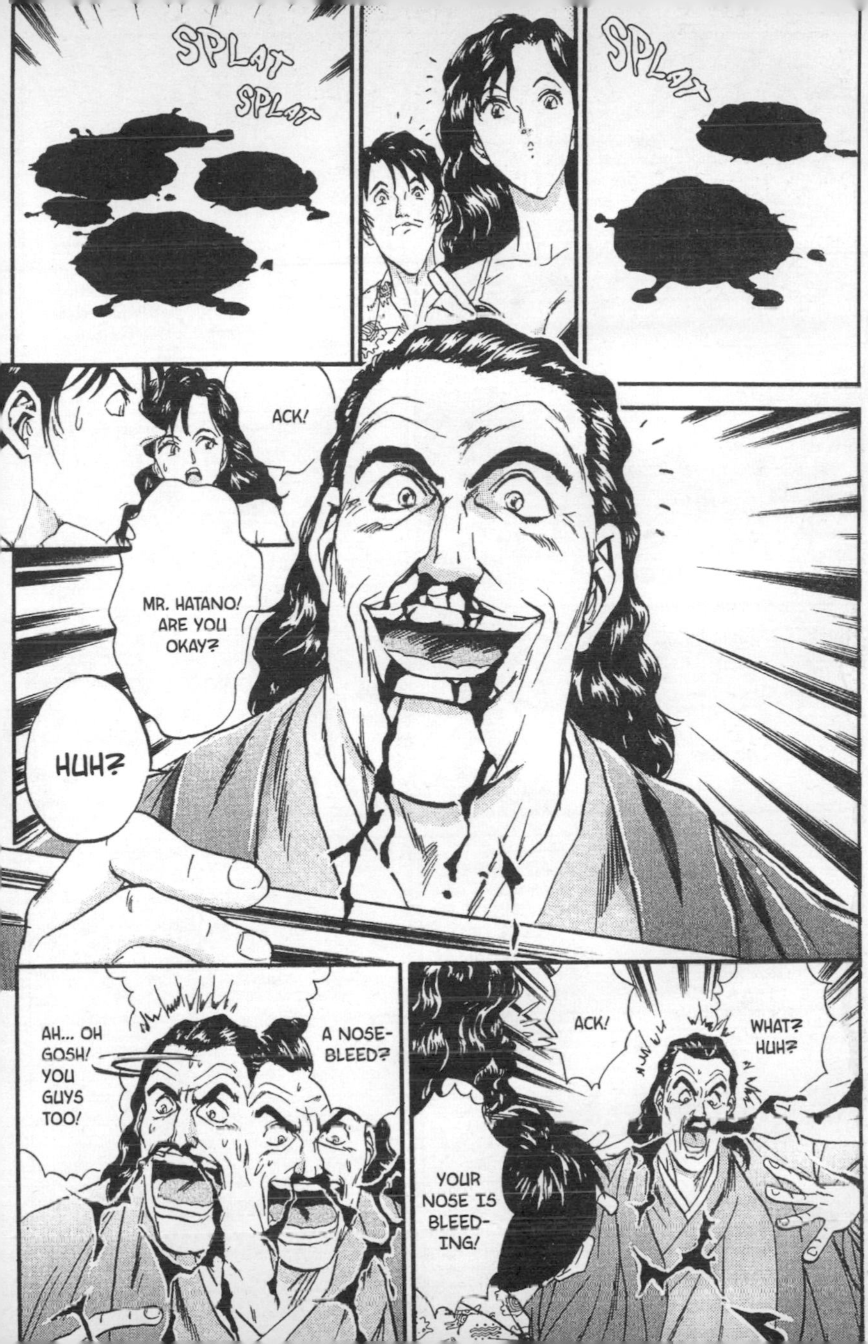
SPLAT
SPLAT
SPLAT
ACK!
MR. HATANO! ARE YOU OKAY?
HUH?
WHAT? HUH?
ACK!
YOUR NOSE IS BLEED-ING!
A NOSE-BLEED?
AH... OH GOSH! YOU GUYS TOO!

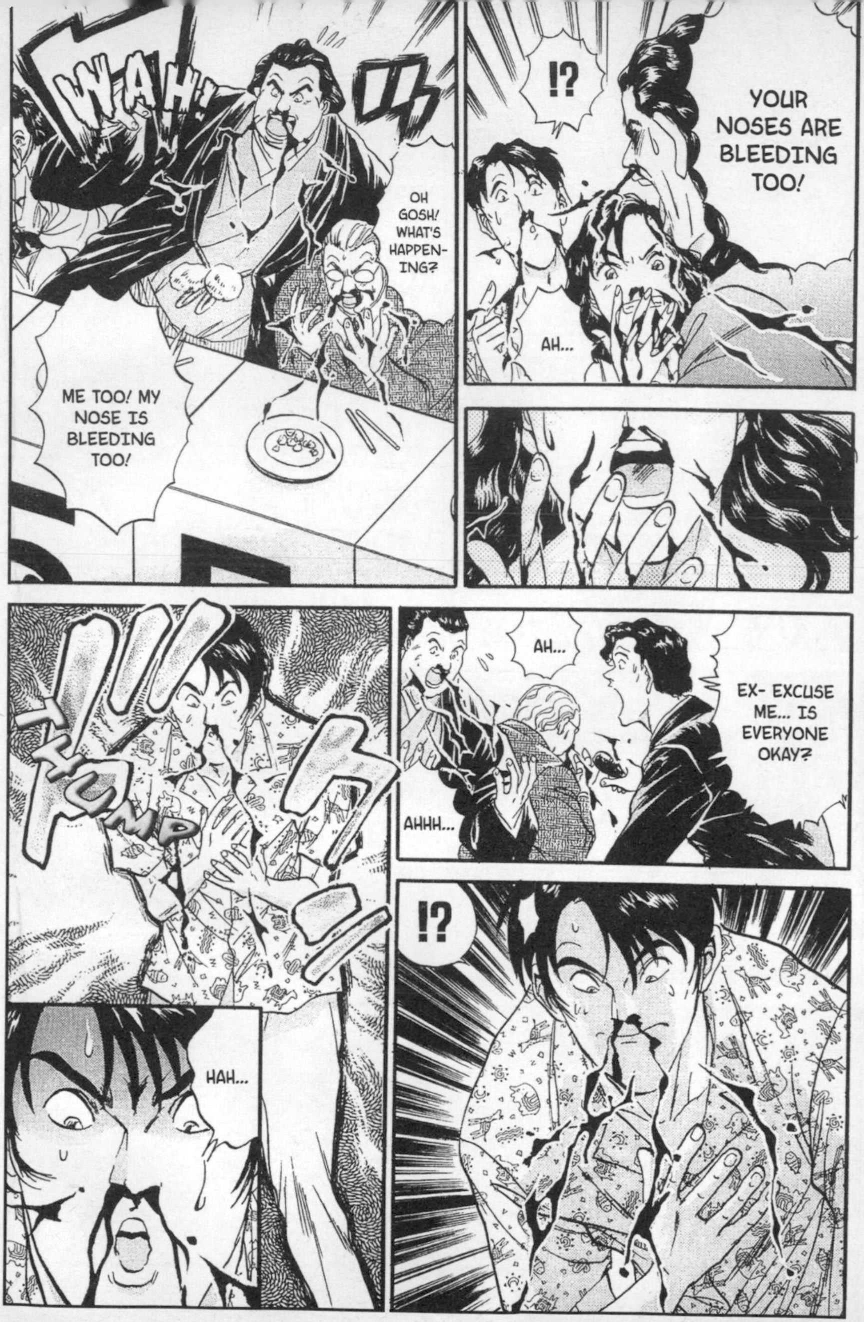
!?
YOUR NOSES ARE BLEEDING TOO!
AH...
WAH!
OH GOSH! WHAT'S HAPPEN-ING?
ME TOO! MY NOSE IS BLEEDING TOO!
AH...
EX- EXCUSE ME... IS EVERYONE OKAY?
AHHH...
!?
THUMP
HAH...

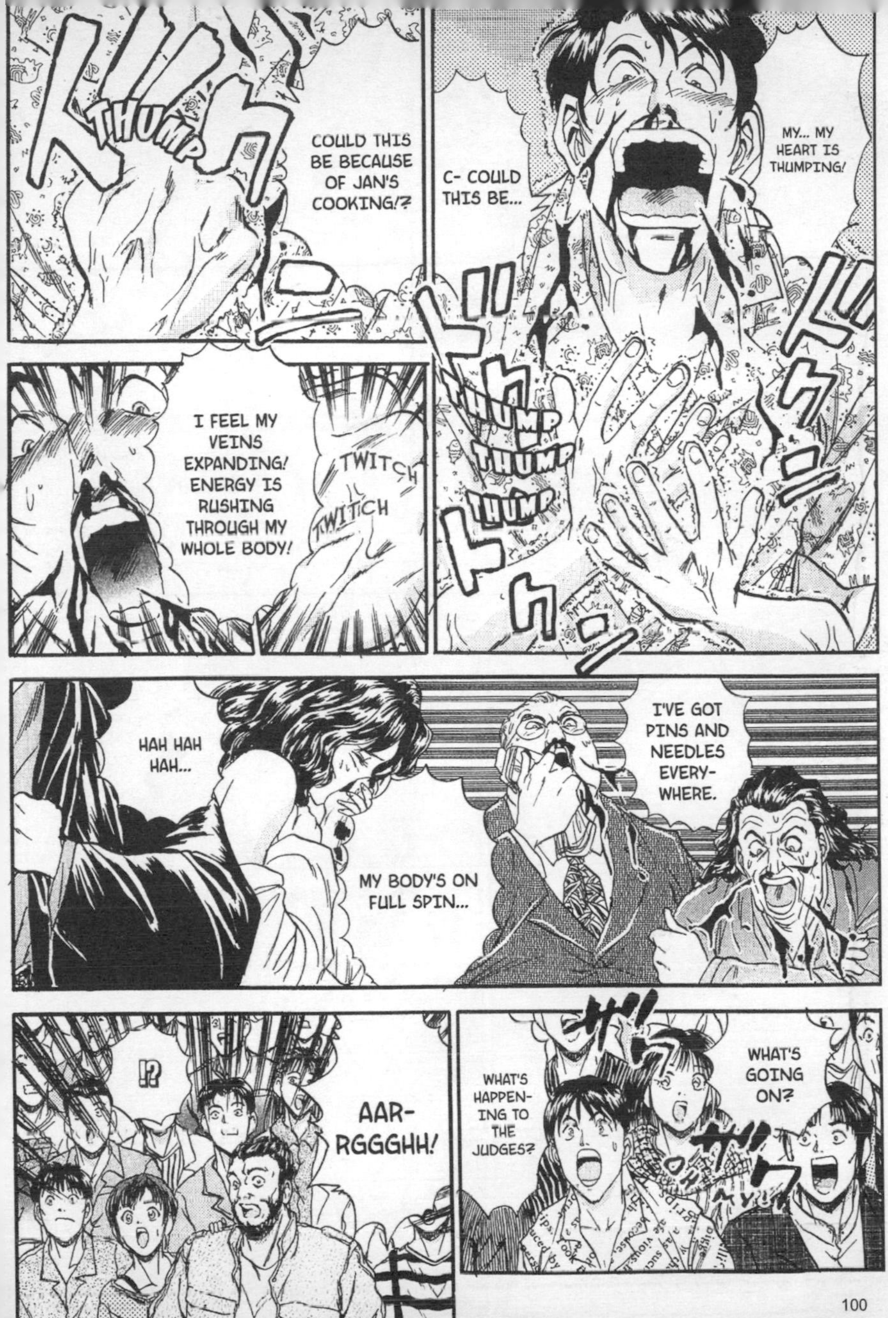
MY... MY HEART IS THUMPING!
C- COULD THIS BE...
THUMP
THUMP
THUMP
THUMP
COULD THIS BE BECAUSE OF JAN'S COOKING!?
TWITCH
TWITCH
I FEEL MY VEINS EXPANDING! ENERGY IS RUSHING THROUGH MY WHOLE BODY!
I'VE GOT PINS AND NEEDLES EVERY-WHERE.
MY BODY'S ON FULL SPIN...
HAH HAH HAH...
WHAT'S GOING ON?
WHAT'S HAPPENING TO THE JUDGES?
AAR-RGGGHH!
!?

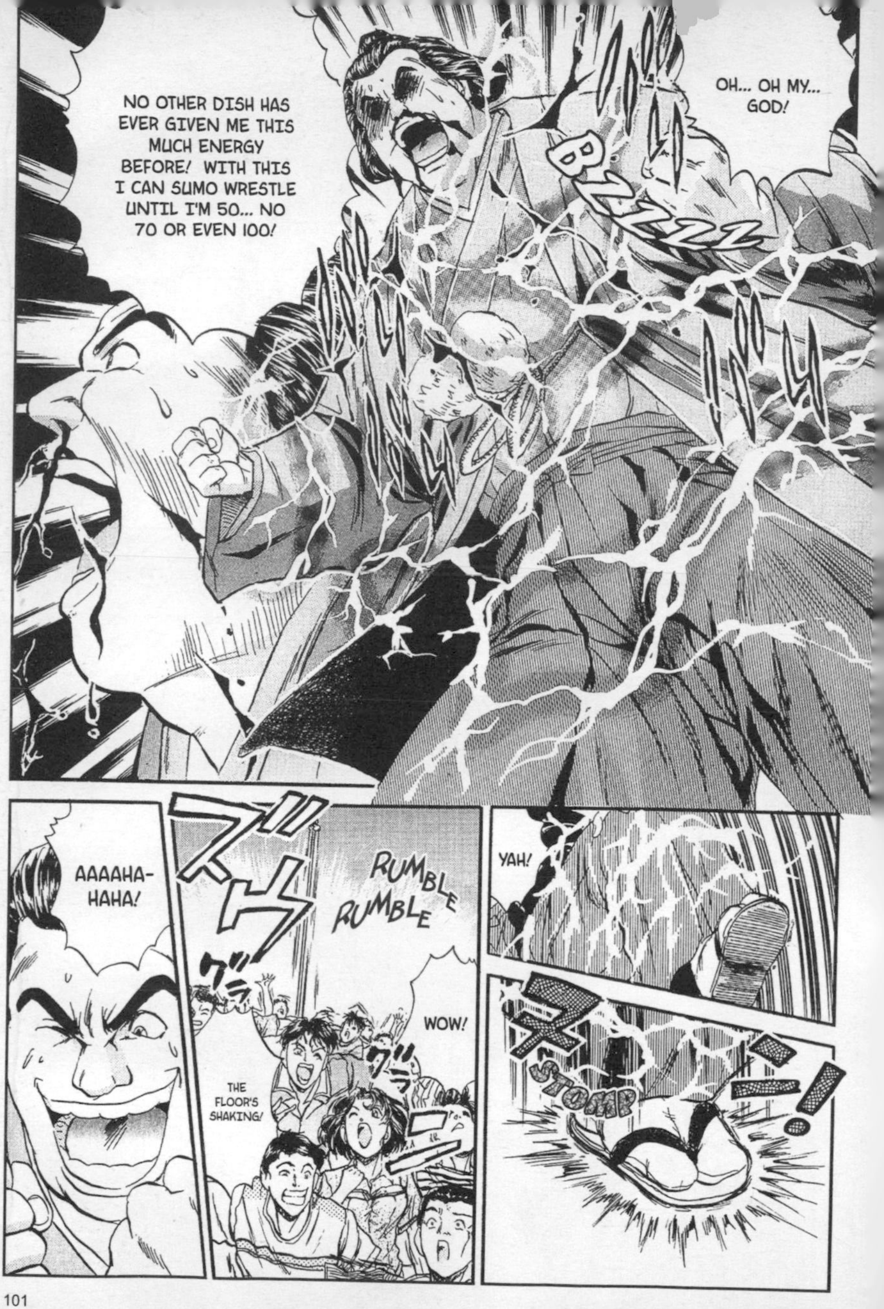
OH... OH MY... GOD!
BZZZZZ
NO OTHER DISH HAS EVER GIVEN ME THIS MUCH ENERGY BEFORE! WITH THIS I CAN SUMO WRESTLE UNTIL I'M 50... NO 70 OR EVEN 100!
YAH!
STOMP
RUMBLE RUMBLE
WOW!
THE FLOOR'S SHAKING!
AAAAHA-HAHA!

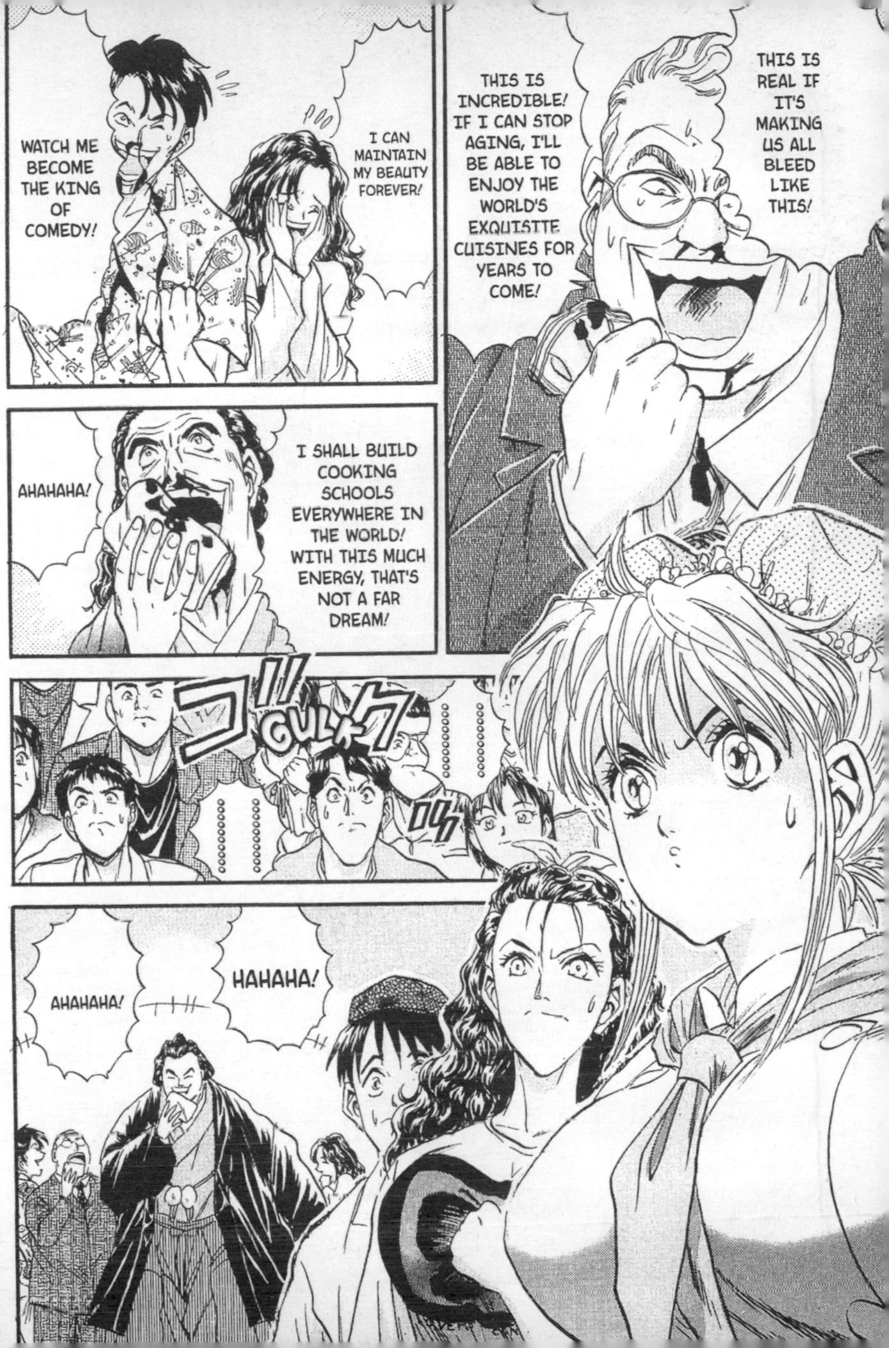
THIS IS REAL IF IT'S MAKING US ALL BLEED LIKE THIS!
THIS IS INCREDIBLE! IF I CAN STOP AGING, I'LL BE ABLE TO ENJOY THE WORLD'S EXQUISITE CUISINES FOR YEARS TO COME!
I CAN MAINTAIN MY BEAUTY FOREVER!
WATCH ME BECOME THE KING OF COMEDY!
I SHALL BUILD COOKING SCHOOLS EVERYWHERE IN THE WORLD! WITH THIS MUCH ENERGY, THAT'S NOT A FAR DREAM!
AHAHAHA!
GULK
HAHAHA!
AHAHAHA!

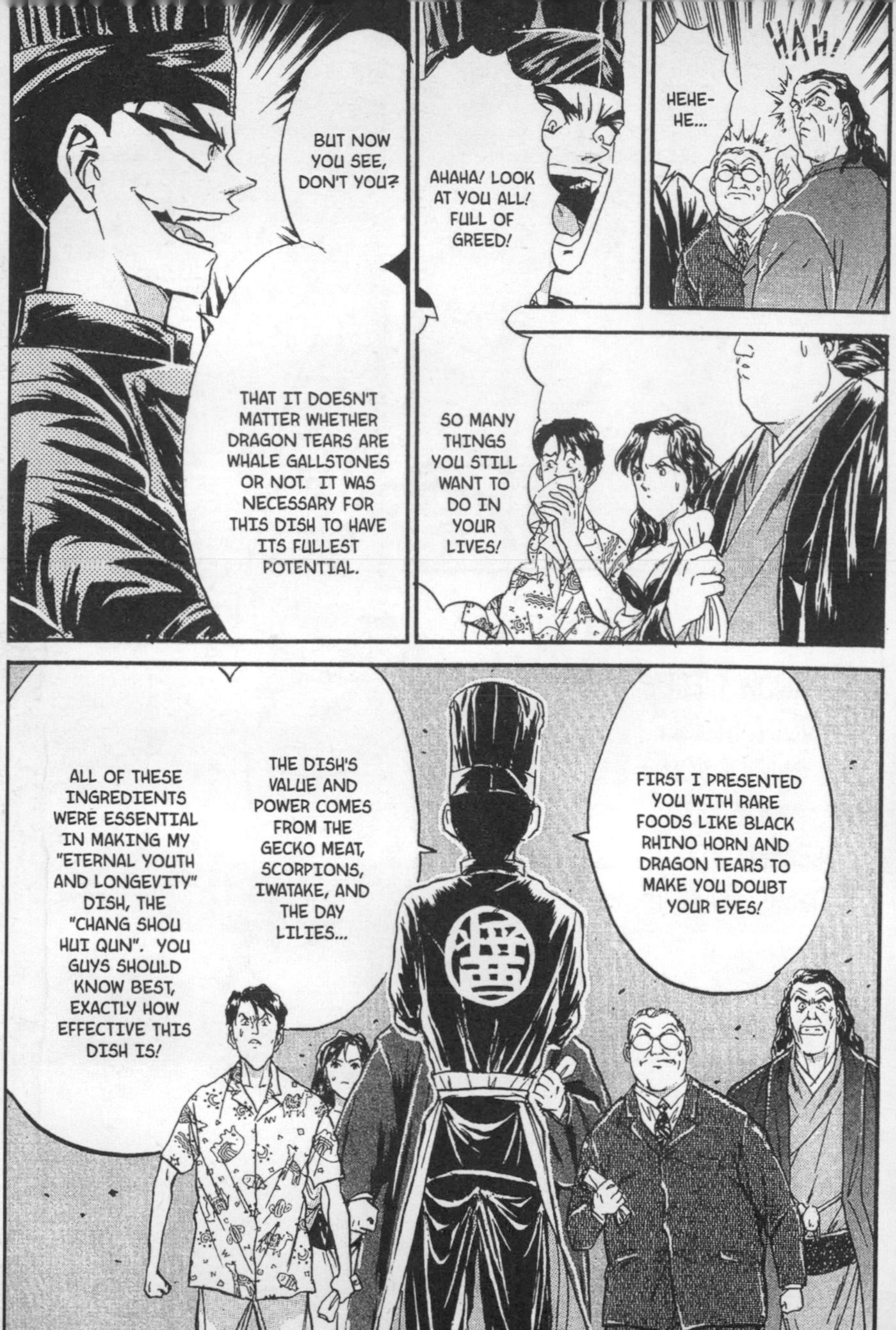
HAH!
HEHE-HE...
AHAHA! LOOK AT YOU ALL! FULL OF GREED!
SO MANY THINGS YOU STILL WANT TO DO IN YOUR LIVES!
BUT NOW YOU SEE, DON'T YOU?
THAT IT DOESN'T MATTER WHETHER DRAGON TEARS ARE WHALE GALLSTONES OR NOT. IT WAS NECESSARY FOR THIS DISH TO HAVE ITS FULLEST POTENTIAL.
FIRST I PRESENTED YOU WITH RARE FOODS LIKE BLACK RHINO HORN AND DRAGON TEARS TO MAKE YOU DOUBT YOUR EYES!
THE DISH'S VALUE AND POWER COMES FROM THE GECKO MEAT, SCORPIONS, IWATAKE, AND THE DAY LILIES...
ALL OF THESE INGREDIENTS WERE ESSENTIAL IN MAKING MY "ETERNAL YOUTH AND LONGEVITY" DISH, THE "CHANG SHOU HUI QUN". YOU GUYS SHOULD KNOW BEST, EXACTLY HOW EFFECTIVE THIS DISH IS!

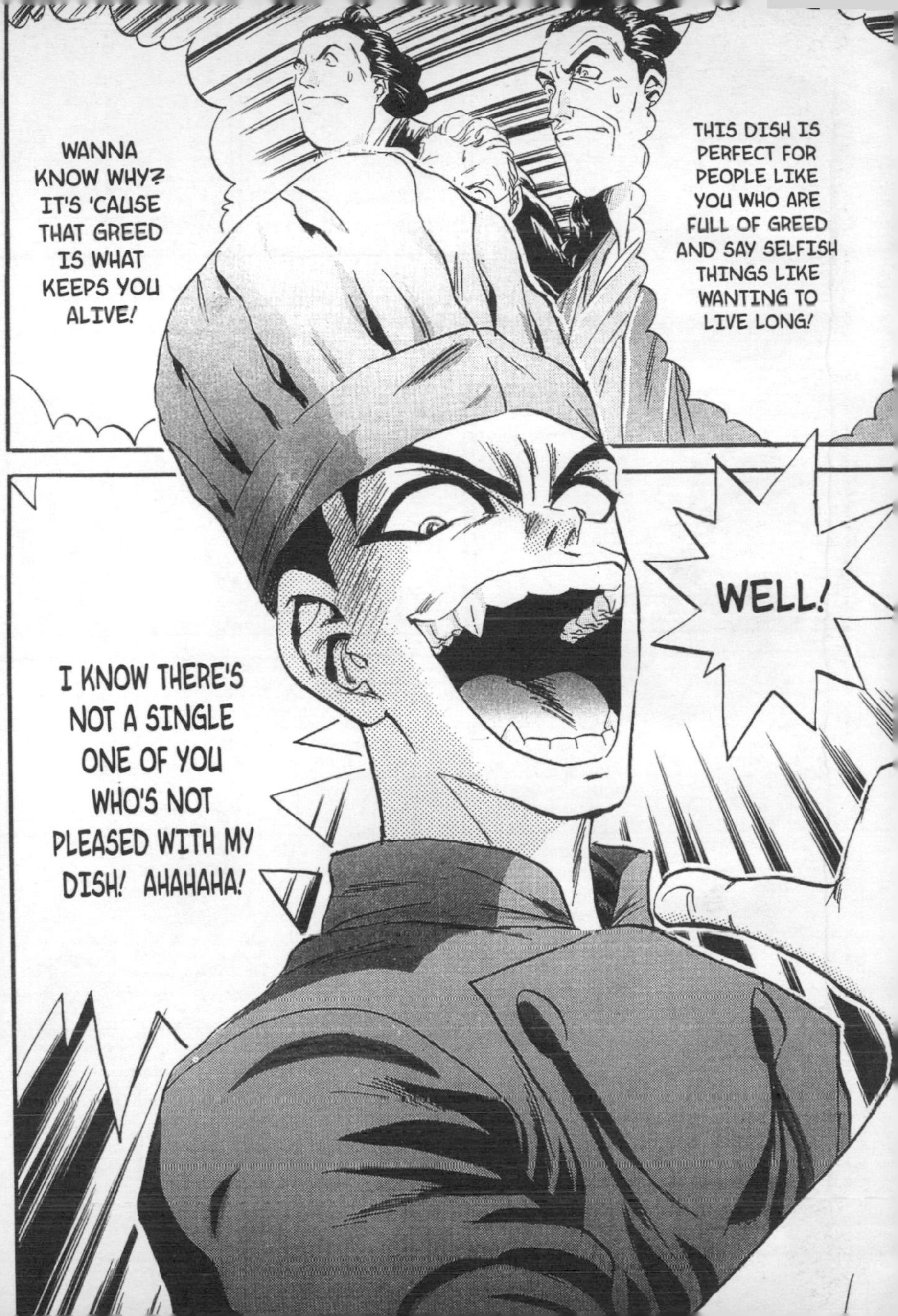
THIS DISH IS PERFECT FOR PEOPLE LIKE YOU WHO ARE FULL OF GREED AND SAY SELFISH THINGS LIKE WANTING TO LIVE LONG!
WANNA KNOW WHY? IT'S 'CAUSE THAT GREED IS WHAT KEEPS YOU ALIVE!
WELL!
I KNOW THERE'S NOT A SINGLE ONE OF YOU WHO'S NOT PLEASED WITH MY DISH! AHAHAHA!

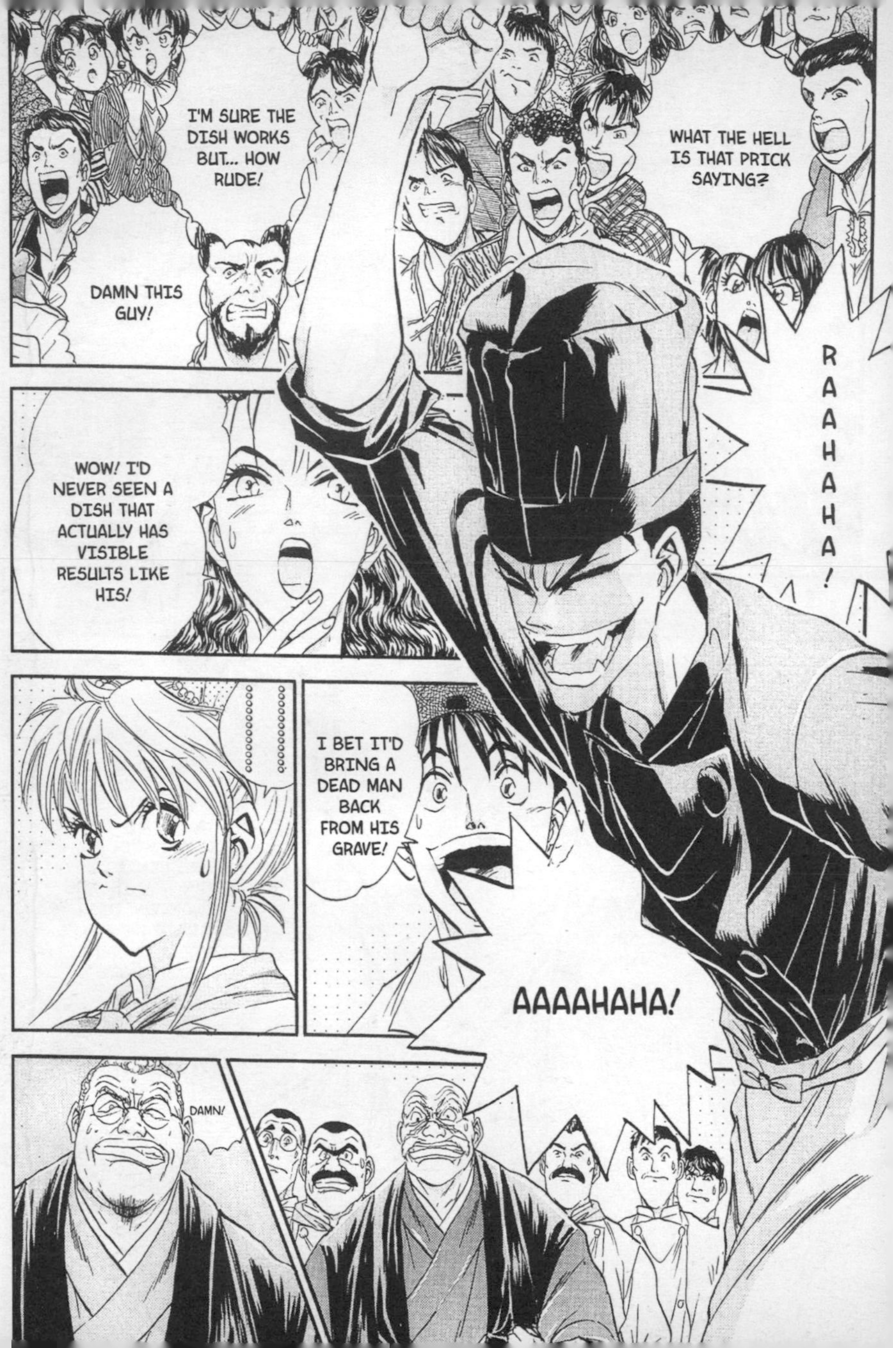
WHAT THE HELL IS THAT PRICK SAYING?
I'M SURE THE DISH WORKS BUT... HOW RUDE!
DAMN THIS GUY!
RAAHAHAHA!
WOW! I'D NEVER SEEN A DISH THAT ACTUALLY HAS VISIBLE RESULTS LIKE HIS!
I BET IT'D BRING A DEAD MAN BACK FROM HIS GRAVE!
AAAAHAHA!
DAMN!

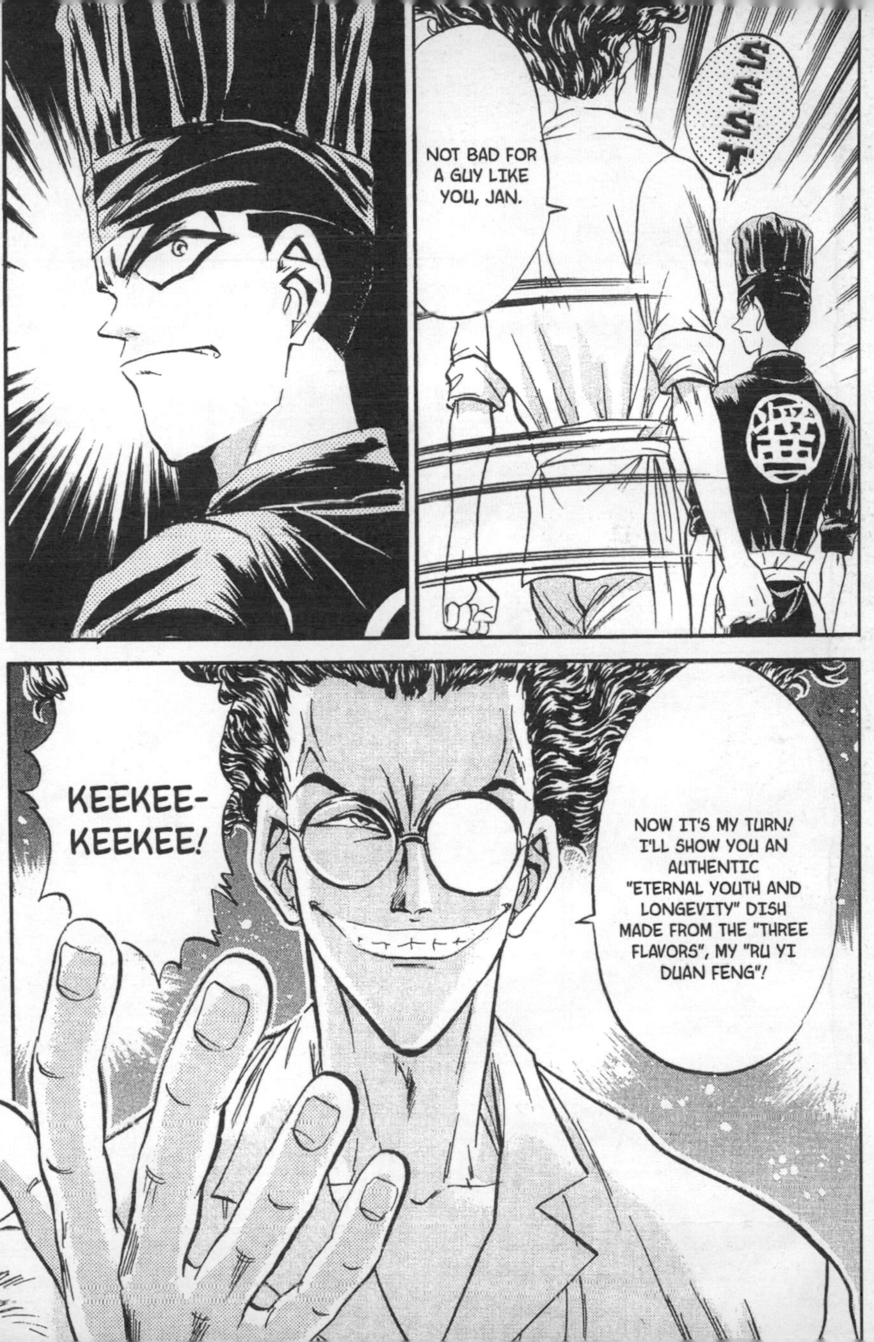
SSST
NOT BAD FOR A GUY LIKE YOU, JAN.
NOW IT'S MY TURN! I'LL SHOW YOU AN AUTHENTIC "ETERNAL YOUTH AND LONGEVITY" DISH MADE FROM THE "THREE FLAVORS", MY "RU YI DUAN FENG"!
KEEKEE-KEEKEE!

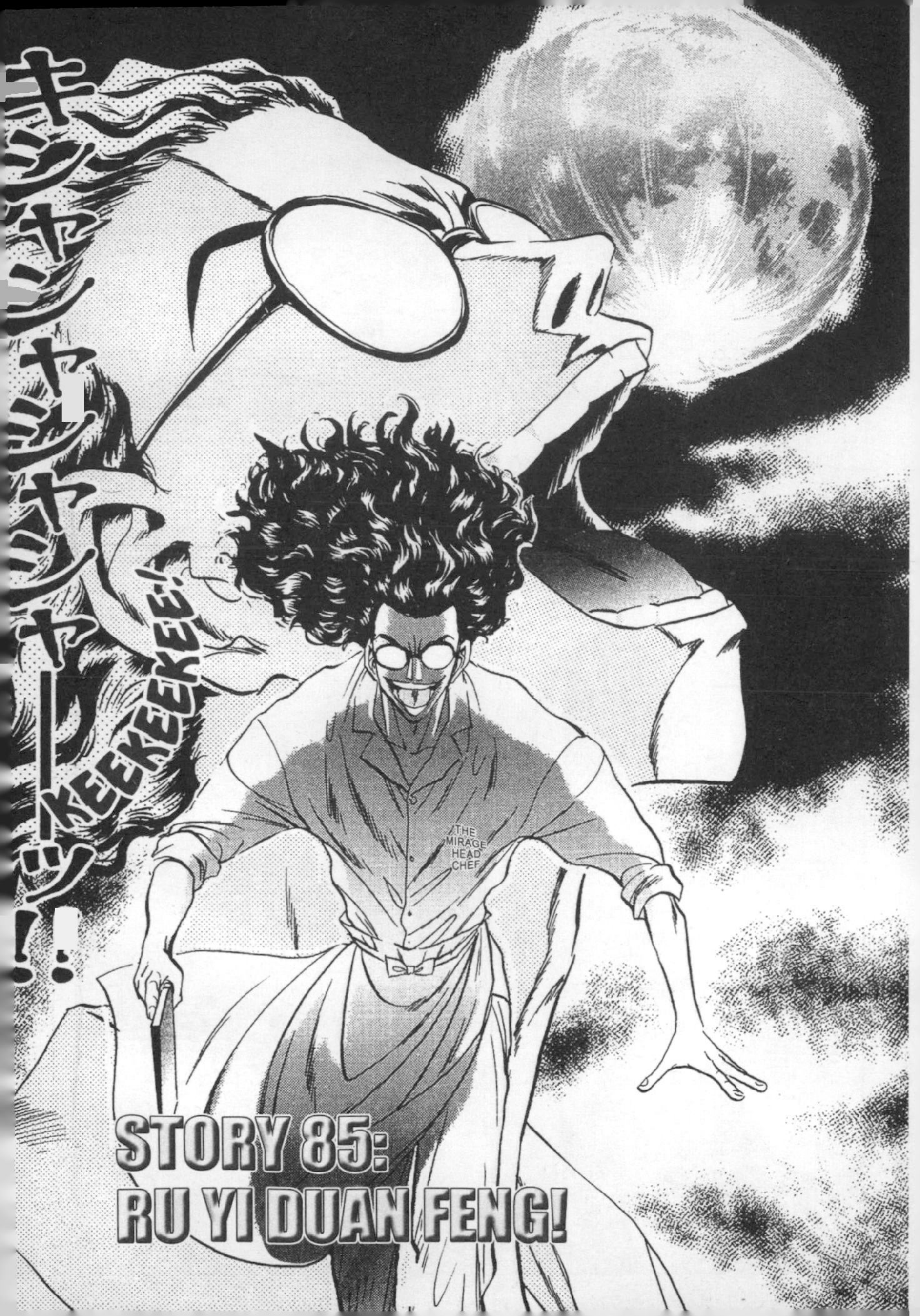
キシャシャシャシャシャーッ!!
KEEKEEKEEKEE!
THE MIRAGE HEAD CHEF
STORY 85:
RU YI DUAN FENG!

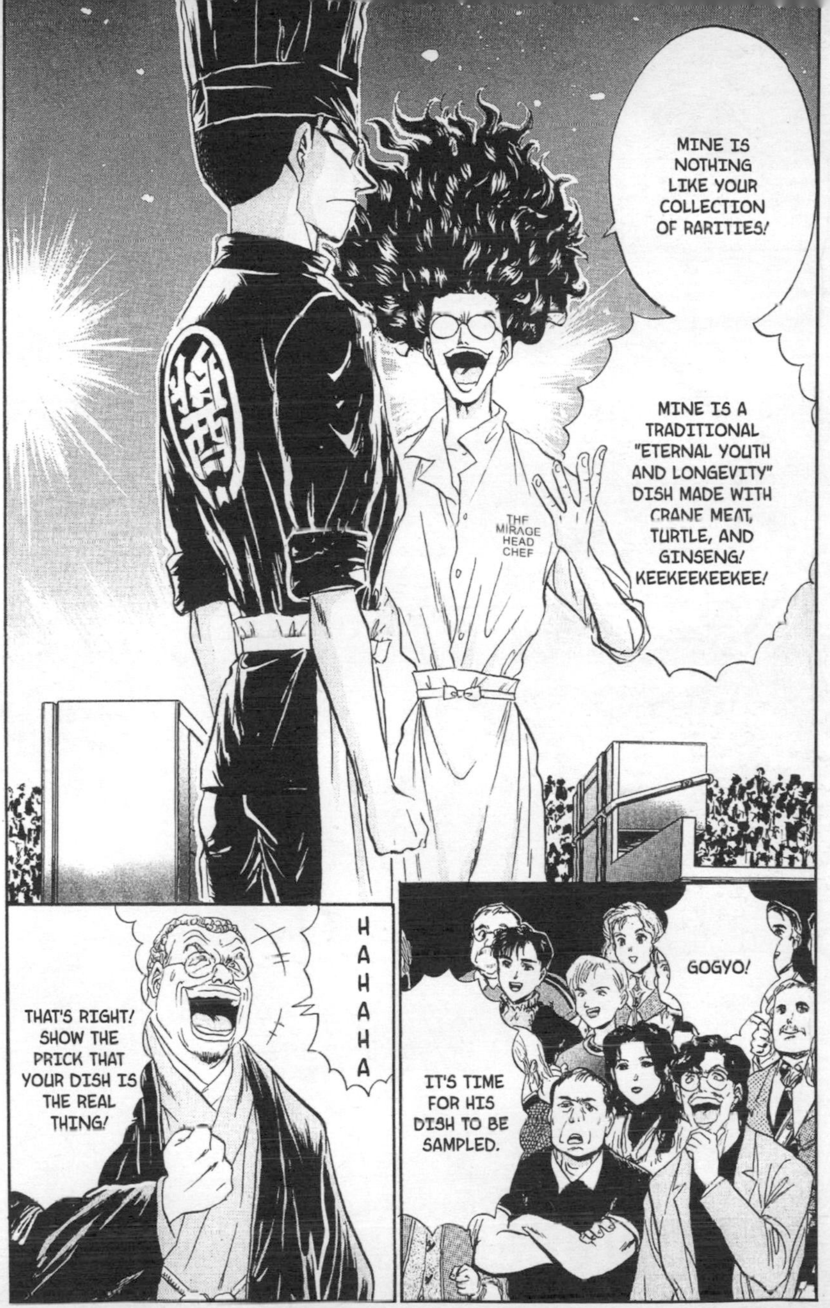
MINE IS NOTHING LIKE YOUR COLLECTION OF RARITIES!
THE MIRAGE HEAD CHEF
MINE IS A TRADITIONAL "ETERNAL YOUTH AND LONGEVITY" DISH MADE WITH CRANE MEAT, TURTLE, AND GINSENG! KEEKEEKEEKEE!
GOGYO!
IT'S TIME FOR HIS DISH TO BE SAMPLED.
HAHAHAHAHA
THAT'S RIGHT! SHOW THE PRICK THAT YOUR DISH IS THE REAL THING!

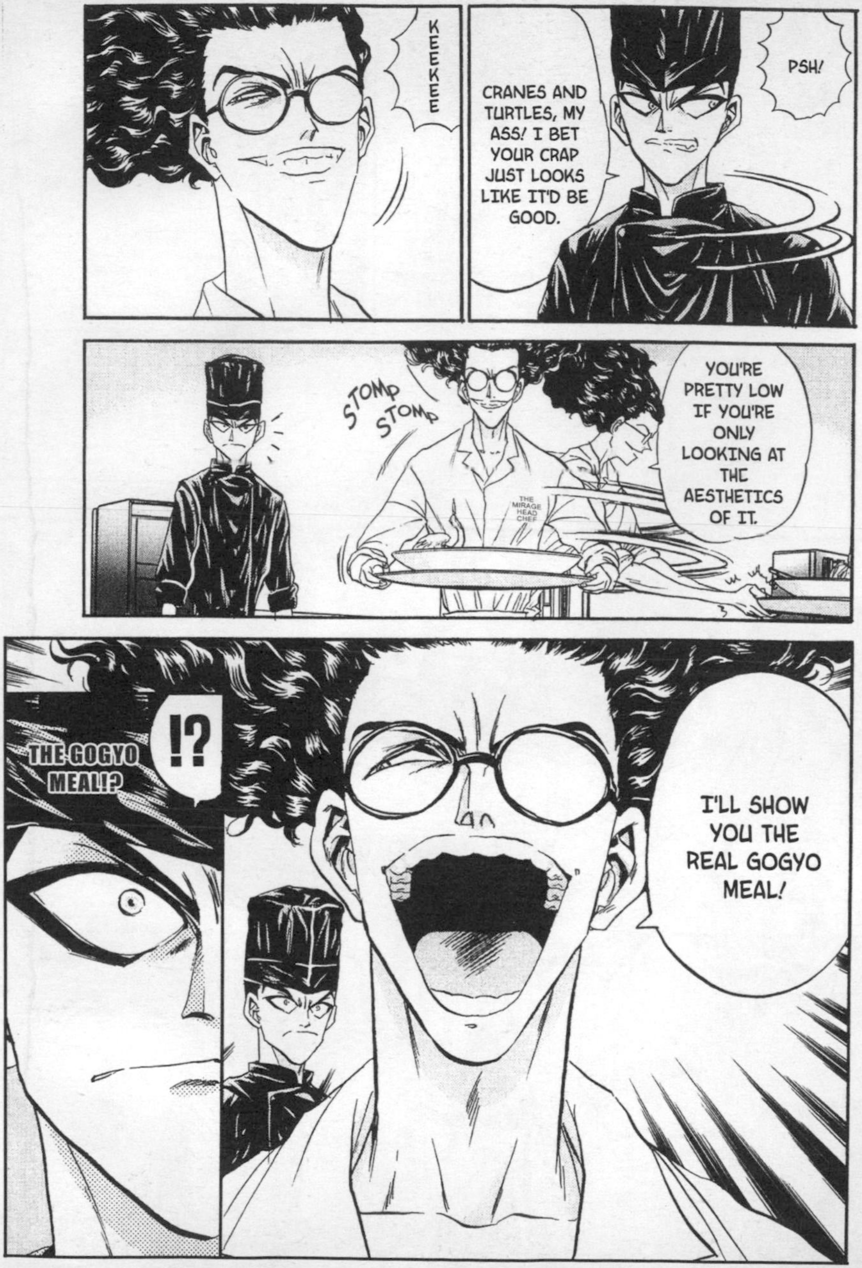
PSH!
CRANES AND TURTLES, MY ASS! I BET YOUR CRAP JUST LOOKS LIKE IT'D BE GOOD.
KEEEKEE
YOU'RE PRETTY LOW IF YOU'RE ONLY LOOKING AT THE AESTHETICS OF IT.
STOMP STOMP
THE MIRAGE HEAD CHEF
I'LL SHOW YOU THE REAL GOGYO MEAL!
!?
THE GOGYO MEAL!?

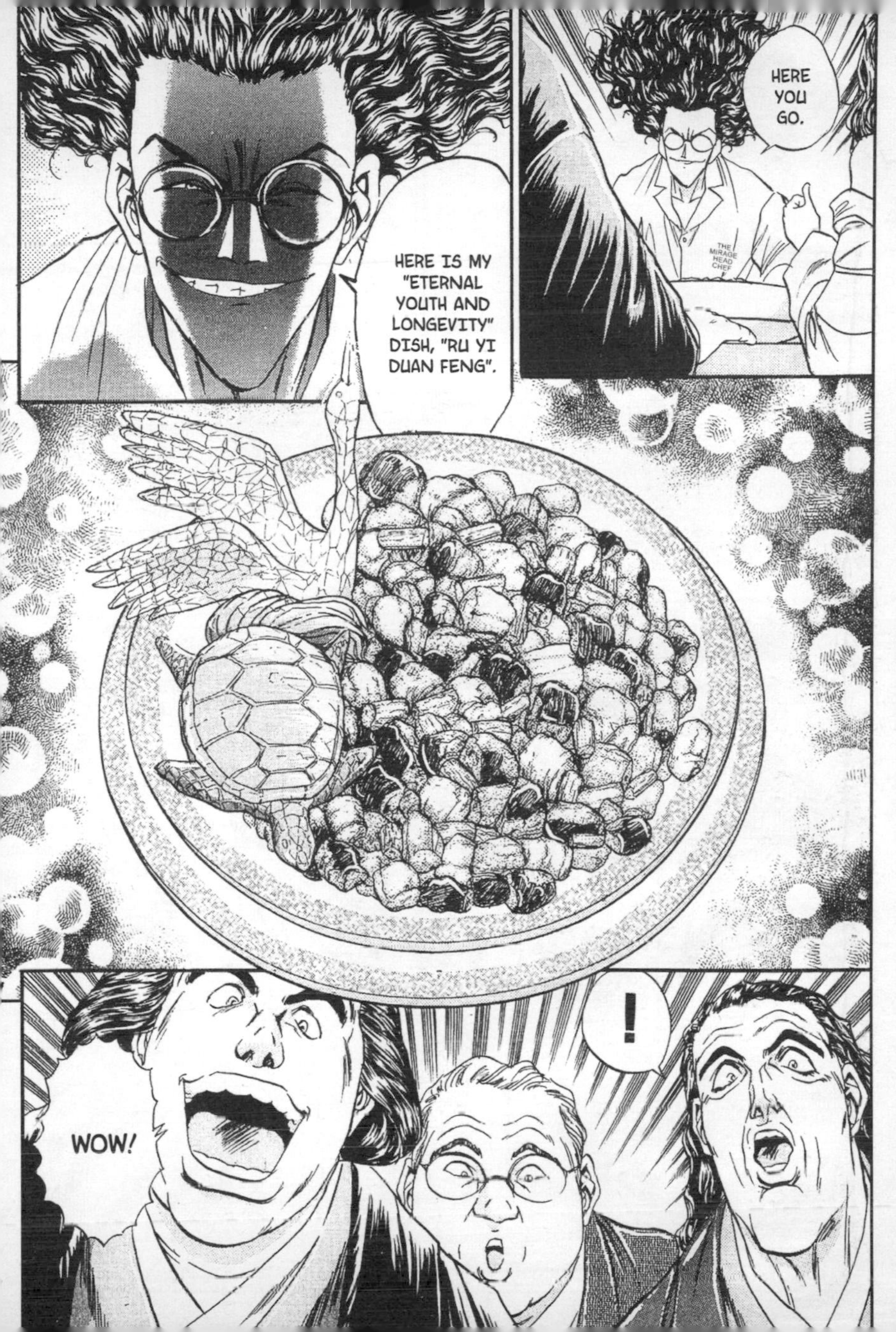
HERE YOU GO.
THE MIRAGE HEAD CHEF
HERE IS MY "ETERNAL YOUTH AND LONGEVITY" DISH, "RU YI DUAN FENG".
!
WOW!

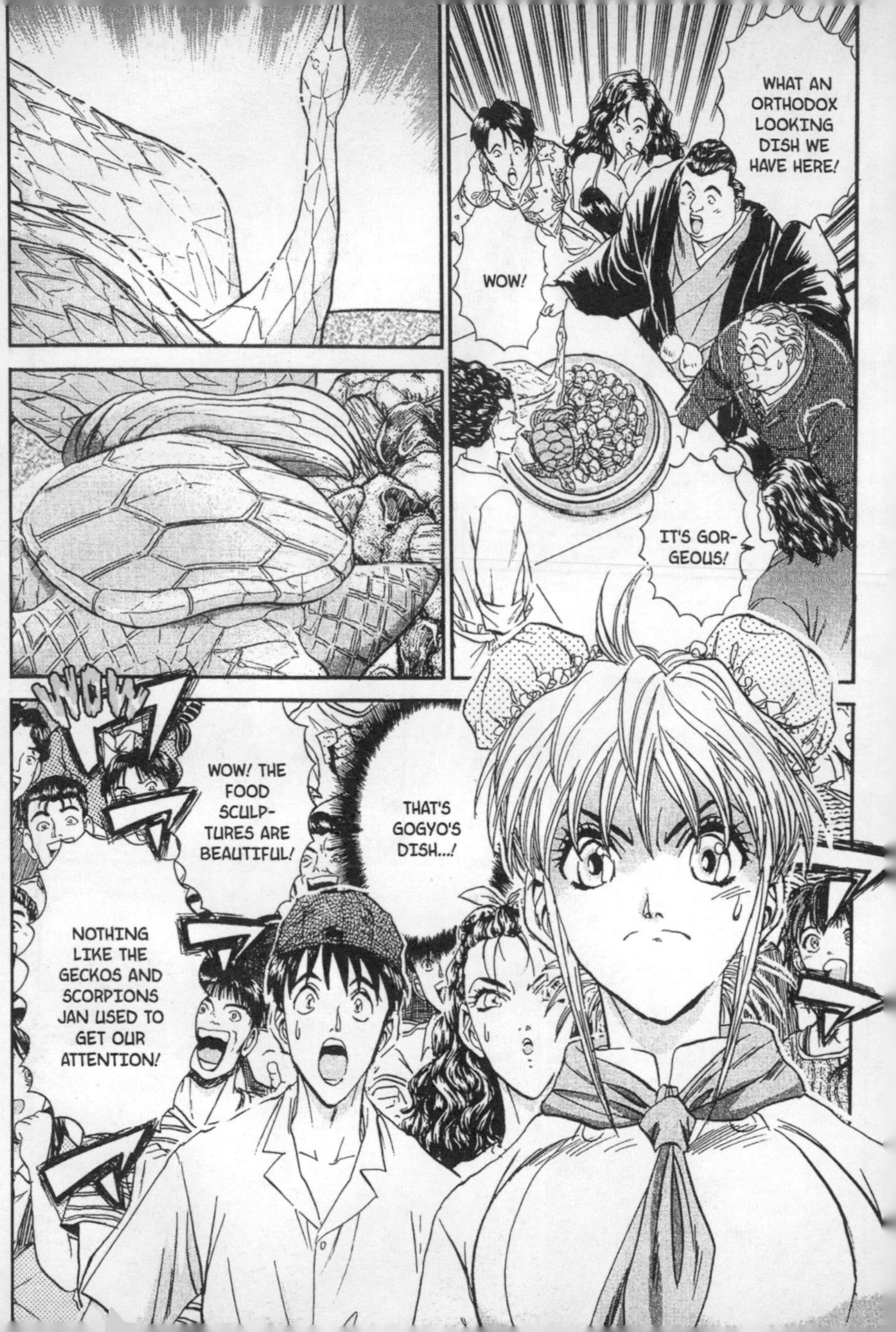
WHAT AN ORTHODOX LOOKING DISH WE HAVE HERE!
WOW!
IT'S GOR-GEOUS!
THAT'S GOGYO'S DISH...!
WOW! THE FOOD SCULP-TURES ARE BEAUTIFUL!
WOW
NOTHING LIKE THE GECKOS AND SCORPIONS JAN USED TO GET OUR ATTENTION!

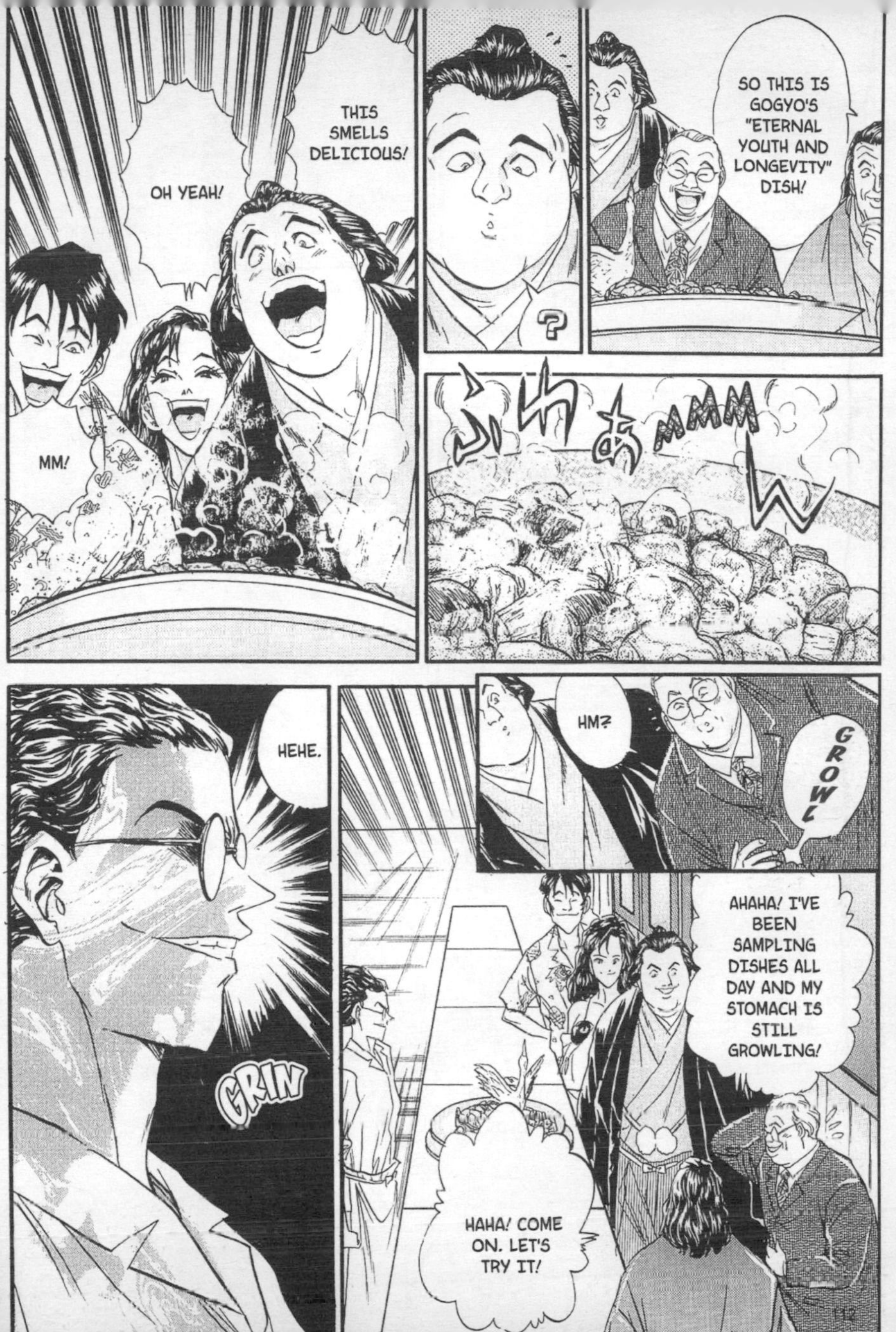
SO THIS IS GOGYO'S "ETERNAL YOUTH AND LONGEVITY" DISH!
?
ふわあ MMMW
THIS SMELLS DELICIOUS!
OH YEAH!
MM!
HM?
GROWL
AHAHA! I'VE BEEN SAMPLING DISHES ALL DAY AND MY STOMACH IS STILL GROWLING!
HAHA! COME ON. LET'S TRY IT!
HEHE.
GRIN

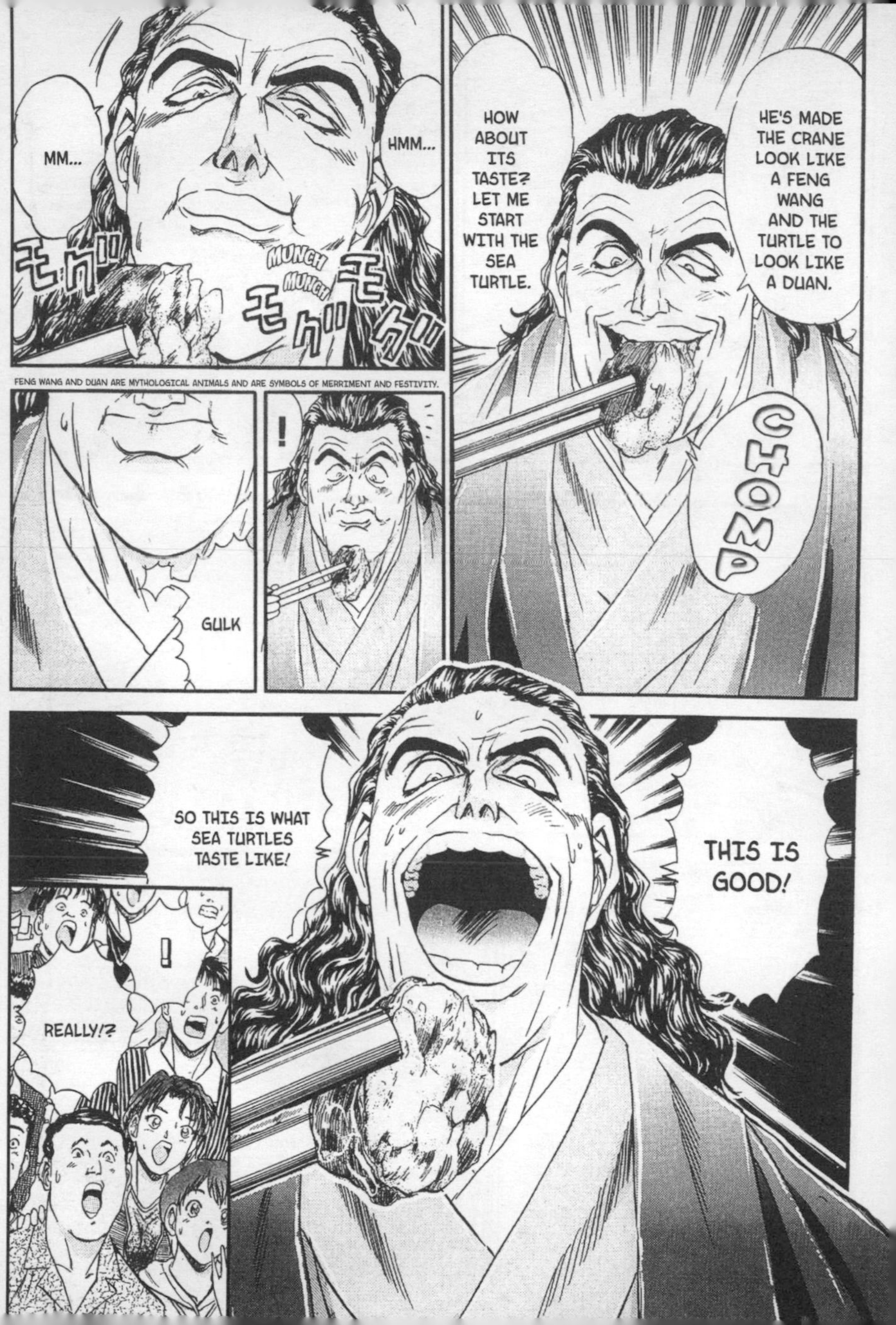
HE'S MADE THE CRANE LOOK LIKE A FENG WANG AND THE TURTLE TO LOOK LIKE A DUAN.
HOW ABOUT ITS TASTE? LET ME START WITH THE SEA TURTLE.
CHOMP
HMM...
MM...
MUNCH
MUNCH
FENG WANG AND DUAN ARE MYTHOLOGICAL ANIMALS AND ARE SYMBOLS OF MERRIMENT AND FESTIVITY.
!
GULK
THIS IS GOOD!
SO THIS IS WHAT SEA TURTLES TASTE LIKE!
!
REALLY!?

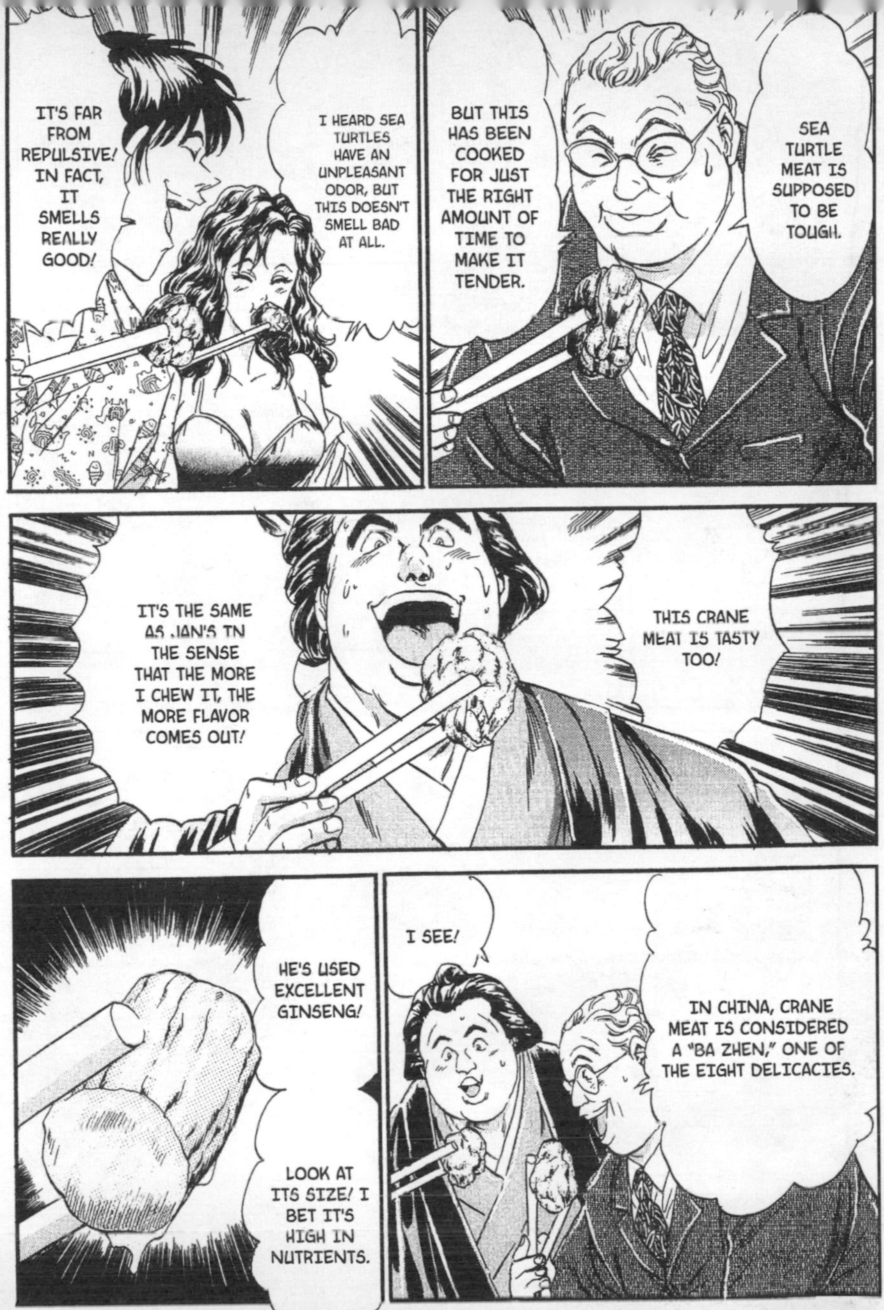
SEA TURTLE MEAT IS SUPPOSED TO BE TOUGH.
BUT THIS HAS BEEN COOKED FOR JUST THE RIGHT AMOUNT OF TIME TO MAKE IT TENDER.
I HEARD SEA TURTLES HAVE AN UNPLEASANT ODOR, BUT THIS DOESN'T SMELL BAD AT ALL.
IT'S FAR FROM REPULSIVE! IN FACT, IT SMELLS REALLY GOOD!
THIS CRANE MEAT IS TASTY TOO!
IT'S THE SAME AS JAN'S IN THE SENSE THAT THE MORE I CHEW IT, THE MORE FLAVOR COMES OUT!
IN CHINA, CRANE MEAT IS CONSIDERED A "BA ZHEN," ONE OF THE EIGHT DELICACIES.
I SEE!
HE'S USED EXCELLENT GINSENG!
LOOK AT ITS SIZE! I BET IT'S HIGH IN NUTRIENTS.

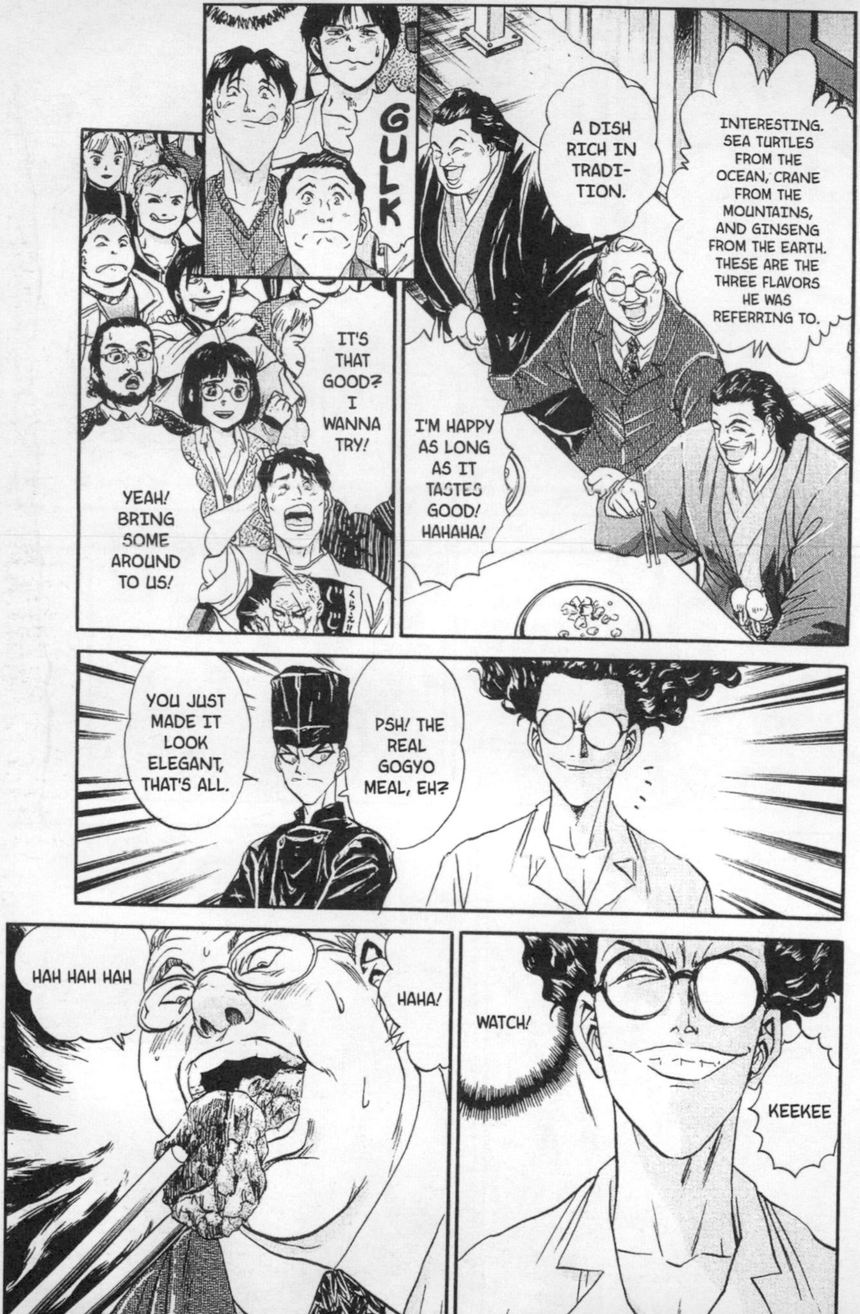
INTERESTING. SEA TURTLES FROM THE OCEAN, CRANE FROM THE MOUNTAINS, AND GINSENG FROM THE EARTH. THESE ARE THE THREE FLAVORS HE WAS REFERRING TO.
A DISH RICH IN TRADITION.
I'M HAPPY AS LONG AS IT TASTES GOOD! HAHAHA!
GULK
IT'S THAT GOOD? I WANNA TRY!
YEAH! BRING SOME AROUND TO US!
PSH! THE REAL GOGYO MEAL, EH?
YOU JUST MADE IT LOOK ELEGANT, THAT'S ALL.
KEEKEE
WATCH!
HAHA!
HAH HAH HAH

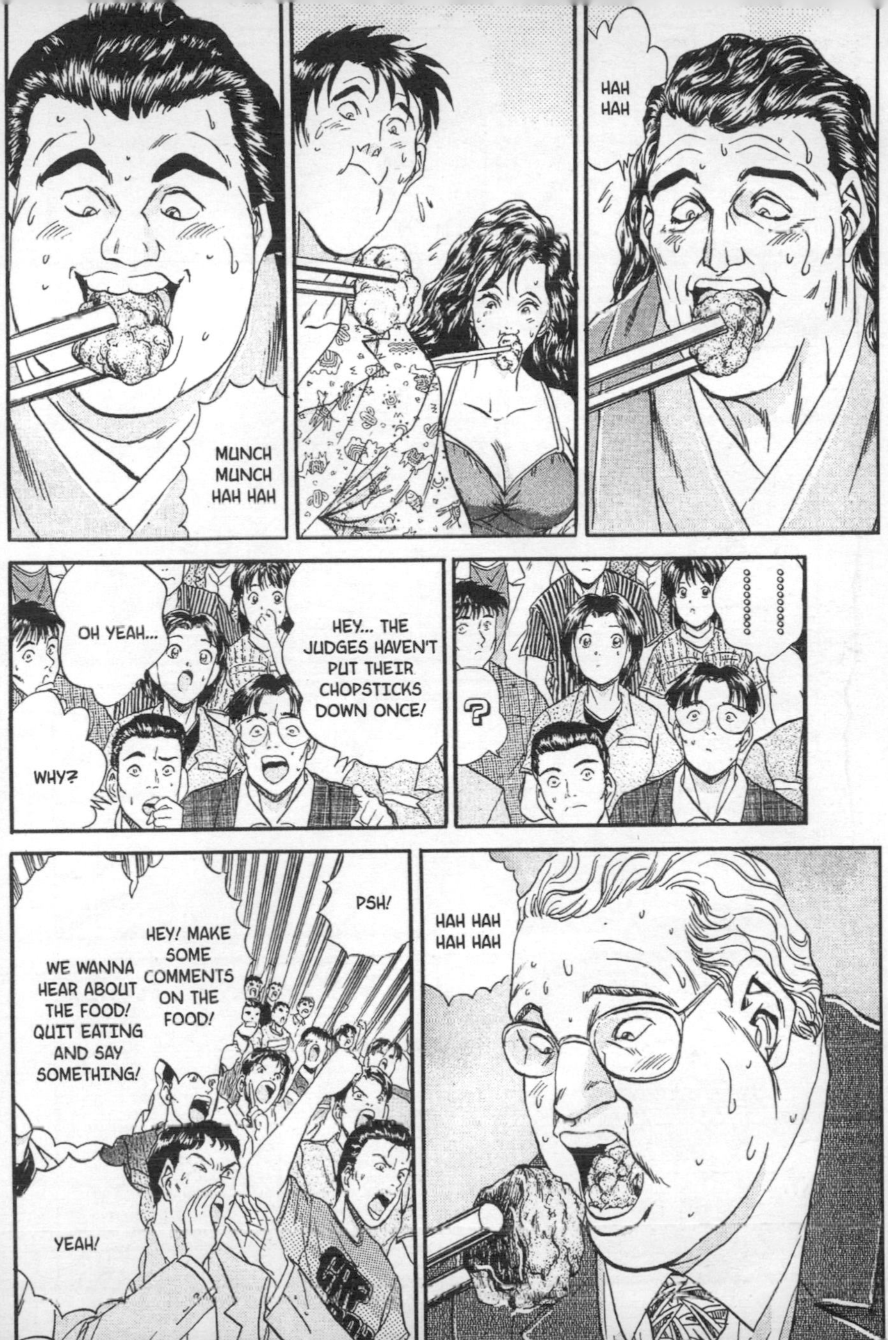
HAH HAH
MUNCH MUNCH HAH HAH
?
HEY... THE JUDGES HAVEN'T PUT THEIR CHOPSTICKS DOWN ONCE!
OH YEAH...
WHY?
HAH HAH HAH HAH
PSH!
HEY! MAKE SOME COMMENTS ON THE FOOD!
WE WANNA HEAR ABOUT THE FOOD! QUIT EATING AND SAY SOMETHING!
YEAH!

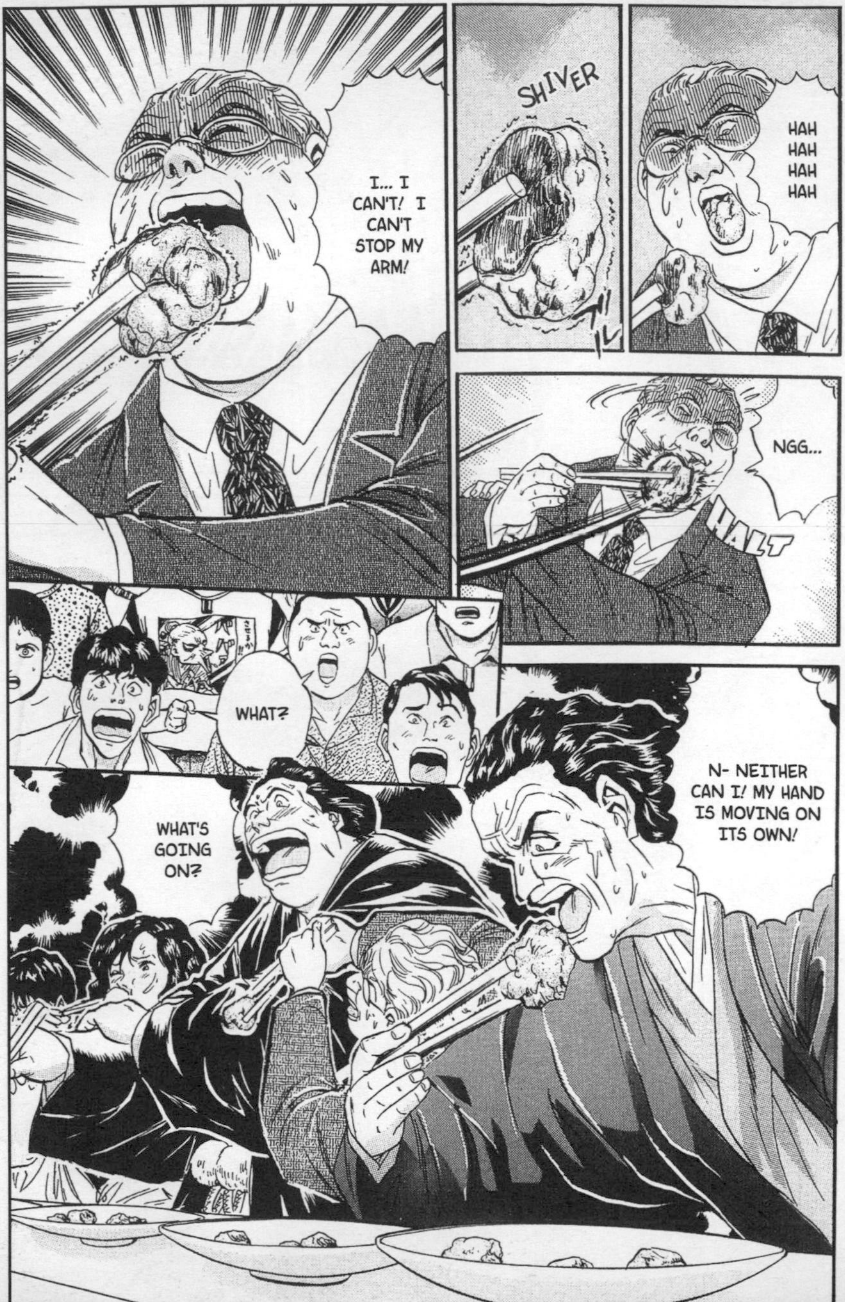

HAH HAH HAH HAH
SHIVER
NGG...
HALT
I... I CAN'T! I CAN'T STOP MY ARM!
WHAT?
N- NEITHER CAN I! MY HAND IS MOVING ON ITS OWN!
WHAT'S GOING ON?

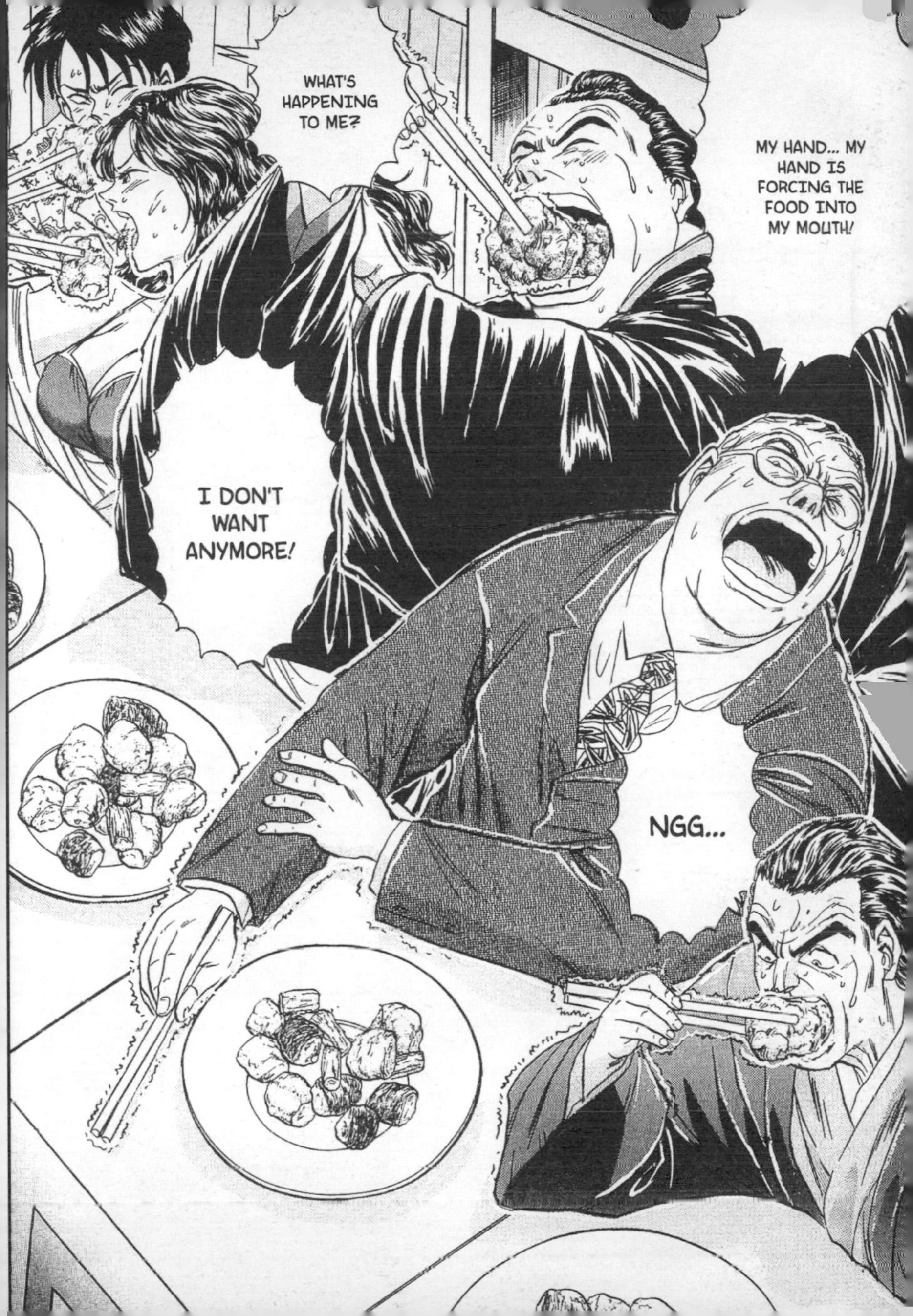
MY HAND... MY HAND IS FORCING THE FOOD INTO MY MOUTH!
WHAT'S HAPPENING TO ME?
I DON'T WANT ANYMORE!
NGG...

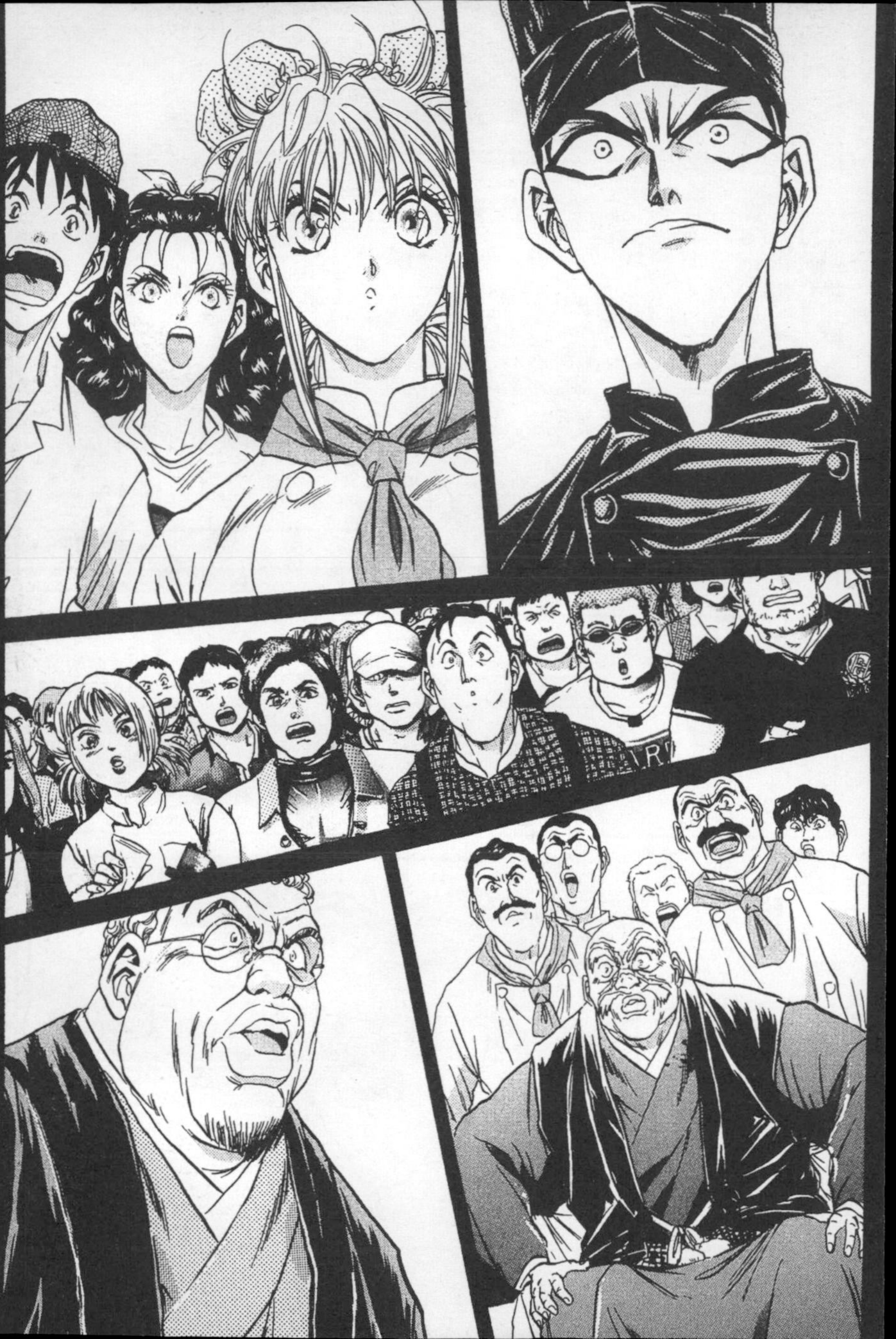

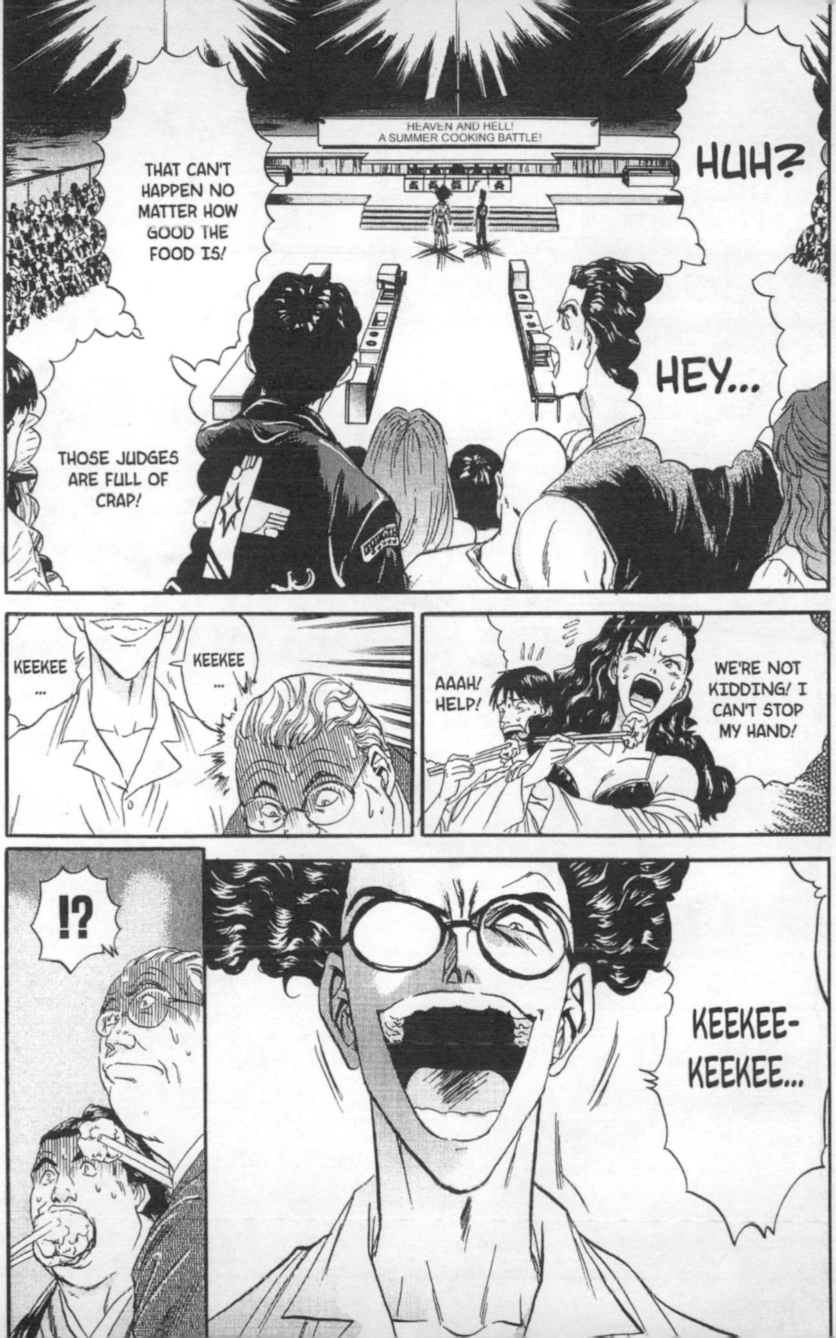
HEAVEN AND HELL! A SUMMER COOKING BATTLE!
HUH?
THAT CAN'T HAPPEN NO MATTER HOW GOOD THE FOOD IS!
HEY...
THOSE JUDGES ARE FULL OF CRAP!
WE'RE NOT KIDDING! I CAN'T STOP MY HAND!
AAAH! HELP!
KEEKEE ...
KEEKEE ...
KEEKEE-KEEKEE...
!?

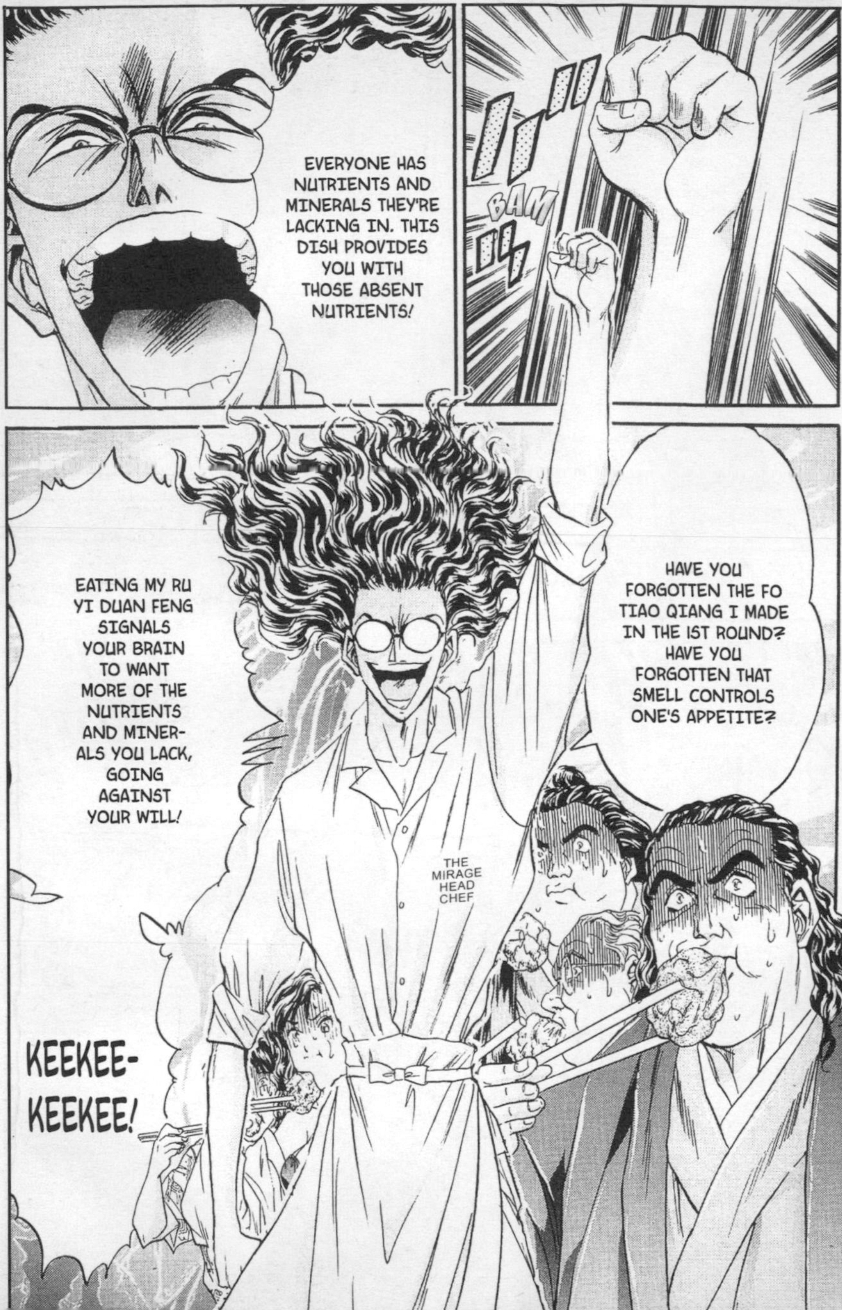
BAM
EVERYONE HAS NUTRIENTS AND MINERALS THEY'RE LACKING IN. THIS DISH PROVIDES YOU WITH THOSE ABSENT NUTRIENTS!
HAVE YOU FORGOTTEN THE FO TIAO QIANG I MADE IN THE 1ST ROUND? HAVE YOU FORGOTTEN THAT SMELL CONTROLS ONE'S APPETITE?
EATING MY RU YI DUAN FENG SIGNALS YOUR BRAIN TO WANT MORE OF THE NUTRIENTS AND MINER-ALS YOU LACK, GOING AGAINST YOUR WILL!
THE MIRAGE HEAD CHEF
KEEKEE-KEEKEE!

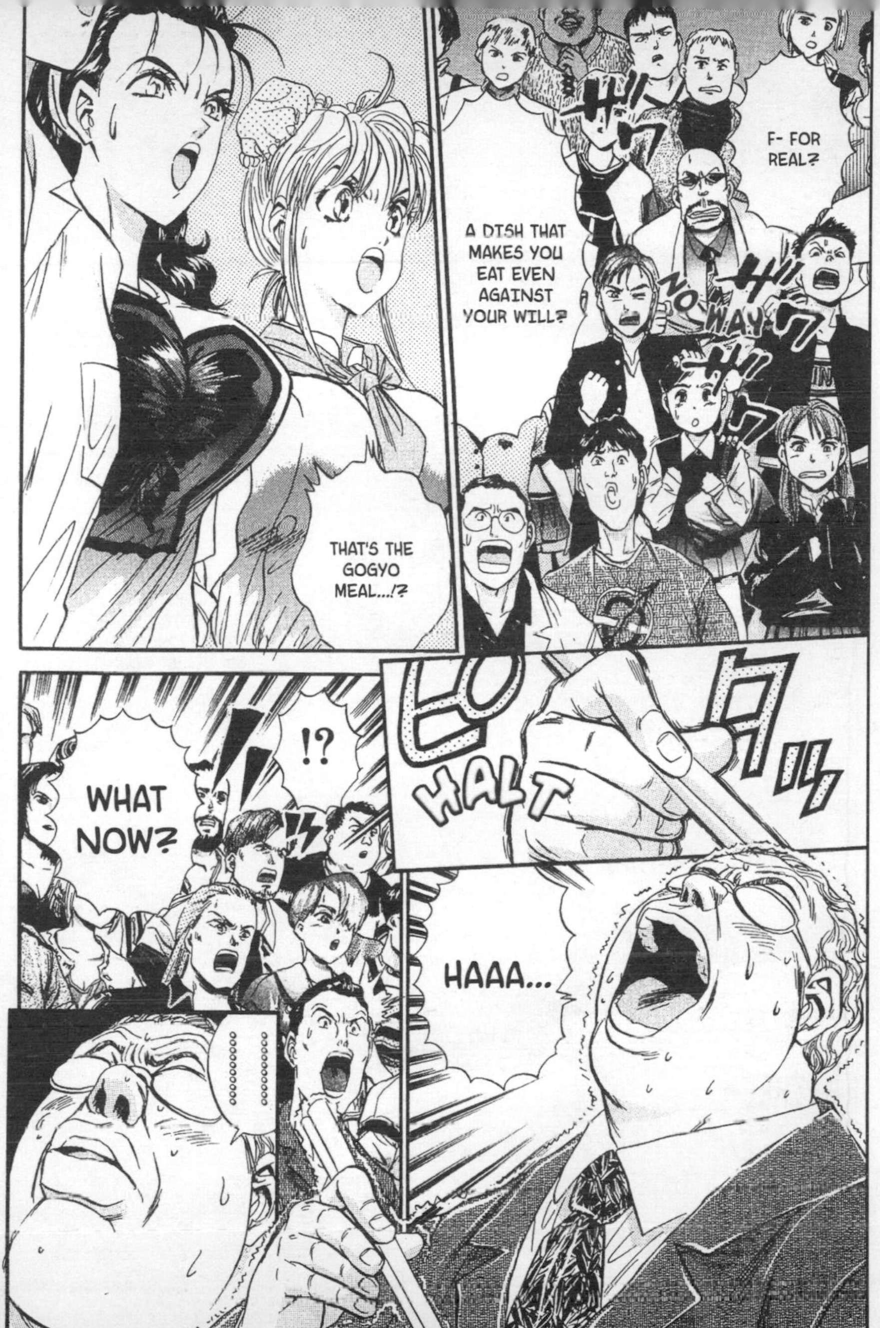
F- FOR REAL?
A DISH THAT MAKES YOU EAT EVEN AGAINST YOUR WILL?
NO WAY
THAT'S THE GOGYO MEAL...!?
HALT
WHAT NOW?
!?
HAAA...
....

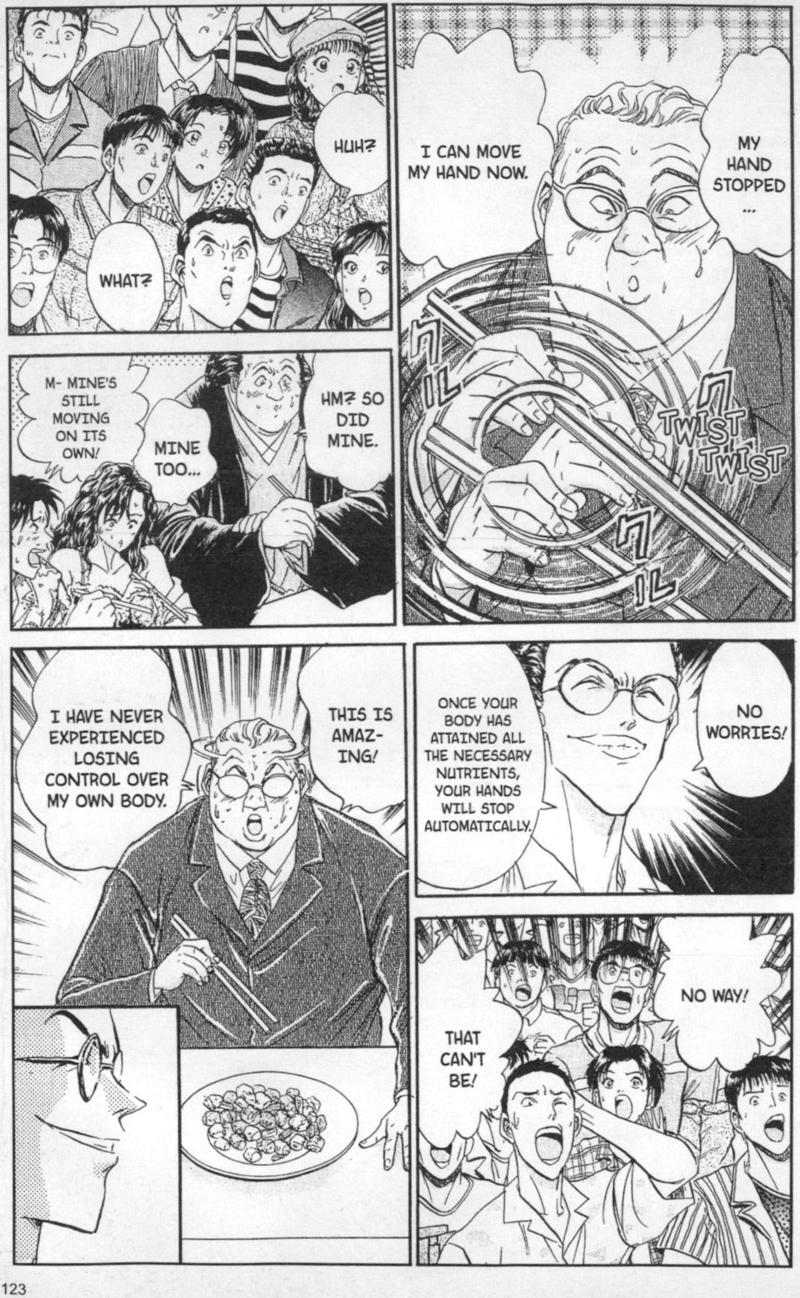

MY HAND STOPPED ...
I CAN MOVE MY HAND NOW.
TWIST TWIST
HUH?
WHAT?
HM? SO DID MINE.
MINE TOO...
M- MINE'S STILL MOVING ON ITS OWN!
NO WORRIES!
ONCE YOUR BODY HAS ATTAINED ALL THE NECESSARY NUTRIENTS, YOUR HANDS WILL STOP AUTOMATICALLY.
NO WAY!
THAT CAN'T BE!
THIS IS AMAZ-ING!
I HAVE NEVER EXPERIENCED LOSING CONTROL OVER MY OWN BODY.

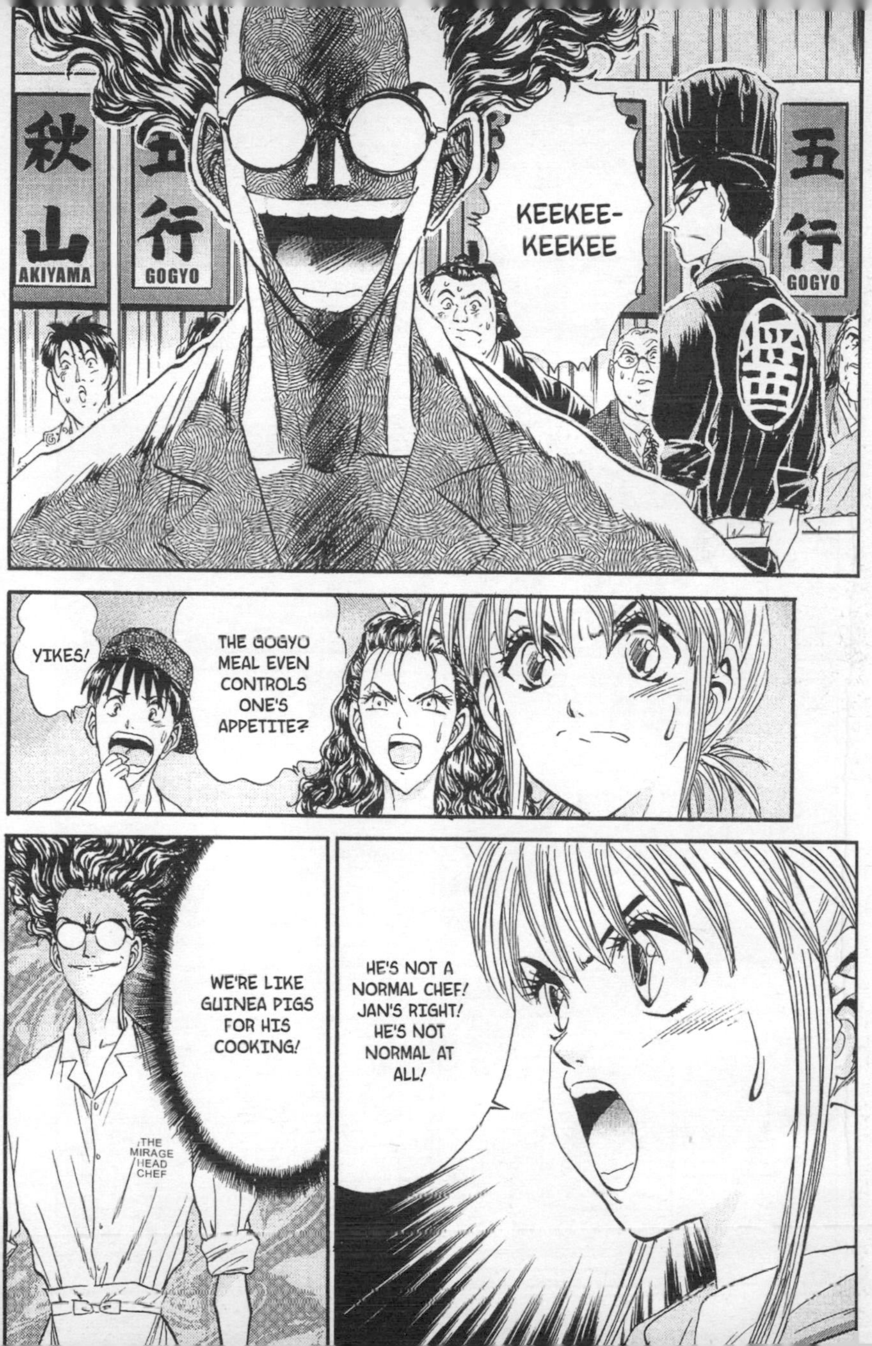
五行
GOGYO
KEEKEE-KEEKEE
五行
GOGYO
秋山
AKIYAMA
THE GOGYO MEAL EVEN CONTROLS ONE'S APPETITE?
YIKES!
HE'S NOT A NORMAL CHEF! JAN'S RIGHT! HE'S NOT NORMAL AT ALL!
WE'RE LIKE GUINEA PIGS FOR HIS COOKING!
THE MIRAGE HEAD CHEF

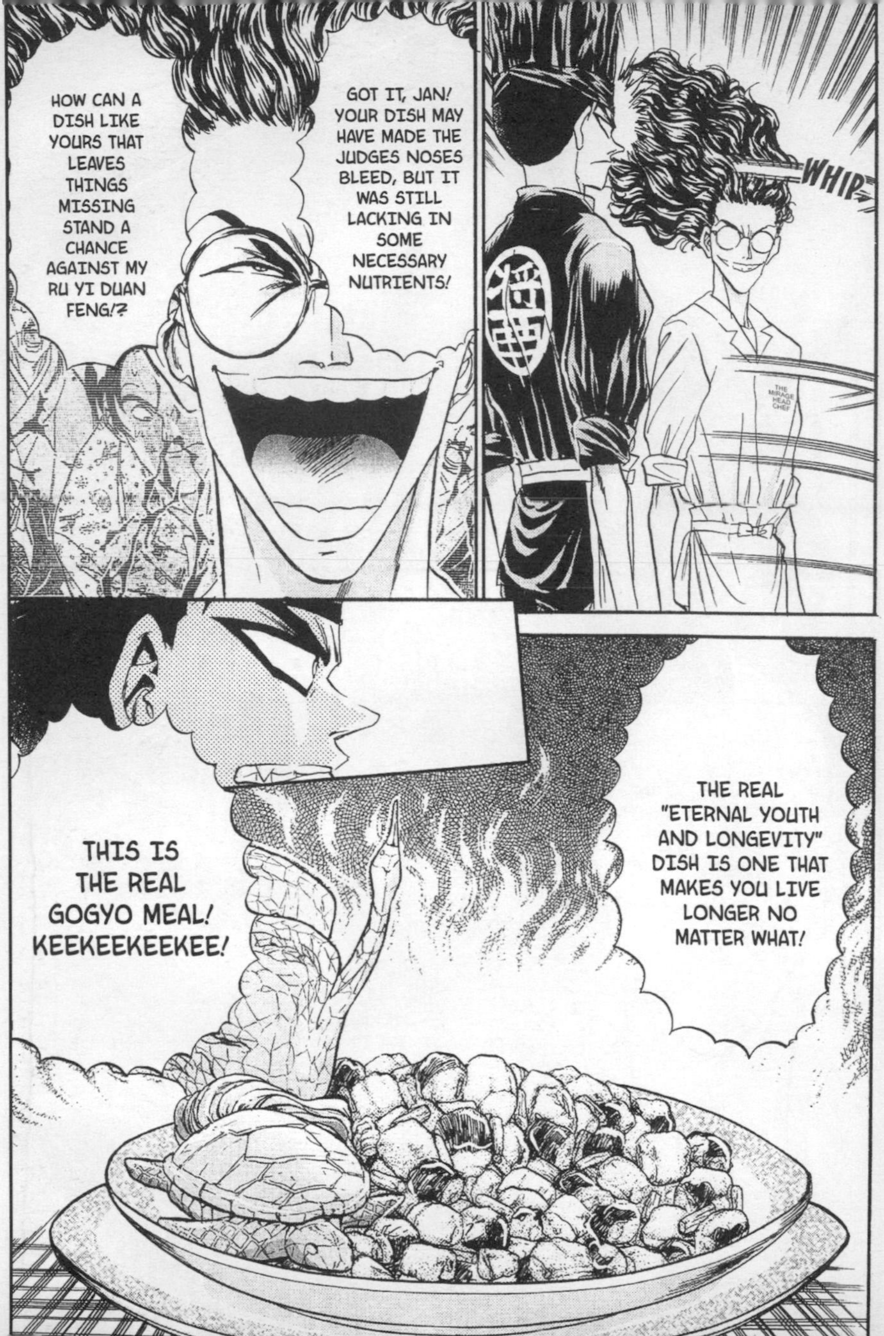
WHIP
THE MIRAGE HEAD CHEF
GOT IT, JAN! YOUR DISH MAY HAVE MADE THE JUDGES NOSES BLEED, BUT IT WAS STILL LACKING IN SOME NECESSARY NUTRIENTS!
HOW CAN A DISH LIKE YOURS THAT LEAVES THINGS MISSING STAND A CHANCE AGAINST MY RU YI DUAN FENG!?
THE REAL "ETERNAL YOUTH AND LONGEVITY" DISH IS ONE THAT MAKES YOU LIVE LONGER NO MATTER WHAT!
THIS IS THE REAL GOGYO MEAL! KEEKEEKEEKEE!

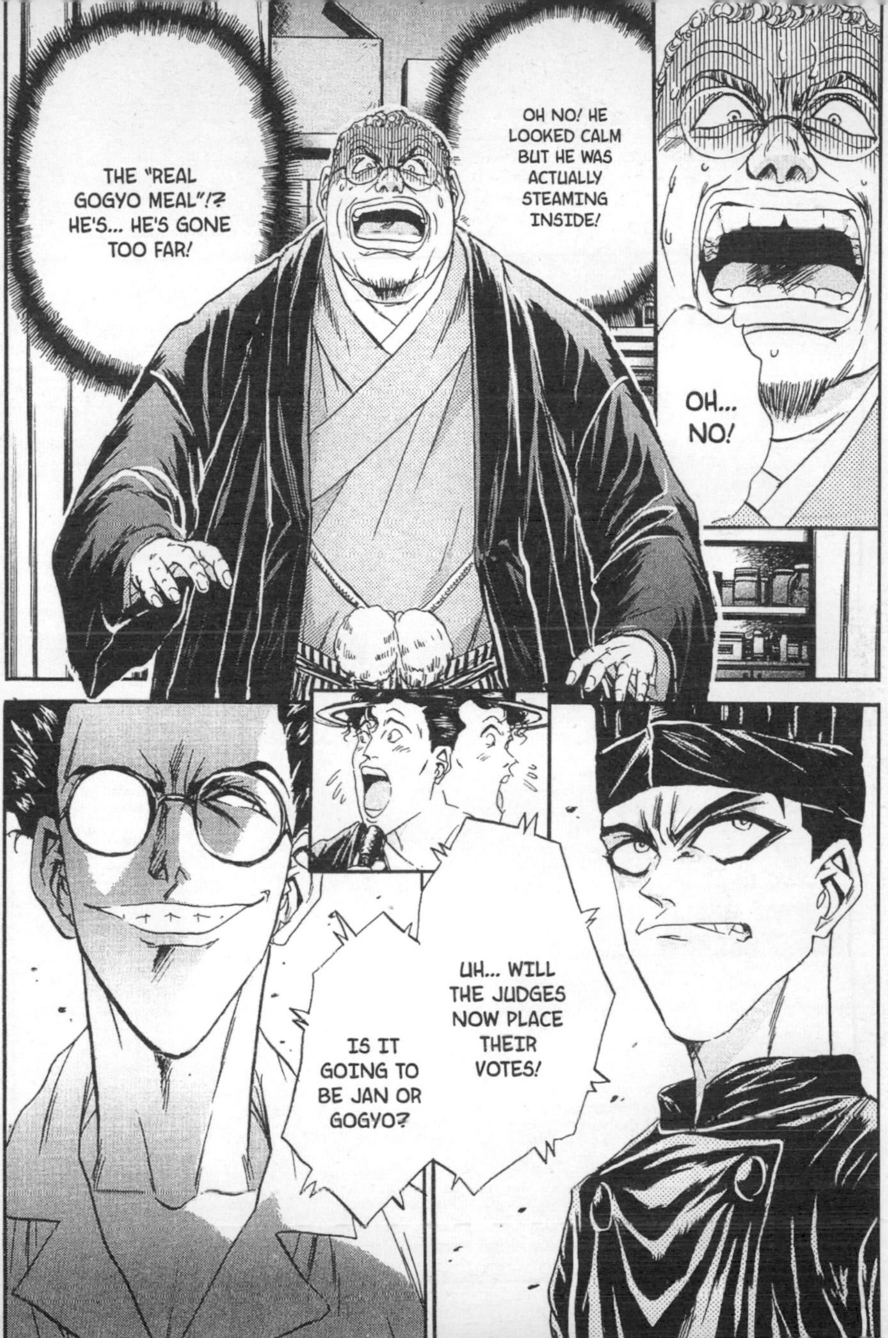
OH... NO!
OH NO! HE LOOKED CALM BUT HE WAS ACTUALLY STEAMING INSIDE!
THE "REAL GOGYO MEAL"!? HE'S... HE'S GONE TOO FAR!
UH... WILL THE JUDGES NOW PLACE THEIR VOTES!
IS IT GOING TO BE JAN OR GOGYO?

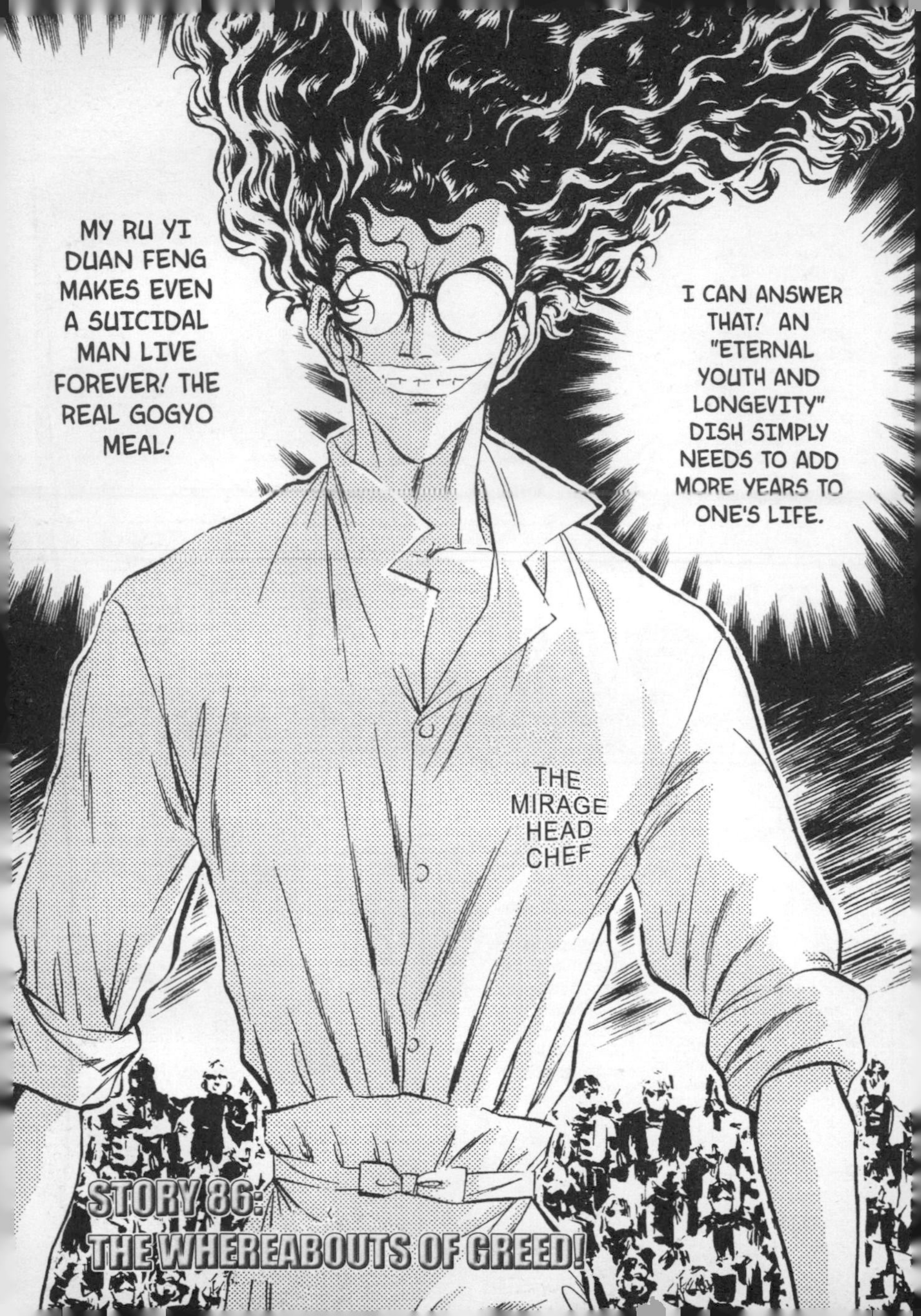
I CAN ANSWER THAT! AN "ETERNAL YOUTH AND LONGEVITY" DISH SIMPLY NEEDS TO ADD MORE YEARS TO ONE'S LIFE.
MY RU YI DUAN FENG MAKES EVEN A SUICIDAL MAN LIVE FOREVER! THE REAL GOGYO MEAL!
THE MIRAGE HEAD CHEF
STORY 86:
THE WHEREABOUTS OF GREED!

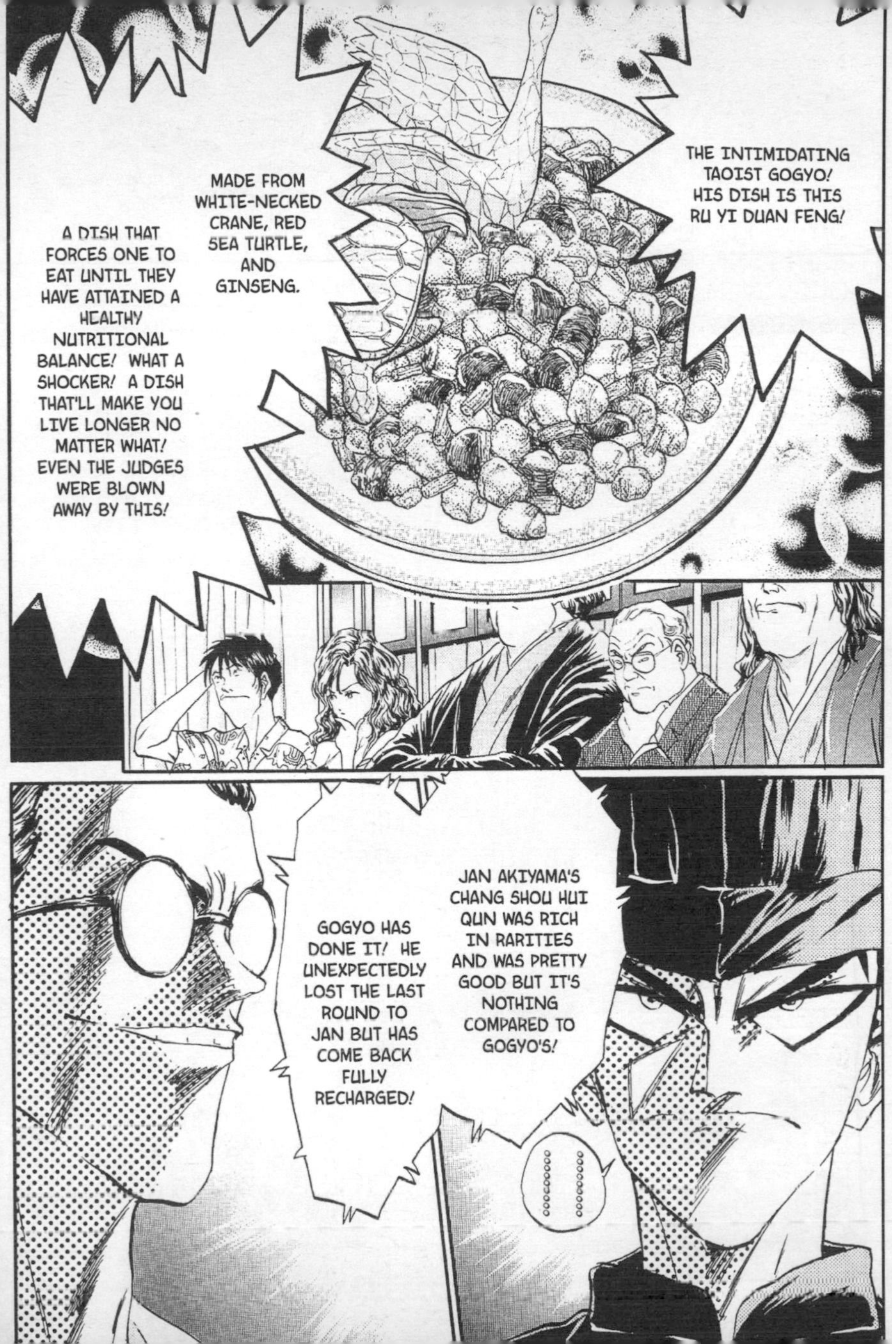
THE INTIMIDATING TAOIST GOGYO! HIS DISH IS THIS RU YI DUAN FENG!
MADE FROM WHITE-NECKED CRANE, RED SEA TURTLE, AND GINSENG.
A DISH THAT FORCES ONE TO EAT UNTIL THEY HAVE ATTAINED A HEALTHY NUTRITIONAL BALANCE! WHAT A SHOCKER! A DISH THAT'LL MAKE YOU LIVE LONGER NO MATTER WHAT! EVEN THE JUDGES WERE BLOWN AWAY BY THIS!
JAN AKIYAMA'S CHANG SHOU HUI QUN WAS RICH IN RARITIES AND WAS PRETTY GOOD BUT IT'S NOTHING COMPARED TO GOGYO'S!
GOGYO HAS DONE IT! HE UNEXPECTEDLY LOST THE LAST ROUND TO JAN BUT HAS COME BACK FULLY RECHARGED!
……

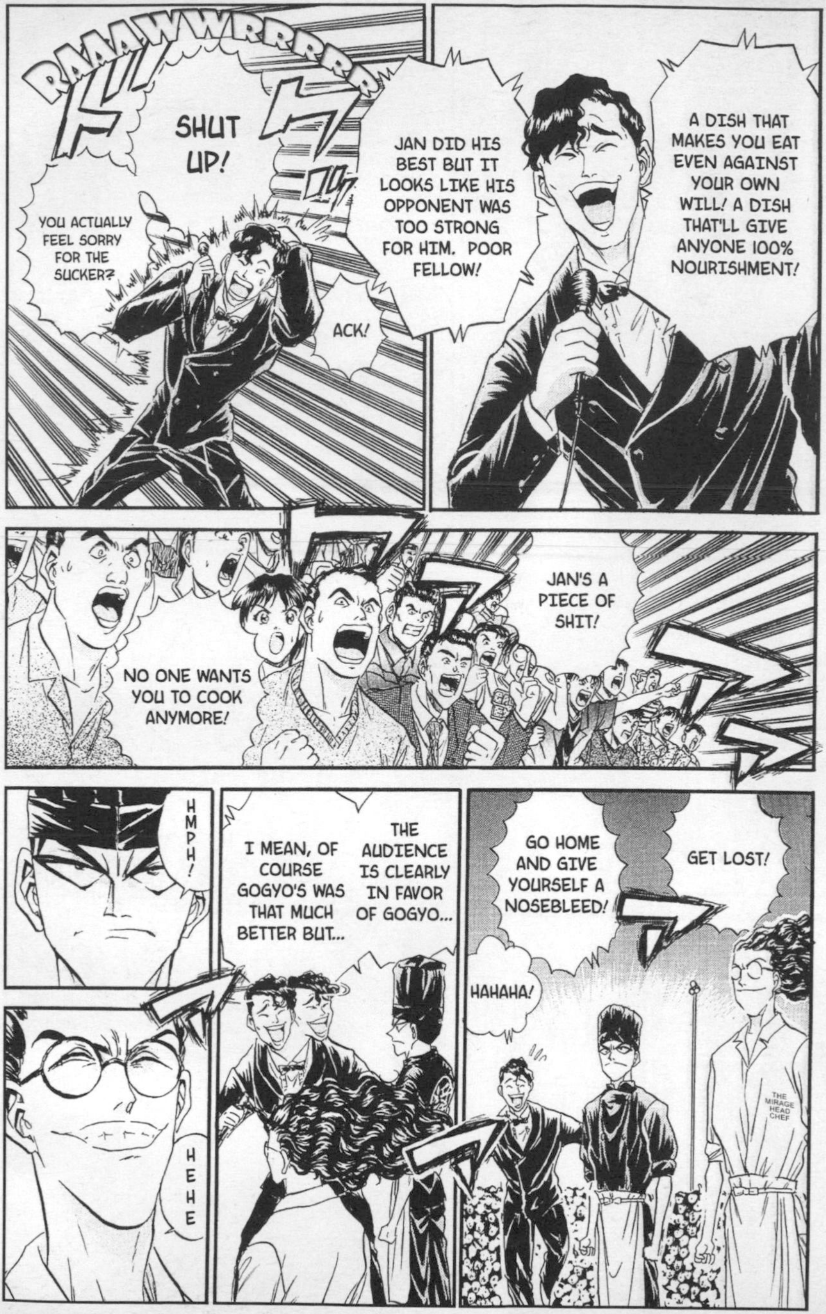
A DISH THAT MAKES YOU EAT EVEN AGAINST YOUR OWN WILL! A DISH THAT'LL GIVE ANYONE 100% NOURISHMENT!
JAN DID HIS BEST BUT IT LOOKS LIKE HIS OPPONENT WAS TOO STRONG FOR HIM. POOR FELLOW!
RAAAWWRRRRR
SHUT UP!
YOU ACTUALLY FEEL SORRY FOR THE SUCKER?
ACK!
JAN'S A PIECE OF SHIT!
NO ONE WANTS YOU TO COOK ANYMORE!
GET LOST!
GO HOME AND GIVE YOURSELF A NOSEBLEED!
HAHAHA!
THE MIRAGE HEAD CHEF
THE AUDIENCE IS CLEARLY IN FAVOR OF GOGYO...
I MEAN, OF COURSE GOGYO'S WAS THAT MUCH BETTER BUT...
HMPH!
HEHE

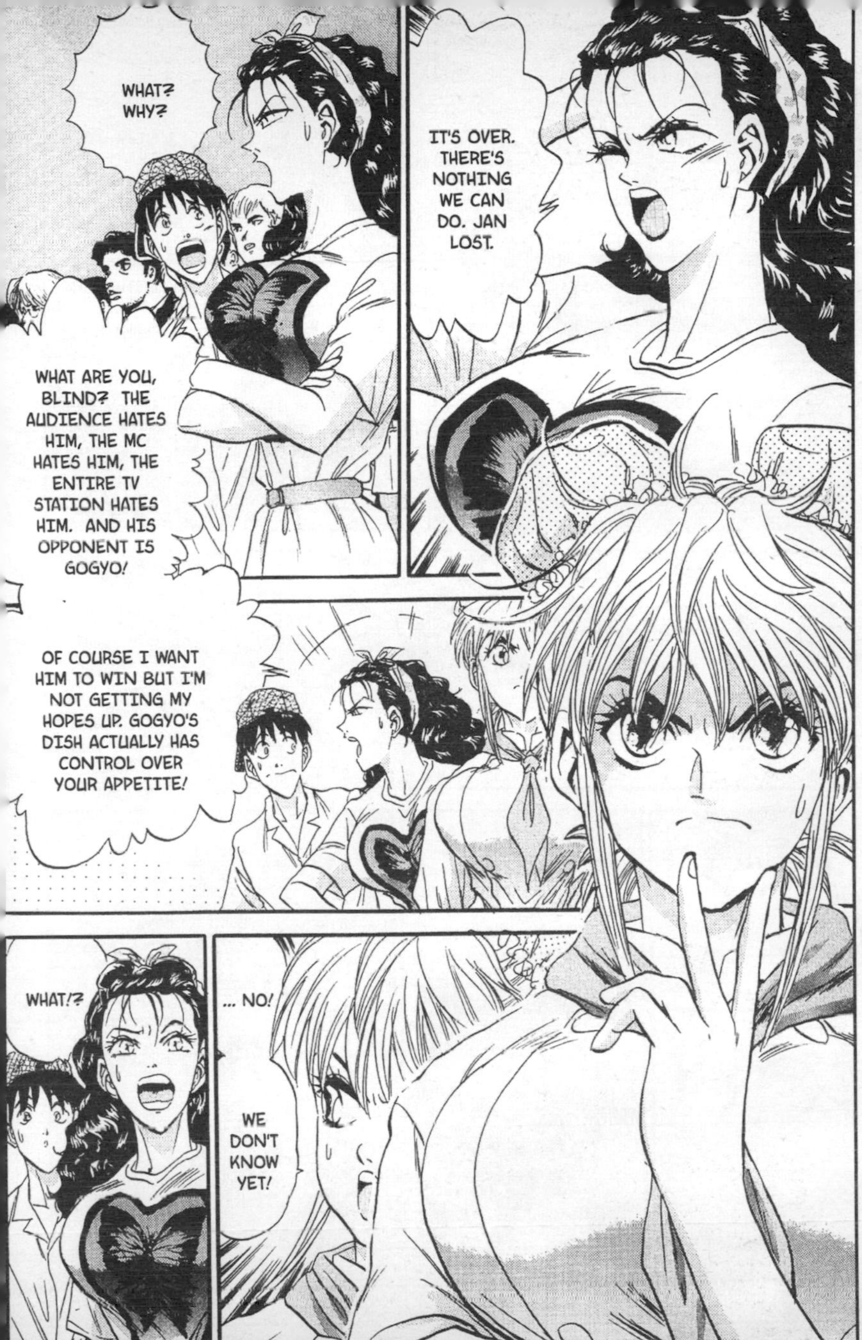
IT'S OVER. THERE'S NOTHING WE CAN DO. JAN LOST.
WHAT? WHY?
WHAT ARE YOU, BLIND? THE AUDIENCE HATES HIM, THE MC HATES HIM, THE ENTIRE TV STATION HATES HIM. AND HIS OPPONENT IS GOGYO!
OF COURSE I WANT HIM TO WIN BUT I'M NOT GETTING MY HOPES UP. GOGYO'S DISH ACTUALLY HAS CONTROL OVER YOUR APPETITE!
... NO!
WE DON'T KNOW YET!
WHAT!?

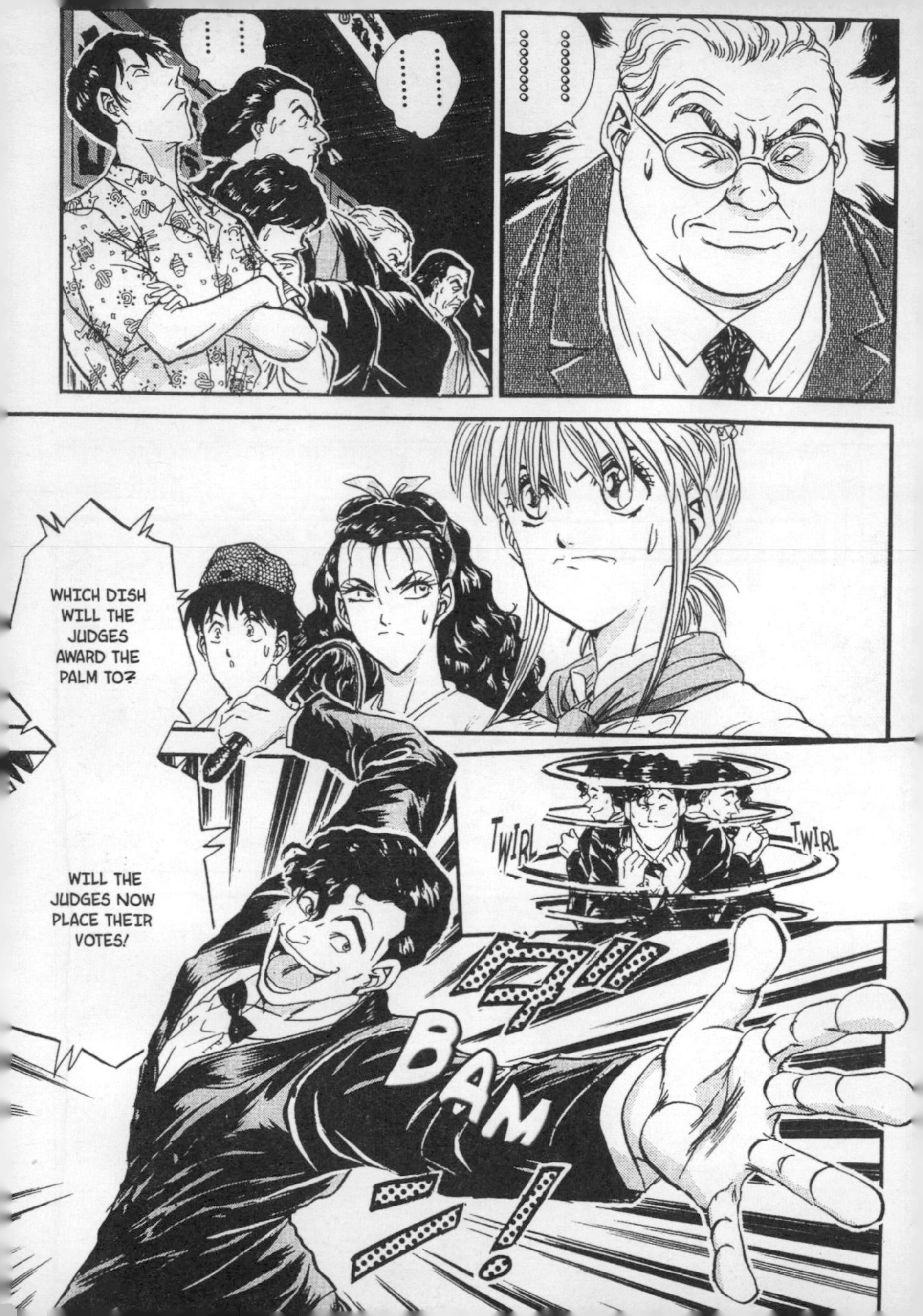

WHICH DISH WILL THE JUDGES AWARD THE PALM TO?
WILL THE JUDGES NOW PLACE THEIR VOTES!
TWIRL
TWIRL
BAM!

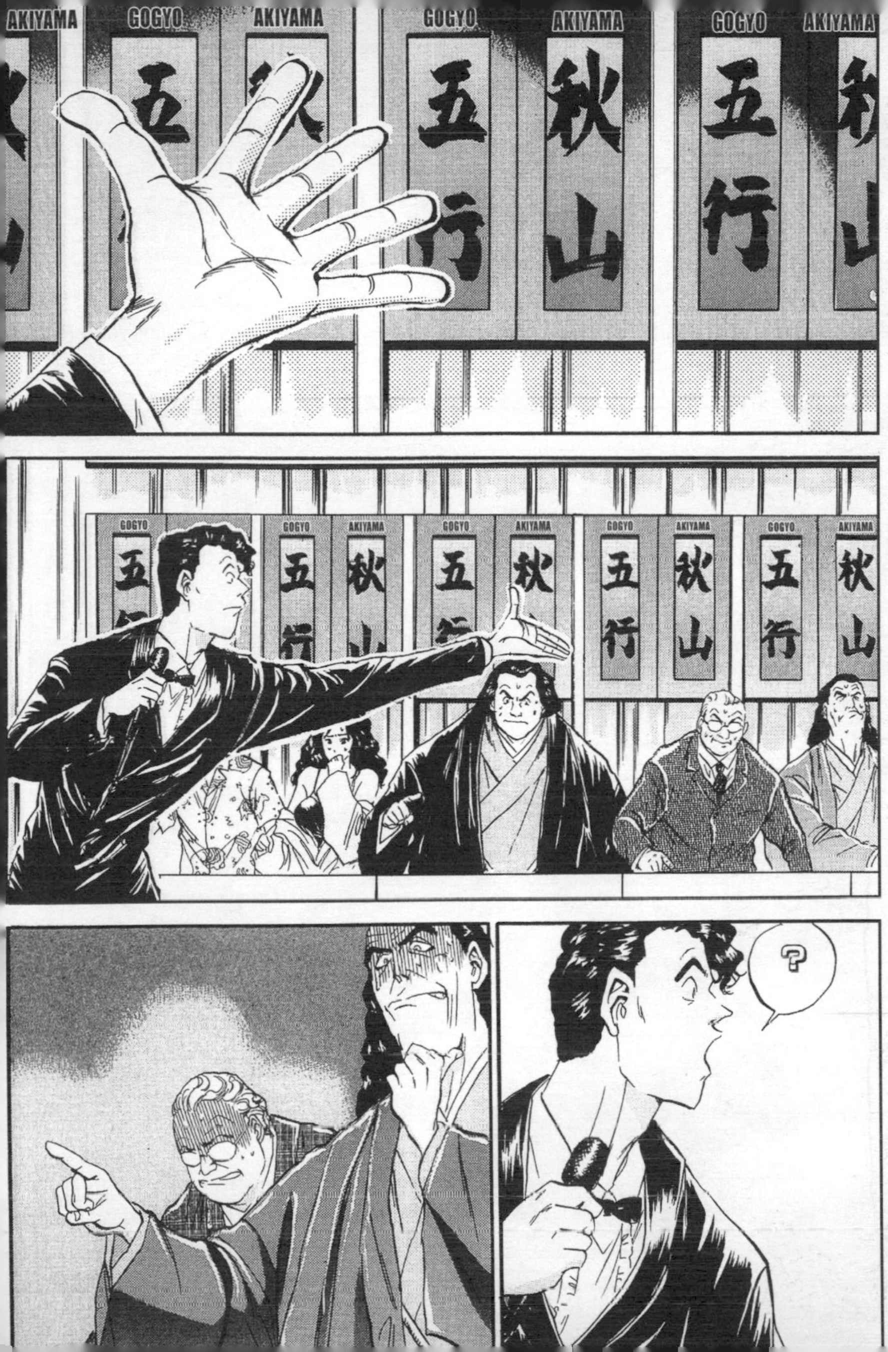
AKIYAMA
GOGYO
五行
AKIYAMA
秋山
GOGYO
五行
AKIYAMA
GOGYO
五
AKIYAMA
AKIYAMA
秋山
GOGYO
五行
AKIYAMA
秋山
GOGYO
五行
AKIYAMA
秋
GOGYO
五
AKIYAMA
秋
GOGYO
GOGYO
五
?

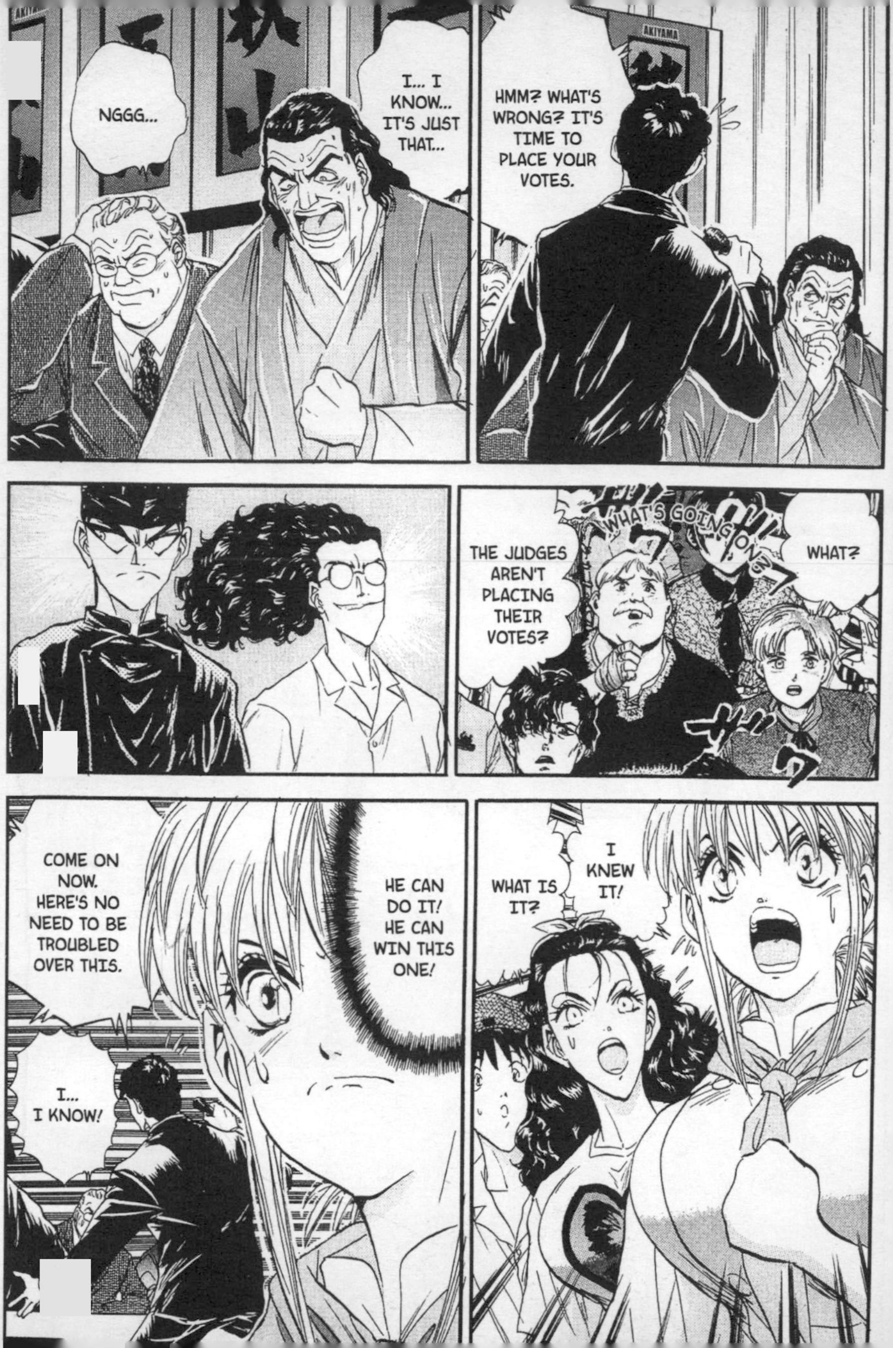
HMM? WHAT'S WRONG? IT'S TIME TO PLACE YOUR VOTES.
I... I KNOW... IT'S JUST THAT...
NGGG...
WHAT?
WHAT'S GOING ON?
THE JUDGES AREN'T PLACING THEIR VOTES?
I KNEW IT!
WHAT IS IT?
HE CAN DO IT! HE CAN WIN THIS ONE!
COME ON NOW. HERE'S NO NEED TO BE TROUBLED OVER THIS.
I... I KNOW!

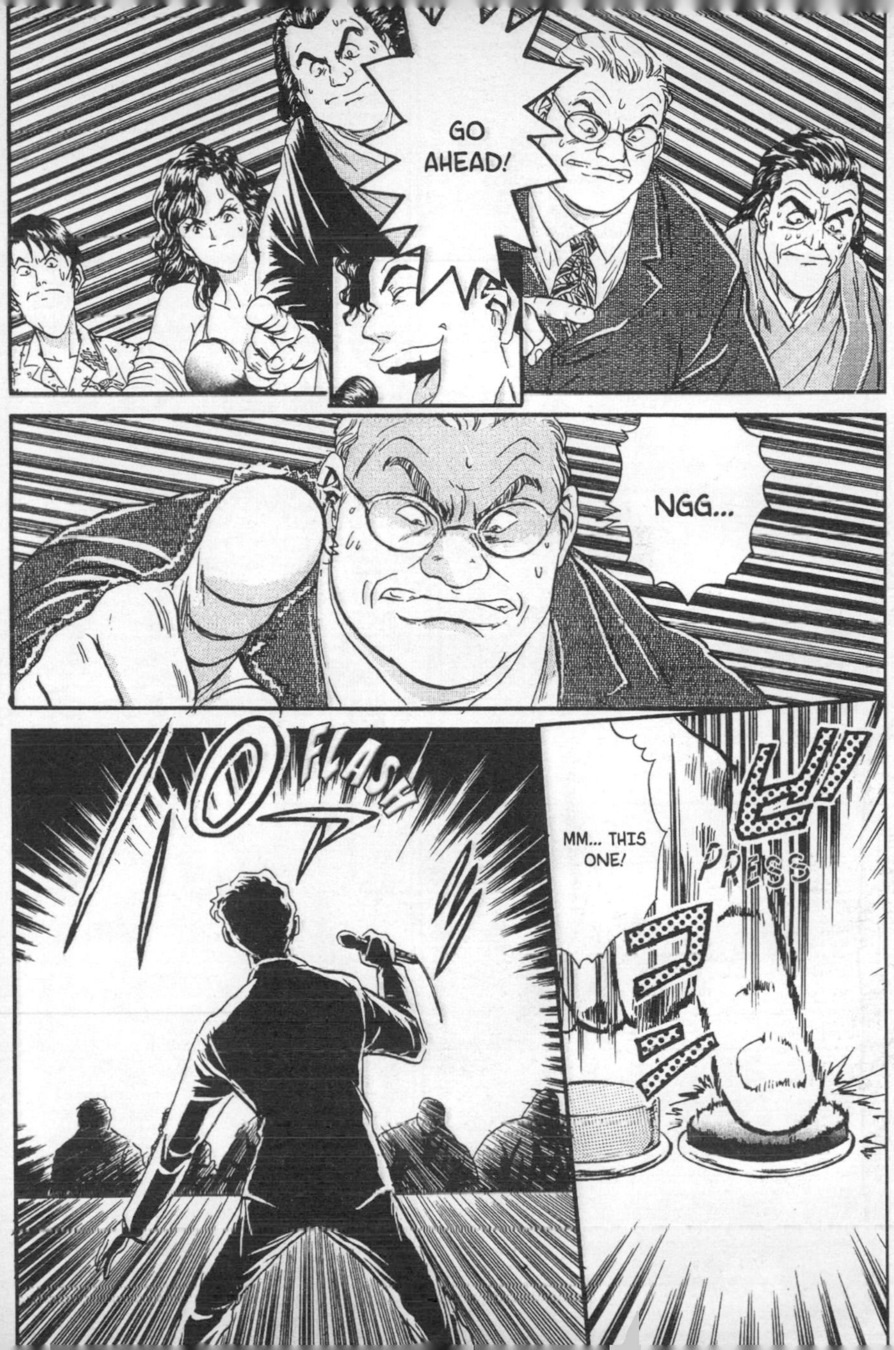
GO AHEAD!
NGG...
MM... THIS ONE!
PRESS
FLASH

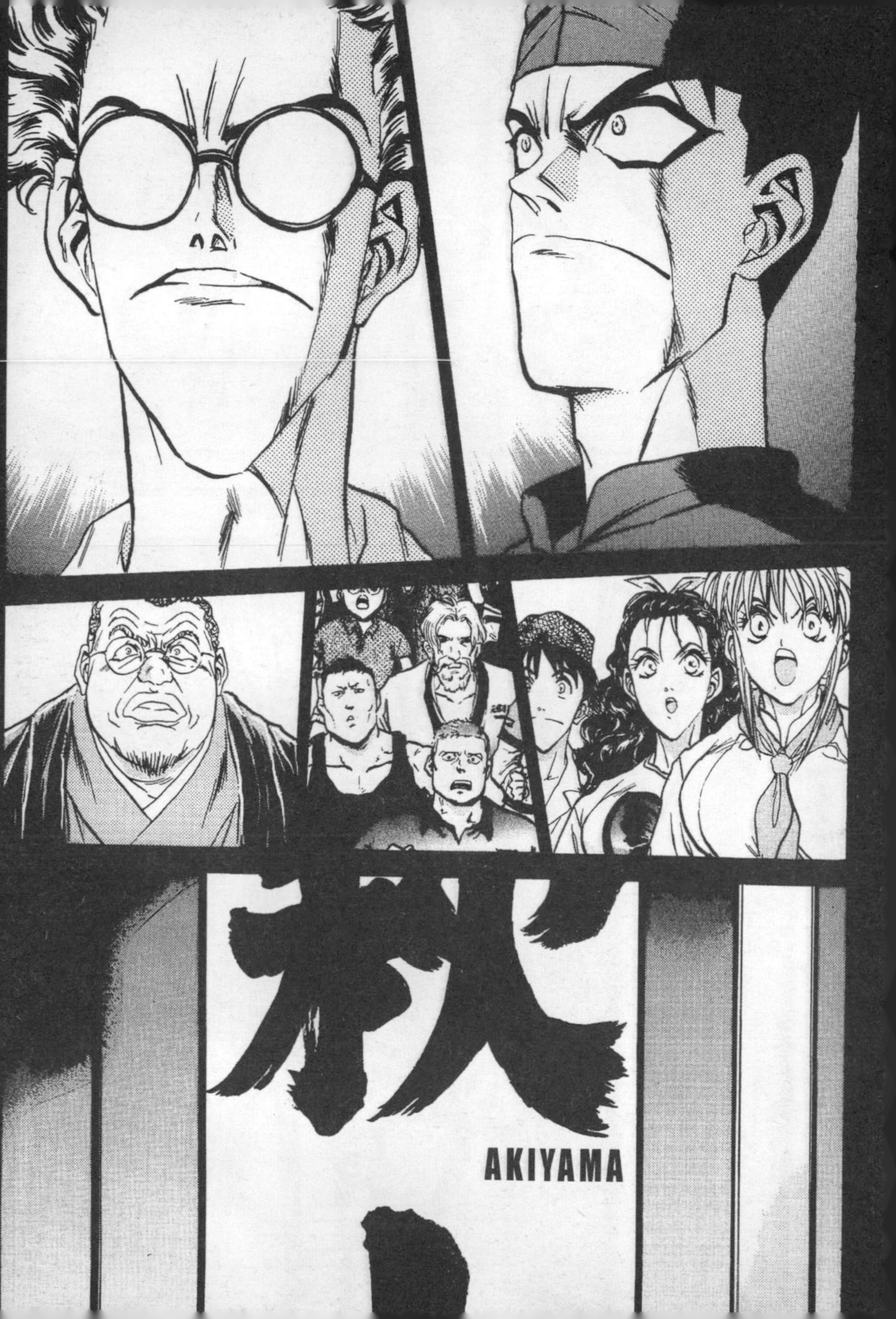
AKIYAMA

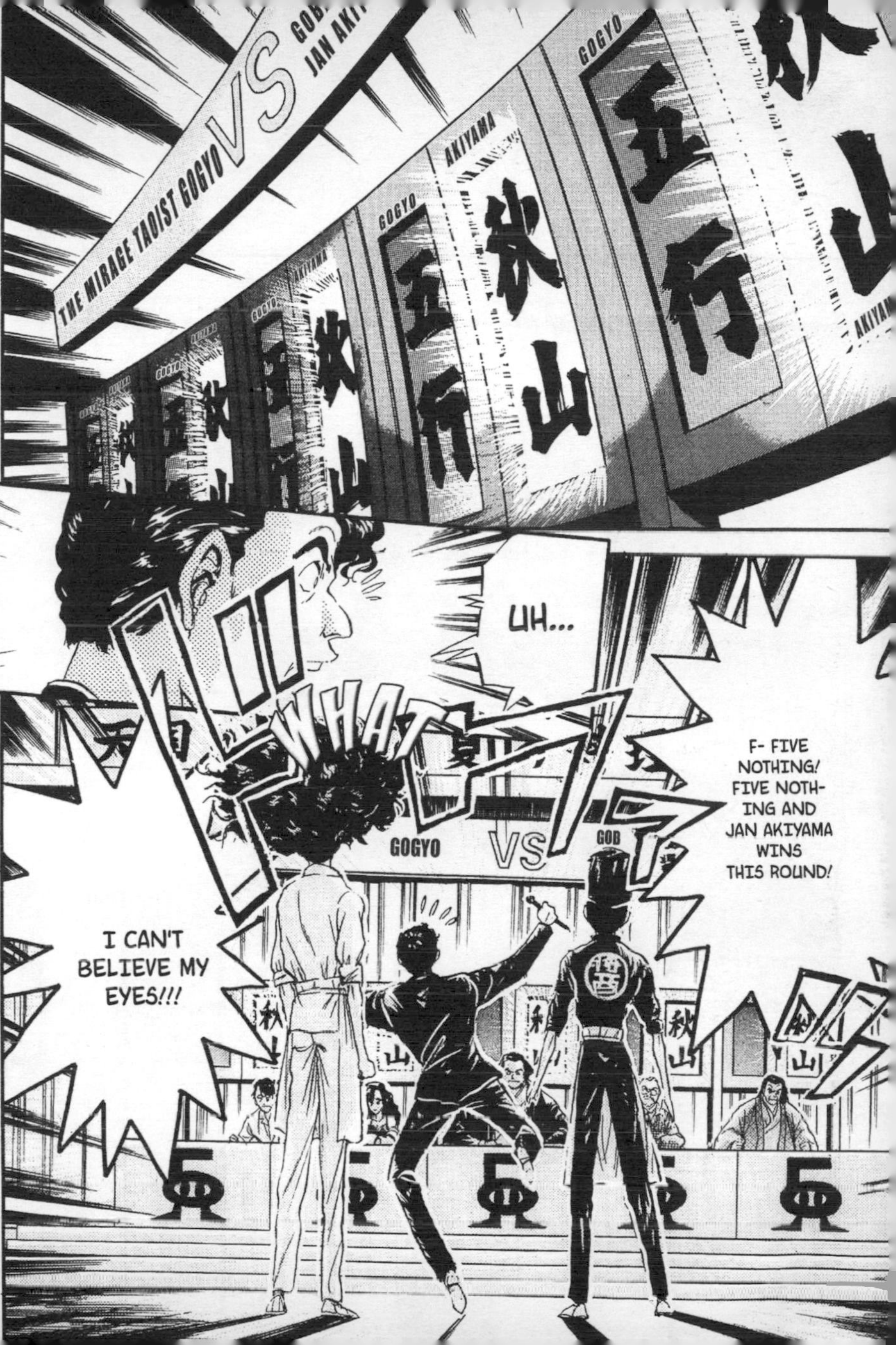
THE MIRAGE TAOIST GOGYO
VS
GOGYO
五行
AKIYAMA
秋山
UH...
WHAT
F- FIVE NOTHING! FIVE NOTH-ING AND JAN AKIYAMA WINS THIS ROUND!
GOGYO
VS
GOB
I CAN'T BELIEVE MY EYES!!!

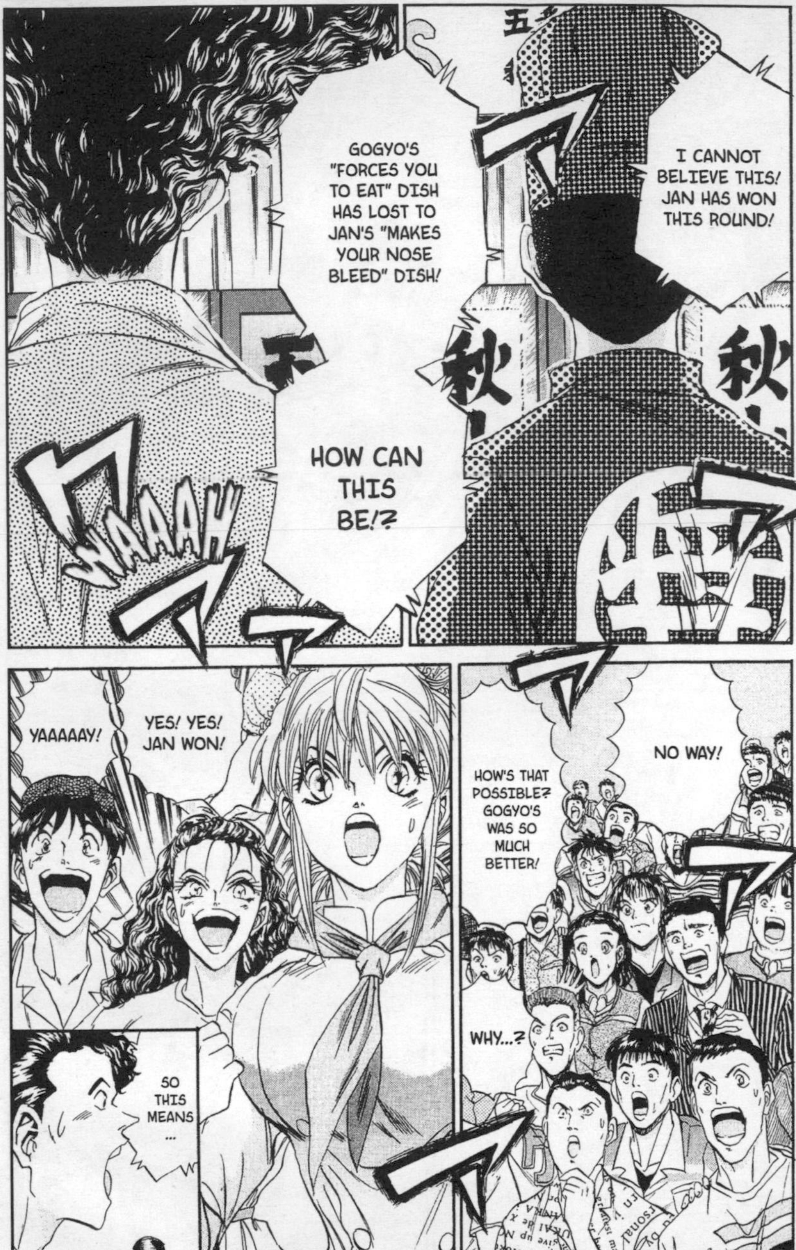
I CANNOT BELIEVE THIS! JAN HAS WON THIS ROUND!
GOGYO'S "FORCES YOU TO EAT" DISH HAS LOST TO JAN'S "MAKES YOUR NOSE BLEED" DISH!
HOW CAN THIS BE!?
NO WAY!
HOW'S THAT POSSIBLE? GOGYO'S WAS SO MUCH BETTER!
WHY...?
YES! YES! JAN WON!
YAAAAAY!
SO THIS MEANS ...

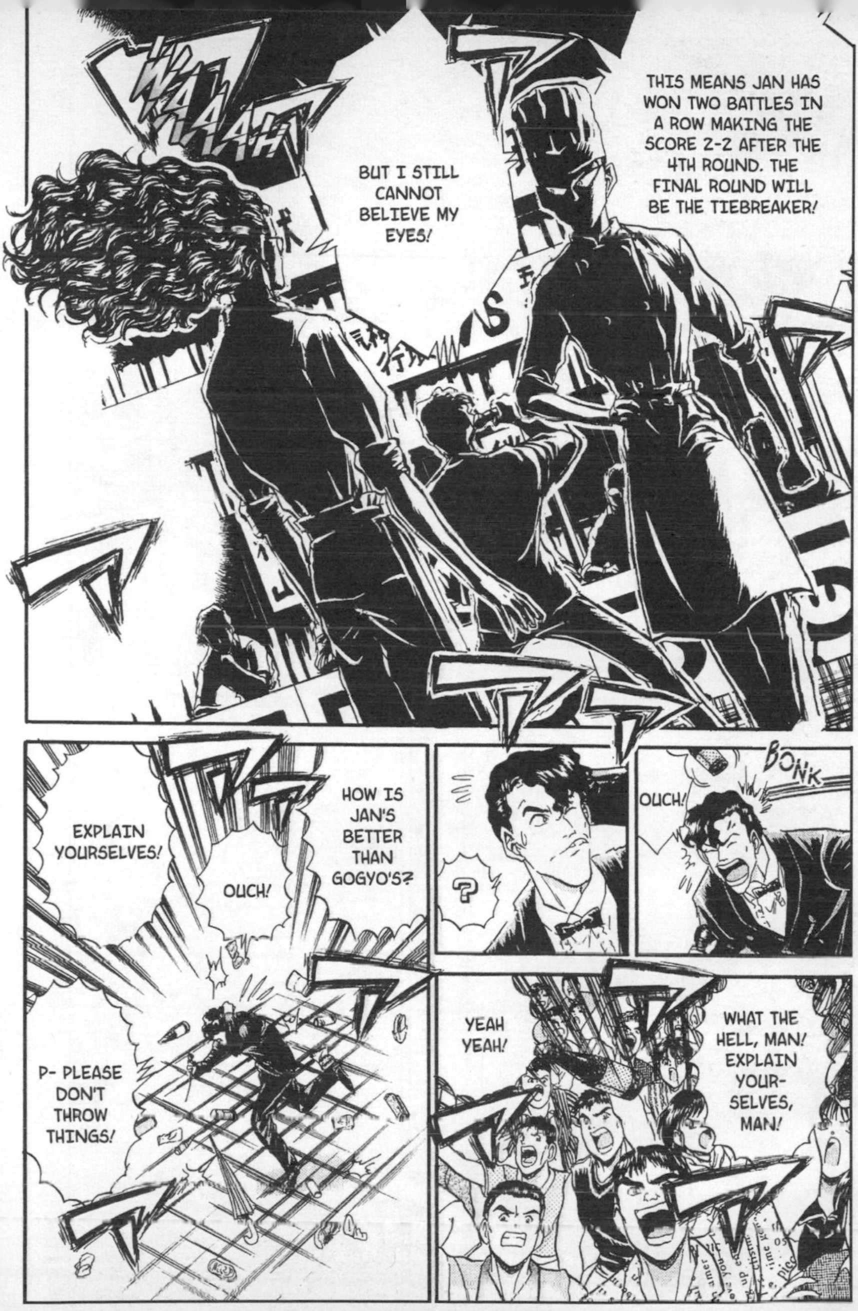
THIS MEANS JAN HAS WON TWO BATTLES IN A ROW MAKING THE SCORE 2-2 AFTER THE 4TH ROUND. THE FINAL ROUND WILL BE THE TIEBREAKER!
BUT I STILL CANNOT BELIEVE MY EYES!
WAAAAH
BONK
OUCH!
?
WHAT THE HELL, MAN! EXPLAIN YOUR-SELVES, MAN!
YEAH YEAH!
HOW IS JAN'S BETTER THAN GOGYO'S?
EXPLAIN YOURSELVES!
OUCH!
P- PLEASE DON'T THROW THINGS!

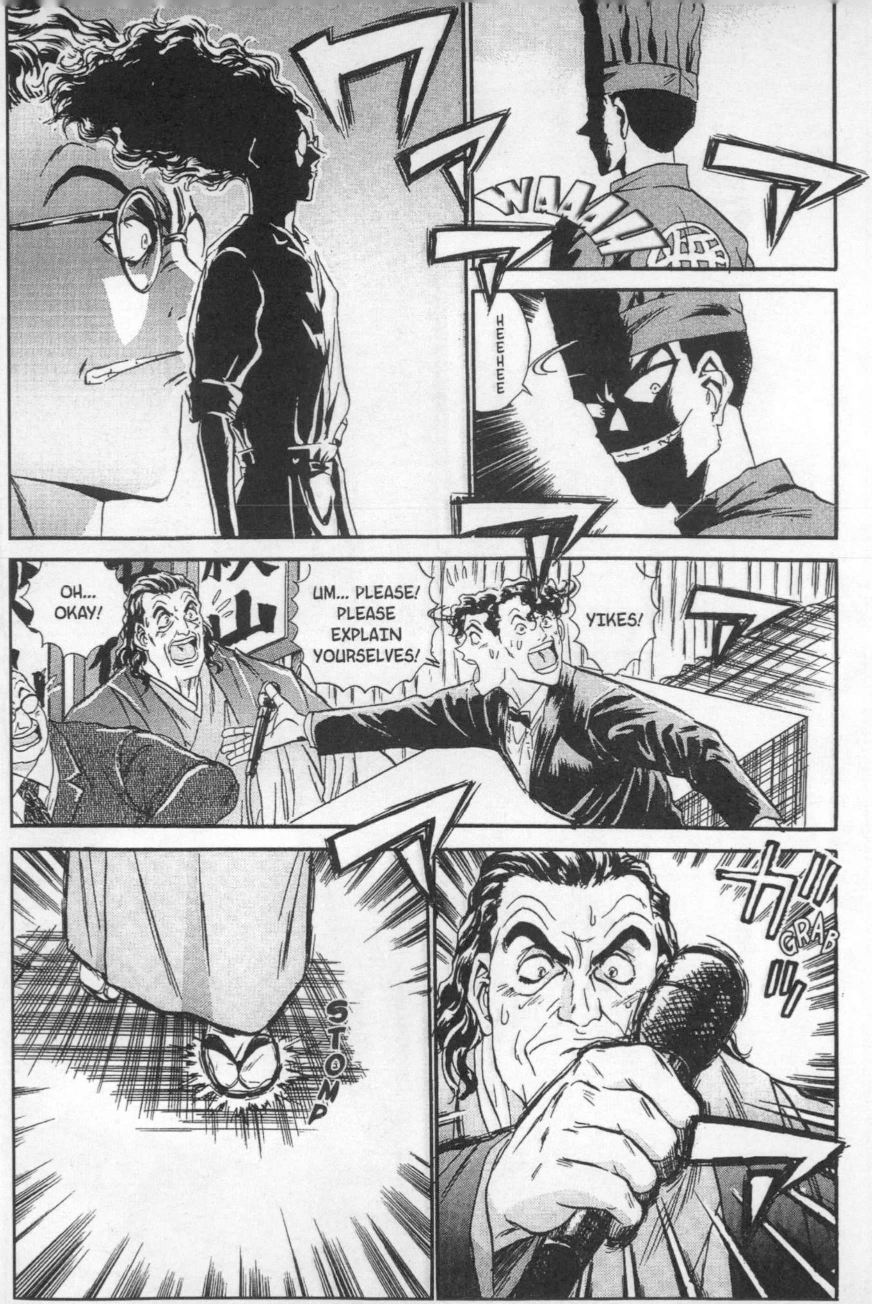
WAAA
HEEHEE
YIKES!
UM... PLEASE! PLEASE EXPLAIN YOURSELVES!
OH... OKAY!
GRAB
STOMP

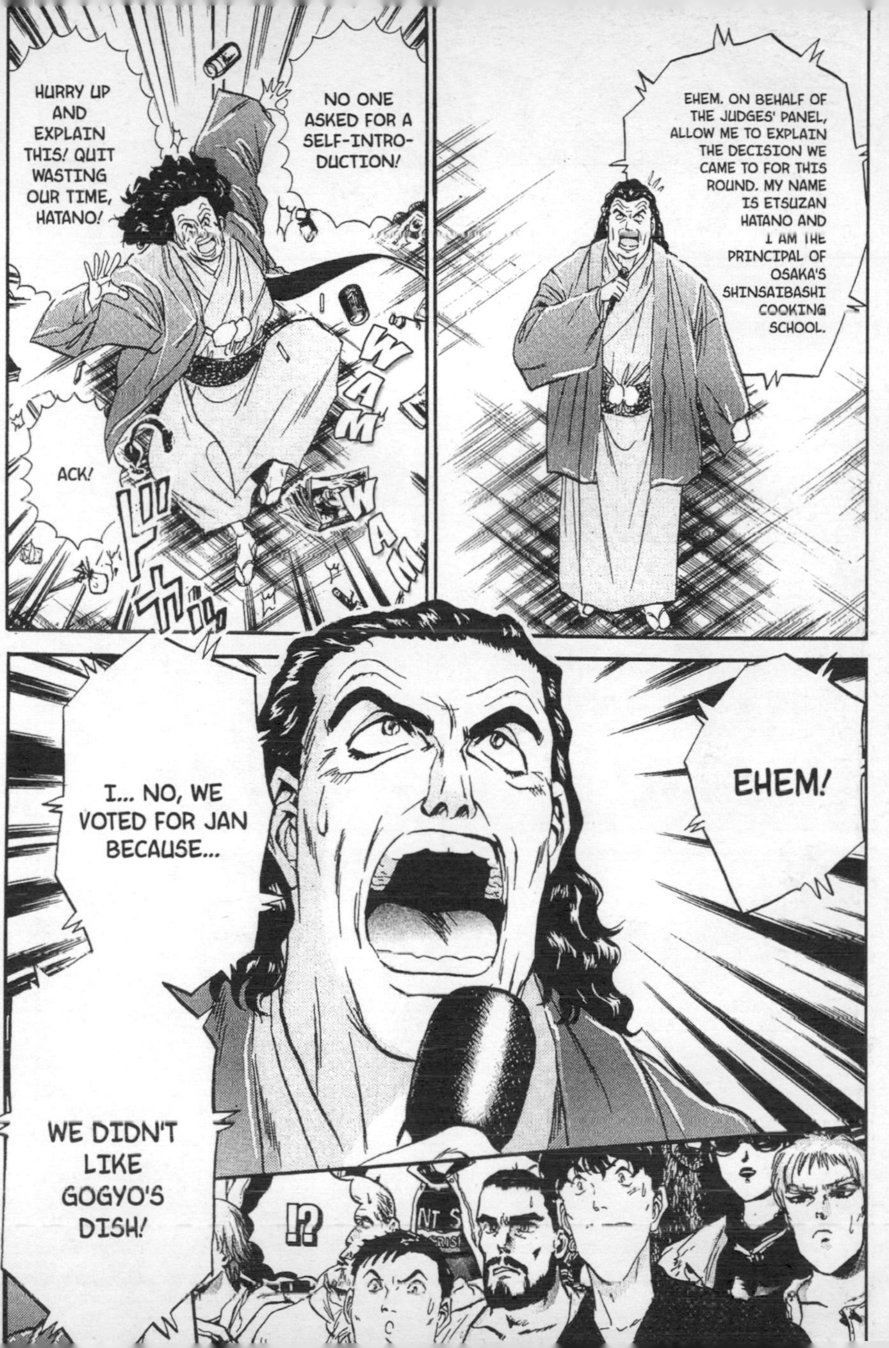

EHEM. ON BEHALF OF THE JUDGES' PANEL, ALLOW ME TO EXPLAIN THE DECISION WE CAME TO FOR THIS ROUND. MY NAME IS ETSUZAN HATANO AND I AM THE PRINCIPAL OF OSAKA'S SHINSAIBASHI COOKING SCHOOL.
NO ONE ASKED FOR A SELF-INTRO-DUCTION!
HURRY UP AND EXPLAIN THIS! QUIT WASTING OUR TIME, HATANO!
WAM
WAM
ACK!
EHEM!
I... NO, WE VOTED FOR JAN BECAUSE...
WE DIDN'T LIKE GOGYO'S DISH!
!?

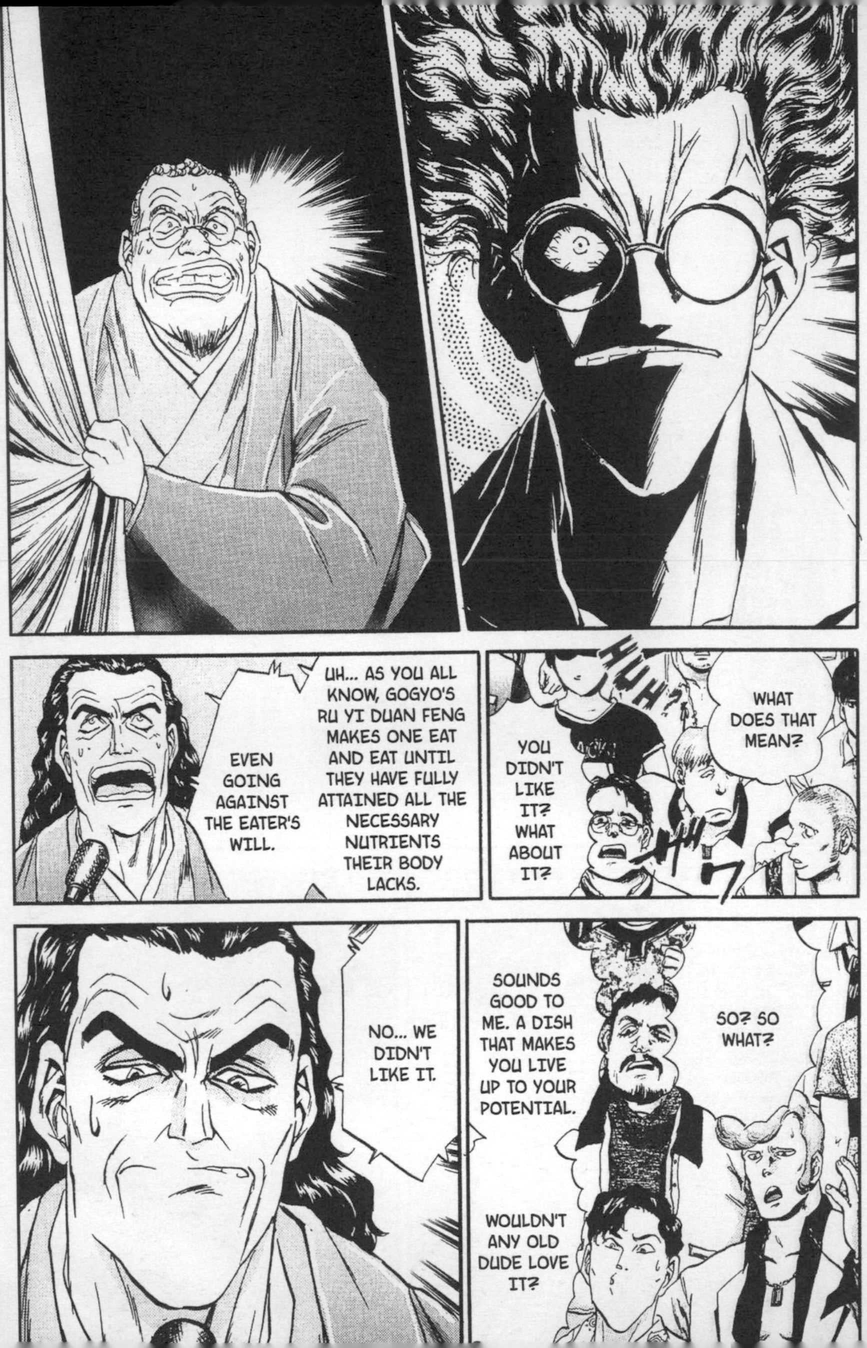
WHAT DOES THAT MEAN?
HUH?
YOU DIDN'T LIKE IT? WHAT ABOUT IT?
UH... AS YOU ALL KNOW, GOGYO'S RU YI DUAN FENG MAKES ONE EAT AND EAT UNTIL THEY HAVE FULLY ATTAINED ALL THE NECESSARY NUTRIENTS THEIR BODY LACKS.
EVEN GOING AGAINST THE EATER'S WILL.
SO? SO WHAT?
SOUNDS GOOD TO ME. A DISH THAT MAKES YOU LIVE UP TO YOUR POTENTIAL.
WOULDN'T ANY OLD DUDE LOVE IT?
NO... WE DIDN'T LIKE IT.

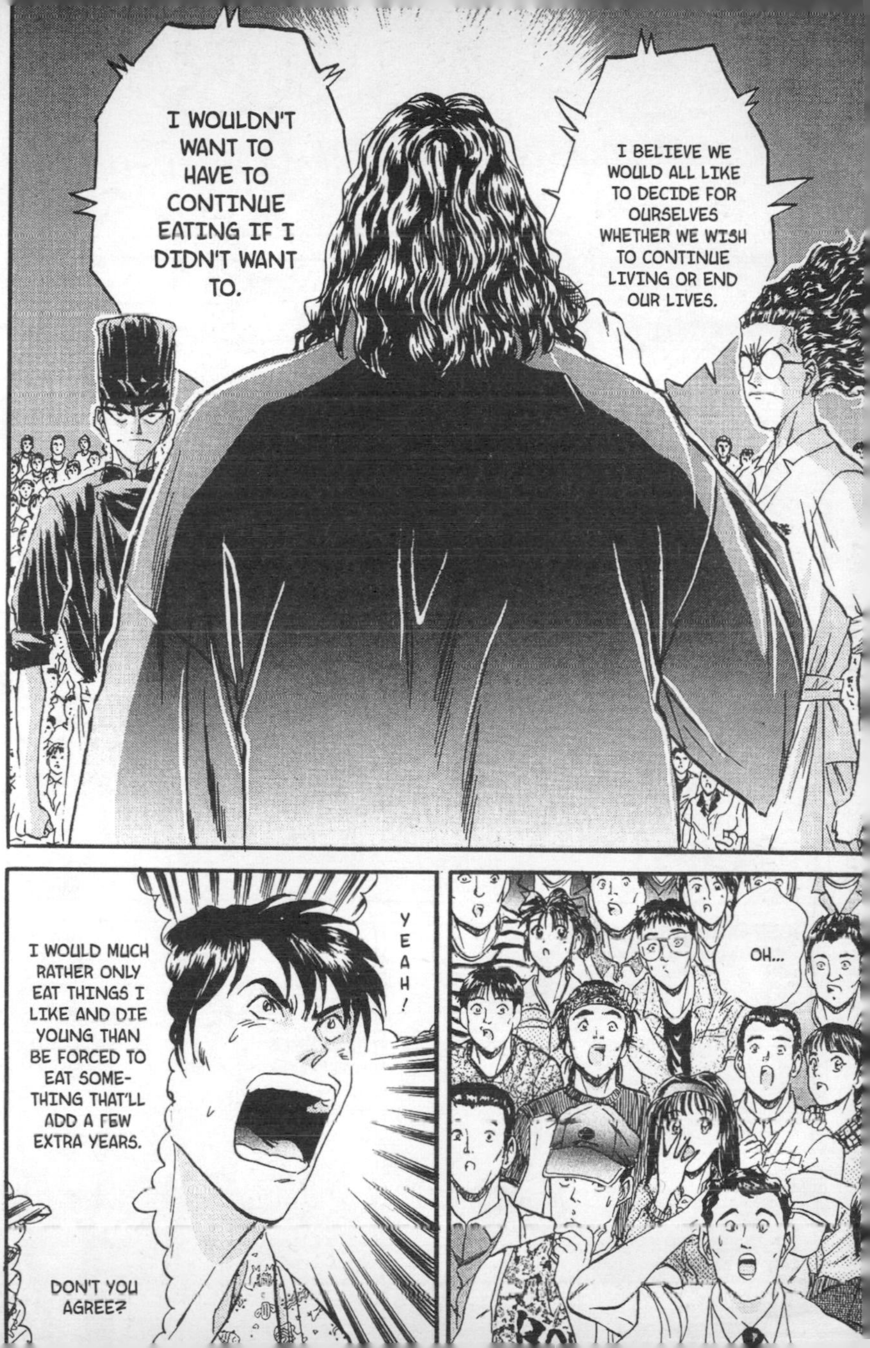
I BELIEVE WE WOULD ALL LIKE TO DECIDE FOR OURSELVES WHETHER WE WISH TO CONTINUE LIVING OR END OUR LIVES.
I WOULDN'T WANT TO HAVE TO CONTINUE EATING IF I DIDN'T WANT TO.
OH...
YEAH!
I WOULD MUCH RATHER ONLY EAT THINGS I LIKE AND DIE YOUNG THAN BE FORCED TO EAT SOME-THING THAT'LL ADD A FEW EXTRA YEARS.
DON'T YOU AGREE?

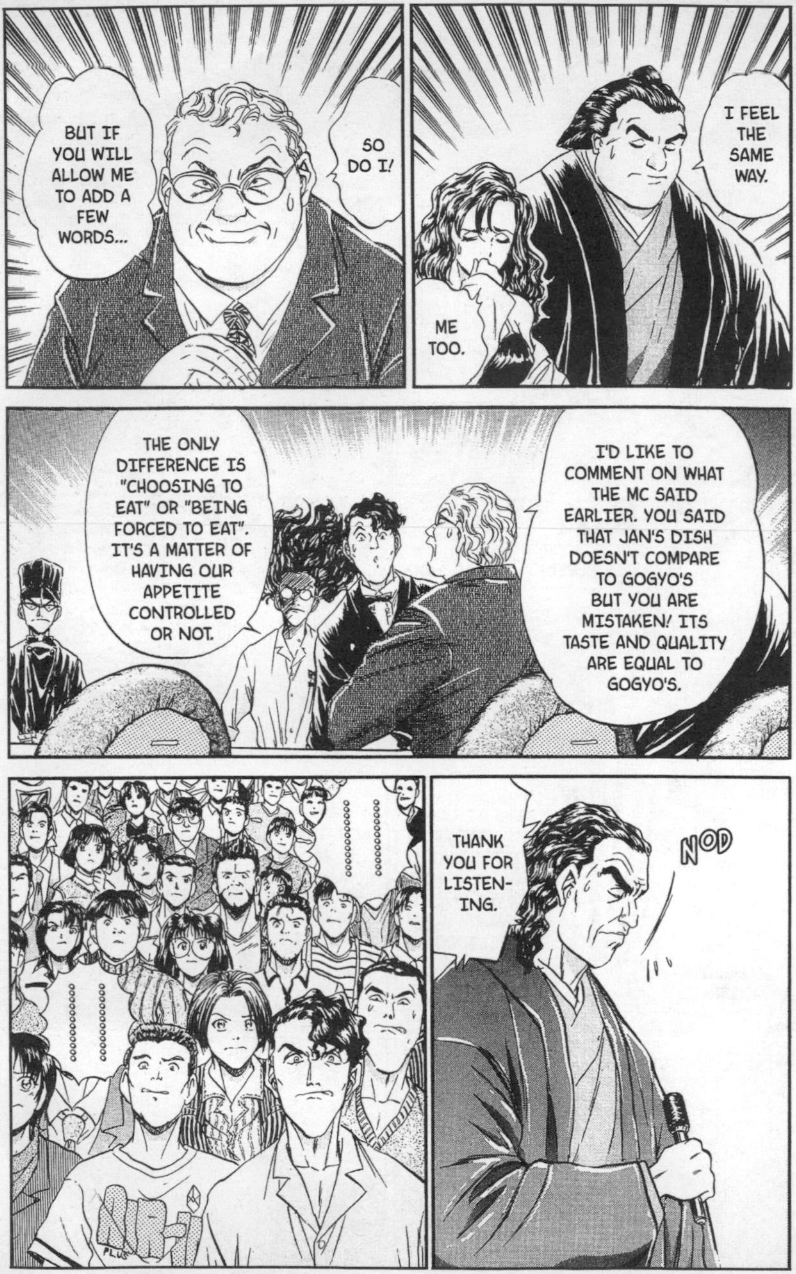
I FEEL THE SAME WAY.
ME TOO.
SO DO I!
BUT IF YOU WILL ALLOW ME TO ADD A FEW WORDS...
I'D LIKE TO COMMENT ON WHAT THE MC SAID EARLIER. YOU SAID THAT JAN'S DISH DOESN'T COMPARE TO GOGYO'S BUT YOU ARE MISTAKEN! ITS TASTE AND QUALITY ARE EQUAL TO GOGYO'S.
THE ONLY DIFFERENCE IS "CHOOSING TO EAT" OR "BEING FORCED TO EAT". IT'S A MATTER OF HAVING OUR APPETITE CONTROLLED OR NOT.
THANK YOU FOR LISTEN-ING.
NOD

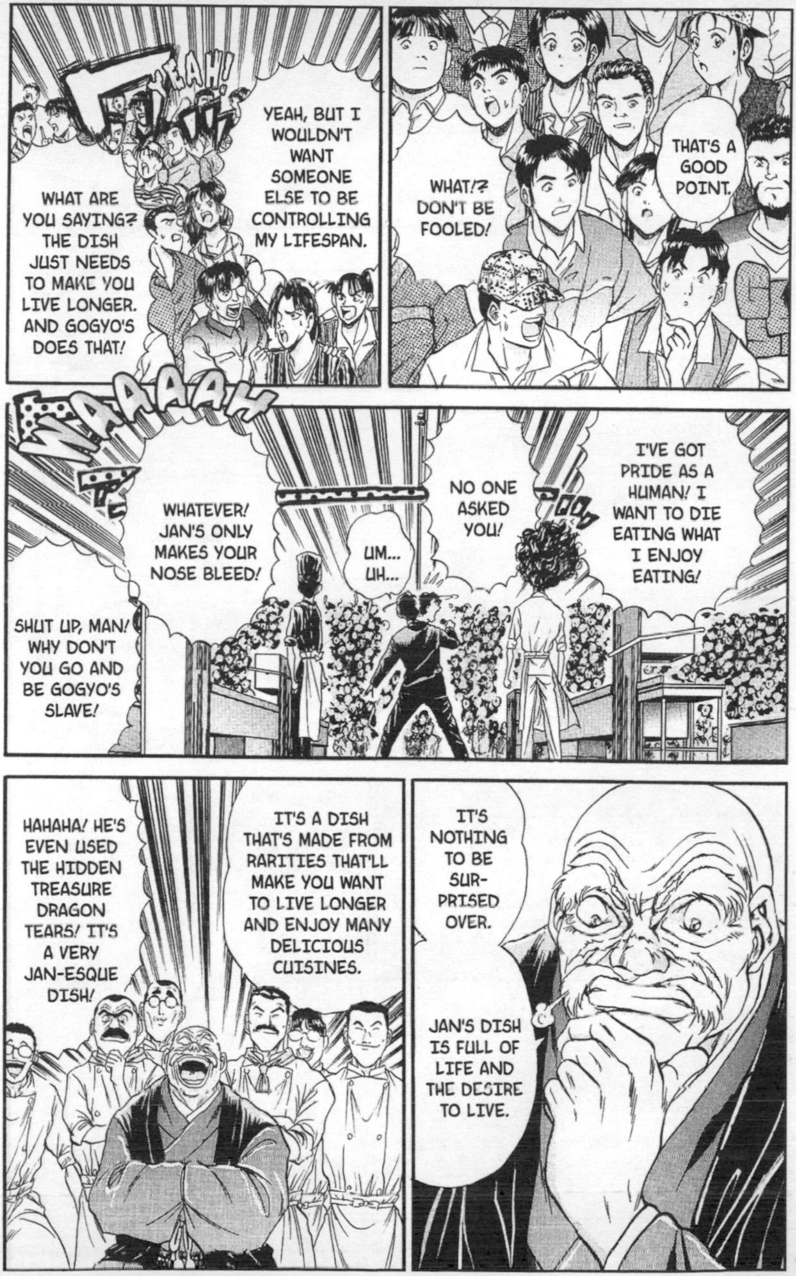
THAT'S A GOOD POINT.
WHAT!? DON'T BE FOOLED!
YEAH!
YEAH, BUT I WOULDN'T WANT SOMEONE ELSE TO BE CONTROLLING MY LIFESPAN.
WHAT ARE YOU SAYING? THE DISH JUST NEEDS TO MAKE YOU LIVE LONGER. AND GOGYO'S DOES THAT!
I'VE GOT PRIDE AS A HUMAN! I WANT TO DIE EATING WHAT I ENJOY EATING!
NO ONE ASKED YOU!
UM... UH...
WHATEVER! JAN'S ONLY MAKES YOUR NOSE BLEED!
WAAAAH
SHUT UP, MAN! WHY DON'T YOU GO AND BE GOGYO'S SLAVE!
IT'S NOTHING TO BE SUR-PRISED OVER.
JAN'S DISH IS FULL OF LIFE AND THE DESIRE TO LIVE.
IT'S A DISH THAT'S MADE FROM RARITIES THAT'LL MAKE YOU WANT TO LIVE LONGER AND ENJOY MANY DELICIOUS CUISINES.
HAHAHA! HE'S EVEN USED THE HIDDEN TREASURE DRAGON TEARS! IT'S A VERY JAN-ESQUE DISH!

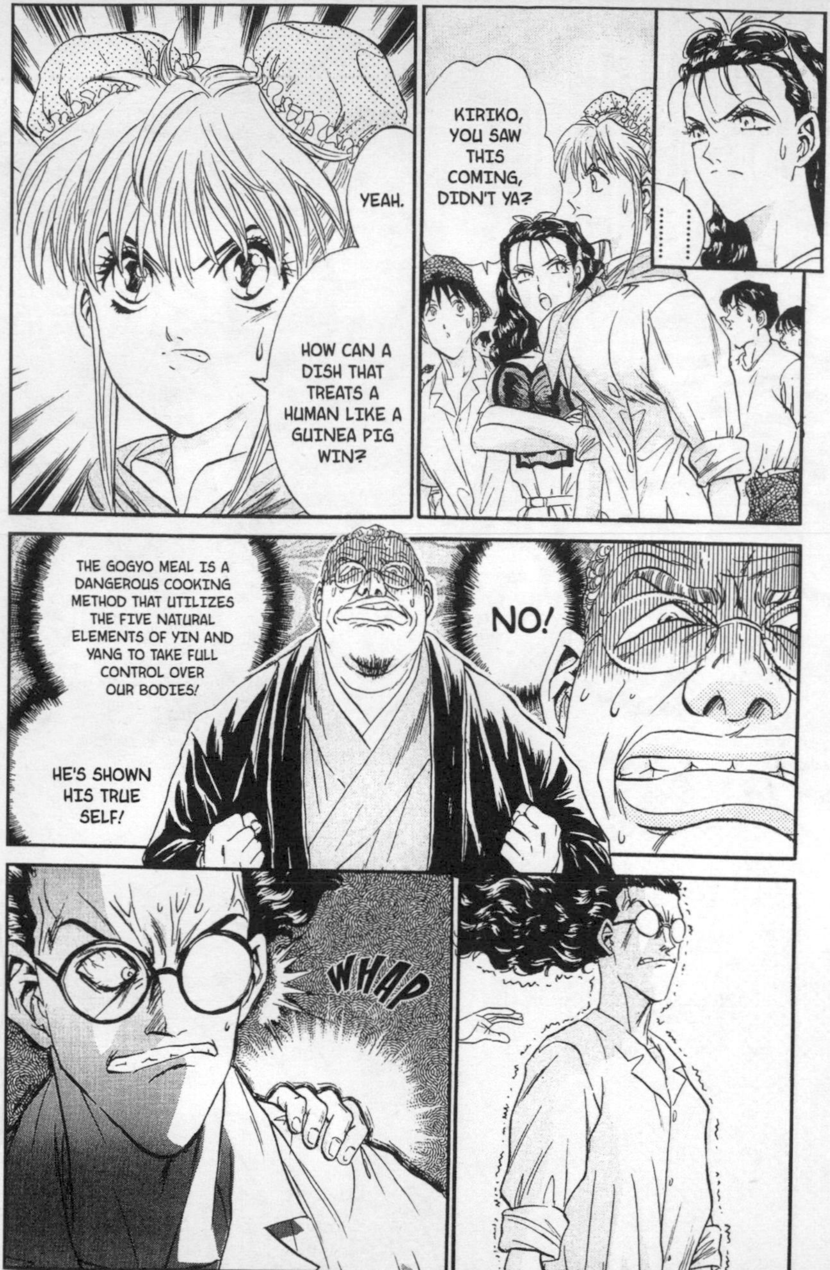
......
KIRIKO, YOU SAW THIS COMING, DIDN'T YA?
YEAH.
HOW CAN A DISH THAT TREATS A HUMAN LIKE A GUINEA PIG WIN?
NO!
THE GOGYO MEAL IS A DANGEROUS COOKING METHOD THAT UTILIZES THE FIVE NATURAL ELEMENTS OF YIN AND YANG TO TAKE FULL CONTROL OVER OUR BODIES!
HE'S SHOWN HIS TRUE SELF!
WHAP

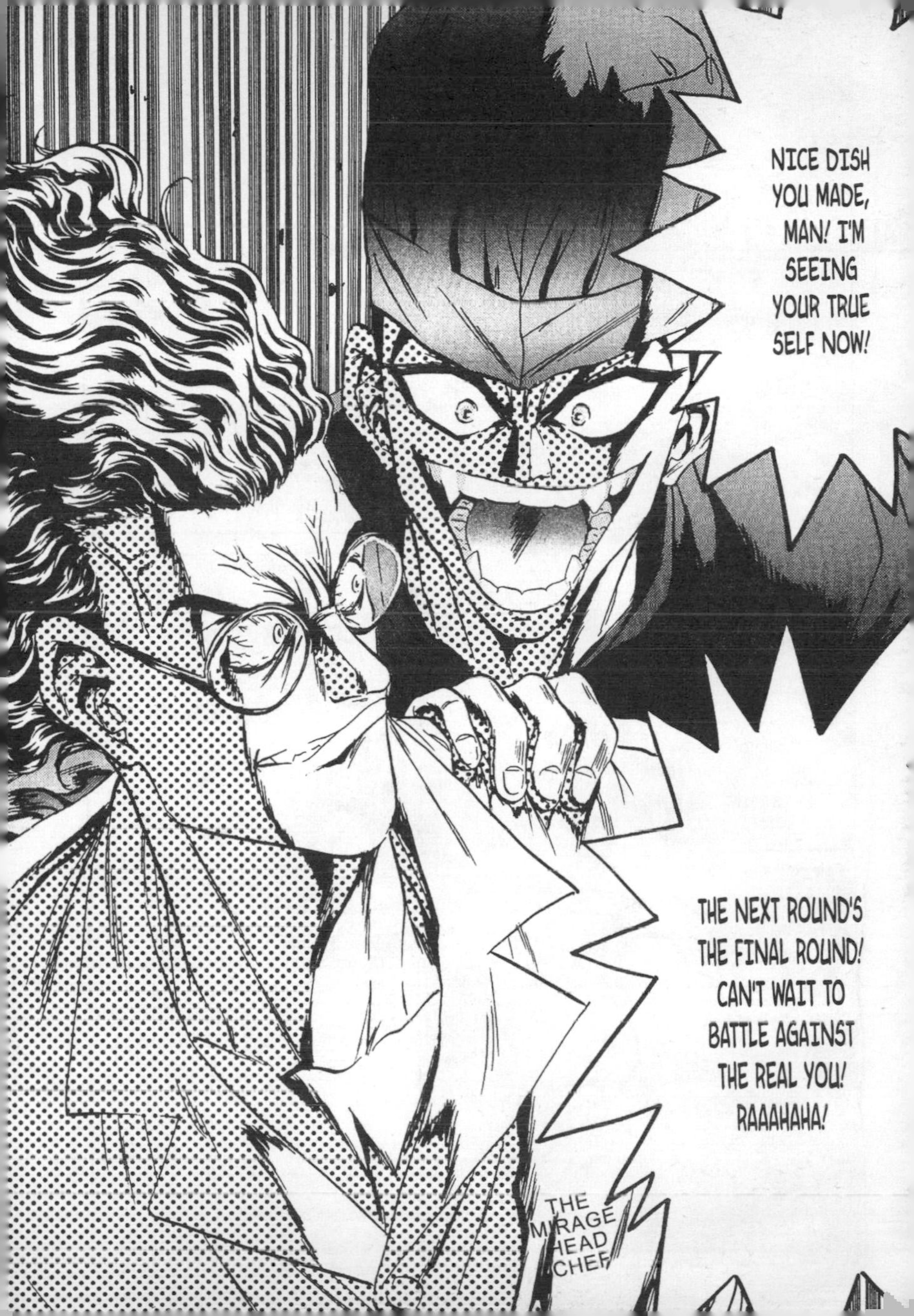
NICE DISH YOU MADE, MAN! I'M SEEING YOUR TRUE SELF NOW!
THE NEXT ROUND'S THE FINAL ROUND! CAN'T WAIT TO BATTLE AGAINST THE REAL YOU! RAAAHAHA!
THE MIRAGE HEAD CHEF

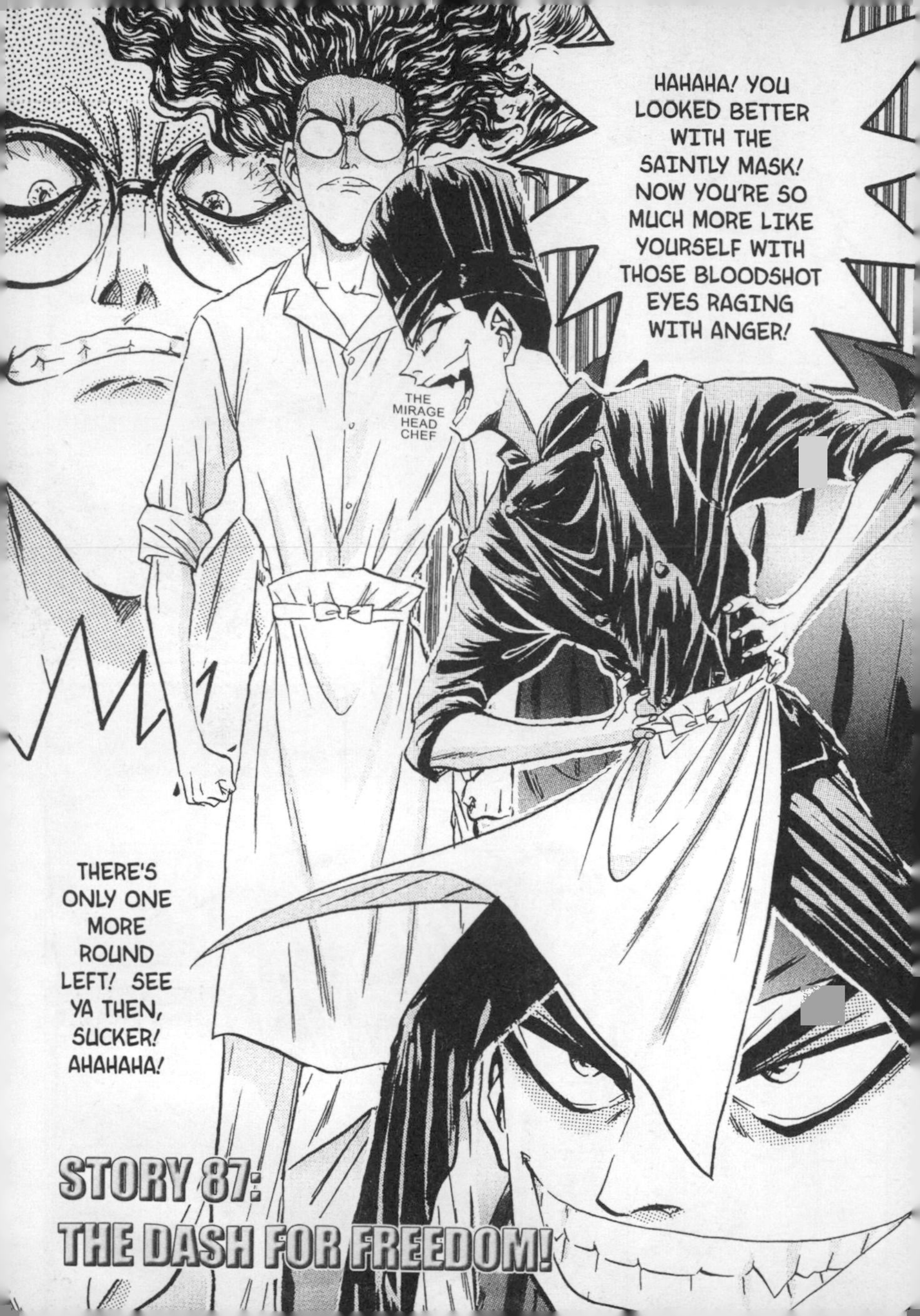
HAHAHA! YOU LOOKED BETTER WITH THE SAINTLY MASK! NOW YOU'RE SO MUCH MORE LIKE YOURSELF WITH THOSE BLOODSHOT EYES RAGING WITH ANGER!
THE MIRAGE HEAD CHEF
THERE'S ONLY ONE MORE ROUND LEFT! SEE YA THEN, SUCKER! AHAHAHA!
STORY 87:
THE DASH FOR FREEDOM!

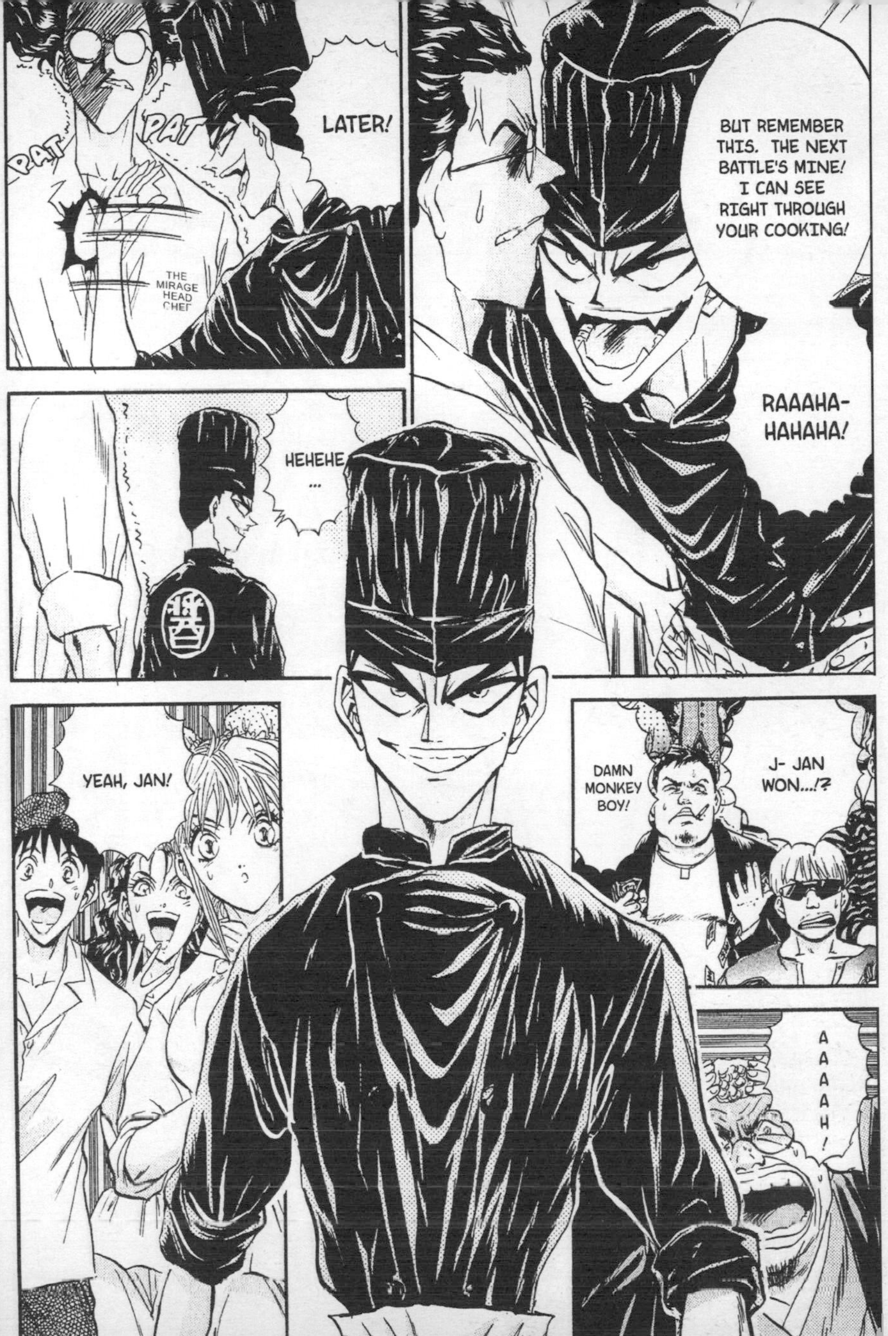
BUT REMEMBER THIS. THE NEXT BATTLE'S MINE! I CAN SEE RIGHT THROUGH YOUR COOKING!
RAAAHA-HAHAHA!
LATER!
PAT PAT
THE MIRAGE HEAD CHEF
HEHEHE ...
J- JAN WON...!?
DAMN MONKEY BOY!
AAAAAH!
YEAH, JAN!

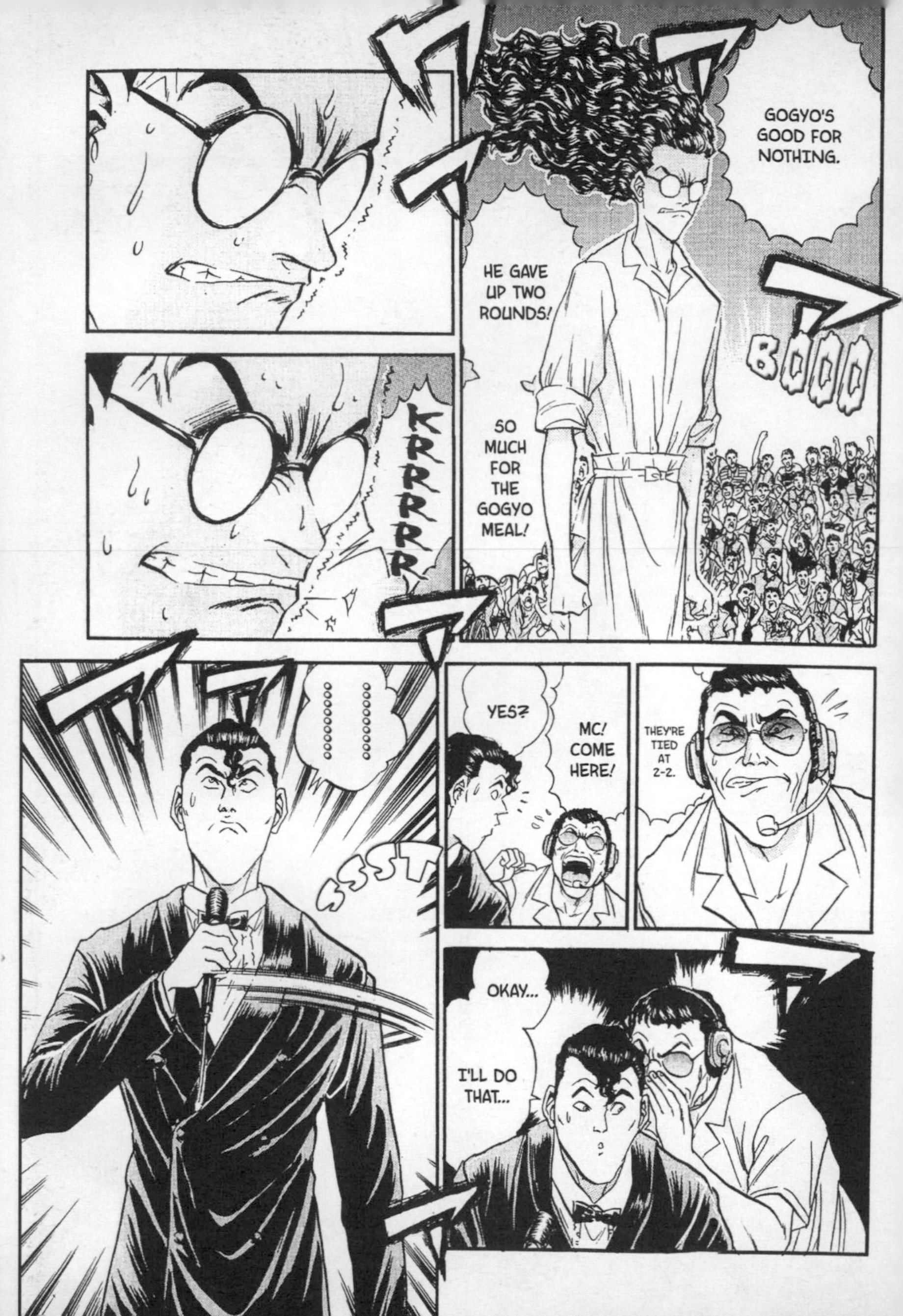
GOGYO'S GOOD FOR NOTHING.
HE GAVE UP TWO ROUNDS!
SO MUCH FOR THE GOGYO MEAL!
BOOO
KRRRRRR
THEY'RE TIED AT 2-2.
MC! COME HERE!
YES?
OKAY...
I'LL DO THAT...
....
SSST

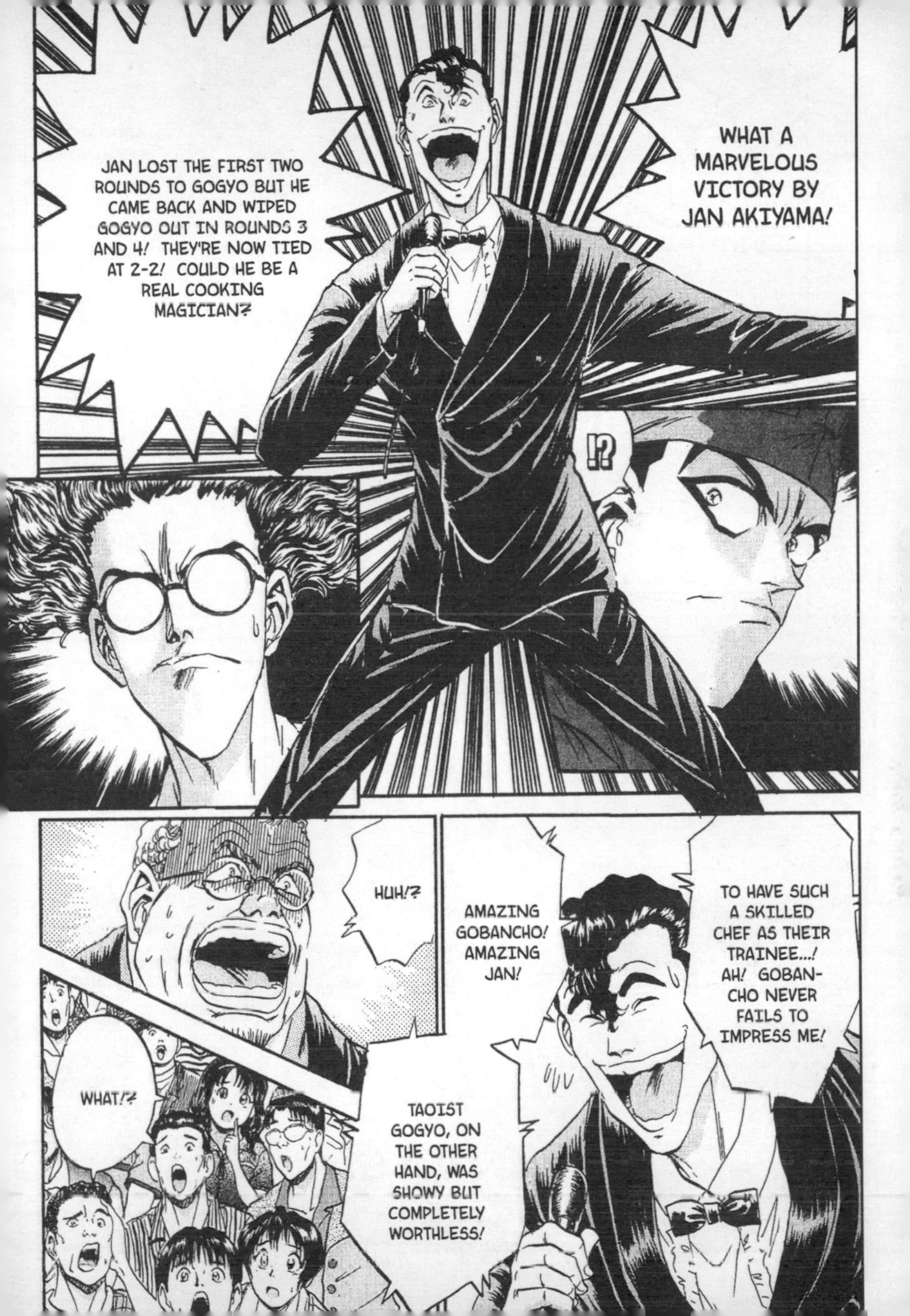
WHAT A MARVELOUS VICTORY BY JAN AKIYAMA!
JAN LOST THE FIRST TWO ROUNDS TO GOGYO BUT HE CAME BACK AND WIPED GOGYO OUT IN ROUNDS 3 AND 4! THEY'RE NOW TIED AT 2-2! COULD HE BE A REAL COOKING MAGICIAN!?
!?
TO HAVE SUCH A SKILLED CHEF AS THEIR TRAINEE...! AH! GOBAN-CHO NEVER FAILS TO IMPRESS ME!
AMAZING GOBANCHO! AMAZING JAN!
TAOIST GOGYO, ON THE OTHER HAND, WAS SHOWY BUT COMPLETELY WORTHLESS!
HUH!?
WHAT!?

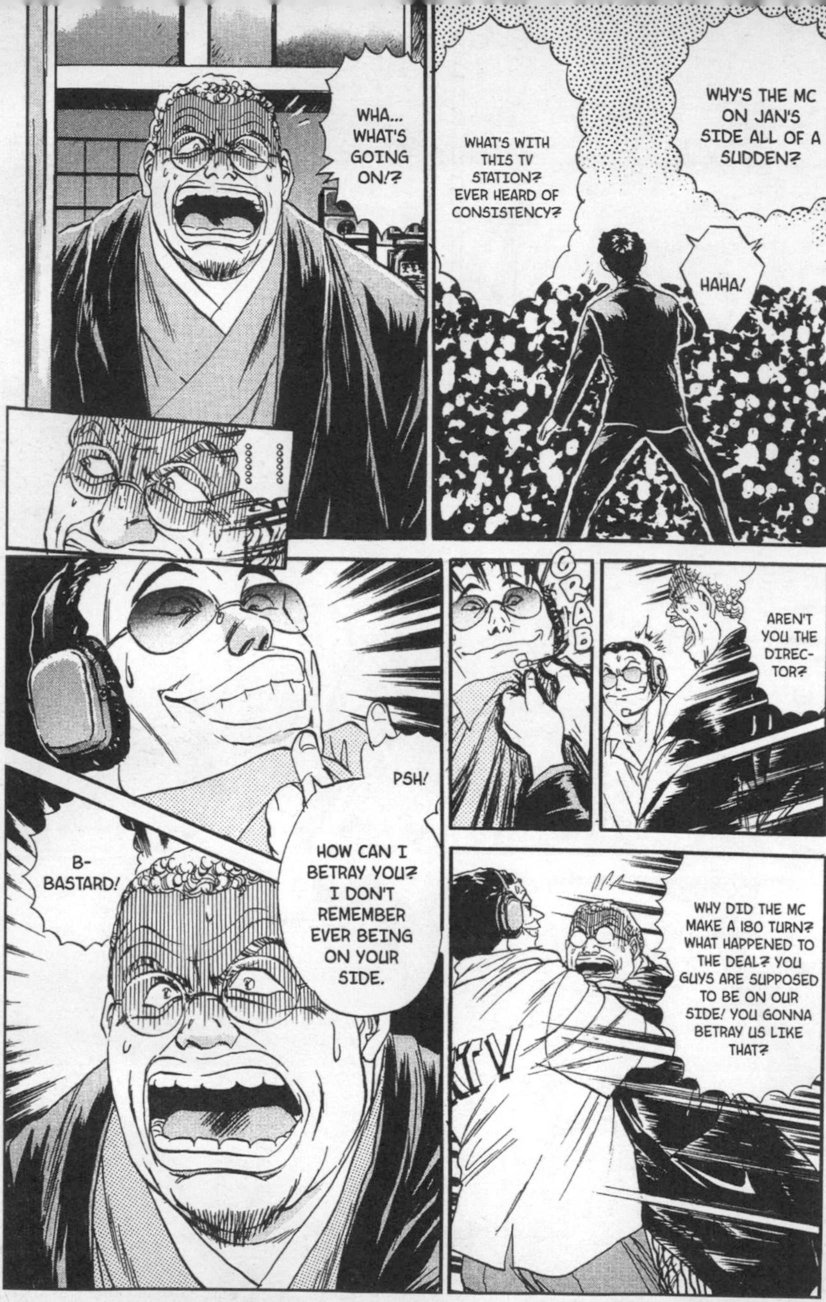
WHY'S THE MC ON JAN'S SIDE ALL OF A SUDDEN?
WHAT'S WITH THIS TV STATION? EVER HEARD OF CONSISTENCY?
HAHA!
WHA... WHAT'S GOING ON!?
AREN'T YOU THE DIRECTOR?
GRAB
WHY DID THE MC MAKE A 180 TURN? WHAT HAPPENED TO THE DEAL? YOU GUYS ARE SUPPOSED TO BE ON OUR SIDE! YOU GONNA BETRAY US LIKE THAT?
PSH!
HOW CAN I BETRAY YOU? I DON'T REMEMBER EVER BEING ON YOUR SIDE.
B- BASTARD!

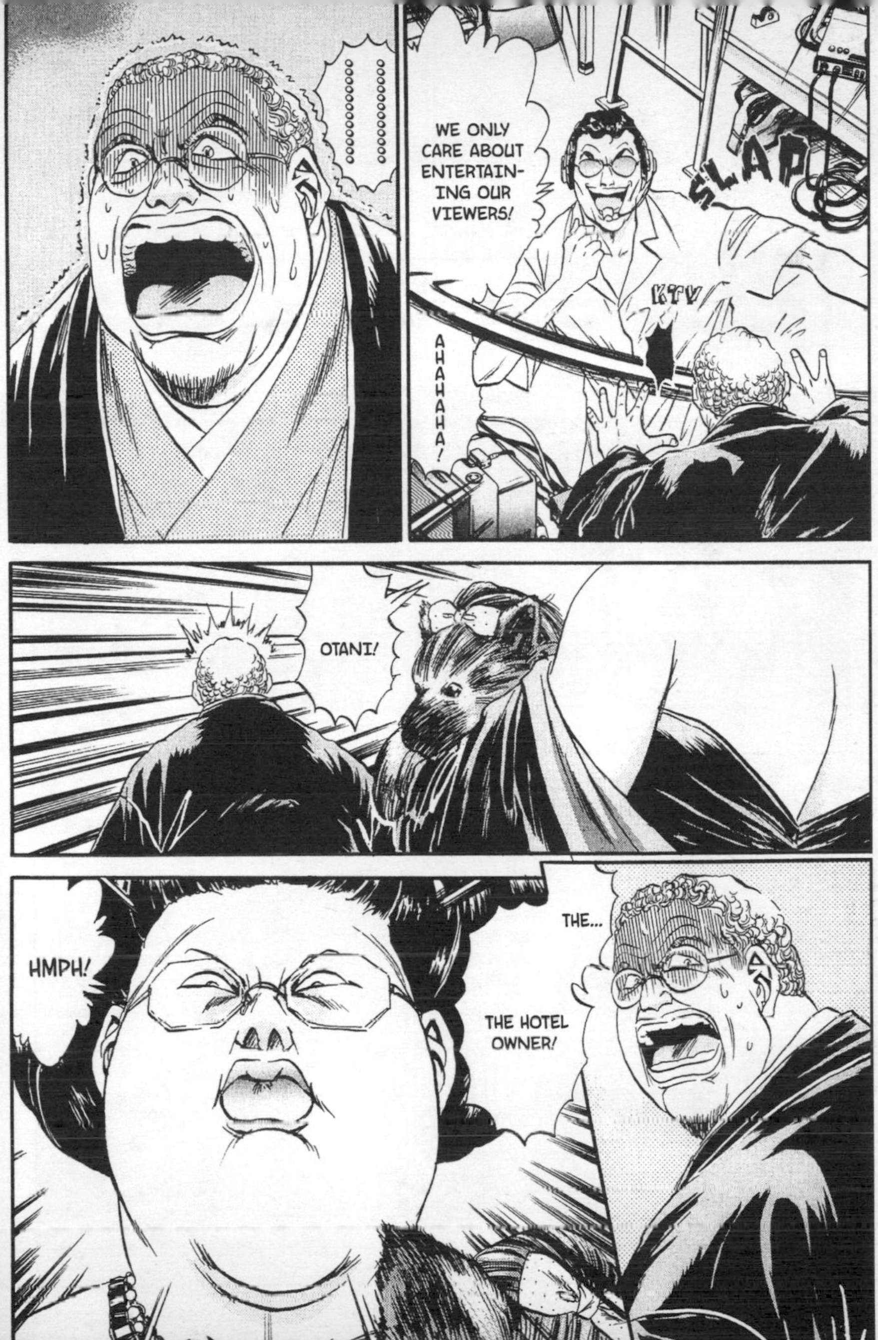
WE ONLY CARE ABOUT ENTERTAINING OUR VIEWERS!
SLAP
KTV
AHAHAHAHA!
OTANI!
THE...
THE HOTEL OWNER!
HMPH!

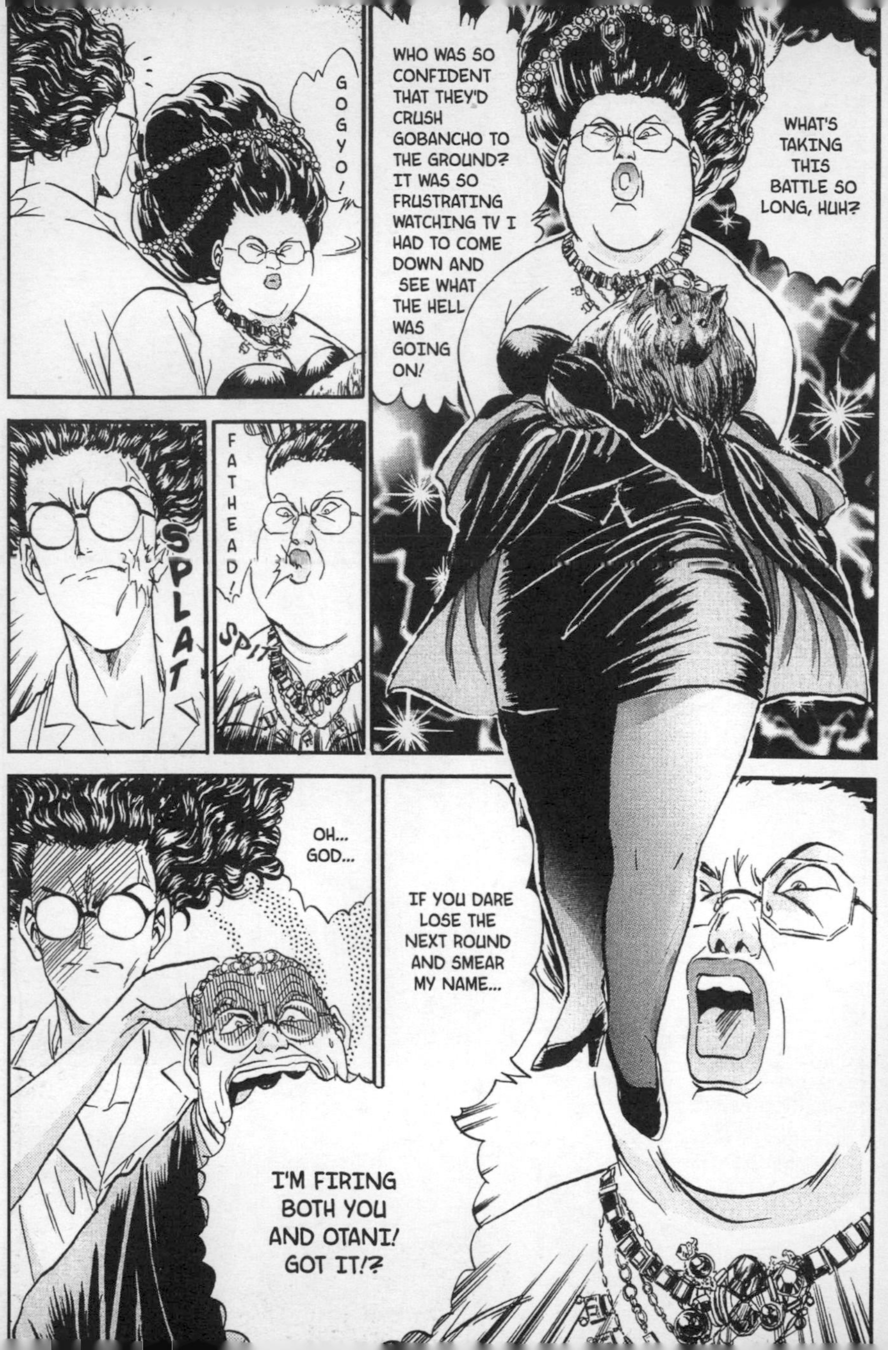
WHAT'S TAKING THIS BATTLE SO LONG, HUH?
WHO WAS SO CONFIDENT THAT THEY'D CRUSH GOBANCHO TO THE GROUND? IT WAS SO FRUSTRATING WATCHING TV I HAD TO COME DOWN AND SEE WHAT THE HELL WAS GOING ON!
GOGYO!
FATHEAD!
SPIT
SPLAT
IF YOU DARE LOSE THE NEXT ROUND AND SMEAR MY NAME...
OH... GOD...
I'M FIRING BOTH YOU AND OTANI! GOT IT!?

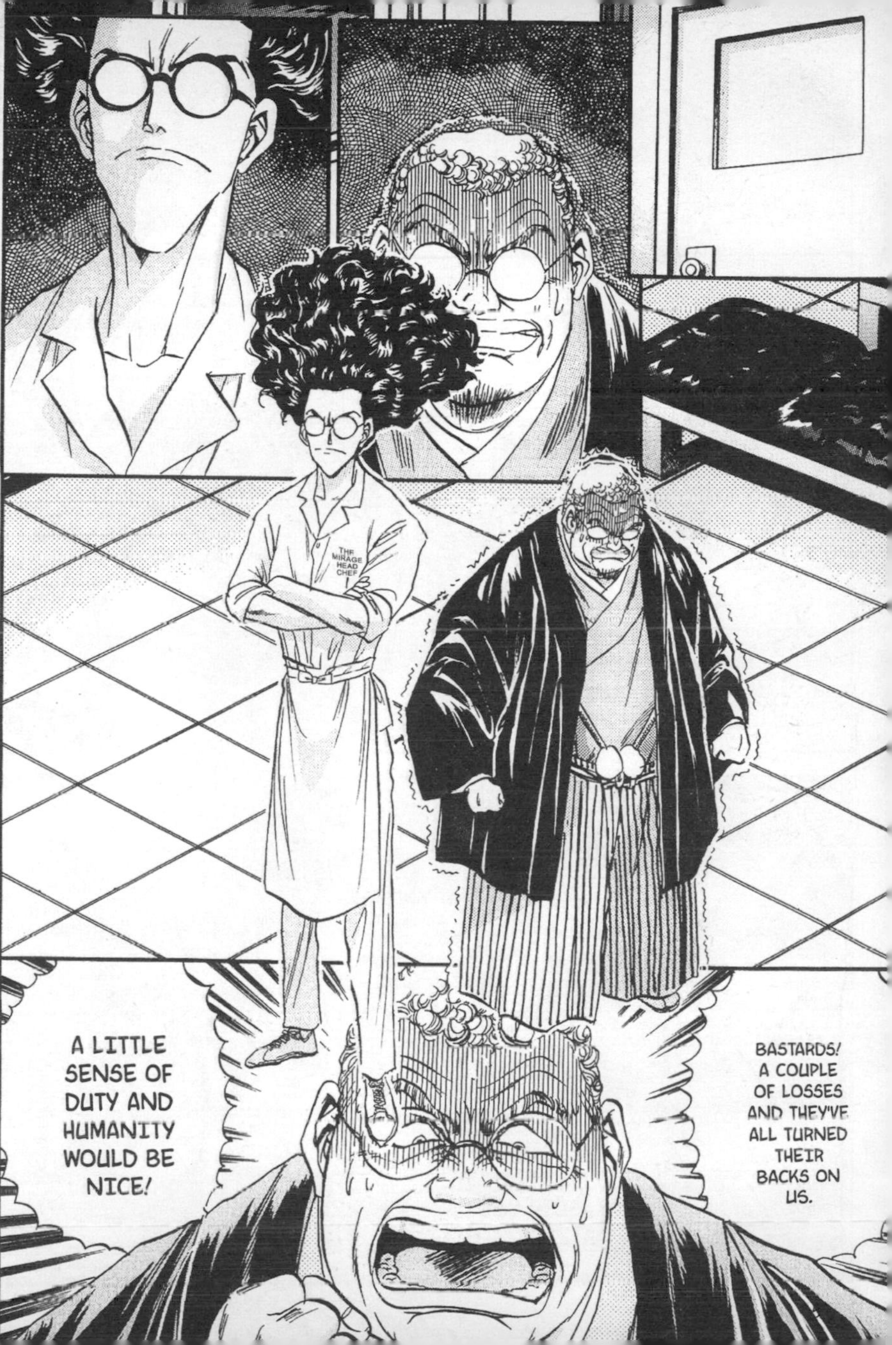
THE MIRAGE HEAD CHEF
BASTARDS! A COUPLE OF LOSSES AND THEY'VE ALL TURNED THEIR BACKS ON US.
A LITTLE SENSE OF DUTY AND HUMANITY WOULD BE NICE!

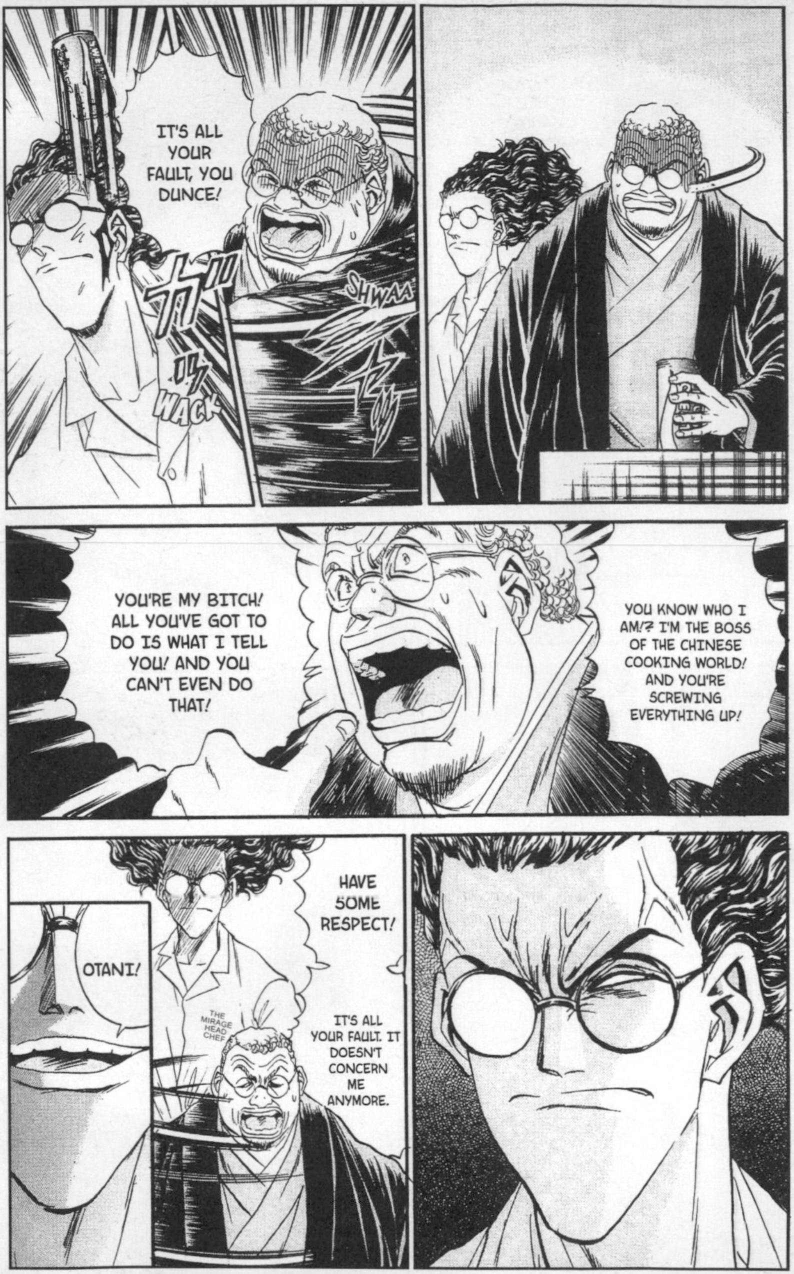
IT'S ALL YOUR FAULT, YOU DUNCE!
SHWAA
WACK
YOU KNOW WHO I AM!? I'M THE BOSS OF THE CHINESE COOKING WORLD! AND YOU'RE SCREWING EVERYTHING UP!
YOU'RE MY BITCH! ALL YOU'VE GOT TO DO IS WHAT I TELL YOU! AND YOU CAN'T EVEN DO THAT!
HAVE SOME RESPECT!
OTANI!
IT'S ALL YOUR FAULT. IT DOESN'T CONCERN ME ANYMORE.
THE MIRAGE HEAD CHEF

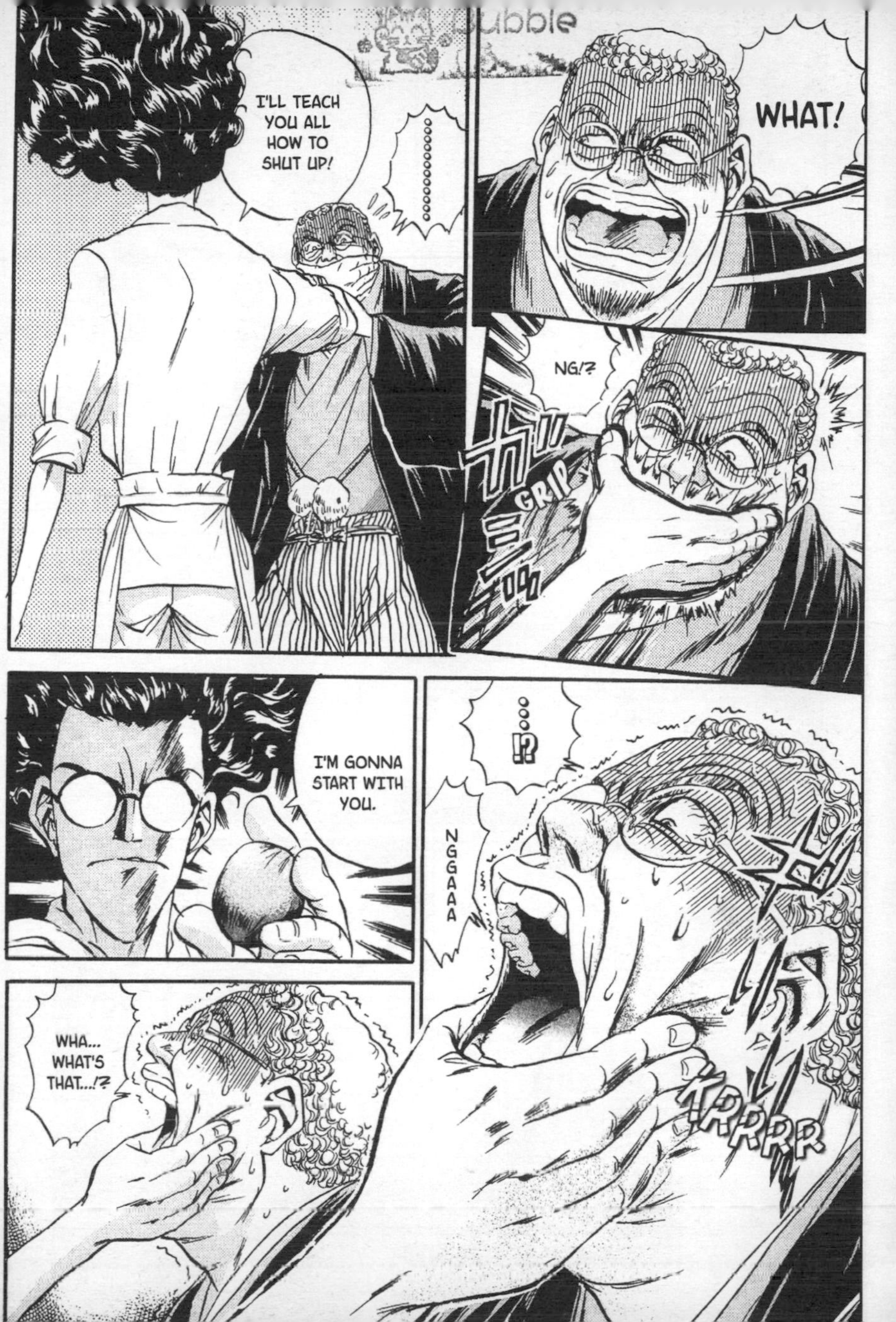
WHAT!
NG!?
GRIP
I'LL TEACH YOU ALL HOW TO SHUT UP!
OOOOOOOOOOOOO...
...!?
NGGAAA
KRRRR
I'M GONNA START WITH YOU.
WHA... WHAT'S THAT...!?

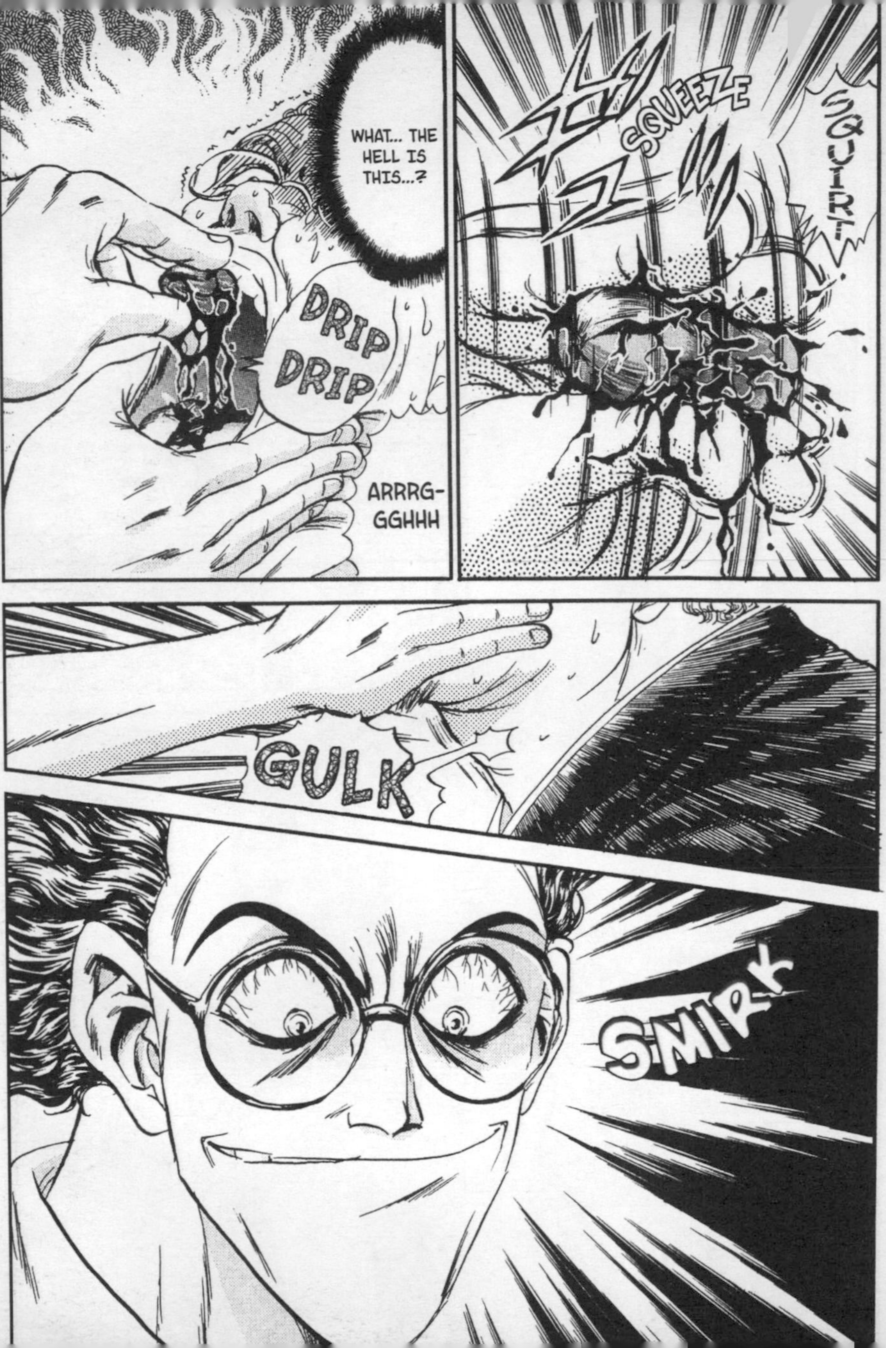
SQUEEZE
SQUIRT
WHAT... THE HELL IS THIS...?
DRIP DRIP
ARRRG-GGHHH
GULK
SMIRK

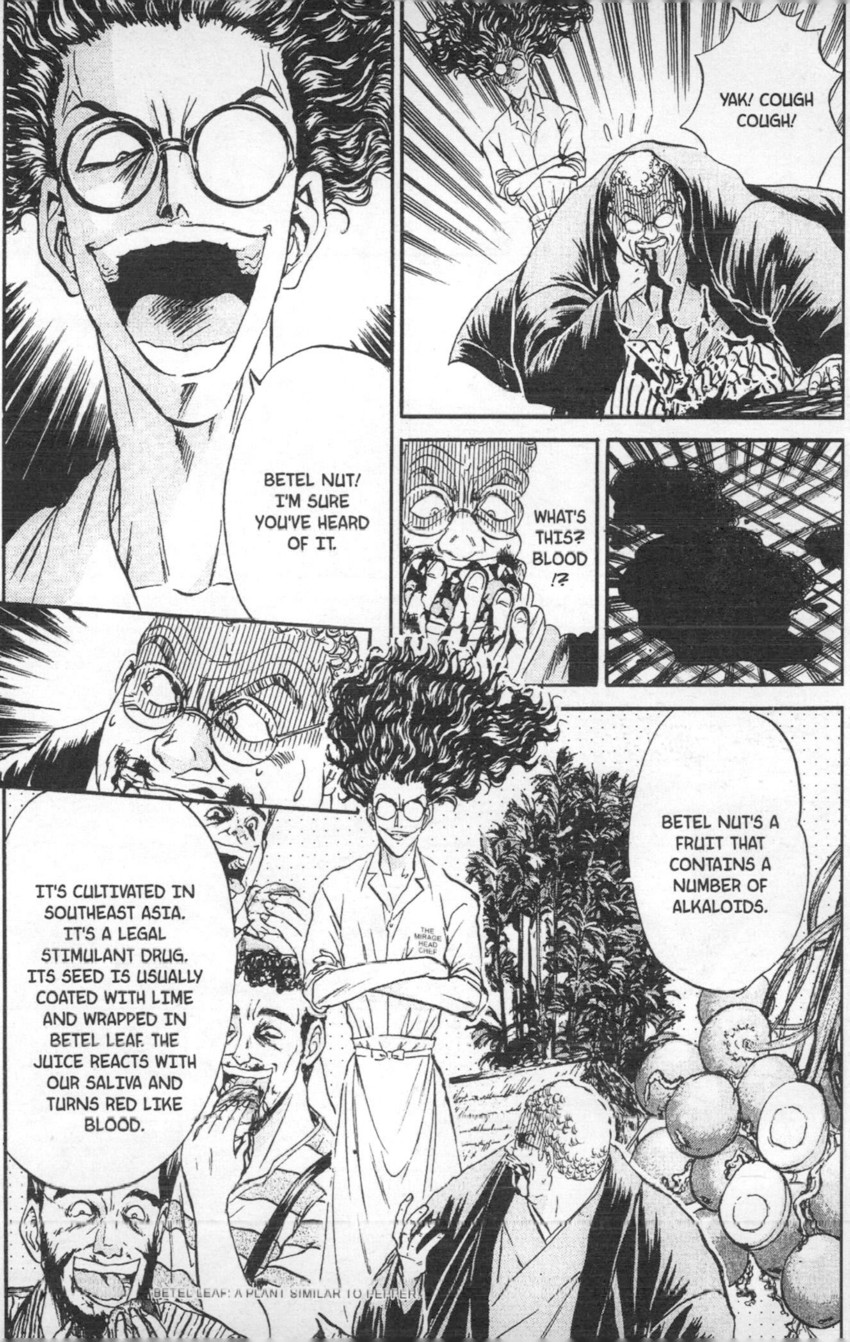
YAK! COUGH COUGH!
WHAT'S THIS? BLOOD !?
BETEL NUT! I'M SURE YOU'VE HEARD OF IT.
BETEL NUT'S A FRUIT THAT CONTAINS A NUMBER OF ALKALOIDS.
THE MIRAGE HEAD CHEF
IT'S CULTIVATED IN SOUTHEAST ASIA. IT'S A LEGAL STIMULANT DRUG. ITS SEED IS USUALLY COATED WITH LIME AND WRAPPED IN BETEL LEAF. THE JUICE REACTS WITH OUR SALIVA AND TURNS RED LIKE BLOOD.
BETEL LEAF: A PLANT SIMILAR TO PEPPER.

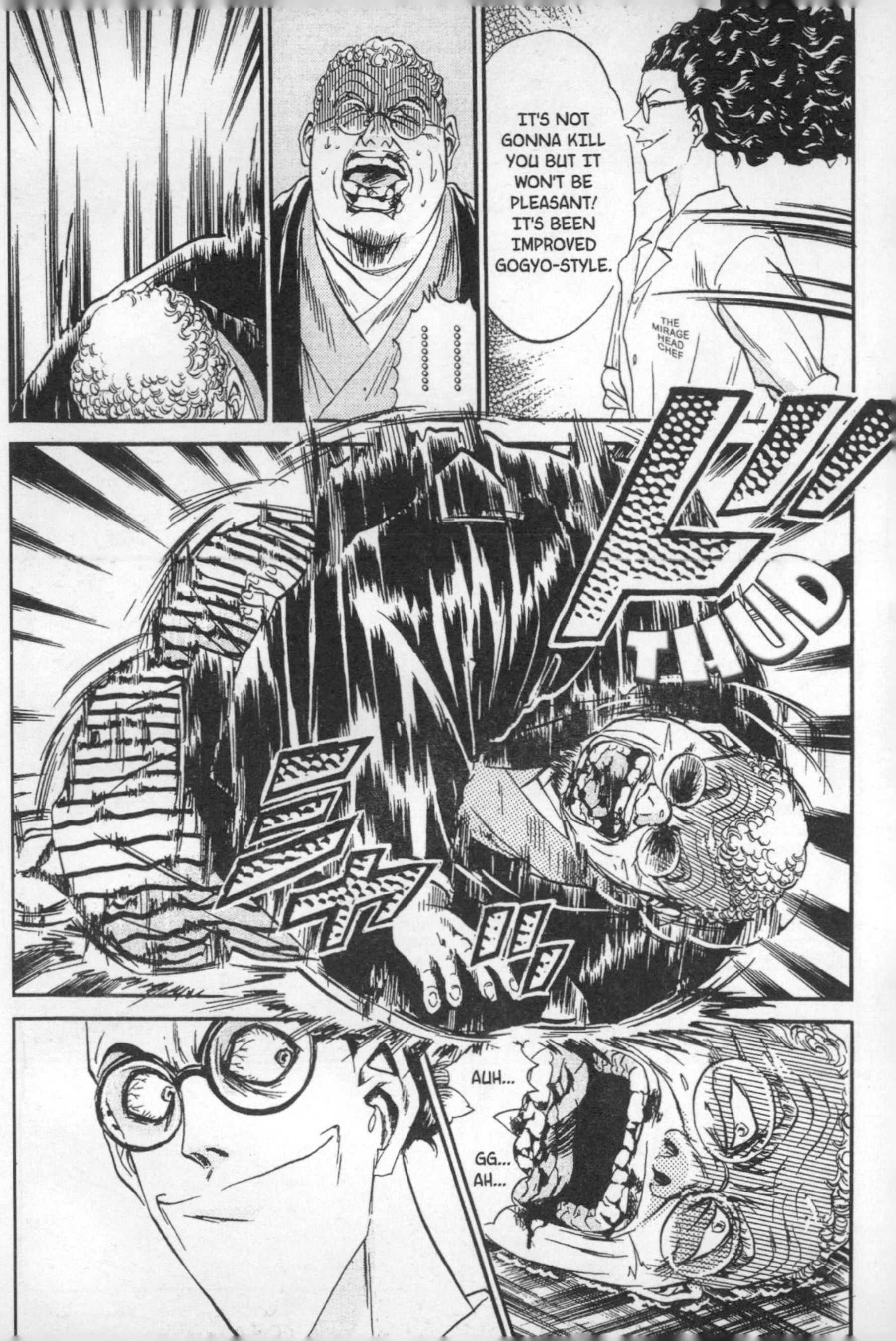
IT'S NOT GONNA KILL YOU BUT IT WON'T BE PLEASANT! IT'S BEEN IMPROVED GOGYO-STYLE.
THE MIRAGE HEAD CHEF
THUD
AUH...
GG... AH...

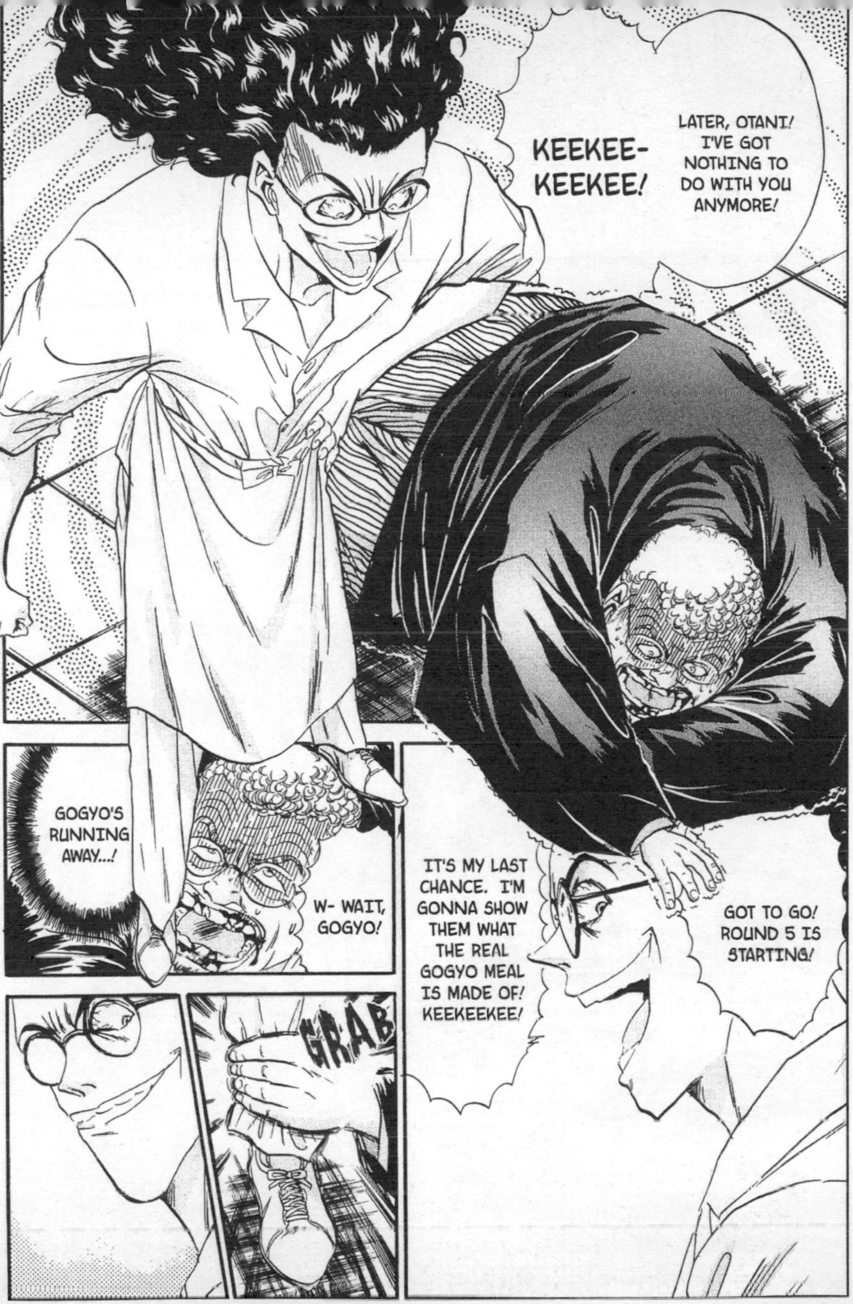
LATER, OTANI! I'VE GOT NOTHING TO DO WITH YOU ANYMORE!
KEEKEE-KEEKEE!
IT'S MY LAST CHANCE. I'M GONNA SHOW THEM WHAT THE REAL GOGYO MEAL IS MADE OF! KEEKEEKEE!
GOT TO GO! ROUND 5 IS STARTING!
W- WAIT, GOGYO!
GOGYO'S RUNNING AWAY...!
GRAB

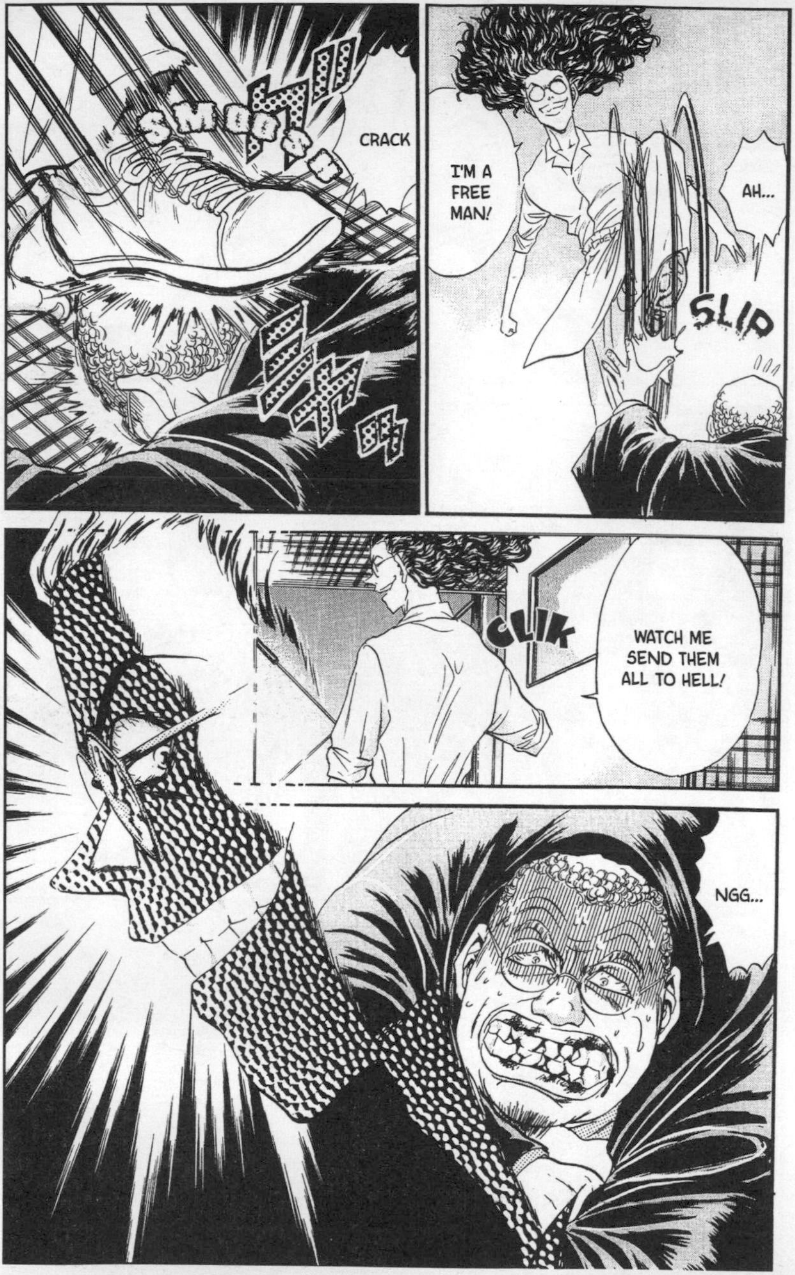
I'M A FREE MAN!
AH...
SLIP
SMOOSH
CRACK
WATCH ME SEND THEM ALL TO HELL!
CLIK
NGG...

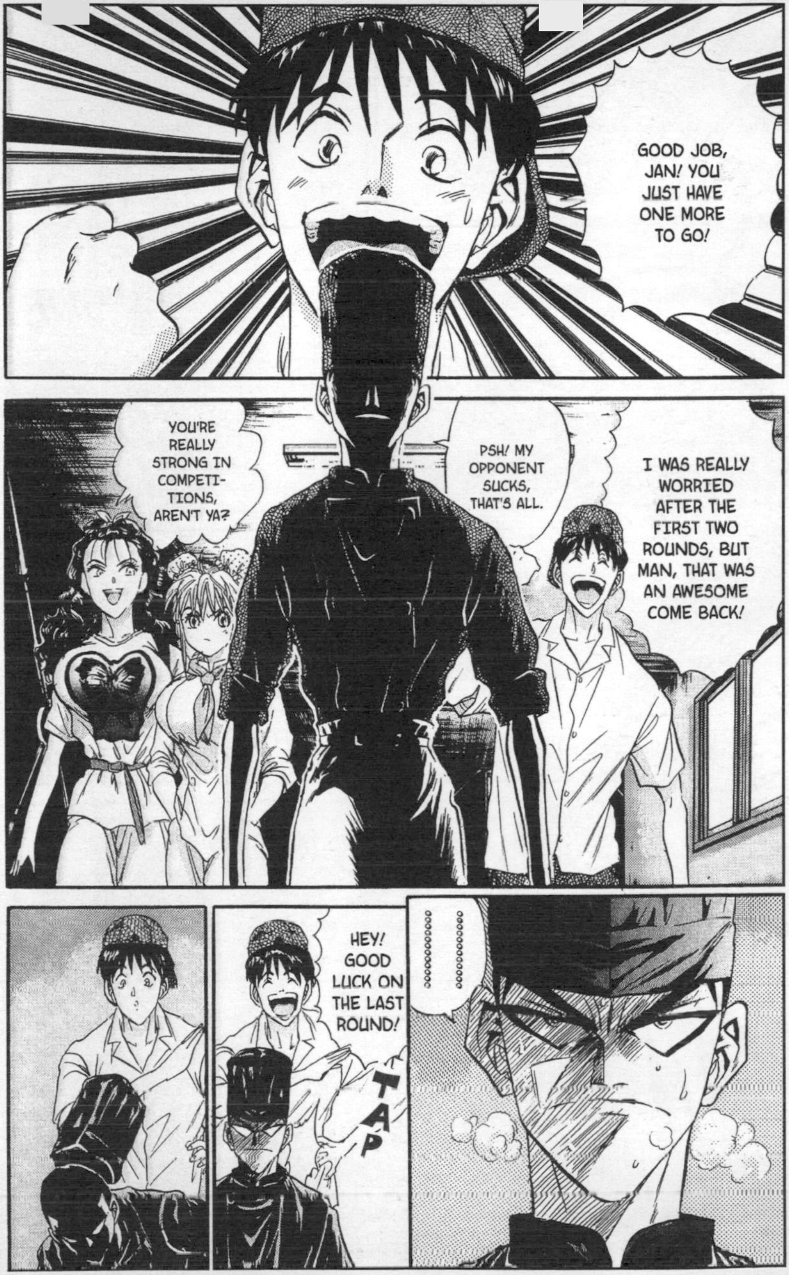
GOOD JOB, JAN! YOU JUST HAVE ONE MORE TO GO!
I WAS REALLY WORRIED AFTER THE FIRST TWO ROUNDS, BUT MAN, THAT WAS AN AWESOME COME BACK!
PSH! MY OPPONENT SUCKS, THAT'S ALL.
YOU'RE REALLY STRONG IN COMPETI-TIONS, AREN'T YA?
....
HEY! GOOD LUCK ON THE LAST ROUND!
TAP

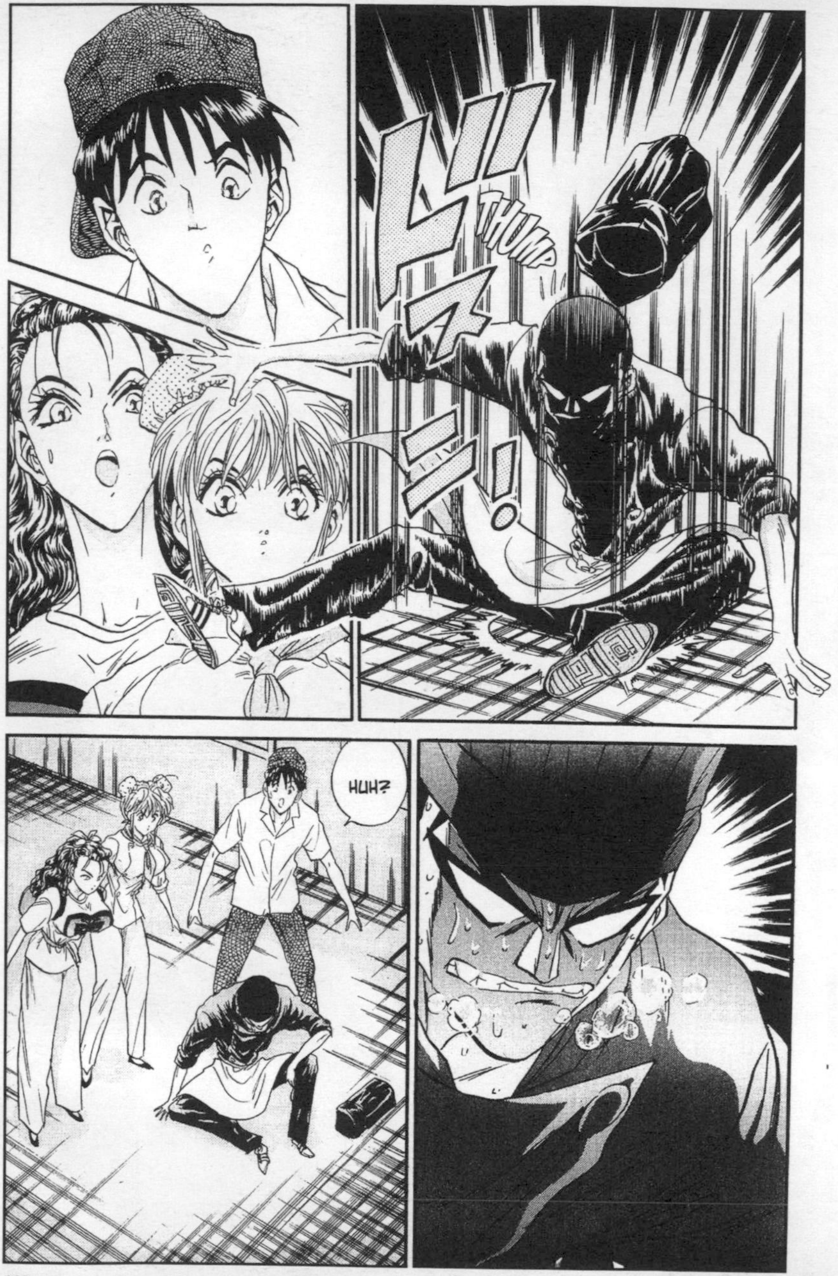
THUMP
HUH?

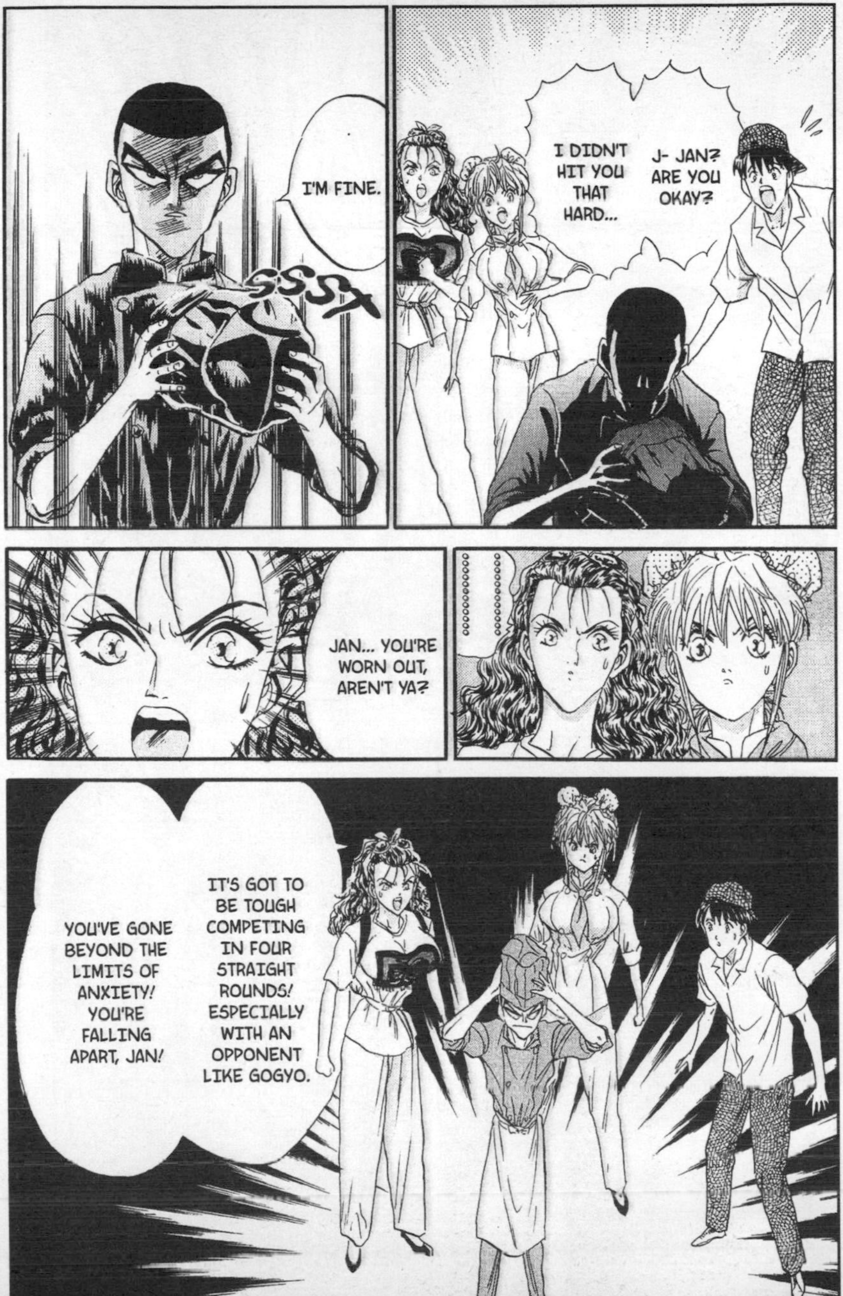
J- JAN? ARE YOU OKAY?
I DIDN'T HIT YOU THAT HARD...
I'M FINE.
SSST
JAN... YOU'RE WORN OUT, AREN'T YA?
IT'S GOT TO BE TOUGH COMPETING IN FOUR STRAIGHT ROUNDS! ESPECIALLY WITH AN OPPONENT LIKE GOGYO.
YOU'VE GONE BEYOND THE LIMITS OF ANXIETY! YOU'RE FALLING APART, JAN!

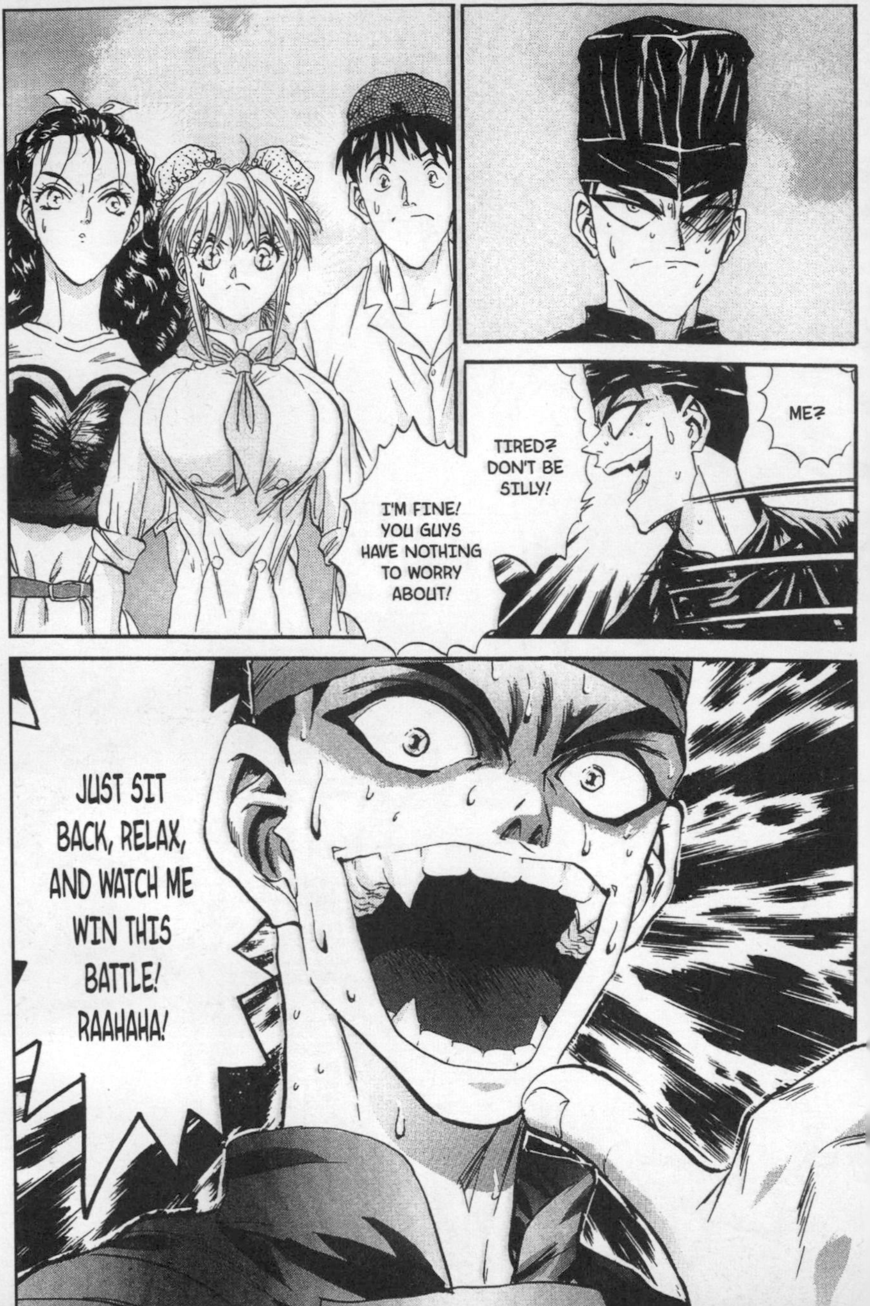
ME?
TIRED? DON'T BE SILLY!
I'M FINE! YOU GUYS HAVE NOTHING TO WORRY ABOUT!
JUST SIT BACK, RELAX, AND WATCH ME WIN THIS BATTLE! RAAHAHA!

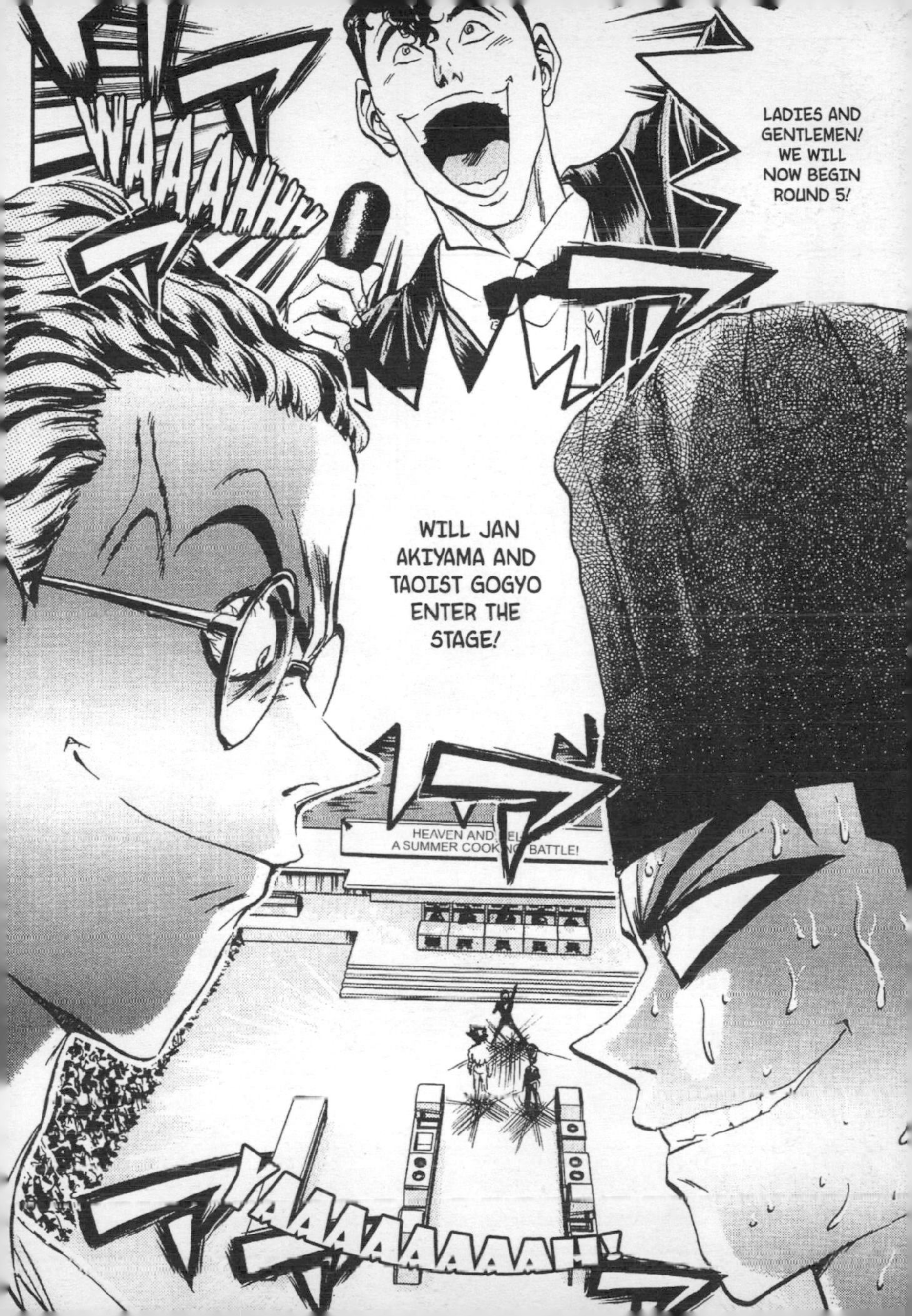
LADIES AND GENTLEMEN! WE WILL NOW BEGIN ROUND 5!
WAAAHHH
WILL JAN AKIYAMA AND TAOIST GOGYO ENTER THE STAGE!
YAAAAAAAAAAH!

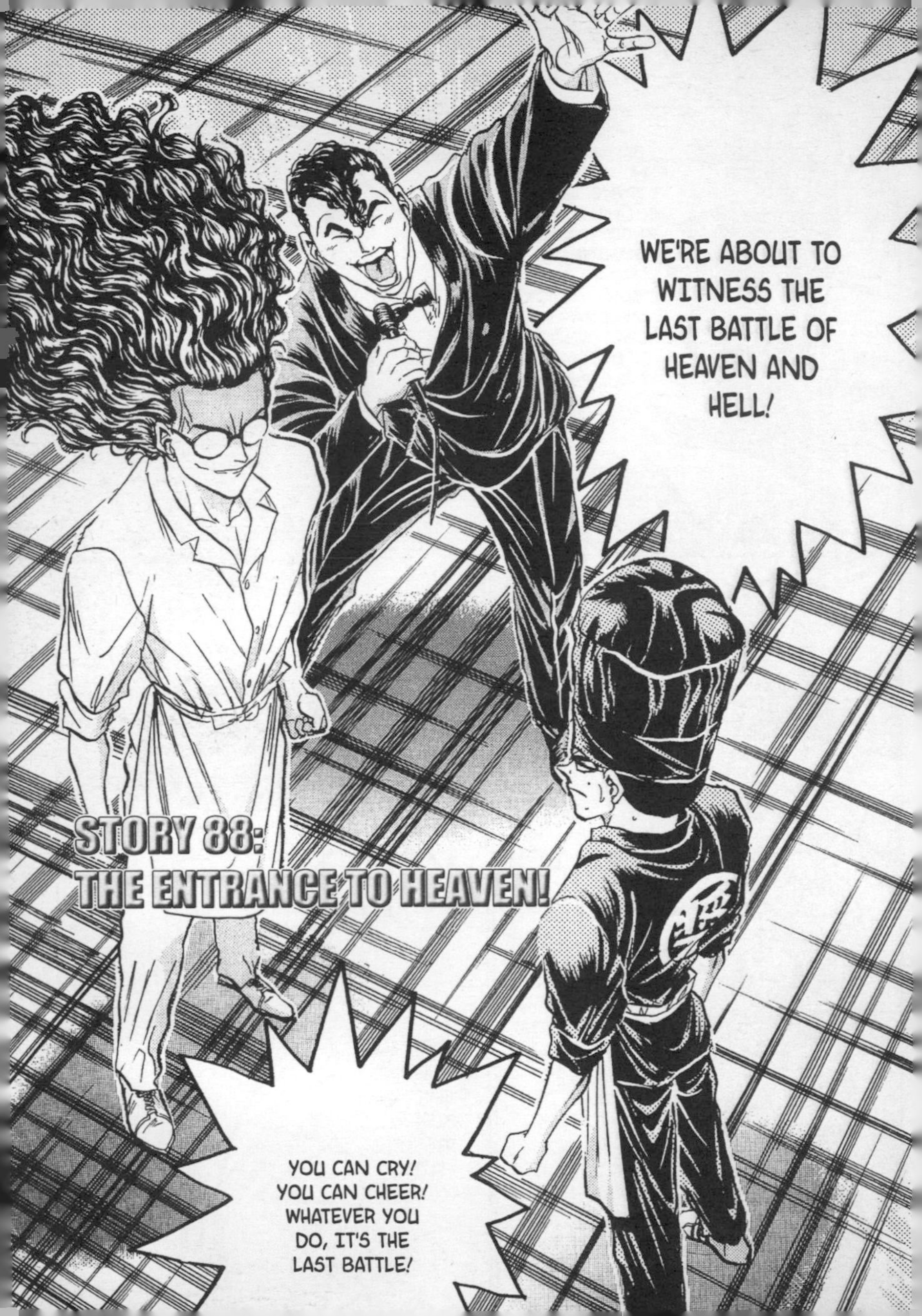
WE'RE ABOUT TO WITNESS THE LAST BATTLE OF HEAVEN AND HELL!
STORY 88: THE ENTRANCE TO HEAVEN!
YOU CAN CRY! YOU CAN CHEER! WHATEVER YOU DO, IT'S THE LAST BATTLE!

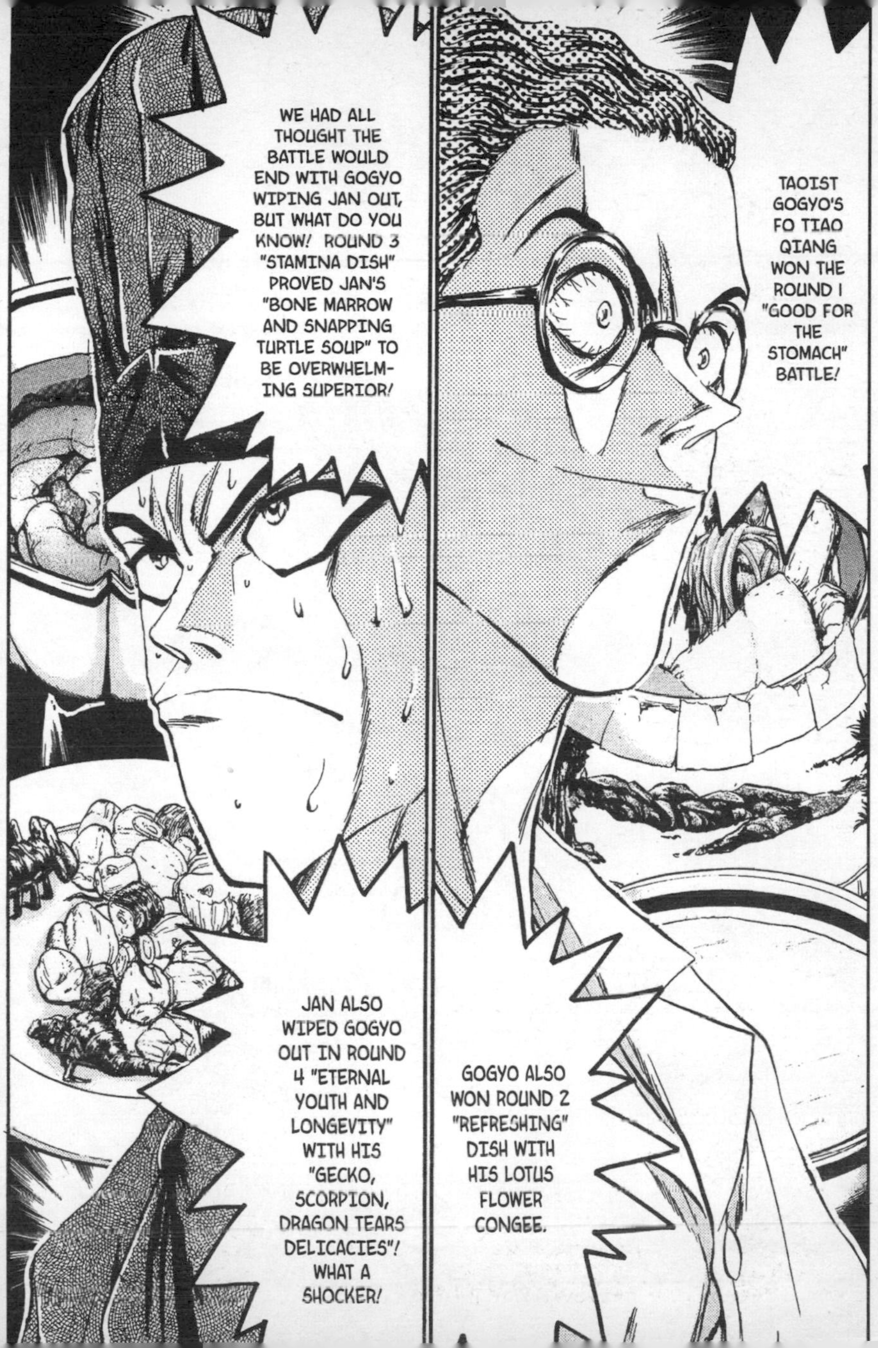
TAOIST GOGYO'S FO TIAO QIANG WON THE ROUND 1 "GOOD FOR THE STOMACH" BATTLE!
GOGYO ALSO WON ROUND 2 "REFRESHING" DISH WITH HIS LOTUS FLOWER CONGEE.
WE HAD ALL THOUGHT THE BATTLE WOULD END WITH GOGYO WIPING JAN OUT, BUT WHAT DO YOU KNOW! ROUND 3 "STAMINA DISH" PROVED JAN'S "BONE MARROW AND SNAPPING TURTLE SOUP" TO BE OVERWHELMING SUPERIOR!
JAN ALSO WIPED GOGYO OUT IN ROUND 4 "ETERNAL YOUTH AND LONGEVITY" WITH HIS "GECKO, SCORPION, DRAGON TEARS DELICACIES"! WHAT A SHOCKER!

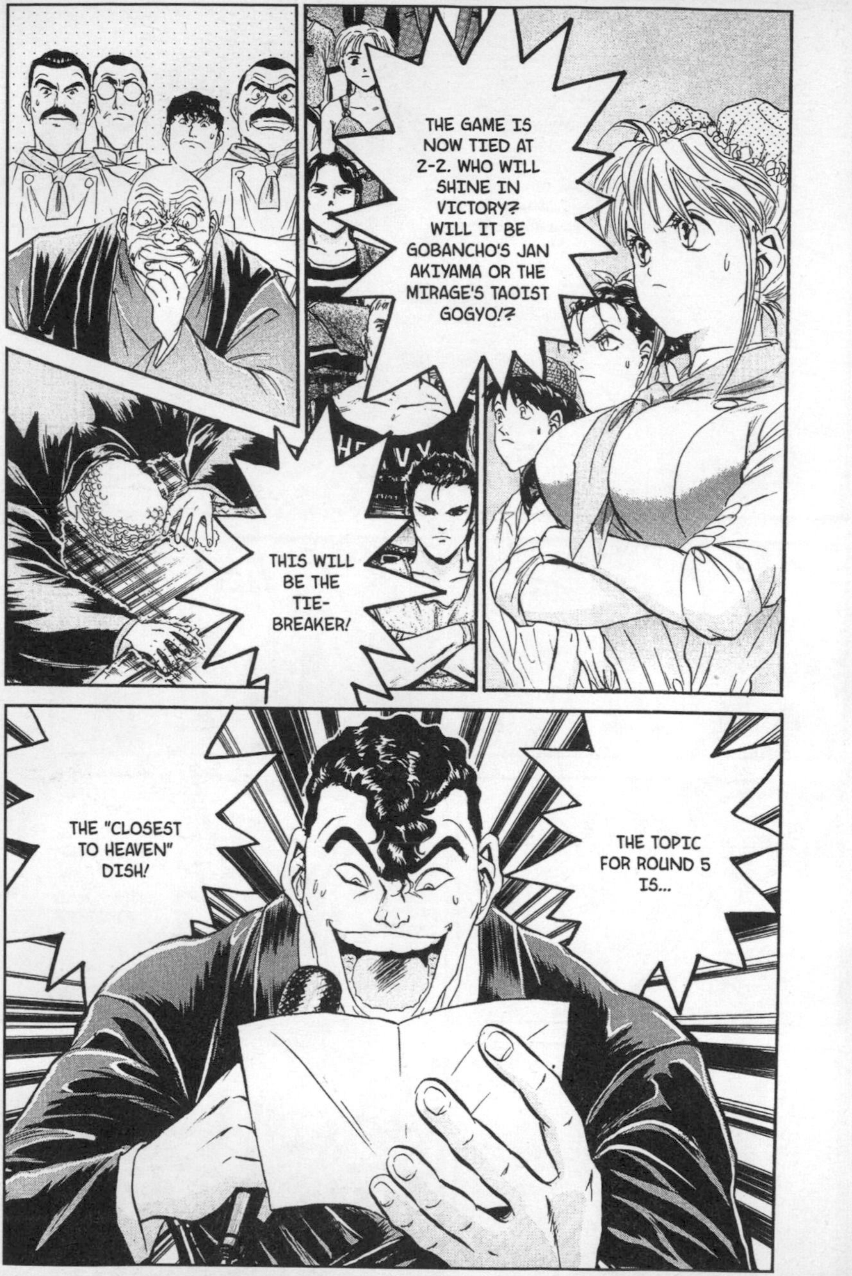
THE GAME IS NOW TIED AT 2-2. WHO WILL SHINE IN VICTORY?! WILL IT BE GOBANCHO'S JAN AKIYAMA OR THE MIRAGE'S TAOIST GOGYO!?
THIS WILL BE THE TIE-BREAKER!
THE TOPIC FOR ROUND 5 IS...
THE "CLOSEST TO HEAVEN" DISH!

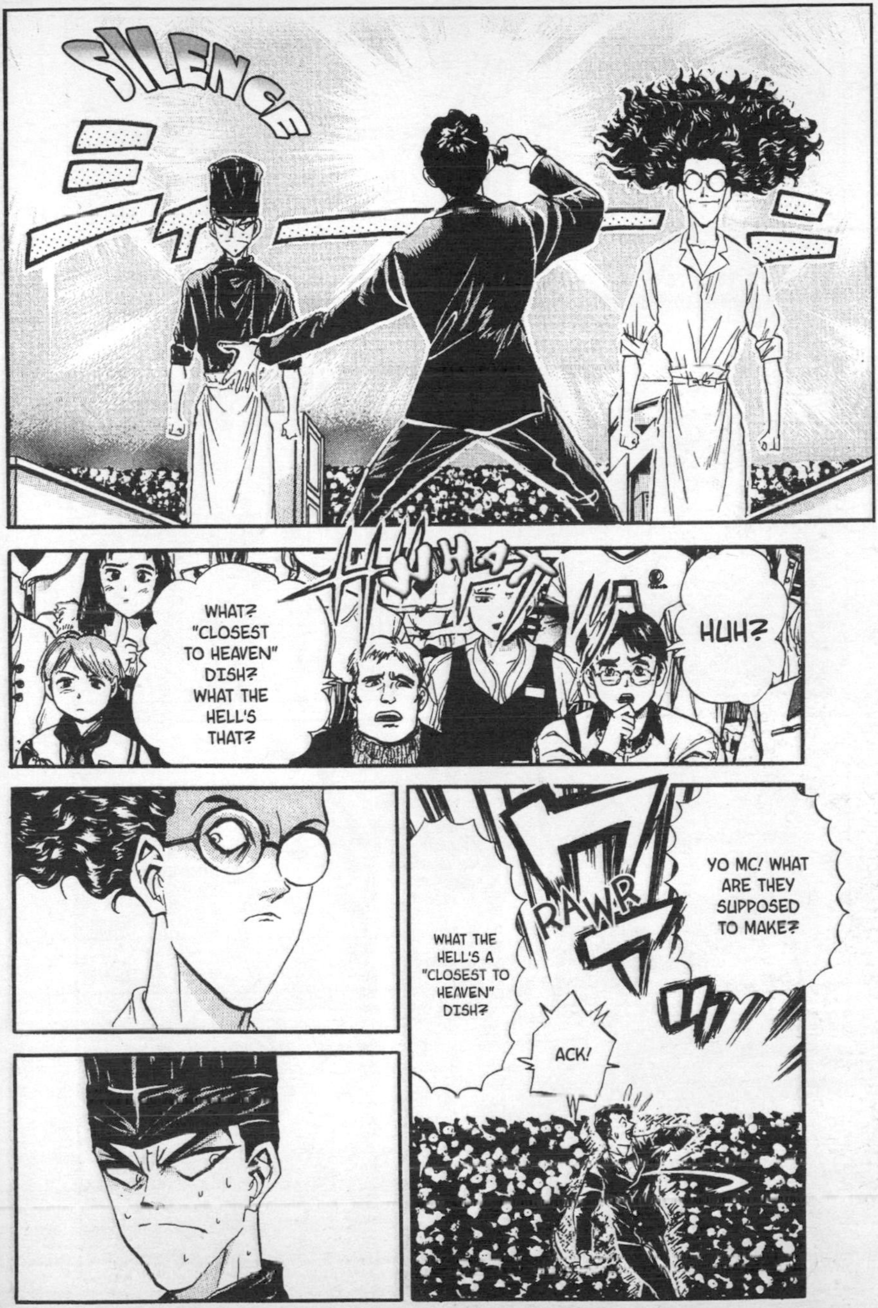
SILENCE
HUH?
WHAT
WHAT? "CLOSEST TO HEAVEN" DISH? WHAT THE HELL'S THAT?
YO MC! WHAT ARE THEY SUPPOSED TO MAKE?
RAWR
WHAT THE HELL'S A "CLOSEST TO HEAVEN" DISH?
ACK!

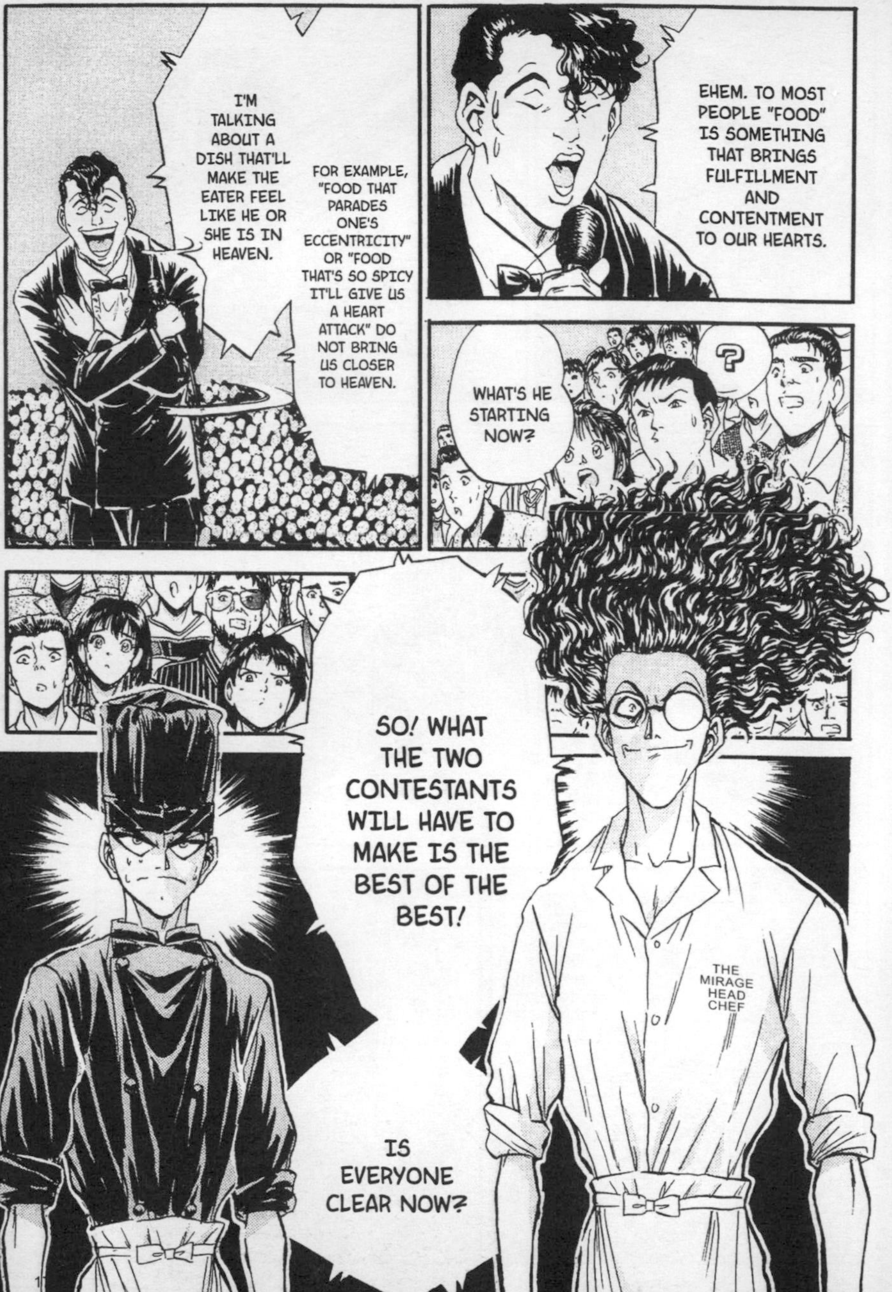
EHEM. TO MOST PEOPLE "FOOD" IS SOMETHING THAT BRINGS FULFILLMENT AND CONTENTMENT TO OUR HEARTS.
I'M TALKING ABOUT A DISH THAT'LL MAKE THE EATER FEEL LIKE HE OR SHE IS IN HEAVEN.
FOR EXAMPLE, "FOOD THAT PARADES ONE'S ECCENTRICITY" OR "FOOD THAT'S SO SPICY IT'LL GIVE US A HEART ATTACK" DO NOT BRING US CLOSER TO HEAVEN.
?
WHAT'S HE STARTING NOW?
SO! WHAT THE TWO CONTESTANTS WILL HAVE TO MAKE IS THE BEST OF THE BEST!
THE MIRAGE HEAD CHEF
IS EVERYONE CLEAR NOW?

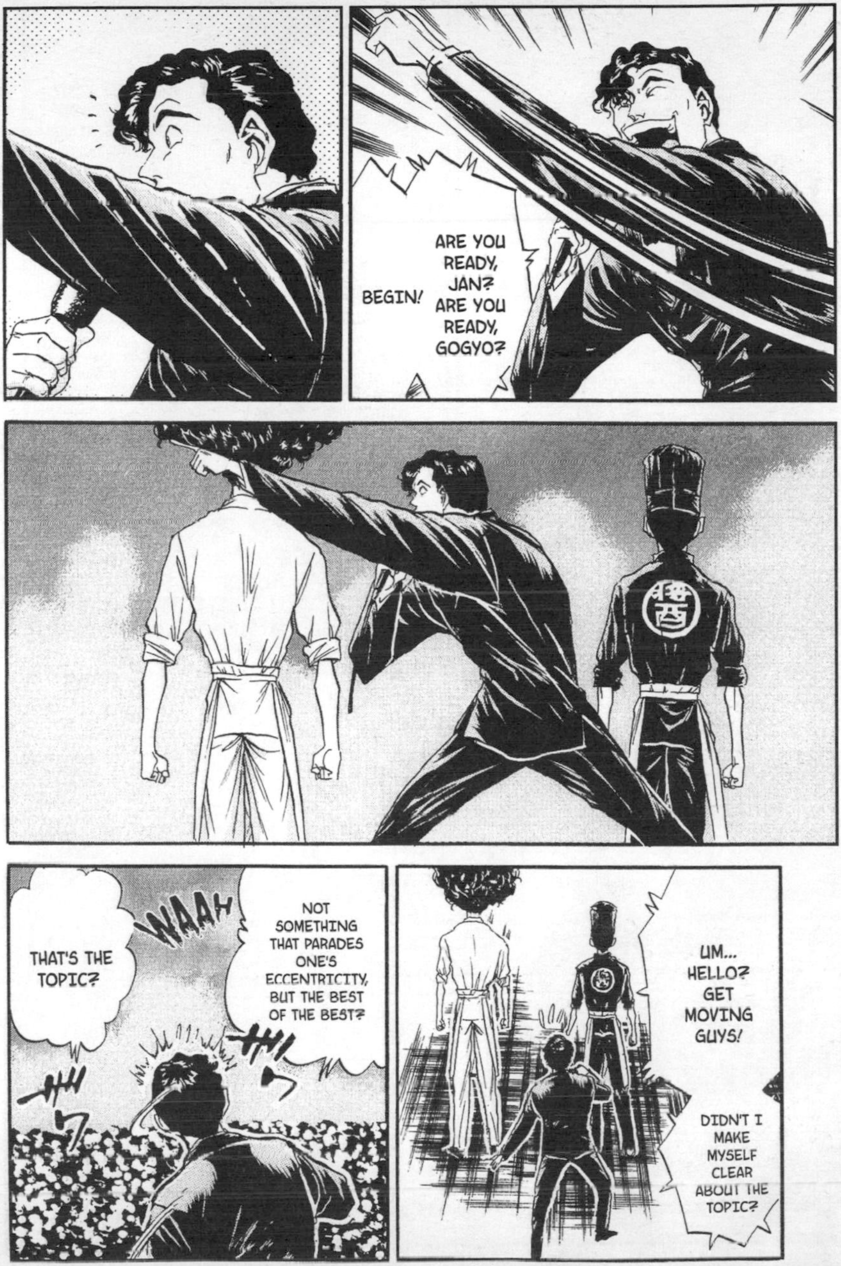
ARE YOU READY, JAN? ARE YOU READY, GOGYO?
BEGIN!
UM... HELLO? GET MOVING GUYS!
DIDN'T I MAKE MYSELF CLEAR ABOUT THE TOPIC?
NOT SOMETHING THAT PARADES ONE'S ECCENTRICITY, BUT THE BEST OF THE BEST?
WAAH
THAT'S THE TOPIC?

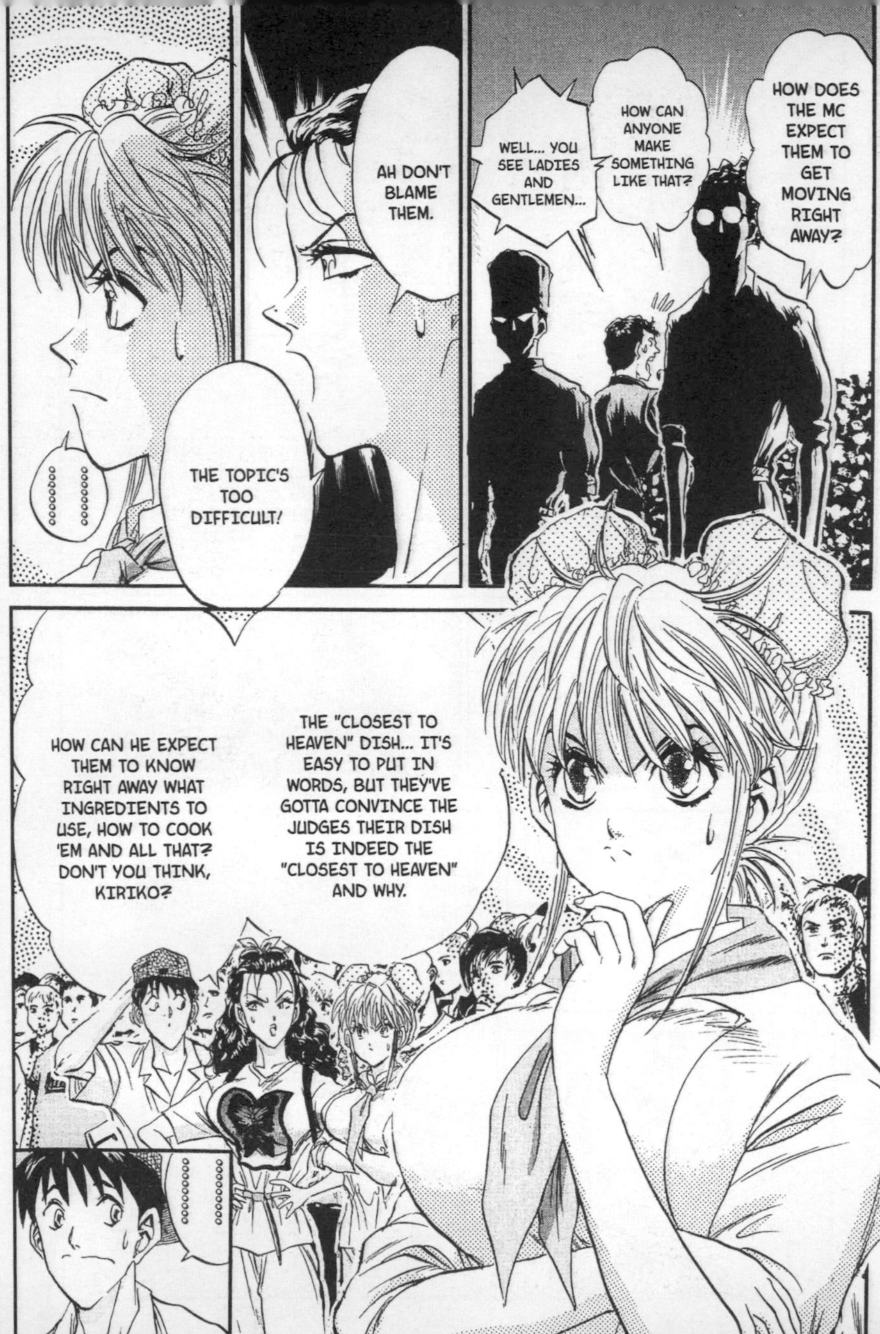
HOW DOES THE MC EXPECT THEM TO GET MOVING RIGHT AWAY?
HOW CAN ANYONE MAKE SOMETHING LIKE THAT?
WELL... YOU SEE LADIES AND GENTLEMEN...
AH DON'T BLAME THEM.
THE TOPIC'S TOO DIFFICULT!
......
THE "CLOSEST TO HEAVEN" DISH... IT'S EASY TO PUT IN WORDS, BUT THEY'VE GOTTA CONVINCE THE JUDGES THEIR DISH IS INDEED THE "CLOSEST TO HEAVEN" AND WHY.
HOW CAN HE EXPECT THEM TO KNOW RIGHT AWAY WHAT INGREDIENTS TO USE, HOW TO COOK 'EM AND ALL THAT? DON'T YOU THINK, KIRIKO?
......

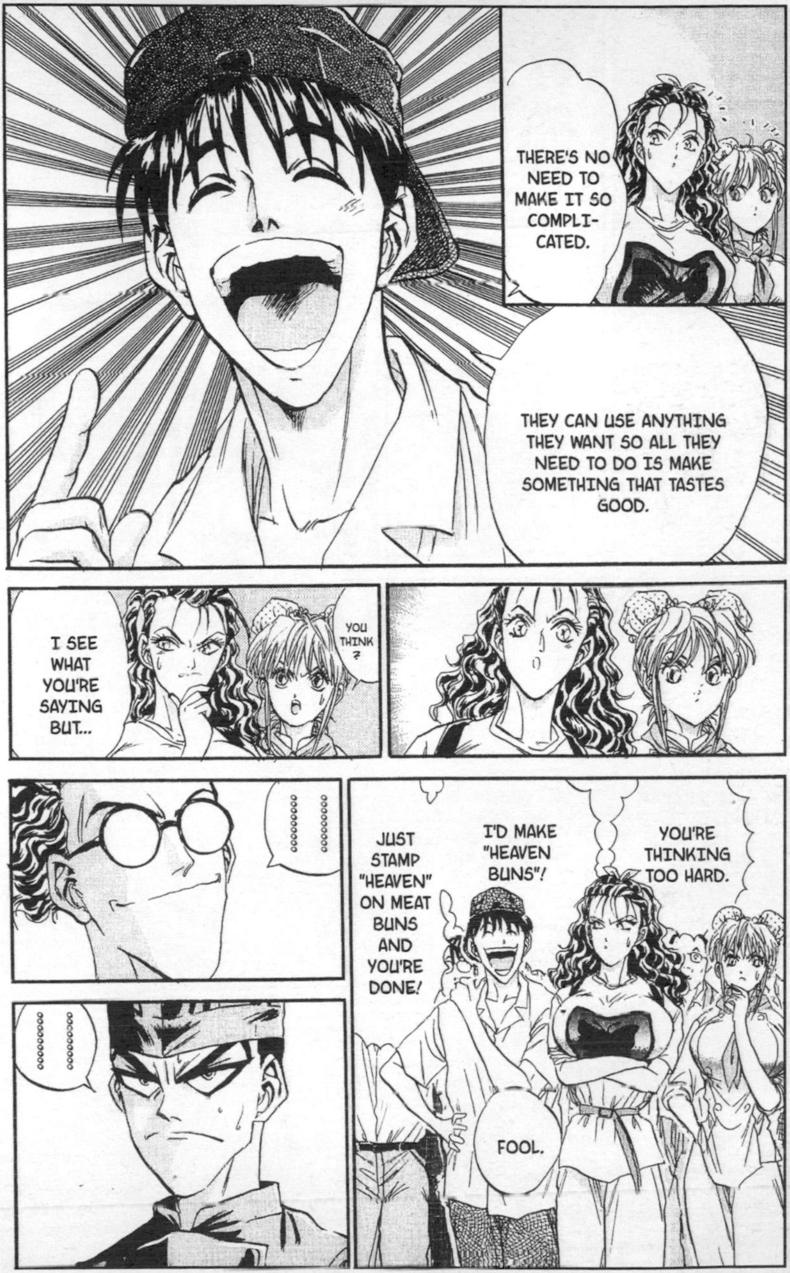
THERE'S NO NEED TO MAKE IT SO COMPLICATED.
THEY CAN USE ANYTHING THEY WANT SO ALL THEY NEED TO DO IS MAKE SOMETHING THAT TASTES GOOD.
YOU THINK?
I SEE WHAT YOU'RE SAYING BUT...
YOU'RE THINKING TOO HARD.
I'D MAKE "HEAVEN BUNS"!
JUST STAMP "HEAVEN" ON MEAT BUNS AND YOU'RE DONE!
FOOL.
....
....

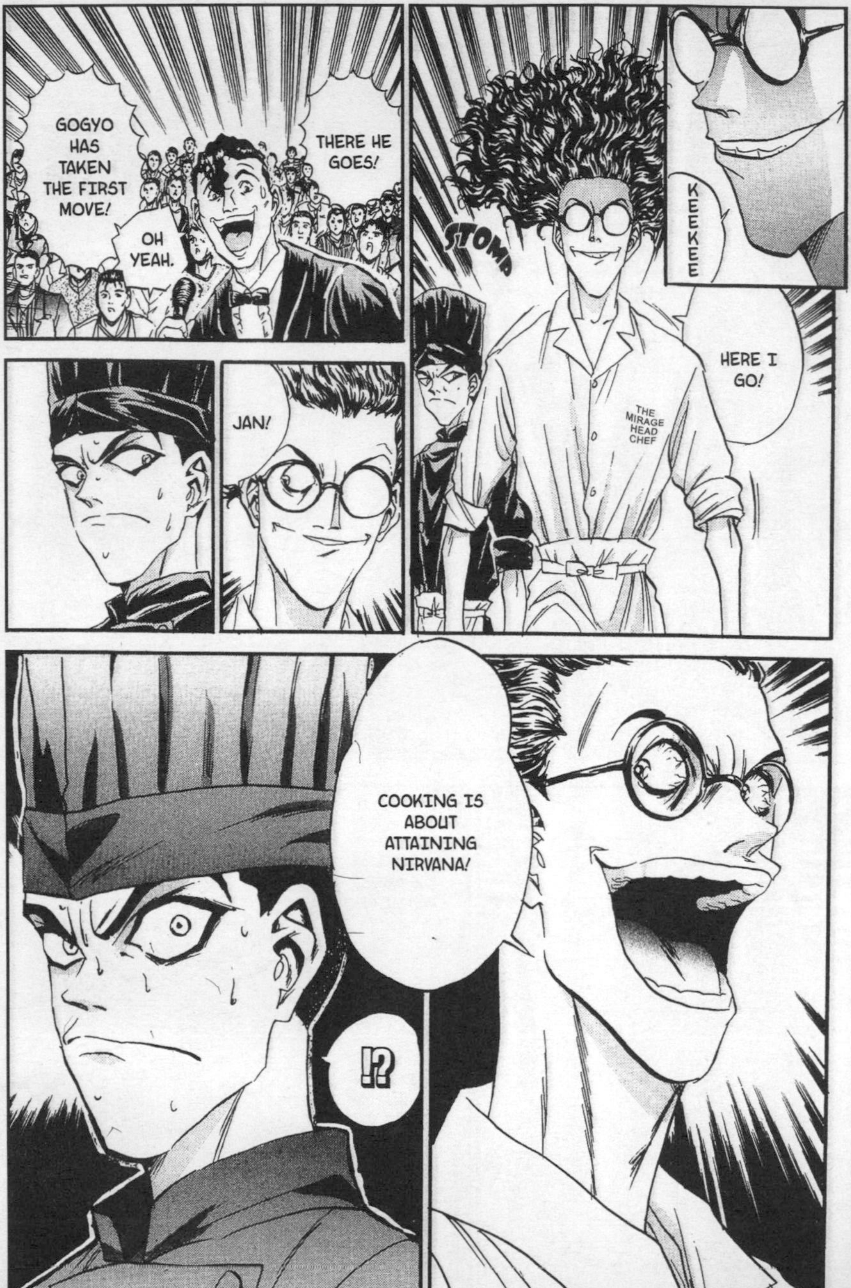
KEEKEE
STOMP
HERE I GO!
THE MIRAGE HEAD CHEF
THERE HE GOES!
GOGYO HAS TAKEN THE FIRST MOVE!
OH YEAH.
JAN!
COOKING IS ABOUT ATTAINING NIRVANA!
!?

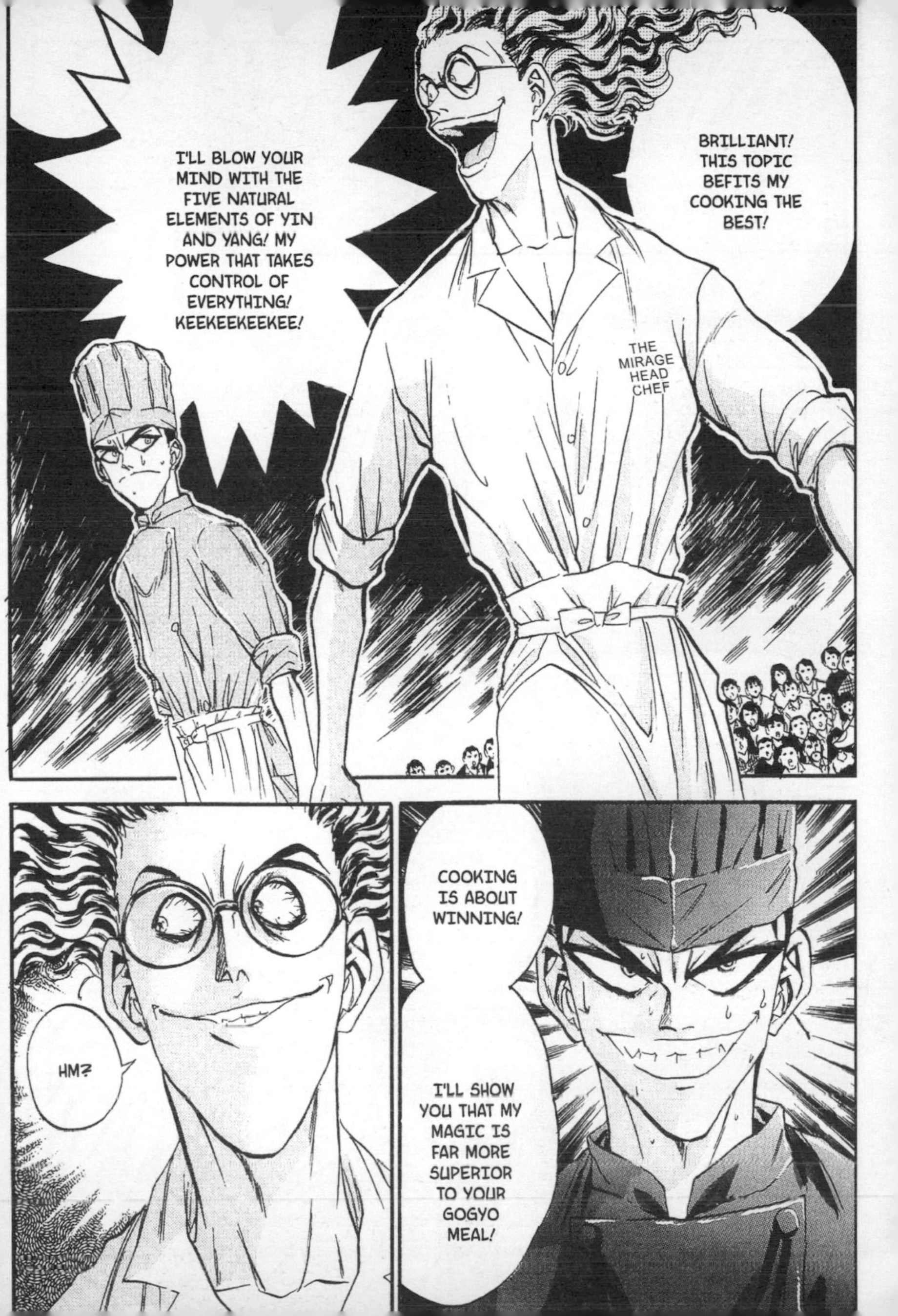
BRILLIANT! THIS TOPIC BEFITS MY COOKING THE BEST!
THE MIRAGE HEAD CHEF
I'LL BLOW YOUR MIND WITH THE FIVE NATURAL ELEMENTS OF YIN AND YANG! MY POWER THAT TAKES CONTROL OF EVERYTHING! KEEKEEKEEKEE!
COOKING IS ABOUT WINNING!
I'LL SHOW YOU THAT MY MAGIC IS FAR MORE SUPERIOR TO YOUR GOGYO MEAL!
HM?

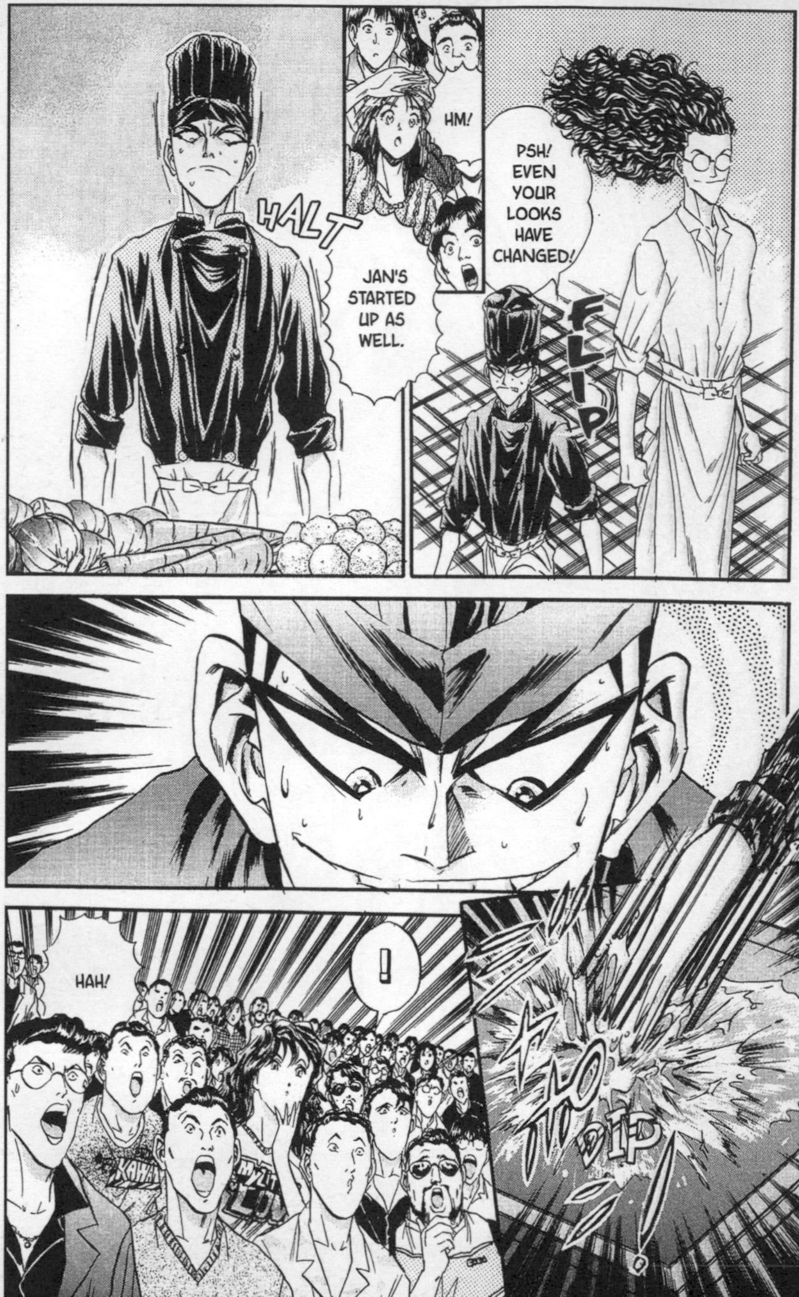
PSH! EVEN YOUR LOOKS HAVE CHANGED!
FLIP
HM!
JAN'S STARTED UP AS WELL.
HALT
DIP
!
HAH!

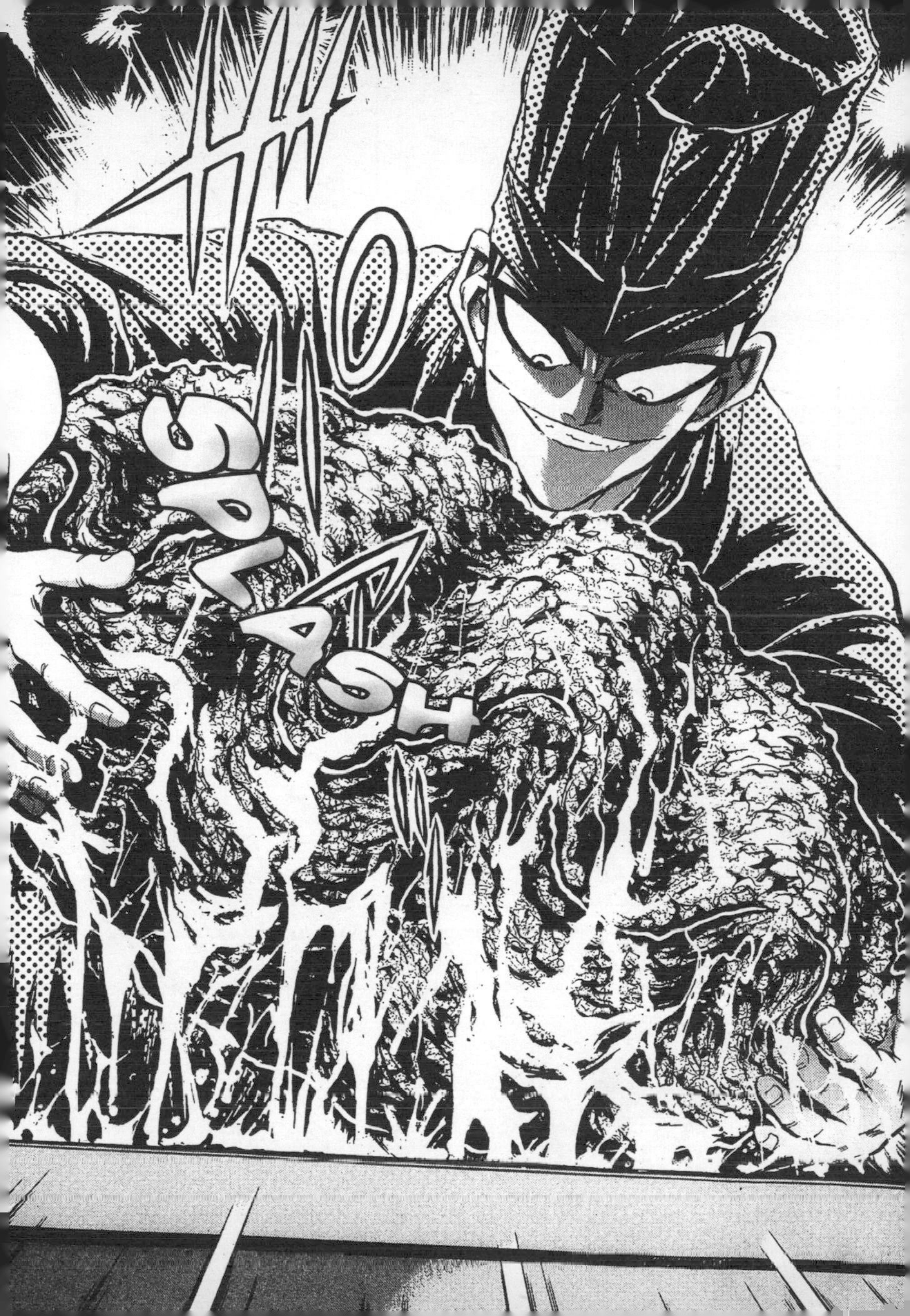
SPLASH

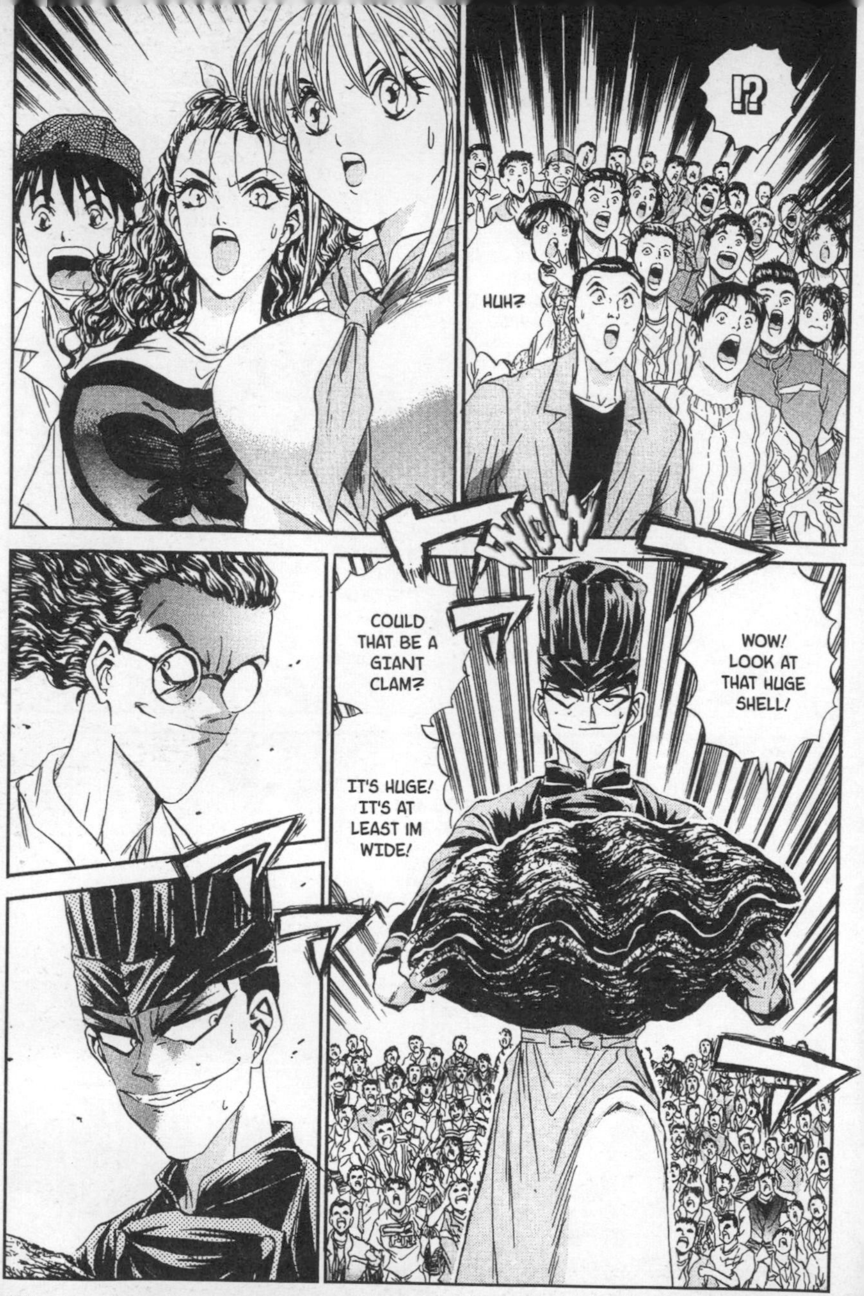
!?
HUH?
WOW! LOOK AT THAT HUGE SHELL!
COULD THAT BE A GIANT CLAM?
IT'S HUGE! IT'S AT LEAST IM WIDE!

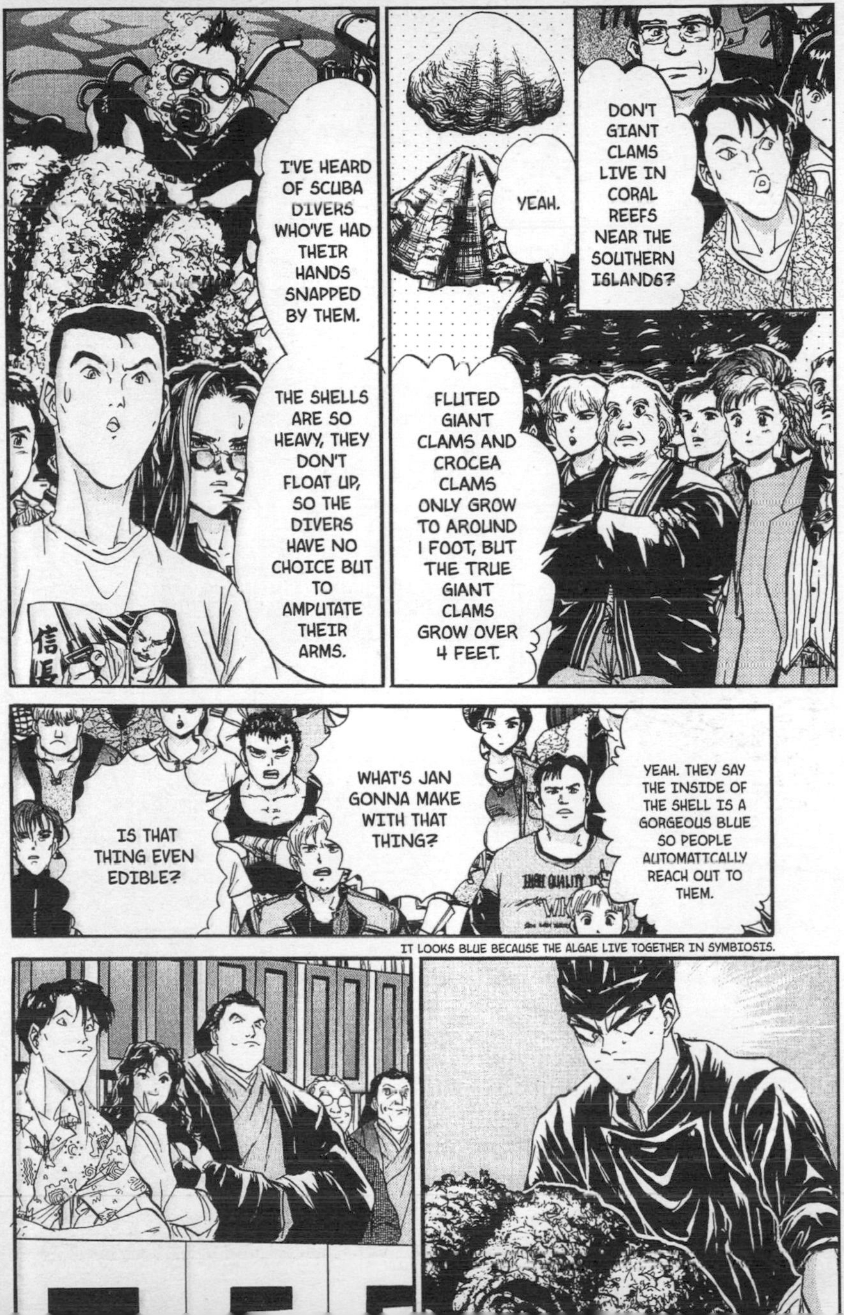
DON'T GIANT CLAMS LIVE IN CORAL REEFS NEAR THE SOUTHERN ISLANDS?
YEAH.
FLUTED GIANT CLAMS AND CROCEA CLAMS ONLY GROW TO AROUND 1 FOOT, BUT THE TRUE GIANT CLAMS GROW OVER 4 FEET.
I'VE HEARD OF SCUBA DIVERS WHO'VE HAD THEIR HANDS SNAPPED BY THEM.
THE SHELLS ARE SO HEAVY, THEY DON'T FLOAT UP, SO THE DIVERS HAVE NO CHOICE BUT TO AMPUTATE THEIR ARMS.
YEAH. THEY SAY THE INSIDE OF THE SHELL IS A GORGEOUS BLUE SO PEOPLE AUTOMATTCALLY REACH OUT TO THEM.
WHAT'S JAN GONNA MAKE WITH THAT THING?
IS THAT THING EVEN EDIBLE?
IT LOOKS BLUE BECAUSE THE ALGAE LIVE TOGETHER IN SYMBIOSIS.

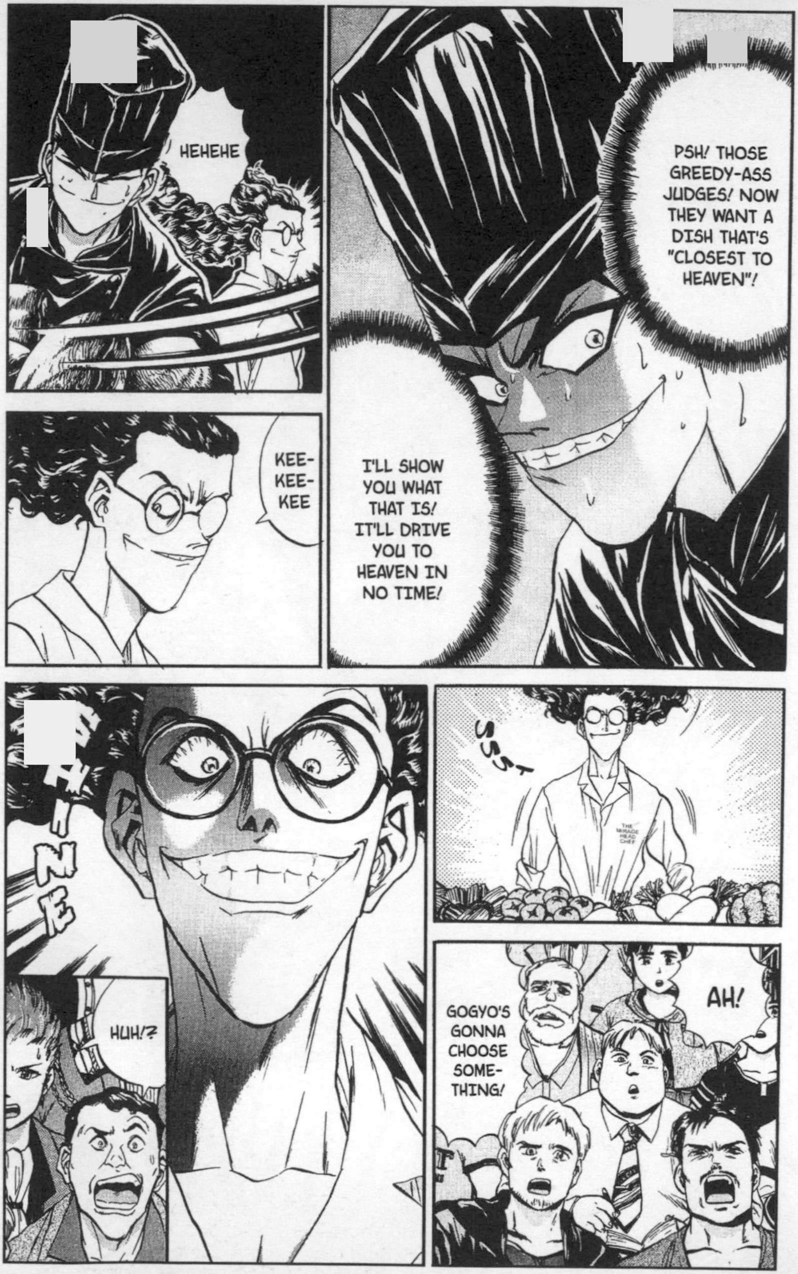
PSH! THOSE GREEDY-ASS JUDGES! NOW THEY WANT A DISH THAT'S "CLOSEST TO HEAVEN"!
I'LL SHOW YOU WHAT THAT IS! IT'LL DRIVE YOU TO HEAVEN IN NO TIME!
HEHEHE
KEE-KEE-KEE
AH!
GOGYO'S GONNA CHOOSE SOME-THING!
HUH!?

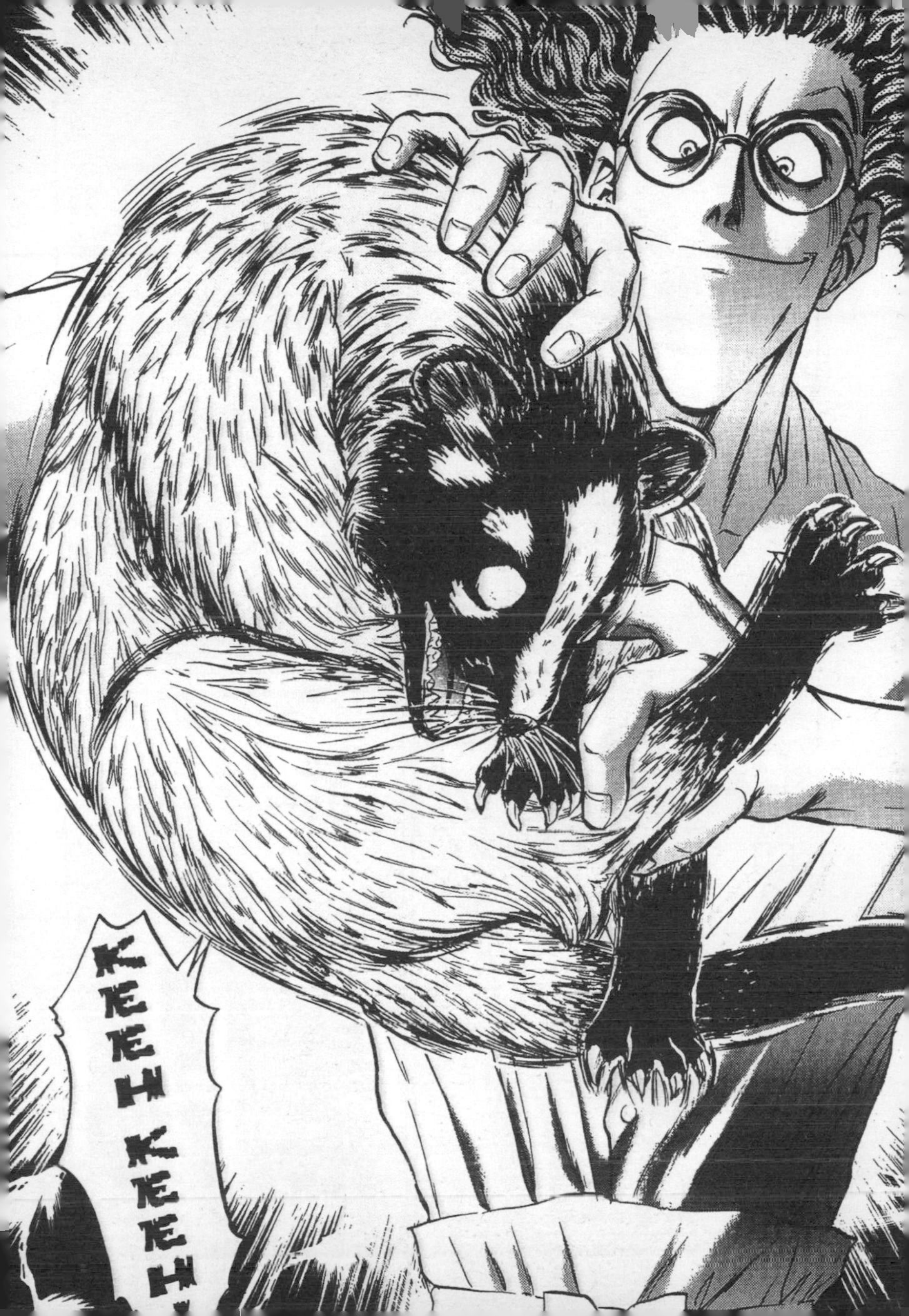
KEEH KEEH

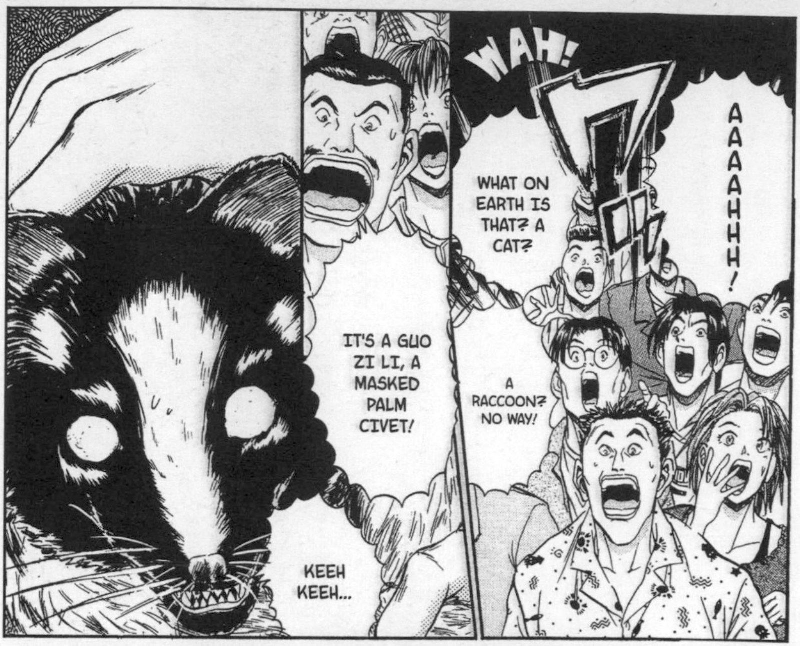
WAH!
AAAAAHHH!
WHAT ON EARTH IS THAT? A CAT?
A RACCOON? NO WAY!
IT'S A GUO ZI LI, A MASKED PALM CIVET!
KEEH KEEH...

MASKED PALM CIVET: OF THE CIVET CAT FAMILY

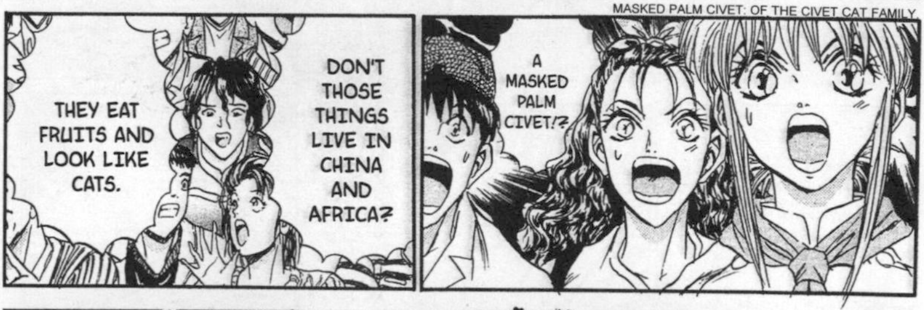
A MASKED PALM CIVET!?
DON'T THOSE THINGS LIVE IN CHINA AND AFRICA?
THEY EAT FRUITS AND LOOK LIKE CATS.

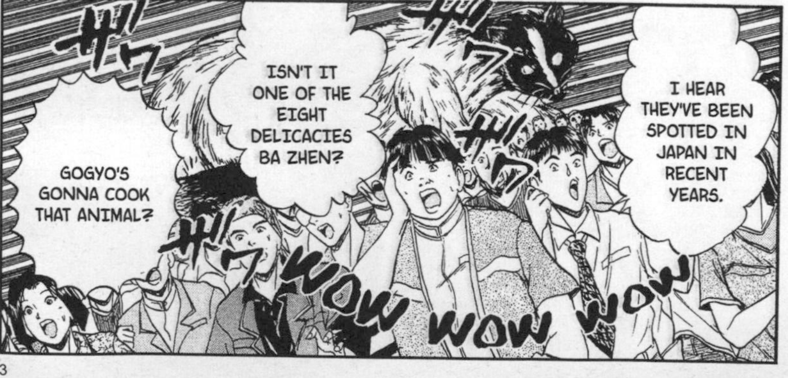
I HEAR THEY'VE BEEN SPOTTED IN JAPAN IN RECENT YEARS.
ISN'T IT ONE OF THE EIGHT DELICACIES BA ZHEN?
GOGYO'S GONNA COOK THAT ANIMAL?
WOW WOW
WOW WOW

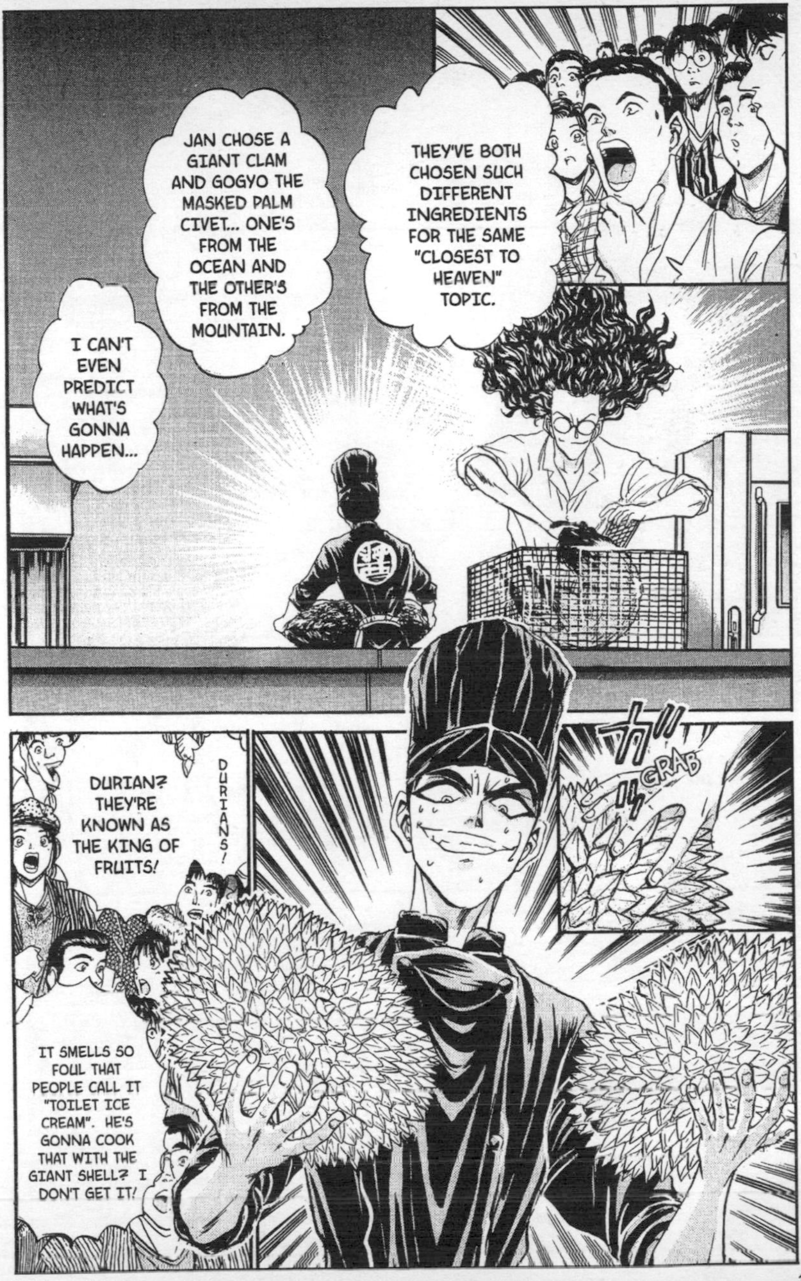
THEY'VE BOTH CHOSEN SUCH DIFFERENT INGREDIENTS FOR THE SAME "CLOSEST TO HEAVEN" TOPIC.
JAN CHOSE A GIANT CLAM AND GOGYO THE MASKED PALM CIVET... ONE'S FROM THE OCEAN AND THE OTHER'S FROM THE MOUNTAIN.
I CAN'T EVEN PREDICT WHAT'S GONNA HAPPEN...
GRAB
DURIANS!
DURIAN? THEY'RE KNOWN AS THE KING OF FRUITS!
IT SMELLS SO FOUL THAT PEOPLE CALL IT "TOILET ICE CREAM". HE'S GONNA COOK THAT WITH THE GIANT SHELL? I DON'T GET IT!

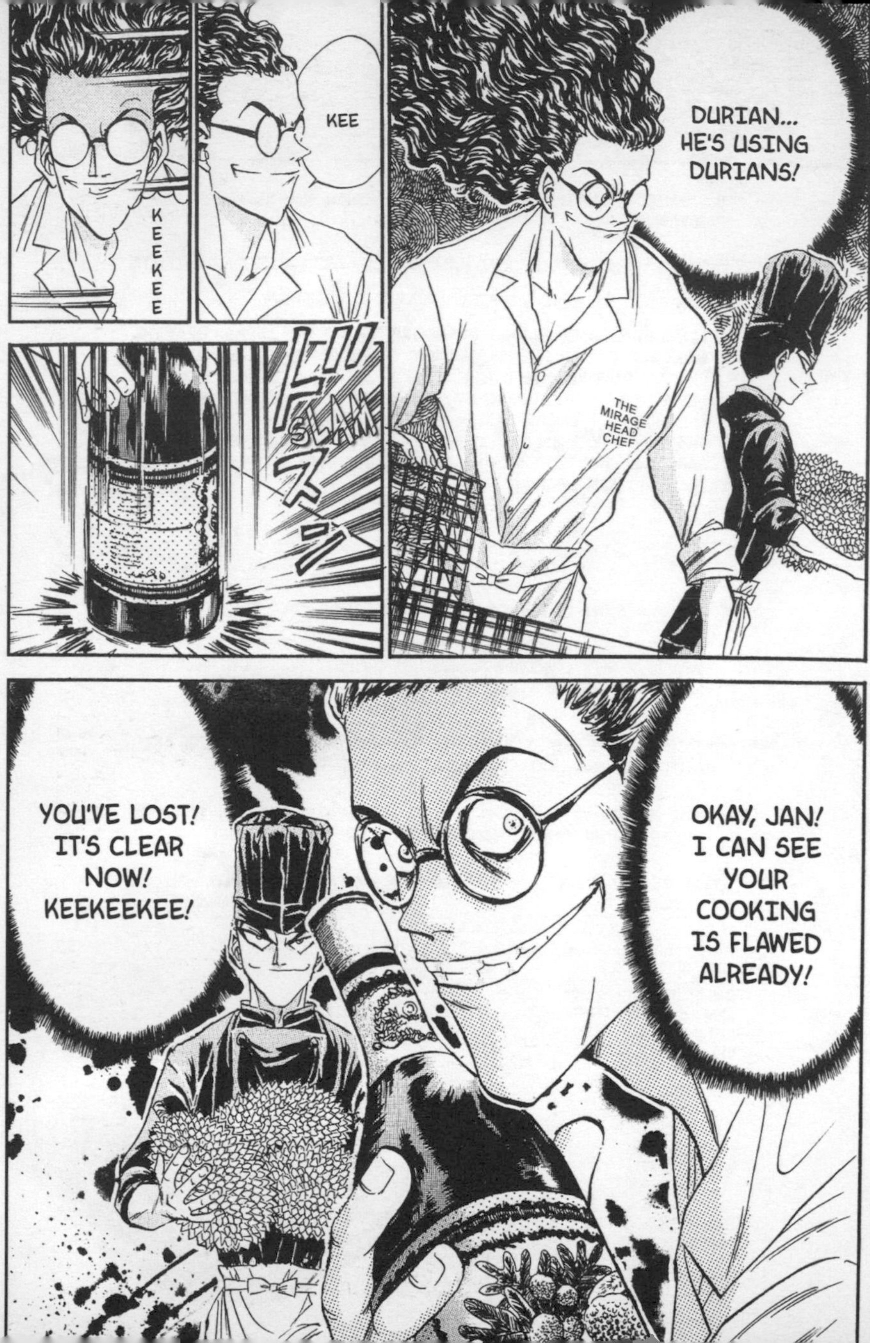
DURIAN... HE'S USING DURIANS!
THE MIRAGE HEAD CHEF
KEE
KEEKEE
SLAM
OKAY, JAN! I CAN SEE YOUR COOKING IS FLAWED ALREADY!
YOU'VE LOST! IT'S CLEAR NOW! KEEKEEKEE!

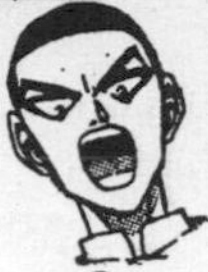

JAN AND OKONOGI'S BEIJING STEAMED DUMPLINGS.

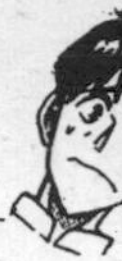

(O) STEAMED DUMPLINGS! THANKS! MUNCH MUNCH. MM! THEY'RE SO JUICY!

(J) D- DUDE! MAKE YOUR OWN, MAN! YOU CAN USE THESE INGREDIENTS.

(O) CAN'T YOU SHOW ME HOW? I WANNA EAT AT LEAST 30!

(J) FINE! WATCH AND LEARN! CHOP UP THE SHRIMP AND LEEKS. BEAT THE EGGS AND FLAVOR IT WITH SALT AND OTHER SEASONINGS. HERE'S THE CRUCIAL PART. YOU NEED TO FRY THE EGGS WITH OIL. THIS IS THE SECRET TO MAKING THE DUMPLINGS JUICY. NEXT, ADD MINCED PORK AND GROUND GINGER IN A BOWL. ADD ALL THE SEASONINGS EXCEPT THE SAKE, AND THEN "MA" IT REAL WELL. THIS IS WHEN WE ADD THE SAKE AND CHOPPED SHRIMP AND LEEKS. THE LAST THING TO ADD ARE THE EGGS. SIMPLE, HUH?

(O) HEY, WHAT'S "MA"? HOW DO YOU "MA" IT? MUNCH MUNCH.

(J) YOU WEREN'T WATCHING, WERE YOU? TO "MA" THE INGREDIENTS MEANS TO MIX IT WITH A NUMBER OF CHOPSTICKS. BUT REMEMBER, NEVER CHANGE THE DIRECTION OF MIXING!

(O) I CAN DO THE REST. I JUST NEED TO WRAP THEM IN THE SKINS AND BOIL 'EM! HAHA! LOOK! THEY'RE RISING! HEY'RE DONE!

(J) NOT YET. YOU ALWAYS WANT TO GIVE IT AN EXTRA SECOND. HUH? WHERE ARE THE ONES I MADE FOR MYSELF?

(O) OH THOSE? I ATE THOSE! I DIDN'T WANT 'EM TO GET COLD, YOU KNOW?

(J:) DAMN YOU, OKONOGI!

INGREDIENTS (FOR 30 DUMPLINGS)

DUMPLING SKINS (30)
MINCED PORK (150G)
SHRIMP (50G)
LEEK (50G)
GINGER (5G)
EGG (2)

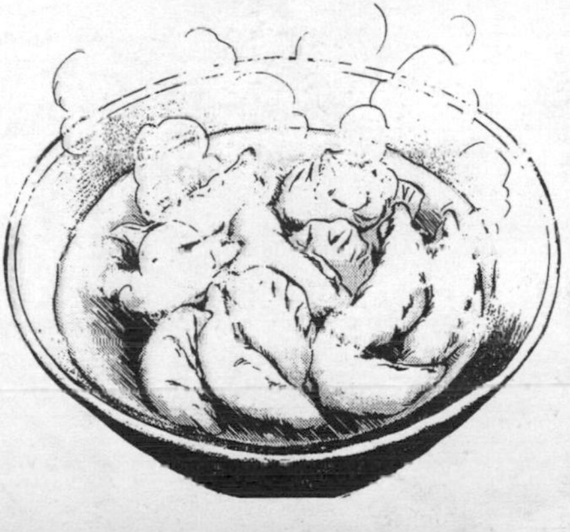

SEASONING

SOY SAUCE (2 TABLESPOONS)
SESAME OIL (2 TABLESPOONS)
WATER (4 TABLESPOONS)
SAKE (1/2 TABLESPOON)
PEPPER

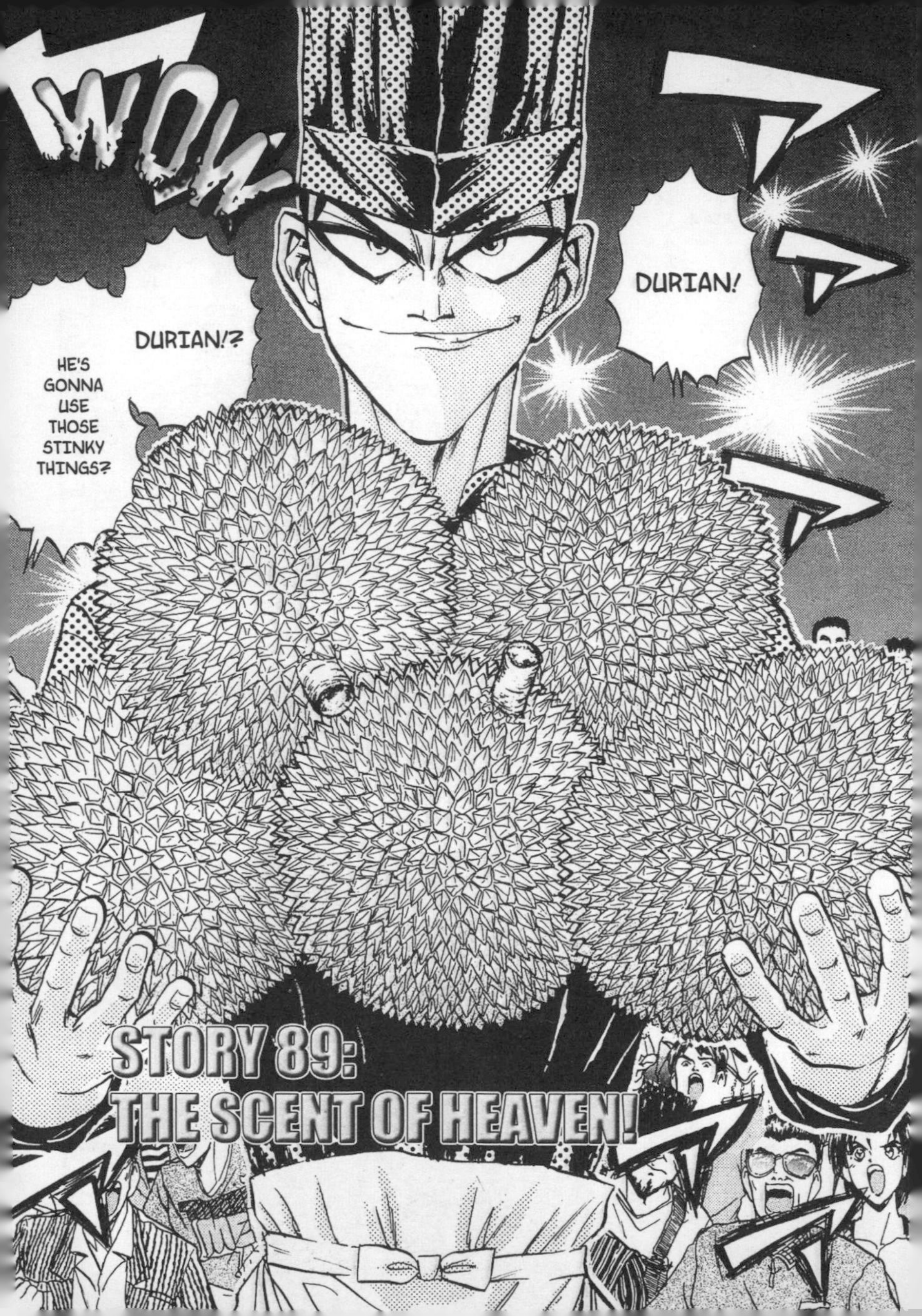
DURIAN!
WOW
DURIAN!?
HE'S GONNA USE THOSE STINKY THINGS?
STORY 89: THE SCENT OF HEAVEN!

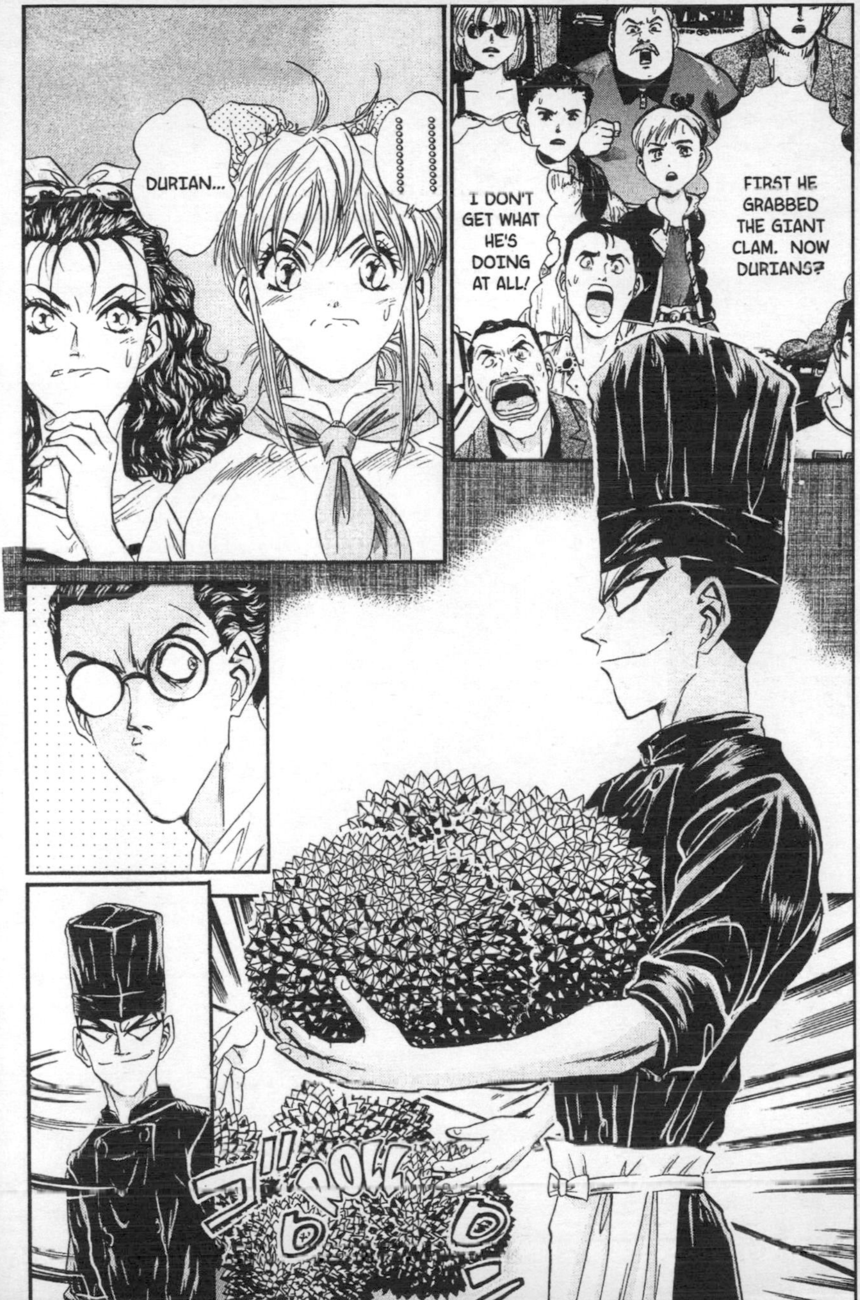
FIRST HE GRABBED THE GIANT CLAM. NOW DURIANS?
I DON'T GET WHAT HE'S DOING AT ALL!
....
DURIAN...
ROLL

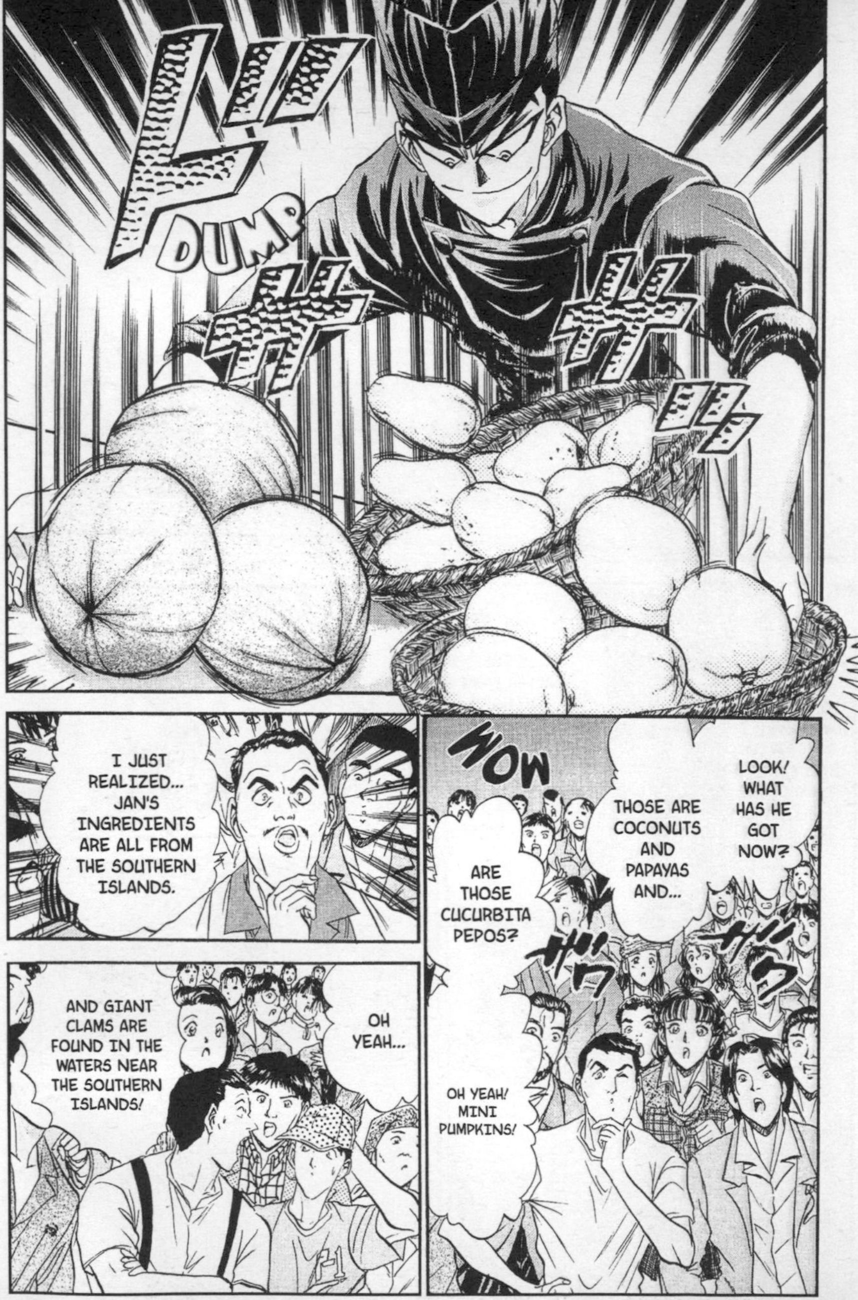
DUMP
WOW
LOOK! WHAT HAS HE GOT NOW?
THOSE ARE COCONUTS AND PAPAYAS AND...
ARE THOSE CUCURBITA PEPOS?
OH YEAH! MINI PUMPKINS!
I JUST REALIZED... JAN'S INGREDIENTS ARE ALL FROM THE SOUTHERN ISLANDS.
OH YEAH...
AND GIANT CLAMS ARE FOUND IN THE WATERS NEAR THE SOUTHERN ISLANDS!

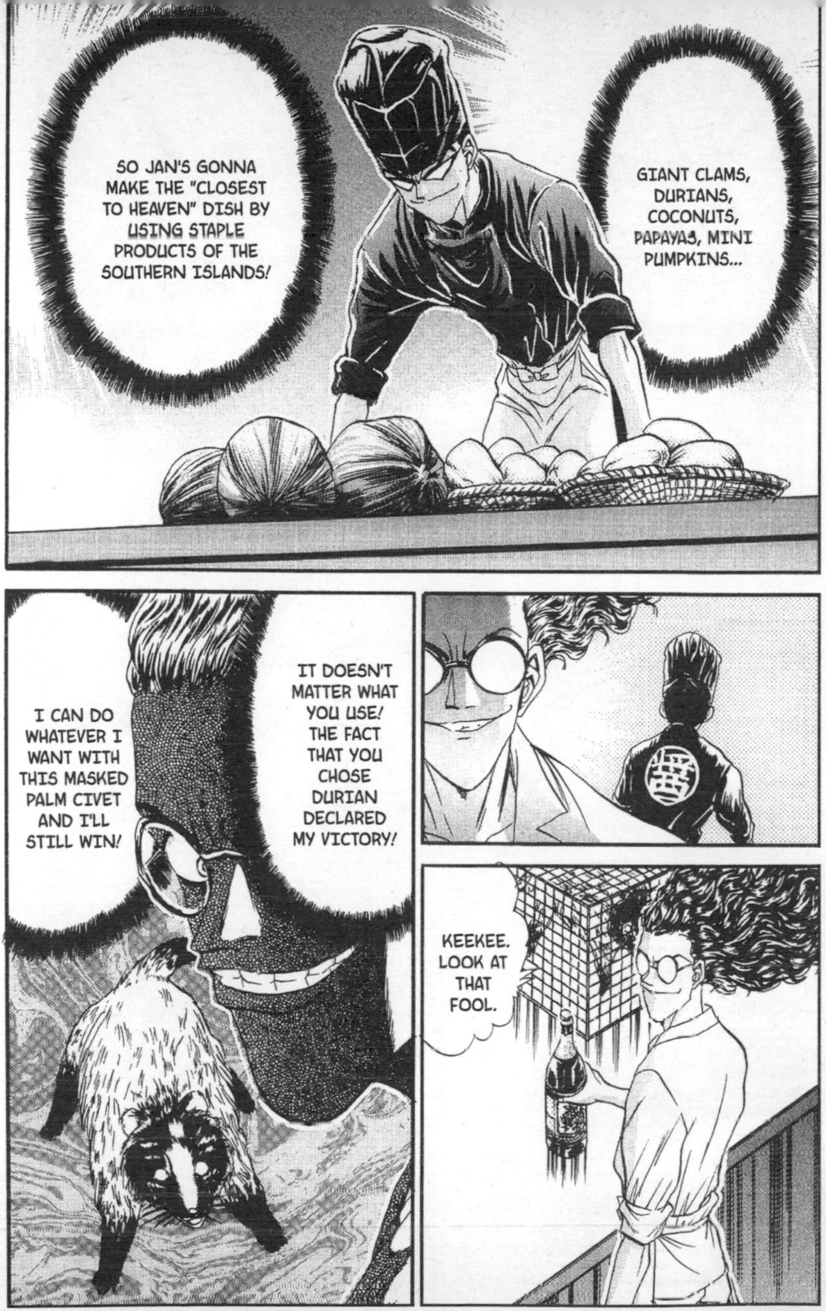
GIANT CLAMS, DURIANS, COCONUTS, PAPAYAS, MINI PUMPKINS...
SO JAN'S GONNA MAKE THE "CLOSEST TO HEAVEN" DISH BY USING STAPLE PRODUCTS OF THE SOUTHERN ISLANDS!
KEEKEE. LOOK AT THAT FOOL.
IT DOESN'T MATTER WHAT YOU USE! THE FACT THAT YOU CHOSE DURIAN DECLARED MY VICTORY!
I CAN DO WHATEVER I WANT WITH THIS MASKED PALM CIVET AND I'LL STILL WIN!

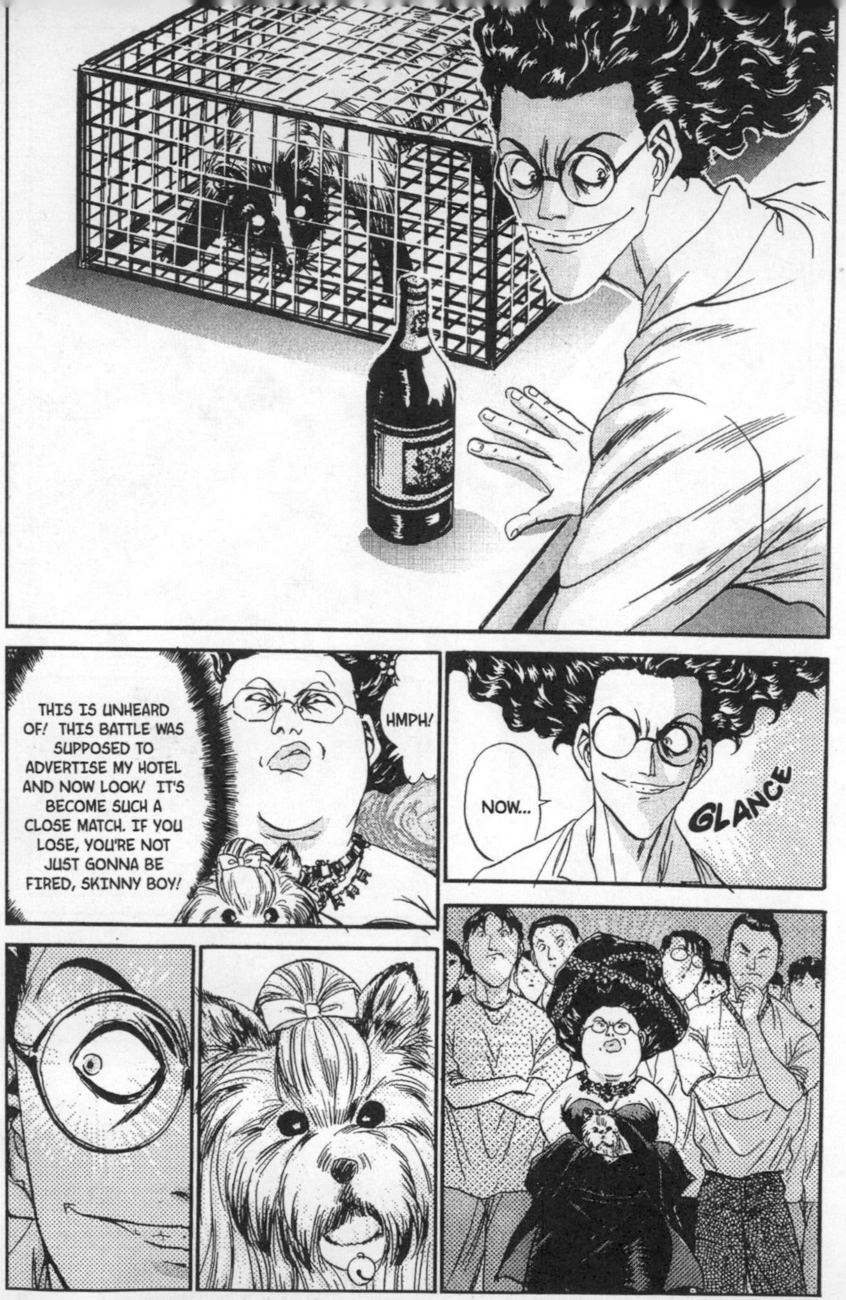
NOW...
GLANCE
HMPH!
THIS IS UNHEARD OF! THIS BATTLE WAS SUPPOSED TO ADVERTISE MY HOTEL AND NOW LOOK! IT'S BECOME SUCH A CLOSE MATCH. IF YOU LOSE, YOU'RE NOT JUST GONNA BE FIRED, SKINNY BOY!

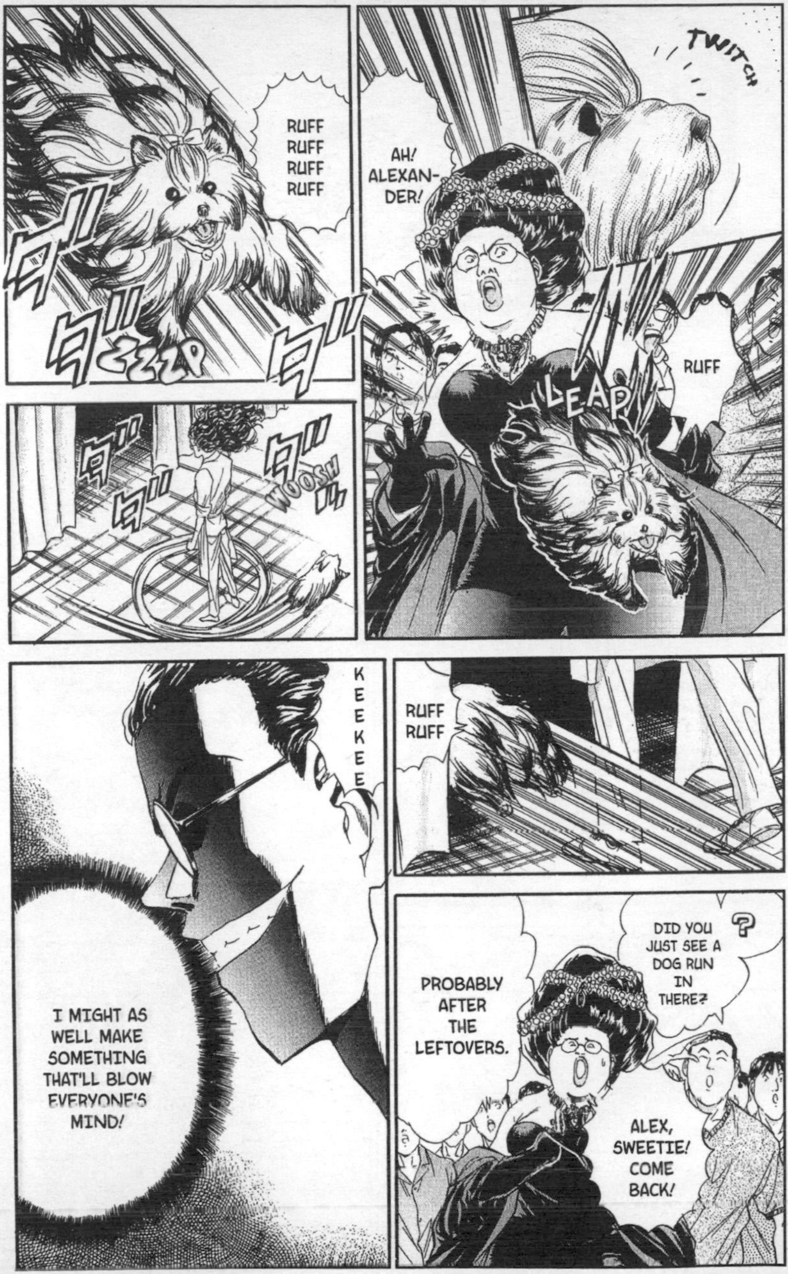
TWITCH
AH! ALEXANDER!
RUFF
LEAP
RUFF RUFF RUFF RUFF
ZZZZP
WOOSH
RUFF RUFF
?
DID YOU JUST SEE A DOG RUN IN THERE?
PROBABLY AFTER THE LEFTOVERS.
ALEX, SWEETIE! COME BACK!
KEEKEE
I MIGHT AS WELL MAKE SOMETHING THAT'LL BLOW EVERYONE'S MIND!

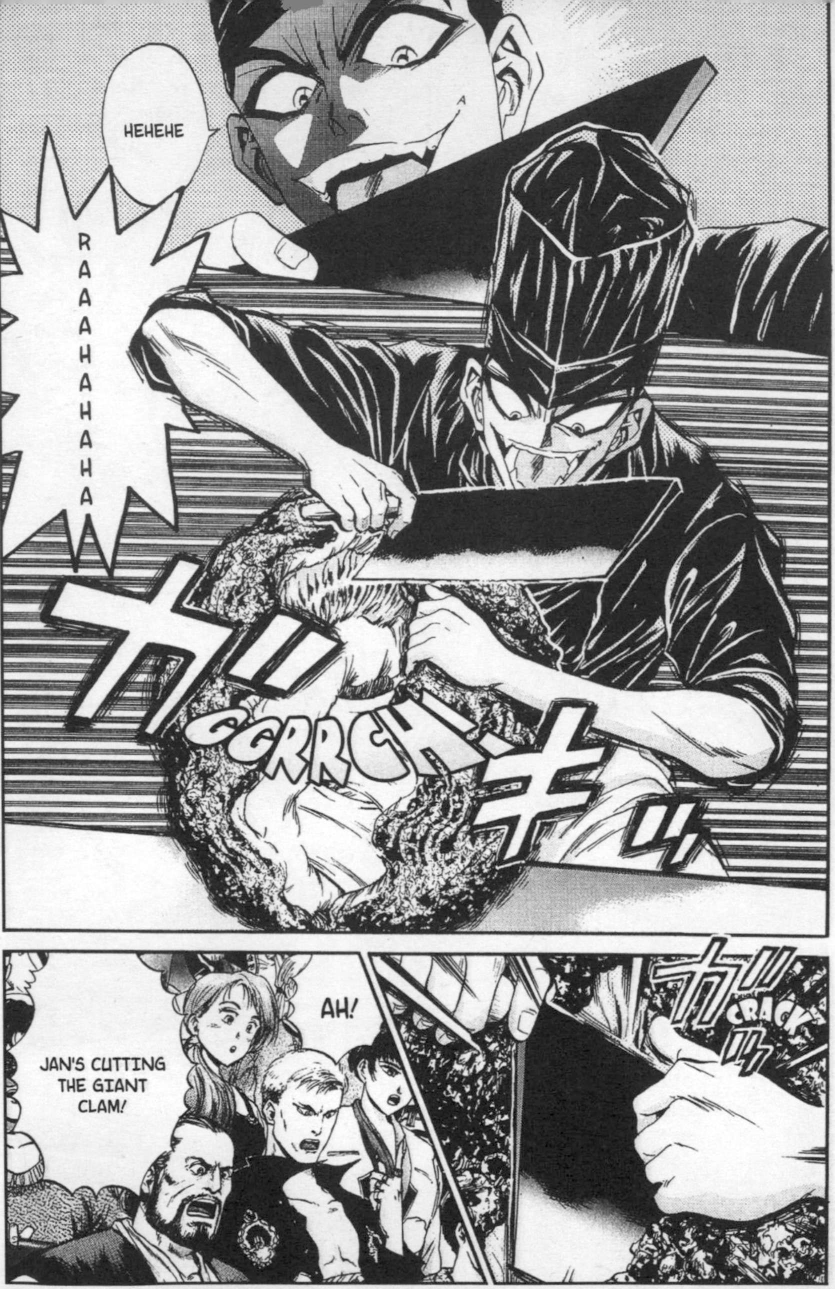
HEHEHE
RAAAAHAHAHAHA
GGRRCH
CRACK
AH!
JAN'S CUTTING THE GIANT CLAM!

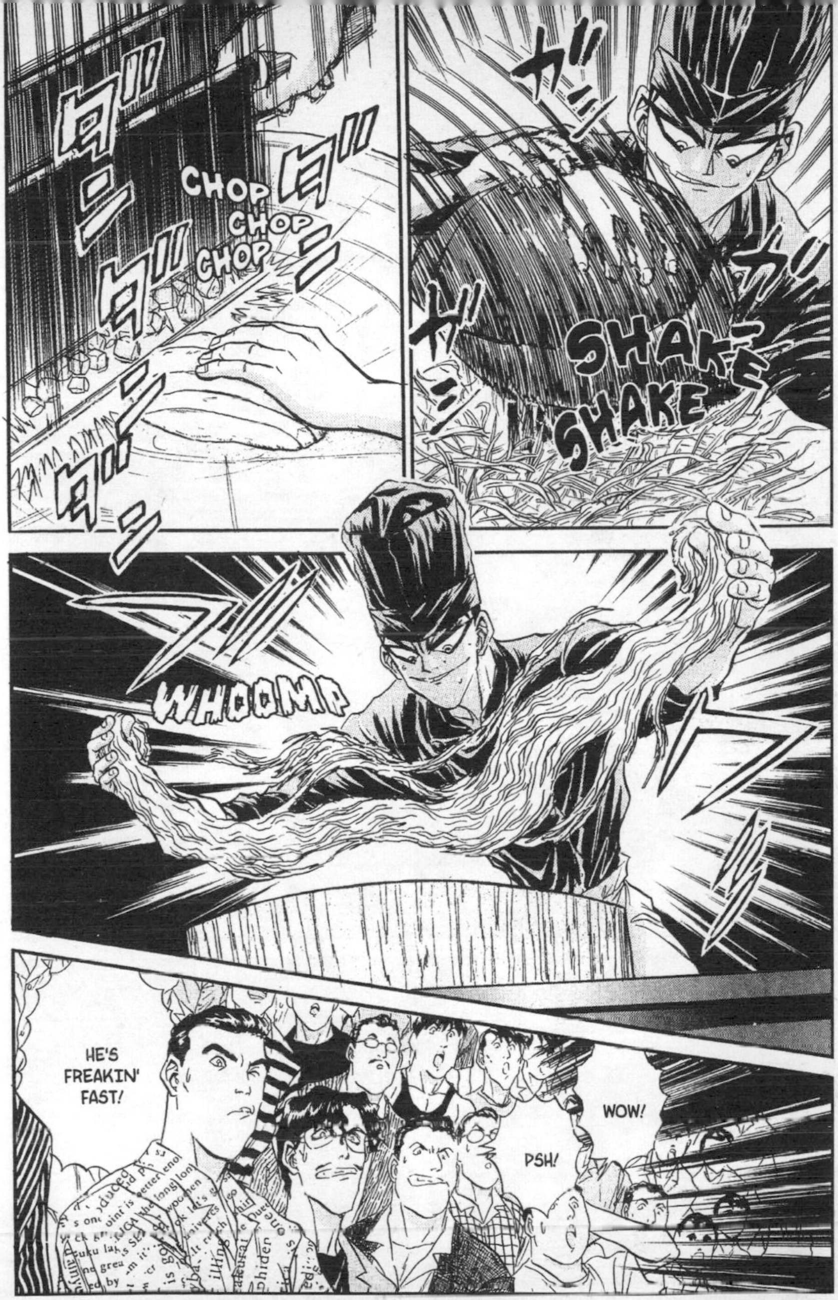
SHAKE
SHAKE
CHOP
CHOP
CHOP
WHOOMP
WOW!
PSH!
HE'S FREAKIN' FAST!

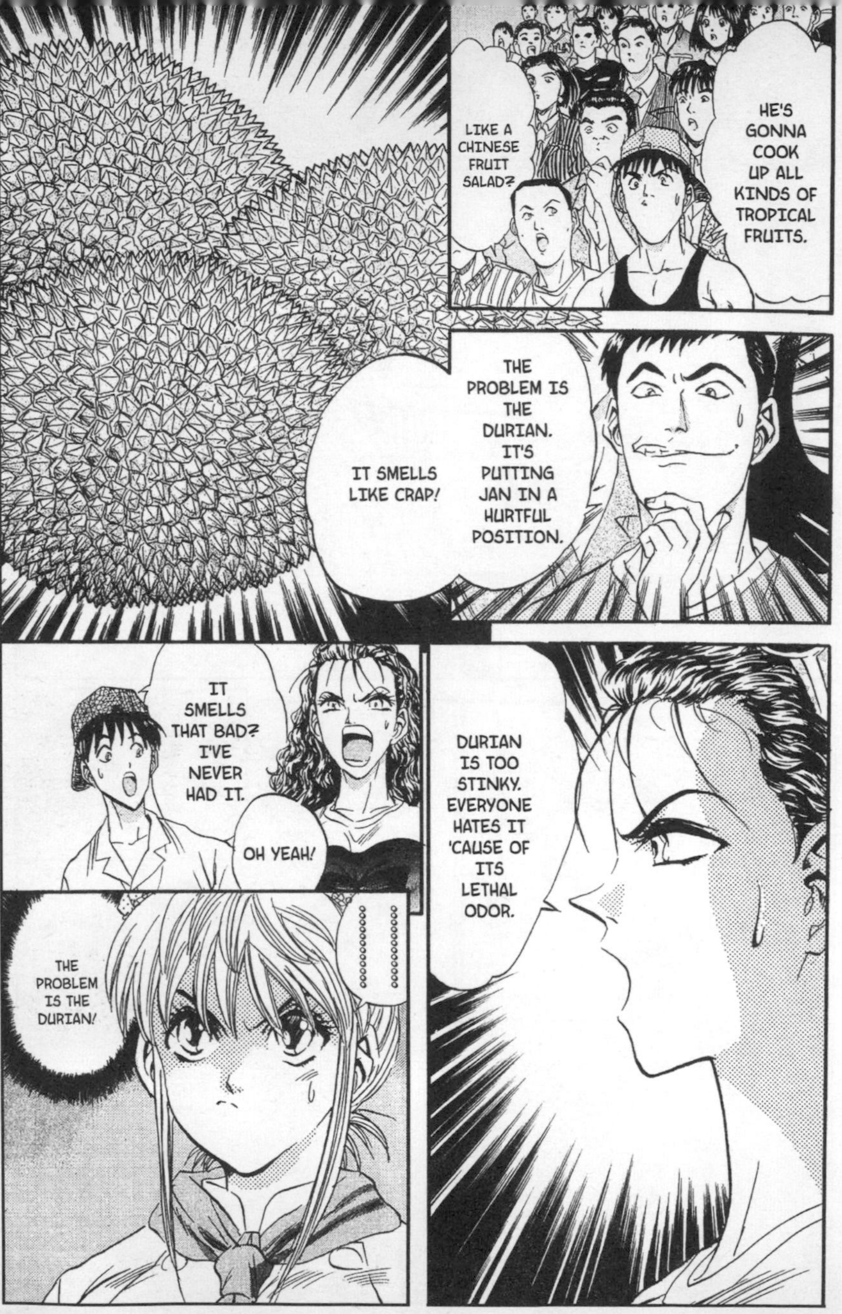

HE'S GONNA COOK UP ALL KINDS OF TROPICAL FRUITS.
LIKE A CHINESE FRUIT SALAD?
THE PROBLEM IS THE DURIAN. IT'S PUTTING JAN IN A HURTFUL POSITION.
IT SMELLS LIKE CRAP!
DURIAN IS TOO STINKY. EVERYONE HATES IT 'CAUSE OF ITS LETHAL ODOR.
IT SMELLS THAT BAD? I'VE NEVER HAD IT.
OH YEAH!
THE PROBLEM IS THE DURIAN!

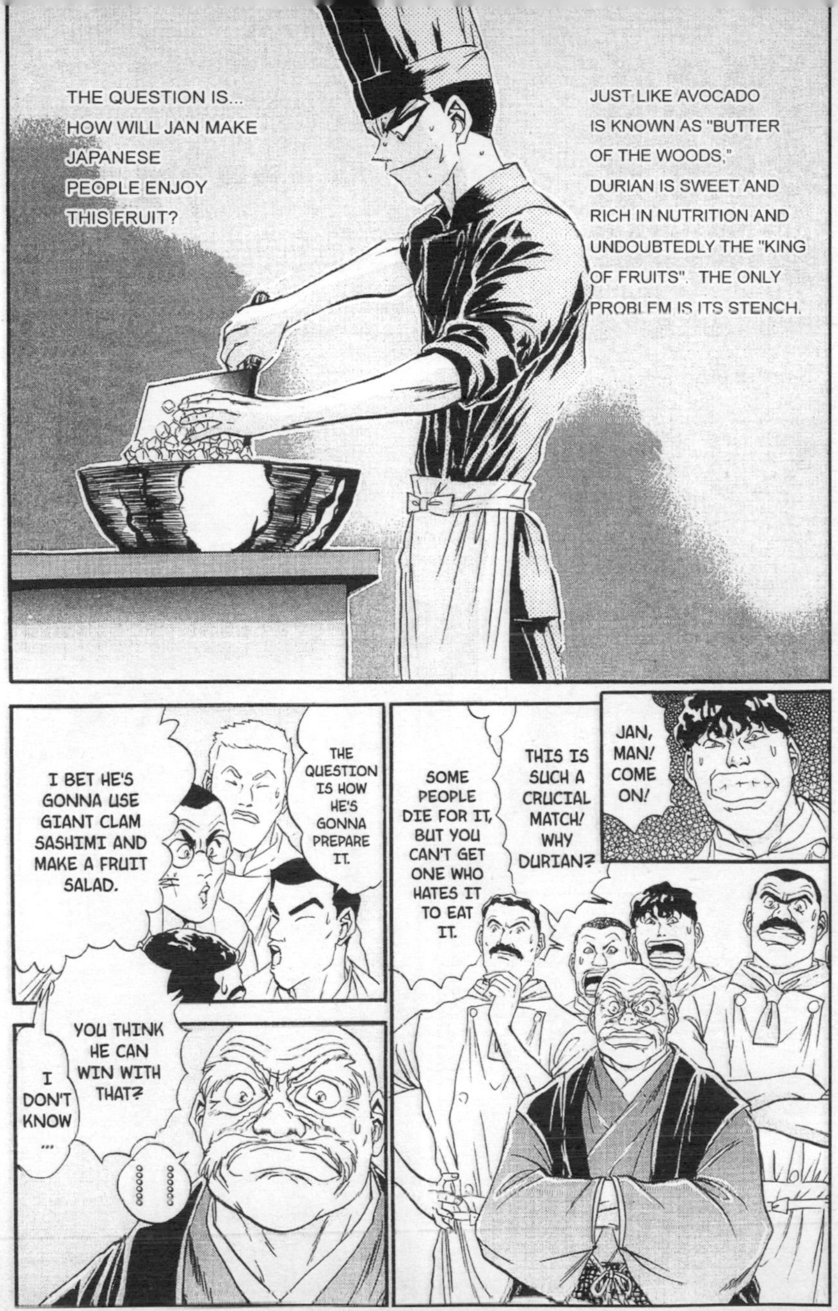
JUST LIKE AVOCADO IS KNOWN AS "BUTTER OF THE WOODS," DURIAN IS SWEET AND RICH IN NUTRITION AND UNDOUBTEDLY THE "KING OF FRUITS". THE ONLY PROBLEM IS ITS STENCH.
THE QUESTION IS... HOW WILL JAN MAKE JAPANESE PEOPLE ENJOY THIS FRUIT?
JAN, MAN! COME ON!
THIS IS SUCH A CRUCIAL MATCH! WHY DURIAN?
SOME PEOPLE DIE FOR IT, BUT YOU CAN'T GET ONE WHO HATES IT TO EAT IT.
THE QUESTION IS HOW HE'S GONNA PREPARE IT.
I BET HE'S GONNA USE GIANT CLAM SASHIMI AND MAKE A FRUIT SALAD.
YOU THINK HE CAN WIN WITH THAT?
I DON'T KNOW ...

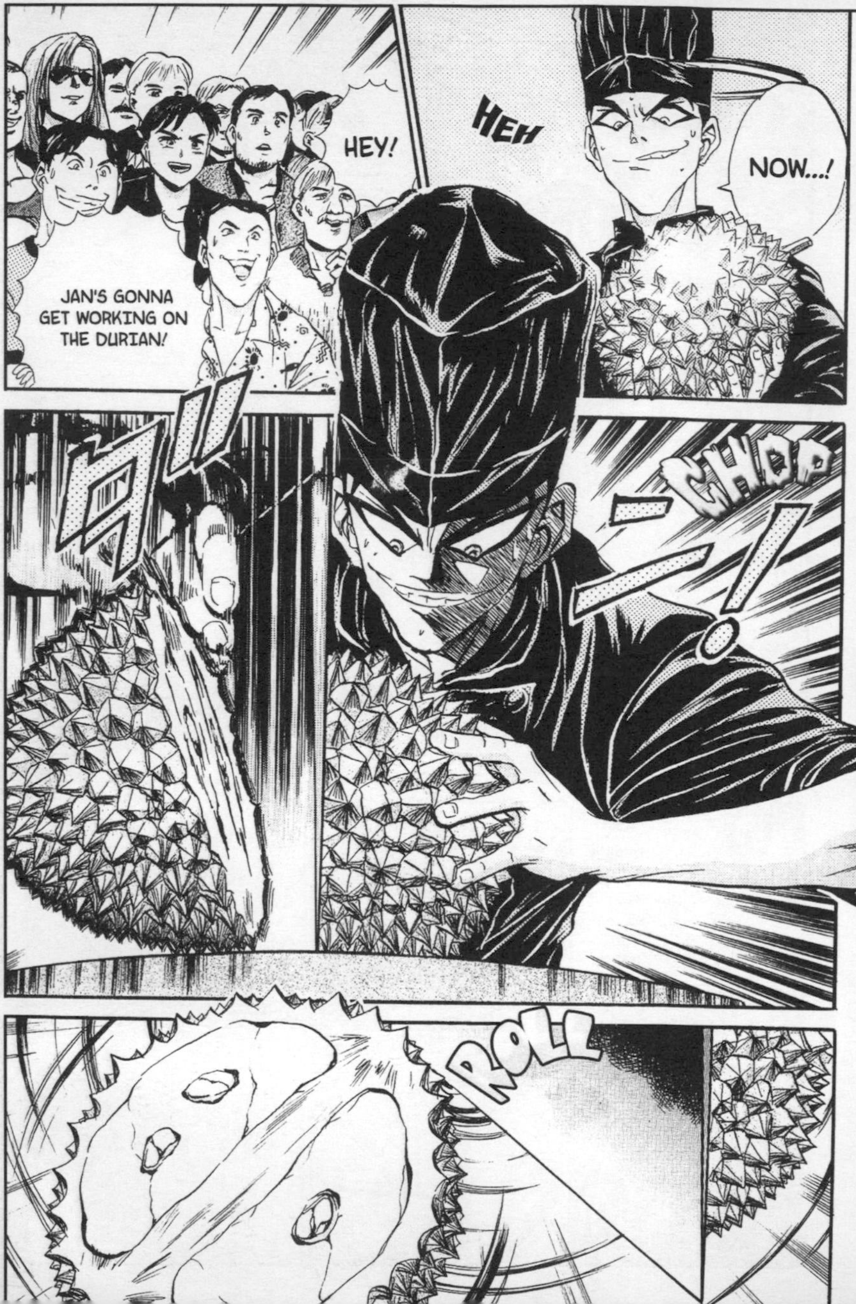
HEH
NOW...!
HEY!
JAN'S GONNA GET WORKING ON THE DURIAN!
CHOP
ROLL

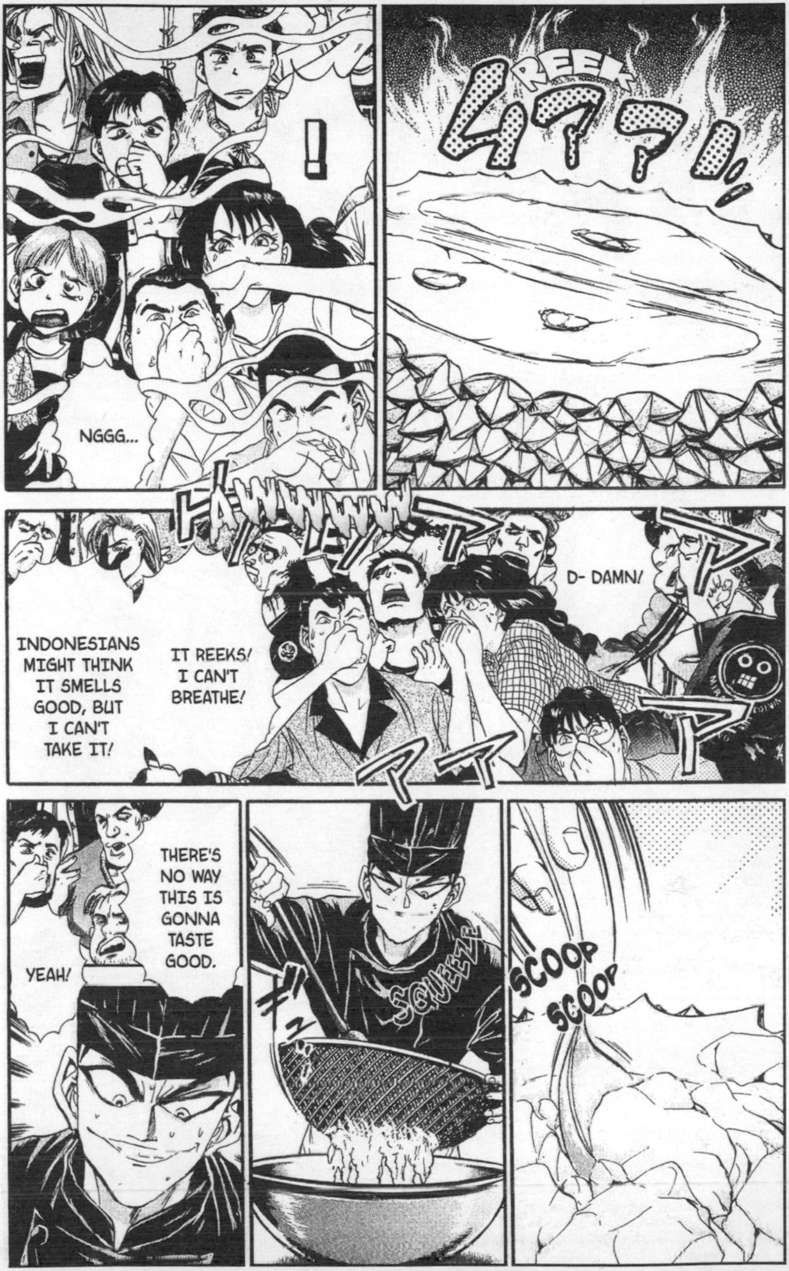
REEK
!
NGGG...
D- DAMN!
IT REEKS! I CAN'T BREATHE!
INDONESIANS MIGHT THINK IT SMELLS GOOD, BUT I CAN'T TAKE IT!
SCOOP SCOOP
SQUEEZE
THERE'S NO WAY THIS IS GONNA TASTE GOOD.
YEAH!

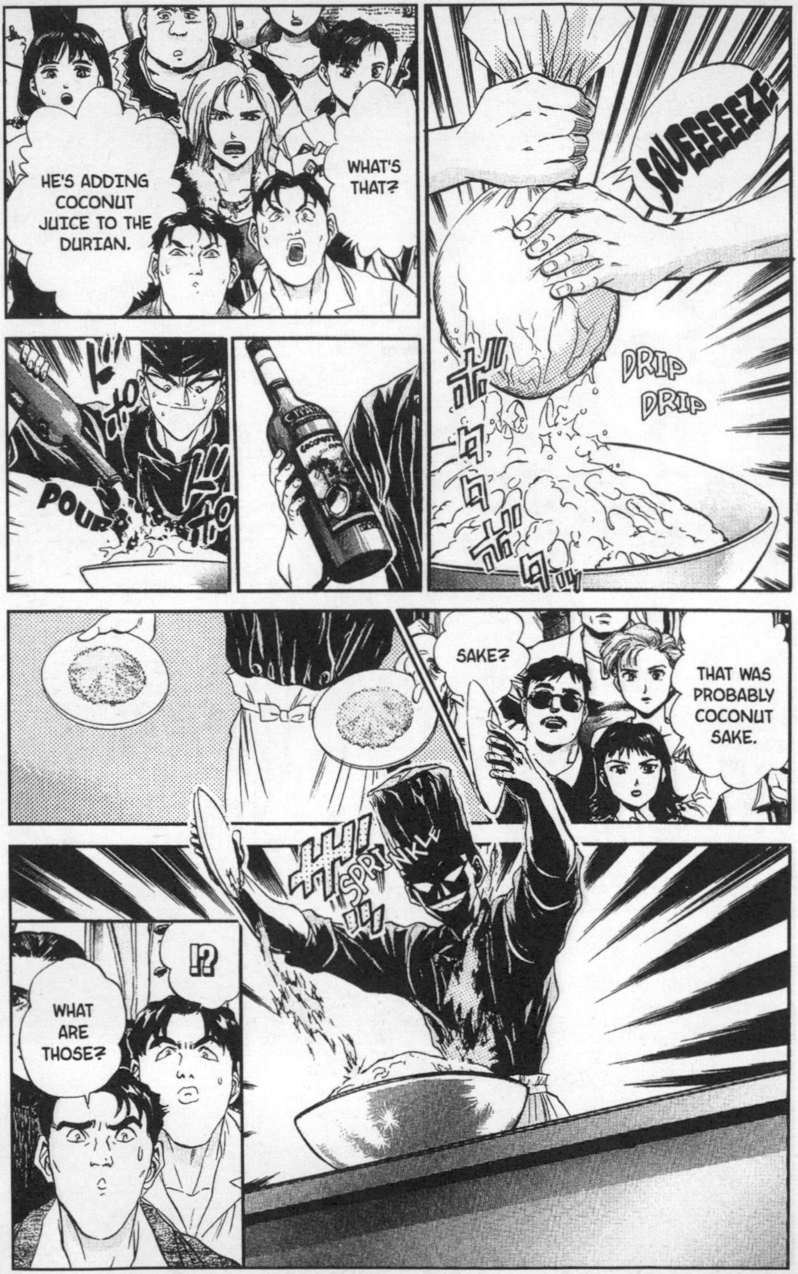

SQUEEEEEZE
DRIP
DRIP
WHAT'S THAT?
HE'S ADDING COCONUT JUICE TO THE DURIAN.
POUR
THAT WAS PROBABLY COCONUT SAKE.
SAKE?
SPRINKLE
!?
WHAT ARE THOSE?

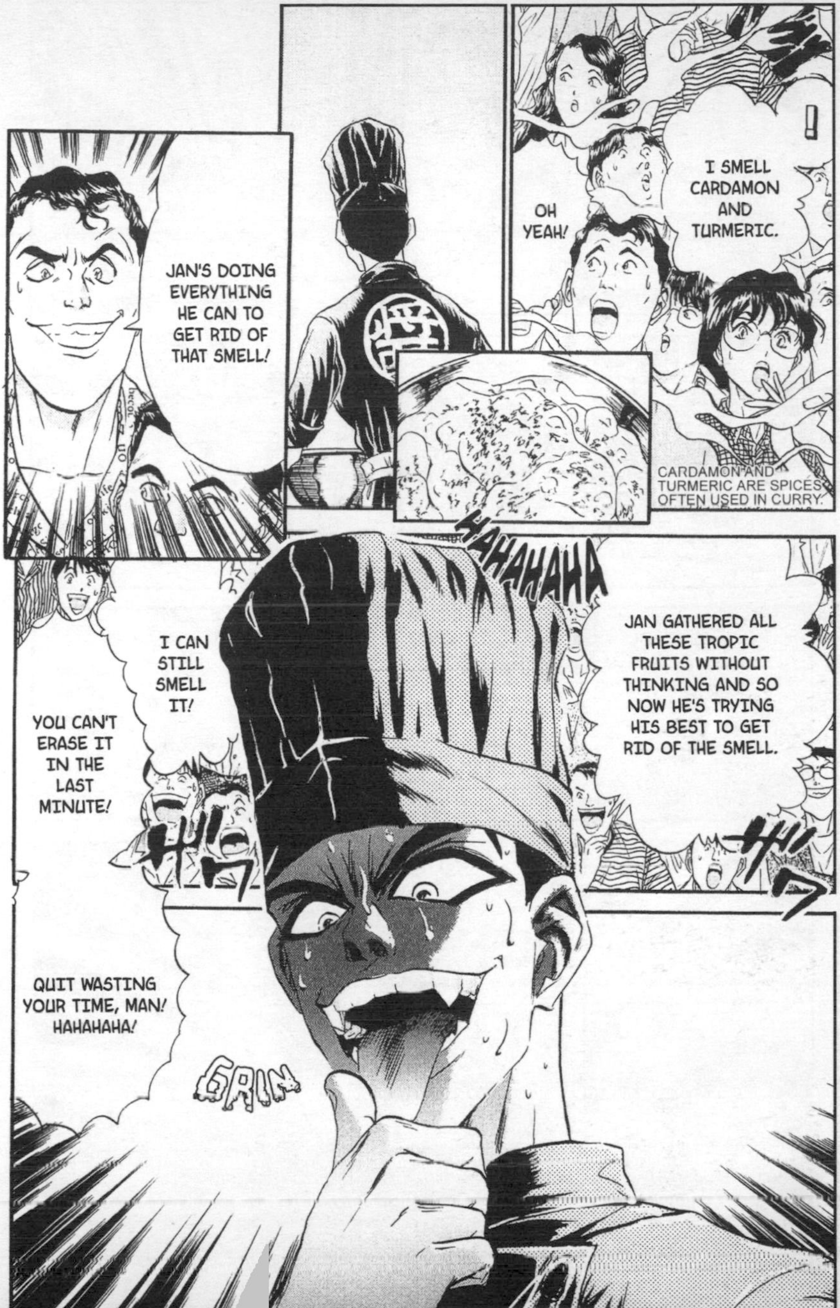
!
I SMELL CARDAMON AND TURMERIC.
OH YEAH!
CARDAMON AND TURMERIC ARE SPICES OFTEN USED IN CURRY.
JAN'S DOING EVERYTHING HE CAN TO GET RID OF THAT SMELL!
HAHAHAHA
JAN GATHERED ALL THESE TROPIC FRUITS WITHOUT THINKING AND SO NOW HE'S TRYING HIS BEST TO GET RID OF THE SMELL.
ザワ
I CAN STILL SMELL IT!
YOU CAN'T ERASE IT IN THE LAST MINUTE!
ザワ
QUIT WASTING YOUR TIME, MAN! HAHAHAHA!
GRIN

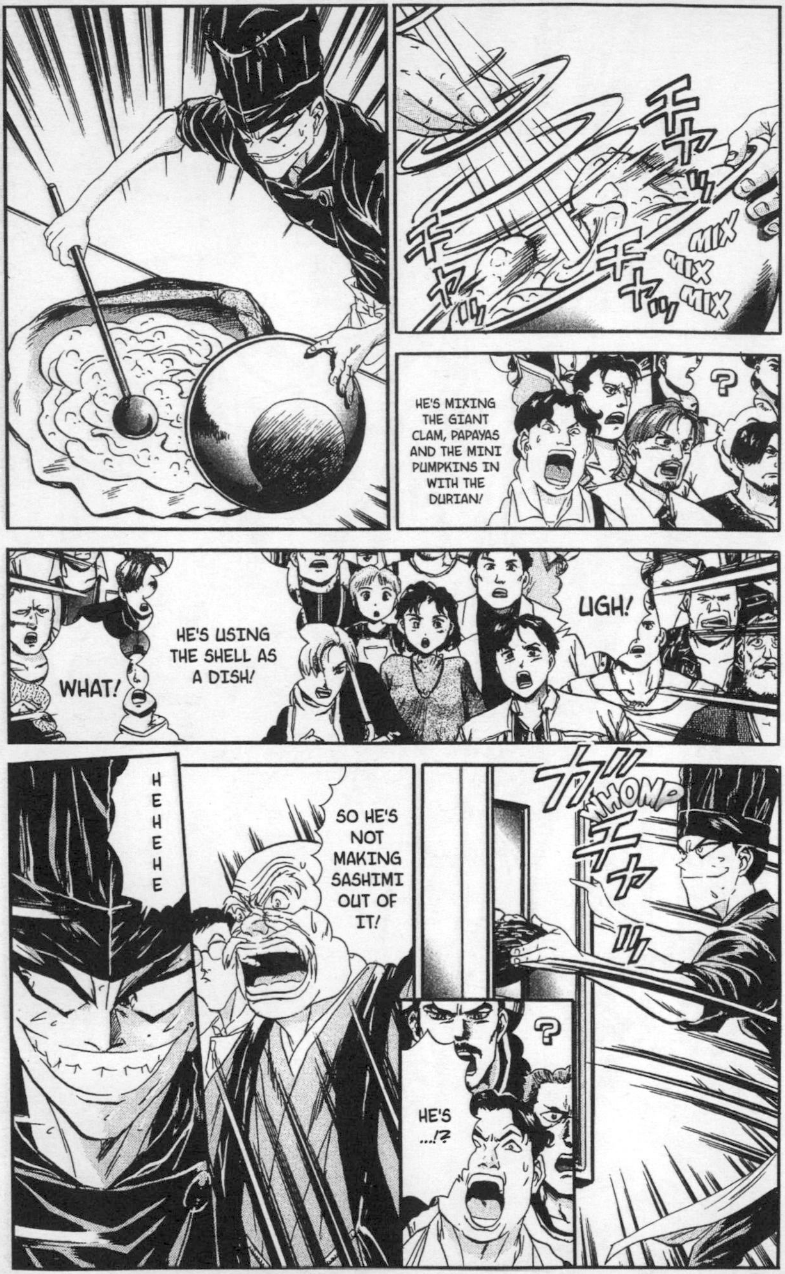
チャッ
チャッ
チャッ
MIX
MIX
MIX
HE'S MIXING THE GIANT CLAM, PAPAYAS AND THE MINI PUMPKINS IN WITH THE DURIAN!
?
UGH!
HE'S USING THE SHELL AS A DISH!
WHAT!
カッ
WHOMP
チャッ
?
HE'S ...!?
SO HE'S NOT MAKING SASHIMI OUT OF IT!
HEHEHEHE

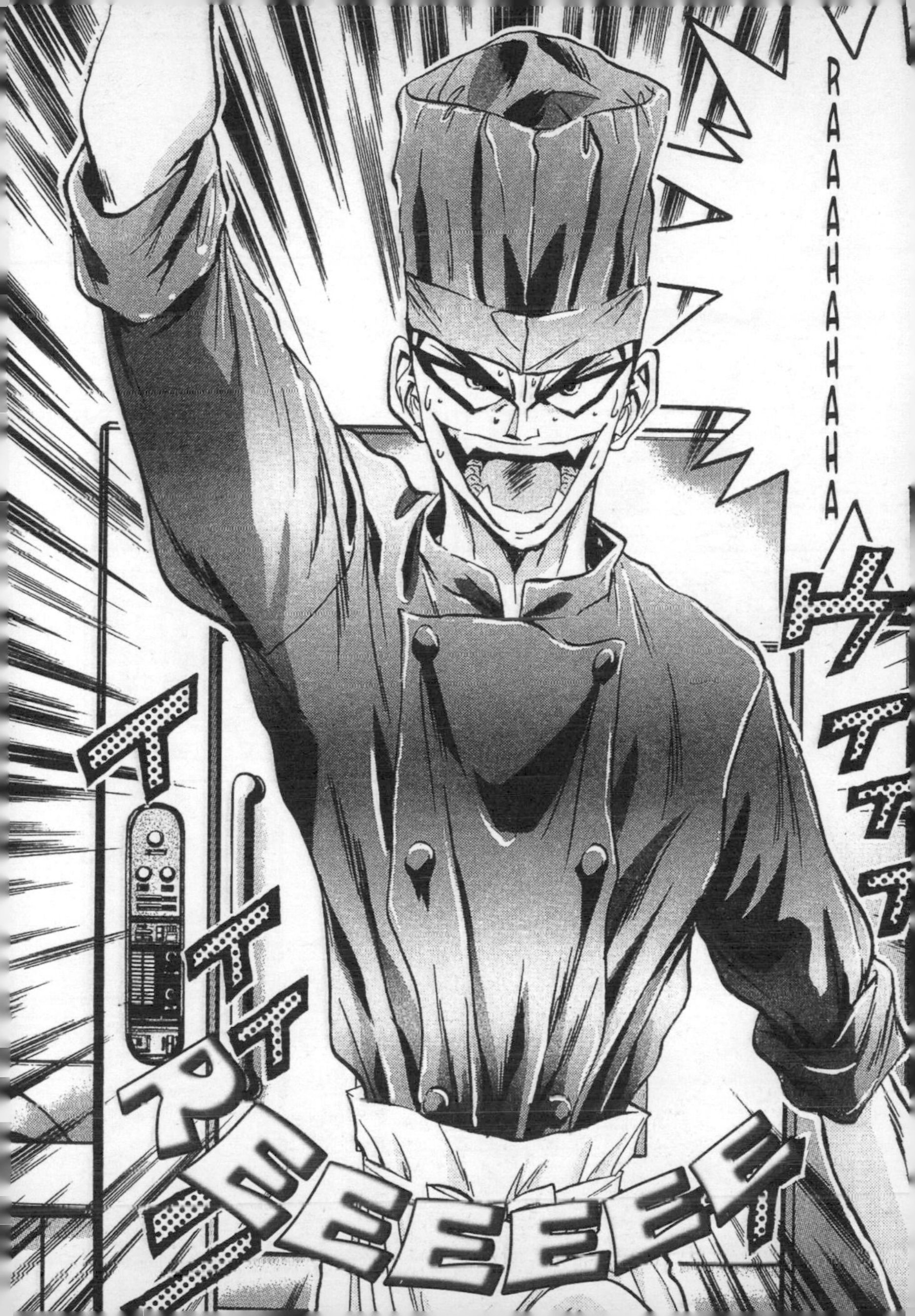
RAAAHAHAHA
REEEEEE

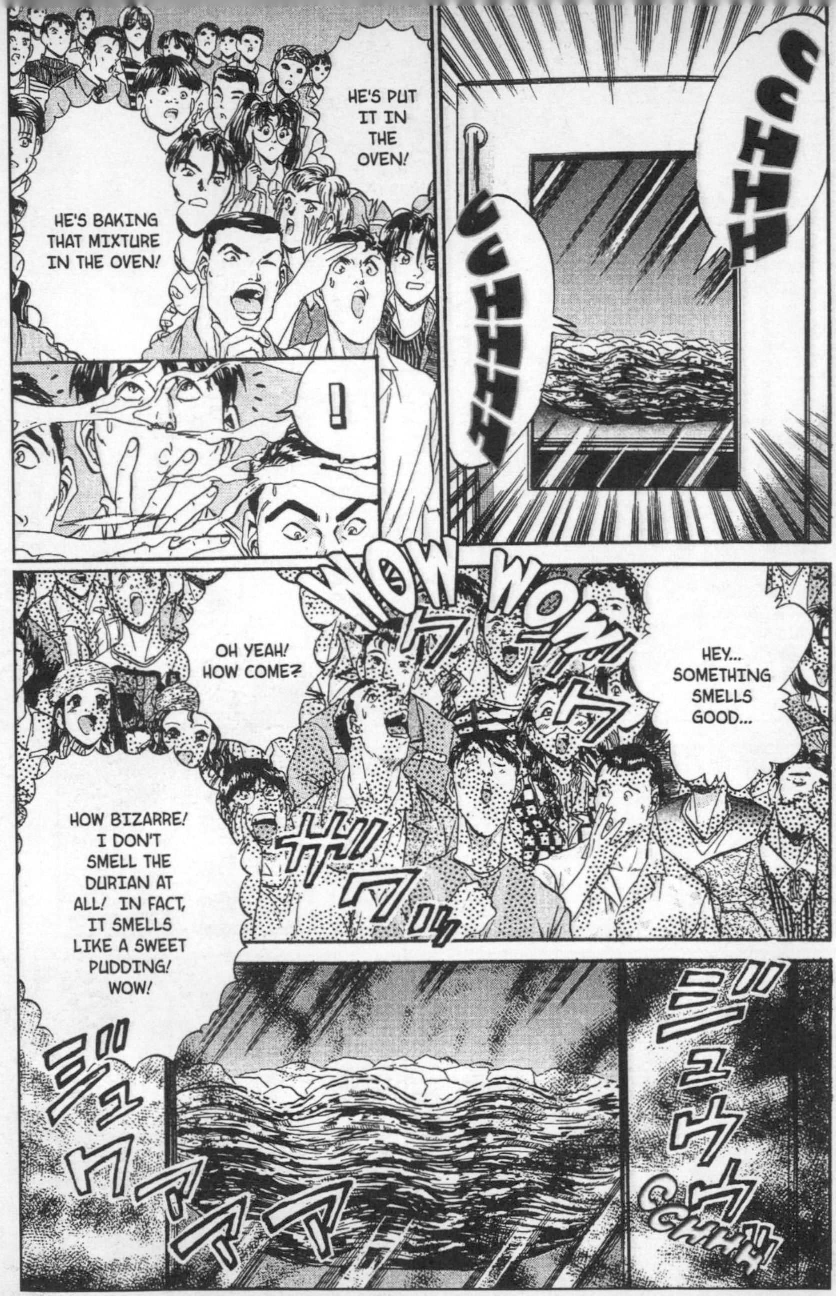
CCHHHH!
CCHHHHHH
HE'S PUT IT IN THE OVEN!
HE'S BAKING THAT MIXTURE IN THE OVEN!
!
WOW WOW
HEY... SOMETHING SMELLS GOOD...
OH YEAH! HOW COME?
HOW BIZARRE! I DON'T SMELL THE DURIAN AT ALL! IN FACT, IT SMELLS LIKE A SWEET PUDDING! WOW!
CHHHH

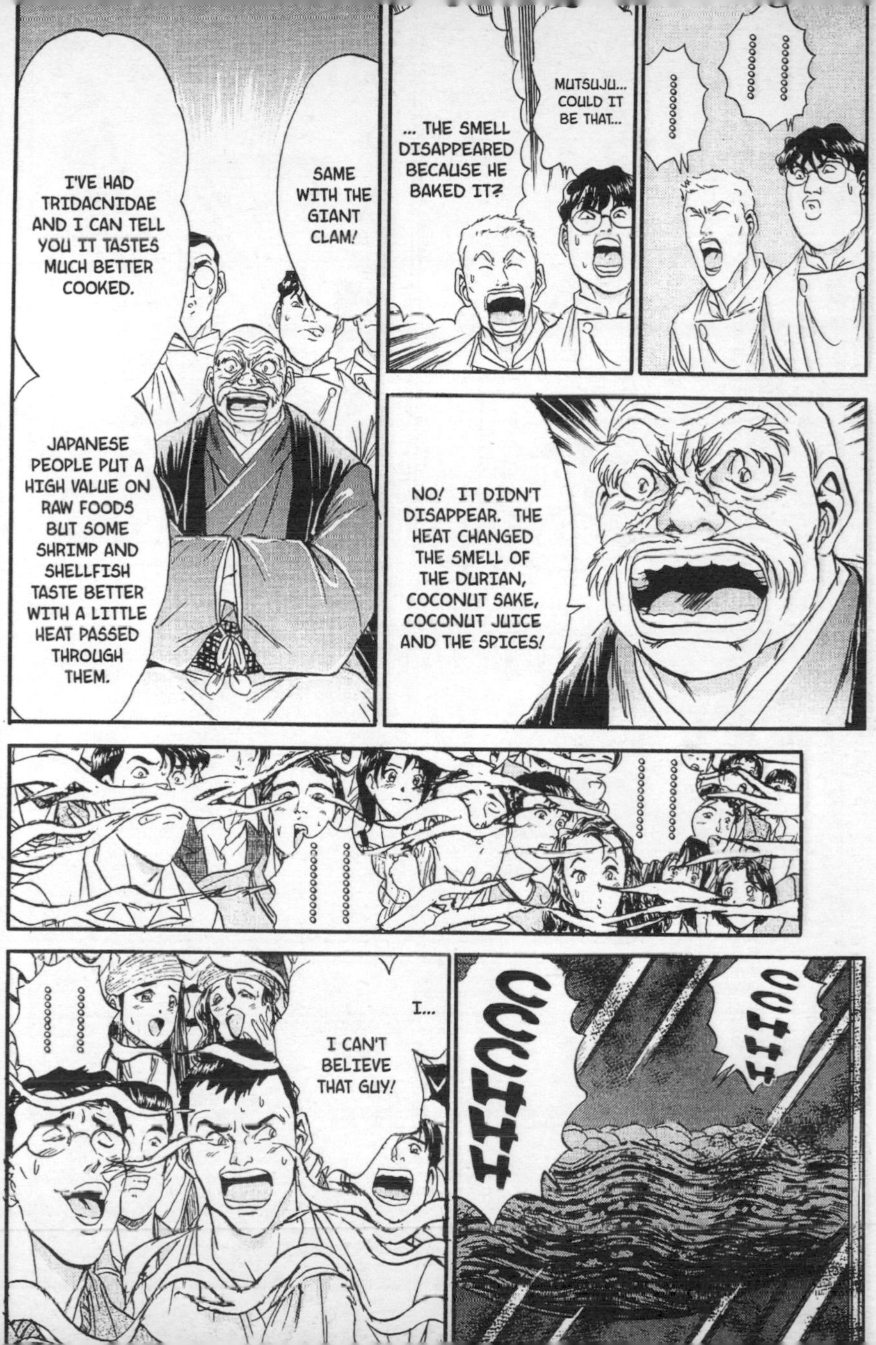
MUTSUJU... COULD IT BE THAT...
... THE SMELL DISAPPEARED BECAUSE HE BAKED IT?
NO! IT DIDN'T DISAPPEAR. THE HEAT CHANGED THE SMELL OF THE DURIAN, COCONUT SAKE, COCONUT JUICE AND THE SPICES!
SAME WITH THE GIANT CLAM!
I'VE HAD TRIDACNIDAE AND I CAN TELL YOU IT TASTES MUCH BETTER COOKED.
JAPANESE PEOPLE PUT A HIGH VALUE ON RAW FOODS BUT SOME SHRIMP AND SHELLFISH TASTE BETTER WITH A LITTLE HEAT PASSED THROUGH THEM.
I...
I CAN'T BELIEVE THAT GUY!

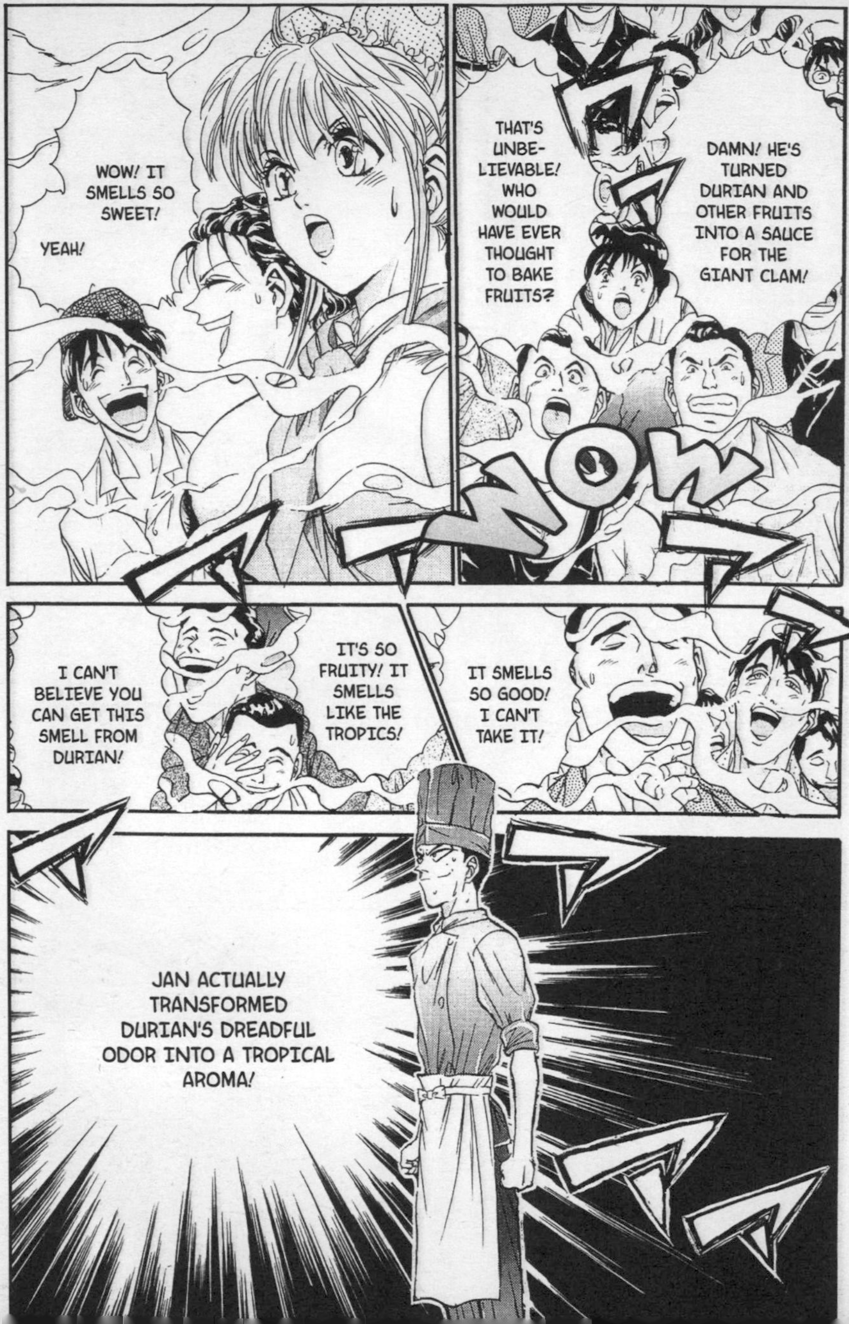
DAMN! HE'S TURNED DURIAN AND OTHER FRUITS INTO A SAUCE FOR THE GIANT CLAM!
THAT'S UNBE-LIEVABLE! WHO WOULD HAVE EVER THOUGHT TO BAKE FRUITS?
WOW
WOW! IT SMELLS SO SWEET!
YEAH!
IT SMELLS SO GOOD! I CAN'T TAKE IT!
IT'S SO FRUITY! IT SMELLS LIKE THE TROPICS!
I CAN'T BELIEVE YOU CAN GET THIS SMELL FROM DURIAN!
JAN ACTUALLY TRANSFORMED DURIAN'S DREADFUL ODOR INTO A TROPICAL AROMA!

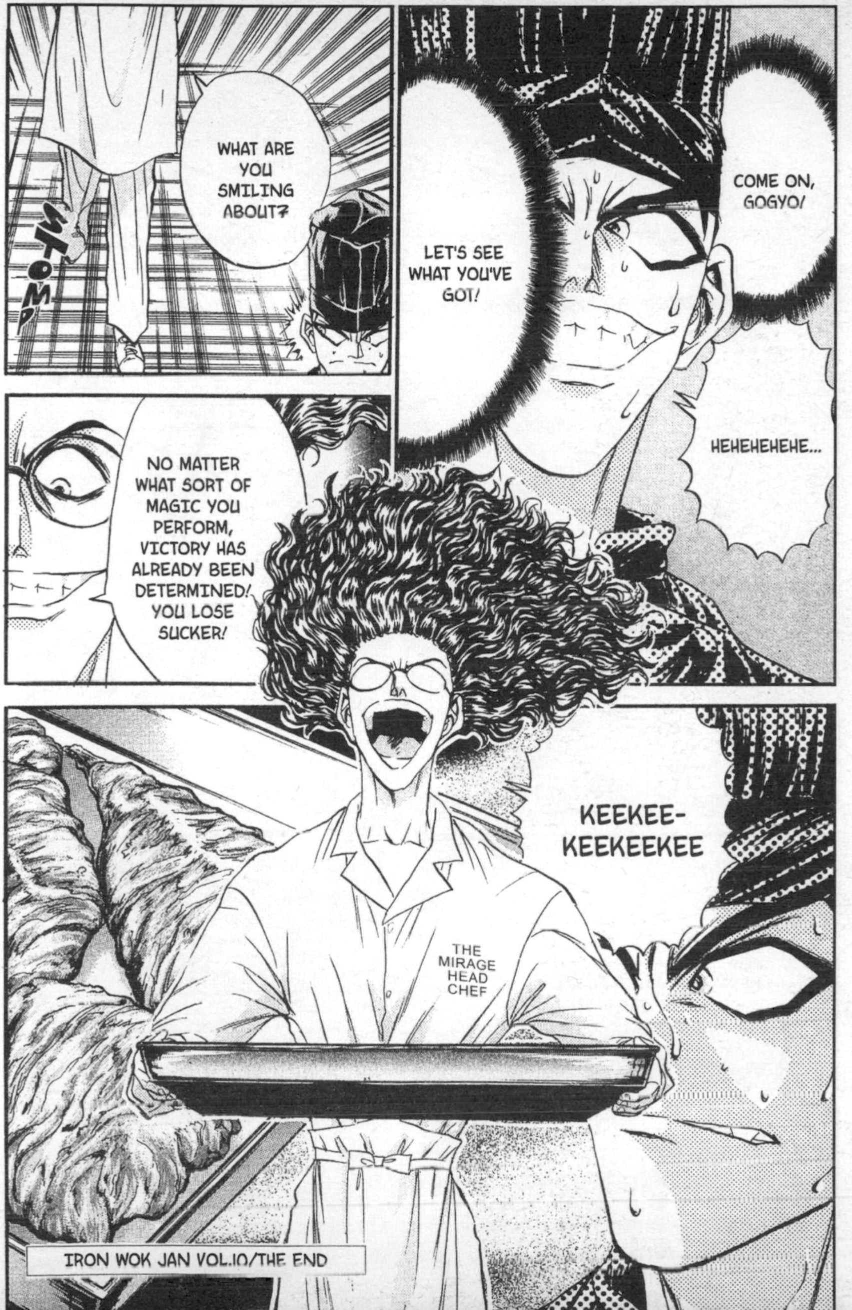
COME ON, GOGYO!
LET'S SEE WHAT YOU'VE GOT!
HEHEHEHEHE...
WHAT ARE YOU SMILING ABOUT?
STOMP
NO MATTER WHAT SORT OF MAGIC YOU PERFORM, VICTORY HAS ALREADY BEEN DETERMINED! YOU LOSE SUCKER!
KEEKEE-KEEKEEKEE
THE MIRAGE HEAD CHEF
IRON WOK JAN VOL.10/THE END

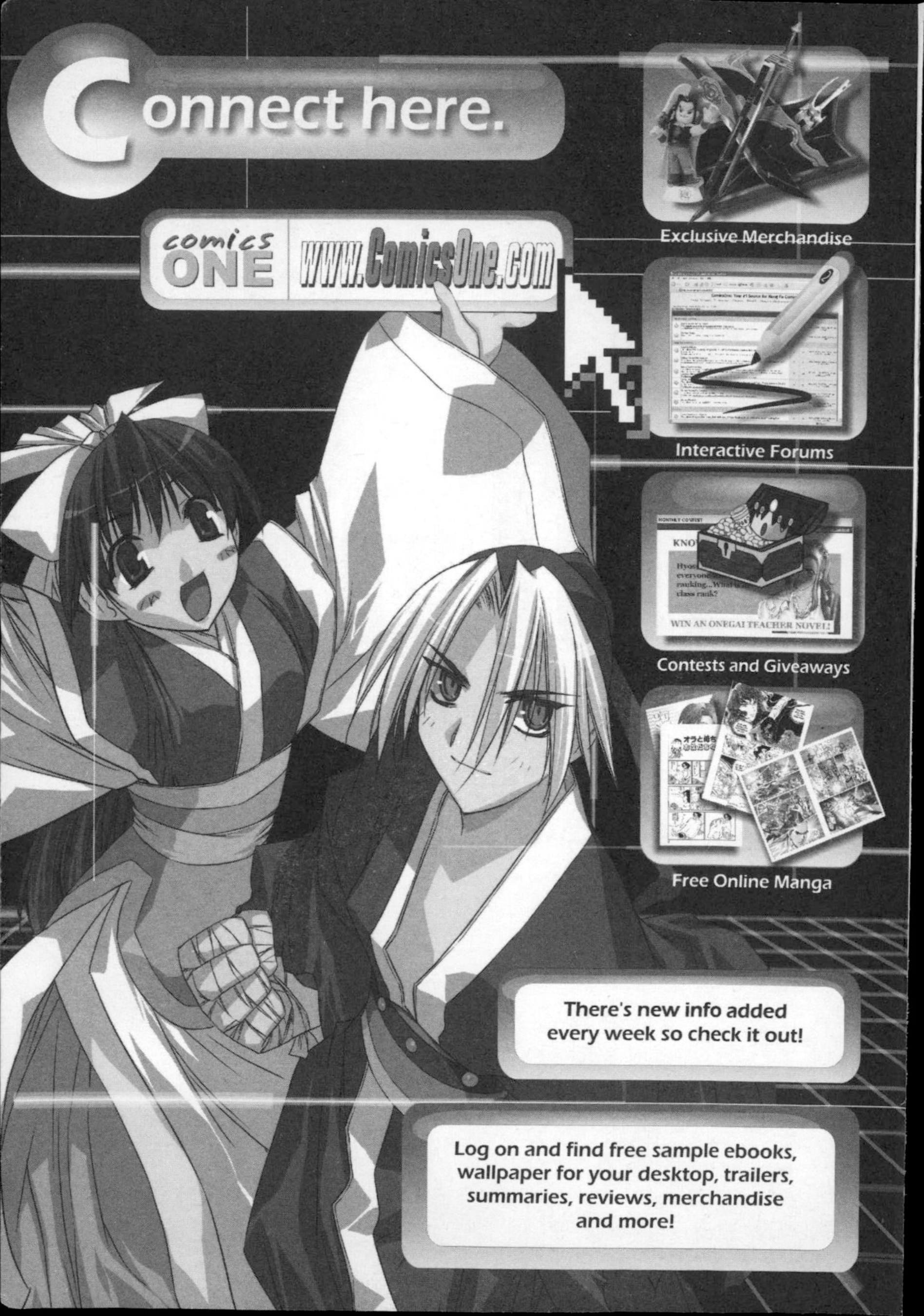
Connect here.
comics ONE
www.ComicsOne.com
Exclusive Merchandise
Interactive Forums
WIN AN ONEGAI TEACHER NOVEL!
Contests and Giveaways
Free Online Manga
There's new info added every week so check it out!
Log on and find free sample ebooks, wallpaper for your desktop, trailers, summaries, reviews, merchandise and more!

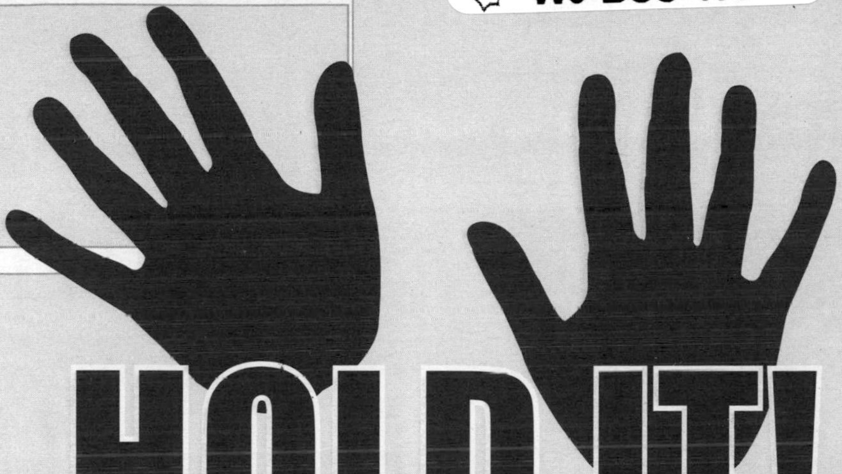

HOLD IT!

This book was printed in the original Japanese format. Please flip the book over and read right-to-left.

NIPPON ¥80

ORIGINAL
MANGA